Religion
in the Age of
Enlightenment

Religion in the Age of Enlightenment

Religion
in the Age of
Enlightenment
Volume 5

Editor, Brett C. McInelly
Book Review Editor, Kathryn Duncan

AMS Press, Inc.
New York

Religion in the Age of Enlightenment

ISSN: 1947-444X

Set ISBN-10: 0-404-63310-2
Set ISBN-13: 978-0-404-63310-3

Vol. 5 ISBN-10: 0-404-63315-3
Vol. 5 ISBN-13: 978-404-63315-8

All AMS books are printed on acid-free paper that meets the guidelines for performance and durability of the Committee on Production Guidelines for Book
Longevity of the Council on Library Resources.

AMS Press, INC.
Brooklyn Navy Yard, 63 Flushing Avenue–Unit #221
Brooklyn, NY 11205-1073, USA
www.amspressinc.com

MANUFACTURED IN THE UNITED STATES OF AMERICA

Contents

Preface

Articles

1   "To Put the Soul in Motion": Connoisseurship as a Religious Discourse in the Writings of Jonathan Richardson

Clare Haynes

25   Telescopes, Microscopes, and the Problem of Evil

Christopher Fauske

55   Equal Portions of Heavenly Fire: Mary Wollstonecraft and the Sexless Soul

Rachael Givens Johnson

97   Providential Empiricism: Suffering and Shaping the Self in Eighteenth-Century British Children's Literature

Adrianne Wadewitz

123   Sacred Alliance? The Critical Assessment of Revelation in Fichte and Kant

Thomas Spencer

157   Recovering the Rhetorical Tradition: George Campbell's Sympathy and its Augustinian Roots

Brian Fehler

181   American Unitarians and the George B. English Controversy

Bradley Kime

211   The Potential Convergence of Religious and Secular Interests in Voltaire's *Traité sur la tolérance*

John C. O'Neal

231   Sacred or Profane Pleasures? Erotic Ceremonies in Eighteenth-Century French Libertine Fiction

Marine Ganofsky

259   Pentecost 1794: Robespierre's Religious Vision and the Fulfillment of Time

Muriel Schmid

277   Songs without Music: The Hymns of Le Franc De Pompignan

Theodore E. D. Braun

Reviews

295   The Elect Methodists: Calvinistic Methodism in England and Wales, 1735–1811

Isabel Rivers

299   David Hume: The Philosopher as Historian

Richard Kleer

303   Imagining Methodism in Eighteenth-Century Britain: Enthusiasm, Belief, and the Borders of the Self

Robin Runia

307   Philosophy and Religion in Enlightenment Britain: New Case Studies
Bob Tennant

311   The Truth of the Christian Religion, with Jean Le Clerc's Notes and Additions
Robert G. Walker

317   Religious Dissent and the Aikin-Barbauld Circle 1740–1860
Nigel Aston

321   Re-Envisioning Blake
Joshua Davis

325   Anglican Church Policy, Eighteenth Century Conflict, and the American Episcopate
Christopher J. Fauske

Index

331

Preface

As the editor of an academic annual, I have the pleasure of interacting with scholars from across the United States and the world. While most of these interactions take place via e-mail, I feel as if I get to know *RAE*'s contributors, in addition to their work, as I take a manuscript from submission to publication. Of course, some interactions are more personal than others. This was particularly true of my email exchanges with Adrianne Wadewitz, who died in a rock-climbing accident during the production of this volume. I am pleased to include her excellent essay on the ways eighteenth-century writers of children's literature encouraged their young readers "to develop a specifically Christian subjectivity." I dedicate this volume to her and her loved ones who will miss her most.

I also wish to express my heartfelt thanks to Kathryn Duncan, who has served admirably as *RAE*'s book review editor since its founding in 2009 and who will step away from this position following the publication of this volume. More than Kathryn's dedication to the discipline of eighteenth-century studies, I most appreciate her friendship and will miss working with her in her capacity as book review editor. I look forward to working with Samara Cahill of Nanyang Technological University in Singapore, who has graciously accepted the invitation to serve as book review editor, beginning with volume 6.

The articles in the present volume range across a number of disciplinary, intellectual, and geographic boundaries, from children's literature and its Christianizing impulses, to art history and the ways artist and critic Jonathan Richardson conceived of art as a means of bringing people closer to God. Other essays consider the intersections of religious and scientific discourse in grappling with questions of evil, the influence of religion on Mary Wollstonecraft's feminist thought, and Frichte's and Kant's critiques of revelation. Another essay examines the influence of St. Augustine's *De doctrina Christiana* on the thinking of the Scottish rhetorician George Campbell, while another addresses the controversy between George B. English and the American Unitarians in early-nineteenth-century America. And the final four essays deal with French topics: the convergence of religious and secular interests in Voltaire, the intermingling of the sacred and profane in French libertine literature, the role of religion in pre- and postrevolutionary France, and the hymns of Le Franc De Pompignan.

I express my appreciation to the contributors to this volume as well as Melvin J. Thorne of the Brigham Young University Humanities Publication Center and his student editors for their help with copyediting, design, and the layout of this volume. I also wish to thank *RAE*'s editorial board. Finally, I express my appreciation to Gabe Hornstein, President of AMS Press, and Albert Rolls, Editor-in-Chief at AMS, for their continued support of eighteenth-century studies generally and *RAE* specifically.

Brett C. McInelly
Brigham Young University

"To Put the Soul in Motion"[1]: Connoisseurship as a Religious Discourse in the Writings of Jonathan Richardson

Clare Haynes

I t is only relatively recently that the significance of Jonathan Richardson's writings has been properly recognized. Carol Gibson-Wood, in a number of articles and a book, identified two main keys to Richardson's importance: first, Richardson adapted European art theory and "Englished" it for a British audience using a methodology heavily dependent on Locke.[2] In doing so, he developed an approach to art that was distinctive in the European tradition. Second, Richardson, as both a writer and connoisseur, was more influential at home and abroad than was previously recognized.[3] Indeed, Richardson was rightly acclaimed by Gibson-Wood as the "art theorist of the English Enlightenment" (plate 1). However, although Gibson-Wood recognized and attended to Richardson's religious

1. Jonathan Richardson, *A Discourse on the Dignity, Certainty, Pleasure and Advantage of the Science of a Connoisseur* (London: W. Churchill, 1719), 16.

2. The terms *English* and *British* are used interchangeably here, as they were to a great extent in the eighteenth century. Carol Gibson-Wood, *Jonathan Richardson: Art Theorist of the English Enlightenment* (New Haven, CT: Yale University Press, 2000). Also see Carol Gibson-Wood, "Jonathan Richardson and the Rationalization of Connoisseurship," *Art History* 7, no. 1 (1984): 38–56.

3. Carol Gibson-Wood, "Jonathan Richardson, Lord Somers's Collection of Drawings, and Early Art Historical Writing in England," *Journal of the Warburg and Courtauld Institutes* 52 (1989): 167–87.

Plate 1: Jonathan Richardson, Self-Portrait, chalk on blue paper, 1728. © Trustees of the British Museum

beliefs, her arguments underplayed the directing influence of religious concerns on the formation of his writings and the field more generally.[4] Richardson's position was not idiosyncratic: religious questions played a role in all English writing about art after the Reformation.[5] This article does not challenge but rather underscores Gibson-Wood's assessment of Richardson by demonstrating how his writings display the concern for religion that has been recognized as characteristic of the English Enlightenment.[6] In addition, through a new reading of Richardson's theoretical writings, this article reveals how fundamental to Richardson's thinking was the conviction that art could bring man to a closer knowledge of God.[7] Recognition of this principle not only gives us a fuller understanding of these influential works but also shows some of the ways in which, in the early English Enlightenment, art, like science, addressed, and was policed by, religion.

Jonathan Richardson was a sought-after portraitist whose sitters included many of the leading figures of his day: Alexander Pope, John Gay, Robert Walpole, Richard Mead, William Cheselden, Hans Sloane, and Richard Steele (plate 2), as well as Isaac Watts, William Fleetwood (Bishop of Ely), and the theologian William Nicholls. Richardson's success as a portraitist was matched by his work as a writer, which focused both on art and on Milton, for whom he had a passionate enthusiasm. He was also a poet, encouraged by his friends Pope and Matthew Prior. Although he did not publish his poetry separately in his lifetime, he included some of it in his essays on art, often alongside excerpts from Milton. Before Richardson, writings about art in England had been the province of *virtuosi*, men who were not

---

4. Carol Gibson-Wood, "Jonathan Richardson's 'Hymn to God,'" *Man and Nature* 8 (1989): 81–90; and Gibson-Wood, *Jonathan Richardson: Art Theorist*, 38–43.

5. Clare Haynes, "In the Shadow of the Idol: Religion in British Art Theory, 1600–1800," *Art History* 35, no. 1 (2012): 62–85.

6. For two different approaches to the religious nature of the English Enlightenment, see Roy Porter, *Enlightenment: Britain and the Creation of the Modern World* (Harmondsworth: Penguin Books, 2000); and Peter Harrison, *"Religion" and the Religions in the English Enlightenment* (Cambridge: Cambridge University Press, 1990).

7. Richardson also wrote an essay based on his son's grand tour: *An Account of Some of the Statues, Bas-Reliefs, Drawings and Pictures in Italy, Etc., with Remarks* (London: J. Knapton, 1722), for which there is not space to consider here. It is consistent with the works examined in respect of the issues under discussion.

Plate 2: John Smith after Jonathan Richardson, Portrait of Mr. Richard Steele, mezzotint, ca.1713. © Trustees of the British Museum

professional artists but were either gentlemanly collectors or scholars, such as William Aglionby, John Evelyn, Franciscus Junius, William Salmon, and Ashley Cooper, Third Earl of Shaftesbury.[8] Although all writers on art in this period recognized that British art lagged far behind that of its European rivals, particularly Italy and France, in both its quality and its quantity, Richardson's stance was rather different from theirs as it was explicitly that of a professional writing in defense of his own profession.[9] Thus, at the beginning of the first essay he published, *An Essay on the Theory of Painting*, Richardson observed that

> because pictures are universally delightful, and accordingly made one part of our Ornamental Furniture, many, I believe, consider the art of *Painting* but as a pleasing Superfluity; at best, that it holds but a low Rank with respect to its *Usefulness* to Mankind.[10]

Richardson understood that because art's moral status was so insecure in Britain, it was necessary to offer a justification for it. Only once its "usefulness" had been established could art thrive. In the *Theory of Painting* and the *Two Discourses*, which followed, Richardson aimed to give the British a "just Idea of the Art" in order to encourage them to take painting more seriously and thus become greater patrons.[11] Richardson understood that only by improving painting's reputation could it begin to flourish as it had on the Continent. To do this, he attempted to prove two interrelated propositions: first, that painting was religiously sound and second, that connoisseurship was a rational science.

In a markedly distinctive maneuver, Richardson began his endeavor with the first cause: art was a gift from God and thus ought "to hold a place in our esteem accordingly." Art was "judged necessary" by God

8. Craig Ashley Hanson, *The English Virtuoso: Art, Medicine, and Antiquarianism in the Age of Empiricism* (Chicago: University of Chicago Press, 2009).

9. See Iain Pears, *The Discovery of Painting: The Growth of Interest in the Arts in England*, 1680–1768 (New Haven, CT: Yale University Press, 1988).

10. Jonathan Richardson, *An Essay on the Theory of Painting* (London: J. Churchill, 1715), 3–4.

11. Richardson, *Science of a Connoisseur*, 10.

for man, and even if it was just a "pleasant, *innocent* Amusement," it ought to be valued more than it had been.[12] However, because it was emphatically more than that, the gift did not just entail an obligation or gratitude but gave art its main purpose: just as with nature, the best art, if looked at properly, would bring the viewer closer to God. This was the foundation of Richardson's proposal to the British public, and the word *innocent* was critical to it.

In a period when extensive iconoclasm was a matter of living memory and when religious art was still substantially associated with Roman Catholicism, or popery, as it was derogatively called, Richardson's insistence on art's innocence demonstrates how estranged he believed the public was from understanding and valuing the power of art to effect moral good.[13] He acknowledged, both in the *Theory* and the *Two Discourses*, that in the past, painting had been made "subservient to Impiety, and Immorality." However, he noted that in the same way other "excellent things . . . Poetry, Music, Learning, Religion, &c" had been abused too.[14] In a passage of high drama, quoting and adapting Job 31: 26–28, Richardson declared,

> I plead for the art not its abuses. . . . If when I see a *Madonna* tho' painted by Rafaelle I be drawn away to Idolatry; Or if the Subject of a Picture, tho' painted by Annibale Carracci pollutes my Mind with impure Images, and transforms me into a Brute . . . *May my Tongue cleave to the Roof of my Mouth, and my Right hand forget its Cunning* If I am its Advocate as 'tis Instrumental to such Detested Purposes.[15]

Thus Richardson sought to separate art from its popish associations and to reclaim art for Protestantism. Art's innocence is essential to its power, which he expressed most clearly in an important passage in the second of the *Two Discourses*:

---

12. Richardson, *Theory of Painting*, 4; emphasis added.

13. For anti-Catholicism in relation to art and Richardson's discourse on the subject in particular, see Clare Haynes, *Pictures and Popery: Art and Religion in England, 1660–1760* (Aldershot, UK: Ashgate Press, 2006).

14. Richardson, *Theory of Painting*, 18–19.

15. Richardson, *Science of a Connoisseur*, 39–40.

Not only such Ideas are convey'd to us by the help of This Art as merely give us Pleasure, but such as Enlighten the Understanding, and put the Soul in Motion. From hence are learn'd the Forms, and Properties of Things, and Persons, we are Thus inform'd of Past Events; by This means Joy, Grief, Hope, Fear, Love, Aversion, and the other Passions, and Affections of the Soul are excited, and above all, we are not only Thus Instructed in what we are to Believe, and Practise; but our Devotion is inflamed, and whatever may have happened to the contrary, it may Thus also be Rectify'd.[16]

Here, Richardson offered his readers a new perspective on looking at art, which was a counterbalance to idolatry and almost certainly the most widely discussed idea about art in early modern Britain.[17] He did not deny art's power, as some would, as a strategy for deflecting the charge of its potential for idolatry.[18] Instead, Richardson argued that art can be wholly effective in furthering true devotion. Looked at properly, art was a way of knowing the world and could lead one to God.

Furthermore, Richardson believed that painting could achieve these ends more effectively than sculpture or even poetry.[19] Indeed, painting could be so effective in this regard that it could rival the Bible, as in the work of Richardson's hero Raphael:

I conceive as highly of St. *Paul* by once walking through the Gallery of *Rafaelle* at *Hampton* Court, as by reading the whole Book of the Acts of the Apostles tho' written by Divine Inspiration [plate 3].[20]

In art of the highest ambition, such as Raphael's, which dealt in ideal forms, painting "perfects all that Humane Nature is capable of in the communication of Ideas 'til we arrive to a more Angelical, and Spiritual

---

16. Ibid., 16–17.
17. Jonathan Sheehan, "Sacred and Profane: Idolatry, Antiquarianism and the Polemics of Distinction in the Seventeenth Century," *Past & Present* 192 (2006): 35–66.
18. Horace Walpole, for example, describes religious art as merely "scenery for devotion" in Horace Walpole, ed., *Anecdotes of Painting in England* (1765), xii.
19. Richardson, *Science of a Connoisseur*, 17–25.
20. Ibid., 20.

Plate 3: Simon Gribelin after Raphael, St. Paul Preaching at Athens, engraving, 1707. © Trustees of the British Museum

State in another World."[21] However, for painting to fulfill its potential in the role in the Enlightenment for which God had instituted it, two conditions were necessary. First, painters of the right characters were needed, men such as Raphael who were a "little lower than the angels" and who could discern and express the highest truths. Not only must they educate themselves in the knowledge necessary to perform their art, including anatomy and mathematics, but they also must ennoble their minds by reading the Bible and the most highly esteemed literature. They were certainly practitioners of a liberal art.[22] In fact, the painter had to be master of more than one art—he had to be

---

21. Ibid., 25.

22. Adapting Psalms 8:5, Richardson, *Theory of Painting*, 92. For the liberal arts and their ranking in this period, see Lawrence Lipking, *The Ordering of the Arts in Eighteenth-Century England* (Princeton, NJ: Princeton University Press, 1970).

philosopher, historian, poet, and painter—so that "a Rafaelle . . . [was] not only Equal, but Superior to a *Virgil,* or a *Livy,* a *Thucydides,* or a *Homer.*"[23]

Second, people must be educated in looking at art in order to exploit its extraordinary resources so that their "Devotion . . . [could be] inflamed."[24] Richardson envisaged the spectatorship of art as a science, which he called *connoissance.*[25] He established its scientific credentials in three stages. In *The Theory of Painting* he described the constituent elements of a painting, on which it should be separately judged: invention, expression, composition, coloring, and so on. This provided the foundation for his later works. For example, in the first of the *Two Discourses* published in 1719, called *On the Art of Criticism,* Richardson laid out his method for judging pictures. This included the "Scale of Perfection," adapted from the work of the French theorist Roger de Piles, which involved giving a numerical score to the parts of painting that had been described in *Theory of Painting.*[26] In the final essay and the second of the *Two Discourses, Of the Science of a Connoisseur,* he returned to the justification of painting's claims on the attention of the British that he had addressed first in *Theory of Painting.* He offered further arguments for the rational basis of connoisseurship and the benefits that would accrue to British society from its wider practice, which were far-reaching for economics, morality, and religion as well.[27]

While Richardson's procedures were heavily influenced by his reading of Locke's *Essay Concerning Human Understanding* (1690), his argument was more explicitly religious in its use of biblical quotations and in its ambition. For example, in teaching his audience how to approach and judge a picture in *On the Art of Criticism,* Richardson

---

23. Richardson, *Theory of Painting,* 35–36.

24. Richardson, *Science of a Connoisseur,* 17.

25. This was, as Richardson told his audience, the suggestion of his friend, the poet Matthew Prior. Richardson, *Science of a Connoisseur,* 63–64.

26. Jonathan Richardson, *The Connoisseur: An Essay on the Whole Art of Criticism as it Relates to Painting* (London: W. Churchill, 1719), 55–56.

27. For the social and economic benefits, see Richardson, *Science of a Connoisseur,* 41–62.

began his discussion with a meditation on Matthew 19:17: *Wherefore callest thou me good? There is none Good but One, that is God,*

> Said the Son of God to the young Man who prefac'd a Noble
> Question with that Complement [*sic*]. This is that Goodness
> that is Perfect, Simple, and Properly so call'd, 'tis what is Pecu-
> liar to the Deity, and so to be found no where else. But there is
> another Improper, Imperfect, comparative Goodness, and no
> other than this is to be had in the Works of Men, and this admits
> of various Degrees.[28]

Painting was established immediately as man's work. It had no claim to divinity; therefore, however good a painting was, it was bound to have faults. This was an iconoclastic gesture, placing limits on art, which confirmed "there never was a Picture in the World without some Faults."[29] Even Raphael was not exempt, however close he had come to perfection.[30] Here, we see the full impetus of Richardson's faith in action. Such a rhetorical gesture might, in the scope of the larger project, be seen as unnecessary, and even undermining, but it was essential to the enterprise that Richardson was undertaking: the demonstration that painting was Godly work.

Richardson exemplified the systematic procedure of looking at a painting, which he described in *On the Art of Criticism*, by giving a complete account of Van Dyck's *Countess Dowager of Exeter*, which he owned. He also gave shorter accounts of two paintings owned by his friend Sir James Thornhill, the most prominent painter of the day, one of *Tancred and Erminia* by Nicolas Poussin and the other of *The Virgin and Child in the Clouds* by Annibale Carracci (plate 4). Richardson assessed each painting according to the system and discussed the pleasures they delivered, the noble ideas they communicated, and the further thoughts that flowed from their study. Utilizing this system to analyze Carracci's *Virgin and Child* led Richardson to muse:

---

28. Richardson, *Art of Criticism*, 11–12. See the similar idea expressed in Richardson, *Theory of Painting*, 169–70, in the context of depicting God the Father.

29. Richardson, *Art of Criticism*, 14.

30. For criticism of Raphael's works, see Richardson, *Theory of Painting*, 61; and Richardson, *Art of Criticism*, 112–14.

Plate 4: Annibale Carracci, *The Virgin and Child in the Clouds*, oil on canvas, 1593–94. By permission of the Governing Body of Christ Church, Oxford.

As every thing else in the Picture is Address'd towards her, She in the humblest, and most Devout Manner lifts up her Eyes towards the Invisible Supreme Being, Directing our Thought thither also, with like Humble, Pious and Devout sentiments. If she to whom the Angels appear so vastly Inferiour is in His Presence but a poor Suppliant, What an Exalted Idea must this give us of him![31]

Furthermore, it led to an expression of the sublime idea of God's unknowable perfection in a stanza of his own poetry:

Angelick minds the nearest to thy Self,
Those who conceive of Thee as far beyond
Our low conceptions as the Eagles flight,
Transcends our utmost Stretch, These See Thee not,
Nor canst Thou be discern'd but by Thy Self:
What art Thou then as by Thy Self beheld?
Just as Thou art! Unclouded! Undiminished!
In full Perfection! O the Joy Divine!
Ineffable! Of that Enlightened Mind
Where this Idea shines Eternally!
The Noblest, Loveliest, and most Excellent,
Thy Mind Divine can possibly conceive![32]

In this, Richardson ended his exposition of art criticism as he began it—with the infinite goodness of God.

The security of *connoissance* as a system of knowledge was fundamental to its usefulness to British Protestants. Therefore, Richardson returned to the topic in *On the Dignity of the Science of the Connoisseur*, where, in a long digression on the nature of human understanding, he discussed connoisseurship in relation to a universal model of knowledge. The degree to which Richardson's arguments were precisely dependent on Locke's is beyond the compass of this essay, but Richardson seems to have been conscious of the distinctive, strikingly religious tone of his arguments, remarking, "I ask Pardon of the Divines that I so

---

31. Richardson, *Art of Criticism*, 96–97.
32. Ibid., 97.

often set my foot upon Holy Ground; They will have the Goodness to consider we Painters are a sort of Lay-Brothers by Profession, as well as Historians, Poets, and Philosophers; And besides They may make reprisals upon Us, and talk of Painting as much as They please."[33] While clergy did not take up Richardson's offer until later in the eighteenth century, painting, particularly portraiture, was used quite frequently as an analogy in works of theology and devotion, for example, by John Scott in *The Christian Life*.[34] Richardson was certain that "we are upon an Equality (at least) with Most Other Sciences, if we have not the Advantage of them" in regard to the possibility of determining divine truth and probability.[35]

Although he was confident that he had demonstrated that connoisseurship and, by extension, painting were secure forms of knowledge, Richardson did acknowledge, with more than a little irritation, that there were nevertheless differences in opinion about art, especially over quality and attribution, but he argued that these conflicts were caused solely by differences between men, not by the security of the rules he had discussed.[36] Richardson repeatedly stressed the necessity of an unbiased judgment to the sciences: as with all the sciences, the connoisseur's judgment "avoids prejudices, and false reasoning" and works from first principles. Anything else, he argued, would be "offering Violence to that Light which we receiv'd from Above, and wherein our Resemblance with the Father of Light consists."[37] For painting to be

---

33. Richardson, *Science of a Connoisseur*, 129. For Richardson's debt to Locke, see Gibson-Wood, *Jonathan Richardson: Art Theorist*, passim.

34. See, for example, John Scott, *The Christian Life*, 6th ed. (n.p., 1712), 247–49, in which the presence of a portrait of a stern father that polices the behavior of a son is engaged to discuss the proper effect of remembering the invisible presence of God, who might be vividly imagined. For a different discussion of portraiture, see the introduction to Simon Patrick's influential book on the Eucharist, *Mensa Mystica*, 7th ed. (n.p., 1717), ii–iii, where he discusses the power of images and God's substitution of bread and wine, as symbols, for an image of Christ, which would be unsafe. Patrick quoted the "Tragical and Theatrical Representations which are made by some Papists of Christ's Sufferings" as exemplifying the danger. It was precisely this view of the inevitable connection between art and popery that Richardson was endeavoring to overturn.

35. Richardson, *Science of a Connoisseur*, 140–41.

36. Ibid., 130.

37. Richardson, *Art of Criticism*, 19.

understood correctly and for it to yield its potential for pleasure and improvement, the individual had to approach it with a mind free of prejudice. Therefore, in the short essays "Of the Knowledge of Hands" and "Of Originals and Copies," where he dealt with the questions of attribution and quality, over which there was the most dispute, Richardson reiterated that "'tis as necessary to a *Connoisseur* as to a Philosopher, or Divine to be a good Logician; The Same Faculties are employ'd, and in the Same manner, the Difference is only in the Subject."[38]

As John Barrell and David Solkin have demonstrated, the idea of an unprejudiced judgment, derived from civic humanism, was very significant in art discourse, particularly in the writings of Ashley Cooper, the Third Earl of Shaftesbury.[39] However, as Gibson-Wood recognized, Richardson's conceptualization was different from the aristocratic model Shaftesbury used.[40] Richardson had been intimate with Shaftesbury's friend, the former Lord Chancellor John Somers (plate 5), whose very substantial collection of prints and drawings Richardson had arranged.[41] There are some overlaps in Richardson's and Shaftesbury's arguments, but their positions were essentially different, as Gibson-Wood observed, with regard to the status of the artist. Although Shaftesbury recognized the possibility of a more enlightened practitioner, his view of the artist was largely that of a mechanic, merely performing what someone else had invented before.[42] Richardson's ideal painter was, on the other hand, a man of moral action, a true liberal artist.

A further substantial difference between Shaftesbury and Richardson, more relevant here, is the latter's understanding of the religious foundation of connoisseurship. While Richardson acknowledged that being a faithful Christian was not a precondition for connoisseurship, he did believe that such a person "has a mind at

---

38. Ibid., 203.

39. John Barrell, *The Political Theory of Painting from Reynolds to Hazlitt: The Body of the Public* (New Haven, CT: Yale University Press, 1995); and David Solkin, *Painting for Money: The Visual Arts and the Public Sphere in Eighteenth-Century England* (New Haven, CT: Yale University Press, 1992).

40. For a discussion of Richardson and civic humanism, see Gibson-Wood, *Jonathan Richardson: Art Theorist*, esp. 7–9.

41. Gibson-Wood, "Lord Somers's Collection of Drawings."

42. Gibson-Wood, *Jonathan Richardson: Art Theorist*, 152–53.

The R.ᵗ Hon.ᵇˡᵉ John Lord Sommers.

Plate 5: John Smith after Jonathan Richardson, Portrait of Rt. Hon. Lord Somers, mezzotint, ca.1713. © Trustees of the British Museum

ease, and most apt to receive virtuous pleasure," which was the key to deriving connoisseurship's most important benefits, as will be discussed shortly.[43] Furthermore, he believed that if art was to flourish in Britain, it had to be reconciled with Protestantism. Shaftesbury expressed the common perception about art and religion that Richardson was fighting in his essay *Plastics*:

> Sad to consider that the . . . rise of painting, being chiefly from the popish priesthood, the improvement and culture of it (except for the vicious part for the cabinets of the grandees, etc.) has turned wholly on the nourishment and support of superstition . . . and exaltation of that vile shrivelling passion of beggarly modern devotion.[44]

Shaftesbury's understanding of popery's encouragement of the arts was widely shared and often remarked on.[45] Shaftesbury developed what was essentially a political solution to the alienation of art in Britain, what has been called the "republic of taste."[46] Significantly, Richardson never directly acknowledged this commonplace connection between great art and popery. Instead, he argued that when the arts revived, they would flourish in Britain, not because of the resemblance of the modern British character to that of the ancient Greeks and Romans but, more remarkably, because of the Church of England.[47] It was the church that guaranteed the judgment that would allow connoisseurship to thrive:

> 'Tis the Glory of the Protestant Church, and especially of the Church of *England* as being Indubitably the Head of the Reformed churches; and so upon That Account, as well as the Purity and Excellency of its Doctrines, and the Piety, and Learning of its

43. Richardson, *Science of a Connoisseur*, 197.

44. Anthony Ashley Cooper, Third Earl of Shaftesbury, *Second Characters: Or, The Language of Forms*, ed. Benjamin Rand (New York: Greenwood Press, 1969), 119.

45. For the continuity of this idea, see Haynes, *Pictures and Popery*; and Haynes, "In the Shadow of the Idol."

46. For Shaftesbury's conception of a republic for art and its influence, see Barrell, *Political Theory of Painting*; and Solkin, *Painting for Money*, esp. 1–77.

47. For the specific qualities in which the British resembled the ancient Greeks and Romans, see Richardson, *Theory of Painting*, 209–13; and Richardson, *Science of a Connoisseur*, 3–4.

Clergy (so far as I am able to judge) the Best National Church in the world: I say 'tis the Glory of the Reformation, that thereby Men are set at liberty to judge for Themselves: We are Thus a Body of Free Men; not the Major part in Subjection to the rest. Here we are all *connoisseurs* as we are Protestants; tho' (as it must needs happen) Some are Abler *connoisseurs* than Others. And we have abundantly experienced the Advantages of This, since we have Thus resum'd our Natural Rights as Rational Creatures.[48]

Here, connoisseurship, and thus painting, was completely naturalized for the British Protestant in what was a bold and unprecedented stroke.

If we return to Richardson's discussion of Carracci's *Virgin and Child*, we can see how he freed British reception of European art, through the exercise of Protestant judgment, from the difficulty of having to maintain a distance from Catholic "idolatry." Britons could indeed be the best judges of all art. Richardson believed that Carracci's painting depicted the Virgin as the protectress of Bologna. This idea, alien to Protestant understandings of the saints, Richardson set aside, concentrating not on the relationship between the Virgin and the city but on the Virgin's character as the principal subject. He described the painting as showing the Virgin above a prospect of the city, where she is seated in glory on clouds, "encompass'd with Cherubims, Boy-Angels, and others as usually describ'd. But oh! the Sublimity of Expression!" He continued, "What Dignity, and Devotion appears in the Virgin! What Awful Regard! What Love! What Delight, and Complacency is in these Angelick Beings towards the Virgin Mother of the Son of God!"[49] Significant elements of both the subject and the painter's symbolism (the depiction of the city and the connection to the Virgin) were set aside, but the painting's religious potential was exploited by Richardson in a different way, leading him to think on God. Through this, Richardson demonstrated to his readers that British Protestants could take possession of the whole of the history of art and that they might derive benefit from even the most popish of paintings. Indirectly, of course, Richardson was also answering the question

---

48. Richardson, *Science of a Connoisseur*, 230–31.
49. Richardson, *Art of Criticism*, 95.

Shaftesbury had raised: Was Catholicism a better nursery for the arts than Protestantism? Richardson did not think so. If the British could deploy their natural advantages, including their religion, and provide greater encouragement for British artists, painting would flourish. It would do so because of the security of the Reformation, guaranteed by the Church of England. It was on this basis that Richardson felt confident to suggest, with a tone of deference, that paintings had a place in churches:

> If... our Churches were Adorn'd with proper Histories, or Alle-
> gories well Painted, the People being now so well instructed as
> to be out of Danger of Superstitious Abuses, their Minds would
> be more Sensibly affected than they can possibly be without this
> Efficacious means of Improvement, and Edification. But This
> (as indeed every thing else advanced by me) I humbly submit
> to the Judgment of my Superiors.[50]

Painting, he argued, can lead to reformed ends. Rationalism, not enthusiasm, gives man a more secure hold on God's gift of painting.

In his analysis of the three paintings at the end of the *Art of Criticism*, Richardson showed how the proper approach to paintings can lead to the direct effects of moral improvement and piety. However, his conception of connoisseurship is more far-reaching still, as he claimed in Section III of the *Science of a Connoisseur*, a richly discursive argument on pleasure and its relation to virtue that he called "a Plan for a Happy Life."[51] This has been seen as a long digression from the overall argument about connoisseurship, but it is surely better read as a significant demonstration of Richardson's understanding of the fundamental power of art and, more importantly, as a direct response to Shaftesbury on three distinct issues. Two of these issues relate to Shaftesbury's *A Notion of the Historical Draught or Tablature of the Judgment of Hercules*, which was published in London in 1713. Shaftesbury had dedicated the essay to his friend, and Richardson's patron, Lord Somers. The *Notion* was a remarkable intervention by a

---

50. Ibid., 44.
51. Richardson, *Science of a Connoisseur*, 158.

Plate 6: Simon Gribelin after Paolo de Matteis, Hercules Rejects Pleasure and Chuses Virtue, engraving, 1713. © Trustees of the British Museum

virtuoso, as a very careful analysis and thus prescription for the design of a painting on the subject of the Hercules choosing between vice and virtue derived from Prodicus. Richardson seems to have disapproved of two aspects of the essay's argument. First, Shaftesbury severely constrained, as we have discussed, the painter's intellectual and moral role. Indeed, he enacted this by commissioning the Italian painter Paolo Matteis to produce a painting of Hercules under his direction, which embodied the essay's prescription (plate 6).[52] This was quite alien to Richardson's conception of the artist.

Second, Shaftesbury's notion of pleasure was one that he seems to have had little time for.[53] The essay bears a quotation from the

---

52. Now in the Ashmolean Museum, Oxford.
53. For their quite different models of civic virtue, see Barrell, *Political Theory*, 20–23.

tenth satire of Juvenal on its title page that has been translated such
that one should prefer "the sorrows and grueling labours of Hercules
to all Sardanapalus' downy cushions and women and junketings."[54]
Shaftesbury thus equated pleasure with vice and virtue with hard labor.
Similarly, his painting was to have little to delight the senses. Coloring
should be "reserv'd, severe, and chaste" for it to be morally effective,
Shaftesbury argued in the essay.[55] Richardson rejected Shaftesbury's
interpretation, saying,

> Were I to paint the Fable of *Prodicus*, as *Annibale Caracci* [*sic*]
> has done, I would not make the Way of Virtue Rough, and
> Stony, that of Vice should be so: He, and other Moralists have
> been injurious to Virtue when they have given us such Harsh
> Representations of her. *Her ways are ways of pleasantness, and
> all her paths are peace.*[56]

Using the description of wisdom in Proverbs 3:17, Richardson's
conception of virtue was different from Shaftesbury's in that he
regarded pleasure as motivating all actions, virtuous as well as
vicious. Thus, he claimed, "*Cato* is as great an Epicure as *Apicius*":
Cato had chosen mental pleasures over physical suffering.[57] Given
Richardson's strong religious faith, his position was a logical one.[58]
Happiness, according to Richardson, rested on the knowledge of God
as benevolent. As God was omnipresent, any other comprehension of
him, such as one that was "Confus'd . . . and Doubtful" or one that
saw him as terrible or forbidding, would disallow happiness.[59] After
suffering a period of painful doubt earlier in his life, Richardson had
arrived at the conclusion that God "takes not Delight in our Miseries,

---

54. Juvenal, *The Sixteen Satires*, trans. Peter Green, 3rd rev. ed. (Harmondsworth, UK: Penguin Classics, 1998), 86.

55. Anthony Ashley Cooper, Third Earl of Shaftesbury, *A Notion of the Historical Draught or Tablature of the Judgment of Hercules* (London: A. Baldwin, 1713), 46.

56. Richardson, *Science of a Connoisseur*, 173.

57. Ibid., 162.

58. Shaftesbury's own faith is hard to discern, and the evidence is contradictory. See Lawrence E. Klein, "Cooper, Anthony Ashley, Third Earl of Shaftesbury (1671–1713)," in *Oxford Dictionary of National Biography* (Oxford: Oxford University Press, 2004), http://www.oxforddnb.com/view/article/6209.

59. Richardson, *Science of a Connoisseur*, 163–64.

and Sufferings" but wants our enjoyment for which he has provided.[60] Enjoyment "within the Bounds of Innocence, and Virtue" was therefore a religious duty.[61] This was also a tacit rejection of Shaftesbury. In his *Inquiry Concerning Virtue or Merit*, part of *Characteristicks* (1711), Shaftesbury had argued that the Old Testament Jehovah was a terrible and morally suspect god and that Judaism necessarily encouraged similar traits.[62] This was an early and authoritative statement of the deist critique of Christianity on the basis of its foundations in the Old Testament.[63] The implications of it were obviously not lost on Richardson—section III of the *Science of a Connoisseur* can be read as an antideist text. In this light, the full significance of Richardson's invocation of the Church of England, quoted previously, and which, in fact, followed section III, is revealed.[64] Richardson's essay was written in defense of both art and religion.

As discussed, Richardson began his writings on art with the assertion that painting was a providential gift. In concluding, he started to draw out the implications of this concept in relation to the ideas of virtuous pleasure that he had established. He started with art practice:

> 'Tis a wretched Turn many People's heads have taken; They are perpetually Depreciating every thing in this World; and seem to fancy there is a sort of Merit in so doing; As if the way to express the Esteem we had for what we hope God has provided for us in Another State was by railing at This; Or as if the Present was not also the Effect of his Goodness, and Bounty.[65]

Richardson thus confronted an underlying tension in British responses to the art of painting in relation to its dependence on idealization,

---

60. Ibid., 167. For a discussion of this period of doubt, see Gibson-Wood, *Jonathan Richardson: Art Theorist*, 39–43; and Gibson-Wood, "Hymn to God."

61. Richardson, *Science of a Connoisseur*, 170.

62. Anthony Ashley Cooper, *Characteristicks* (London, 1711), 2:48

63. Ruth Smith, *Handel's Oratorios and Eighteenth-Century Thought* (Cambridge: Cambridge University Press, 1995), 234.

64. The significance of Richardson's reaction to Shaftesbury has perhaps yet to be properly recognized and analyzed.

65. Richardson, *Science of a Connoisseur*, 184.

which was regarded as illegitimate and immodest by some early-modern Christians. This position was expressed most famously in the apocryphal story of Oliver Cromwell insisting on being painted by Peter Lely, "warts and all."[66] Richardson regarded this as profoundly mistaken and obstructive to painting's primary purpose of raising the mind and spirit toward God. In contrast, he argued that art's role was to "Exalt our Species as much as possible to what we conceive of the Angelick State . . . to impregnate our Minds with the most Sublime, and Beautiful Images of things."[67] According to Richardson, there was considerable pleasure to be gained from a stock of mental pictures, "which will finely employ every vacant moment of one's time."[68] However, what perhaps mattered more to Richardson was to recognize God's presence in everything visible:

> A Man must have Gross Conceptions of God if he imagines he can be seen in a Future, Better state in any Corporeal Form: Incorporeally we see him Here, his Wisdom, Goodness, Power, and Providence; and this Beatific Vision brightens More, and More to Pure Minds, . . . and thus 'tis Heaven here on Earth.[69]

Richardson turned on its head the literal interpretation of St. Paul's famous expression of eschatology: "For now we see through a glass, darkly; but then face to face."[70] Through hyperbole, he suggested that God had pulled the veil aside in ways that should do more than simply satisfy humankind's question about God's existence. The potential of connoisseurship to be a religious practice is expressed tacitly but most fervently here. By training the judgment, exercising the sight, and taking pleasure, the connoisseur could not fail to come closer to God. By learning to savor the parts of paintings—the subjects, the coloring, the composition, the particular manners and invention of individual artists, and so on—which were things that gave great

---

66. Laura Lunger Knoppers, "The Politics of Portraiture: Oliver Cromwell and the Plain Style," *Renaissance Quarterly* 51, no. 4 (1998): 1282–1319.

67. Richardson, *Science of a Connoisseur*, 184.

68. Ibid., 191.

69. Ibid., 194.

70. 1 Corinthians 13:12.

pleasure, the connoisseur learned to see the beauties of nature so that to him or her

> the most Common things . . . creates great Delight in his Mind. . . . [T]he Beauties of the Works of the great Author of Nature are not seen but by Enlighten'd Eyes, and to These they appear far otherwise than before they were so; as we hope to see every thing still nearer to its true Beauty, and Perfection in a Better State, when we shall see *what our Eyes have not yet seen, nor our Hearts conceiv'd.*[71]

The rewards of connoisseurship went far beyond the canvas. In learning to look rationally at art, an individual could learn to see the world differently. This was the most significant justification for Richardson of connoisseurship: it placed the individual in a different relationship with God.

Although the role of religion in enlightenment science in Britain is well established, its importance to art remains insecure. Further work, for example, on debates about idolatry, the use of art imagery in theological writings, and the continuity of plain-style portraiture through the eighteenth century, may yield considerable insights into the concerns expressed so vividly by Jonathan Richardson in what remain distinctive art theoretical texts. Richardson's writings emerged from a period of intense religious and political conflict during the reign of Queen Anne, and it is striking to observe that they remained the most sustained attempt to consider painting theoretically on religious terms, until Ruskin's writings in the quite different conditions of the mid-nineteenth century. Although they were formative on Joshua Reynolds, whose *Discourses* were widely read in the later eighteenth century, as well as other artist-writers such as James Barry and Benjamin West, the wider impact of Richardson's manifesto for English art is difficult to measure.[72] Nevertheless, the publication of new editions of his works in 1725, 1773, and 1792 suggests that they continued to be influential.[73]

---

71. Richardson, *Science of a Connoisseur*, 203–4.
72. Barrell, *Theory of Painting*, passim.
73. Apparently persuaded by his son and his friend Ralph Palmer, Richardson removed some of the religious content from the texts for the 1728 French edition and for

By attending more closely to the shape and direction that his own faith gave his arguments, we can clearly see why Richardson expressed his ambitions as a writer in this way:

> Would to God I could be Instrumental in persuading Gentlemen to exchange those trifling, Unmanly, and Criminal Pleasures to which too many are accustomed, for those of the Other, and Better kind: Would to God I could persuade them to manage life well; to get Noble Ideas of the Supreme Being; to apply themselves to the Knowledge and Improvement of Useful and Excellent arts . . . [and] to impregnate their Minds with Pure and Beautiful Images.[74]

Richardson set out to secure painting as a practice suitable for English Protestants. He did this not by setting religion to the side but by demonstrating how God's gift of painting could be reclaimed to encourage moral virtue, piety, and orthodox Christianity.

Jonathan Richardson Jr.'s edition in 1773, but it was restored for the edition published in 1792. See Gibson-Wood, *Jonathan Richardson: Art Theorist*, 253–54.

74. Richardson, *Science of a Connoisseur*, 196.

Telescopes, Microscopes, and the Problem of Evil

Christopher Fauske
Salem State University[1]

Astronomers of the late seventeenth and early eighteenth centuries found themselves for a while at the center of an alignment of scientific, cultural, and religious curiosity. Theirs was an endeavor embraced by significant segments of the established churches of England and Ireland who supported the founding of scientific societies in both countries and who drew on their network of contacts with continental Protestants to keep abreast of current developments abroad. In England, for example, works such as the Reverend William Derham's *Astro-theology* drew on mounting evidence that the universe might well be far larger than could be imagined to raise the possibility that life, for so long thought only to be on the level of the observable, in fact was infinite in scope.[2] At the opposite end of the scale, Anton Van Leeuwenhoek in the Dutch city of Delft was making startling discoveries with the microscope that reinforced the pioneering work Robert Hooke had detailed in studies such as *Micrographia*.[3] Van Leeuwenhoek's observations,

1. I would like to thank Richard Kleer of the Department of Economics at the University of Regina for his thoughtful reading and comments on a late draft of this article.

2. William Derham, *Astro-theology: or, A Demonstration of the Being and Attributes of God, from a Survey of the Heavens Based on the Author's Observations by Means of "Mr. Huygens' Glass"* (London, 1714).

3. Robert Hooke, *Micrographia: or Some Physiological Descriptions of Minute Bodies Made by Magnifying Glasses: With Observations and Inquiries Thereupon. by R. Hooke, Fellow of the Royal Society* (London, 1665).

communicated to the Royal Society in London,[4] revealed a teeming microscopic world so stunning that the Society at first refused to accept his reports on cells. The Dutchman at length prevailed on the Society to commission a team to review his work. Among those asked by the Society to review Van Leeuwenhoek's work were Alexander Petrie, minister to the English Reformed Church in Delft; Benedict Haan, at that time Lutheran minister at Delft; and Henrik Cordes, then Lutheran minister at The Hague. That Petrie, Haan, and Cordes were part of the team sent to review Van Leeuwenhoek's work speaks to the coexistence of scientific inquiry into new realms of knowledge with a religious mind-set independent of, but sympathetic to, the possible implications.

Derham was the rector of St. Laurence's in Upminster, Essex.[5] Two years after the publication of *Astro-theology*, he was appointed canon of Windsor and thus became a member of the ecclesiastical body of St. George's Chapel at Windsor Castle, the chapel of the Order of the Garter and a royal peculiar whose members were exempt from episcopal oversight and were, in theory, answerable only to themselves and the monarch.[6] Derham's appointment to Upminster suggests connections

4. The extent of the correspondence between Leeuwenhoek and the society can be seen in a series of letters gathered and bound in London with the title *Letters to the Royal Society, Extracted from Issues Published between 1673 and 1685*. The contents include letter 94: "A specimen of some observations made by a microscope"; letter 106: "Microscopical observations . . . about blood, milk, bones"; letter 117: "Microscopical observations . . . concerning the optic nerve"; letter 160: "Abstract of a letter . . . concerning scales within the mouth"; letter 165: "Letter . . . containing observations about the cristallin humor of the eye"; letter 168: "Abstract of a letter . . . concerning the parts of the brain of several animals"; letter 173: "Abstract of a letter . . . concerning the various figures of the salts contained in several substances"; letter 174: "Abstract of a letter . . . concerning generation by an insect;" accessed March 28, 2013, http://search.lib.unc.edu/search?R=UNCb3174649. Leeuwenhoek was elected a fellow of the society in 1680.

5. Today, Upminster is the eastern terminus of Transport for London's District Line. Derham succeeded a rector appointed by the Halke family, who would seem to have acquired the right to presentment from their relative William Harvey, discoverer of the circulation of the blood. Presentations in 1662 and 1679 were made by members of the Halke family. I have been unable to determine if there was a Harvey/Halke connection to Derham's presentation in 1688, but it seems likely. Accessed October 23, 2012, http://www.british-history.ac.uk/report.aspx?compid=42831.

6. Biographies of Derham tend to refer to his "election" as canon of Windsor, but then and now "appointment of Canons . . . is by Letters Patent issued by the monarch, so ultimately it [was] the Sovereign's decision. Whether or not Chapter had any involvement

to the family of William Harvey, discoverer of the circulation of the blood, and his appointment as canon of Windsor indicates a degree of royal approval for the intermingling of religious and scientific activity. In addition to his astronomical work, Derham developed an extensive holding of insects, published daily weather reports for Upminster for several years, and experimented with barometric pressure readings to try to ascertain their relation to weather. As part of his meteorological work, he contributed to the discussion of the "Great Storm" of November 26–27, 1703, recording the lowest barometric pressure reading of the event.[7] From Delft, Van Leeuwenhoek offered his recordings of the phenomenon. Derham was elected a fellow of the Royal Society in 1702 and made the first reasonably accurate measurements of the speed of light. In short, he was the embodiment of the royalist, scientific, conforming clergyman who represented both a validation of the post-1688 settlement and an affirmation of the continuity of the church's engagement in both religious and social activity.

This sympathetic alignment of science and faith presented Anglican theologians familiar with such works the opportunity to secure the underpinnings of their faith by demonstrating its compatibility with worlds both greater and smaller than had ever before been seen.[8] Perhaps the most effective demonstration of the ends to which such observations could be put came from the pen of the man who would end his career as archbishop of Dublin, William King, who recognized in the emerging stream of data a means to tackle perhaps the greatest conundrum of monotheistic religion: the nature of evil. Then, as now, the issue was how to reconcile an omniscient, omnipotent God with apparent imperfections in both society ("moral evil"—willful acts of human beings, such

---

in the nomination of candidates at that period is something we are currently investigating, but I am afraid we do not have an answer yet." Personal correspondence with Eleanor Cracknell, Assistant Archivist, St George's Chapel Archives and Chapter Library, October 26, 2012.

7. William Derham, "A Letter for the Reverend Mr. William Derham, F. R. S. Containing His Observations Concerning the Late Storm," *Philosophical Transactions of the Royal Society* 24, no. 289 (1704): 1530–34.

8. I am aware of the anachronistic nature of the word *Anglican* in this article, but it is surely easier than referring each time to "the Church of England and the Church of Ireland" when I am referring to doctrine held in common.

as murder or theft) and nature ("natural evil"—famine, storms, etc.). The "big" question was whether such evils exist as evil, in which case the efficacy of God's creation is up for debate, or whether such evils do not in fact exist but are indicative of failures in human understanding, which raises the question of the reason for God's creation of an imperfect human condition. The result of King's labors, *De origine mali*, received significant attention in Germany and France and had an immediate impact in Britain.[9] At least as important, both *De origine mali* and King's companion piece, *Divine Predestination and Fore-knowledg*,[10] were greeted not as rarified theological expositions but as part of a broad cultural embrace of the idea that life existed on a scale, both great and small, previously only imagined in literature.

Derham's call in *Astro-theology* for consideration of a "new system" consisting of a plurality of worlds, each containing a central star orbited by planets, owed something to previous works published elsewhere in Europe. One of those had first appeared in English in 1698 and came with a British royal imprimatur. It was Christiaan Huygens's *The Celestial Worlds Discover'd*.[11] Huygens, a Dutch polymath who had been secretary to William of Orange, is better remembered for his work on probability theory, but his interest in optics was significant, and he was one of the

---

9. William King, *De origine mali* (Dublin, 1702). The first English translation is referred to throughout this article: *Essay on the Origin of Evil by Dr. William King, Late Lord Archbishop of Dublin. Translated from the Latin, with Large Notes; Tending to Explain and Vindicate Some of the Author's Principles Against: The Objections of Bayle, Leibnitz, the Author of a Philosophical Enquiry Concerning Human Liberty; and Others*, trans. Edward Law (London, 1731) (hereafter cited as *Essay*). Strengthening the connection between the theologian and social philosophers, Law's translation appeared with an introductory thesis by the clergyman John Gay, a cousin of the more famous poet of the same name, titled *Concerning the Fundamental Principle of Virtue or Morality*. For more on the contemporary responses to the work, see Hermann J. Real, "Conversations with a Theodicist: William King's *Essay on the Origin of Evil*, with Some Sidelights on Hobbes, Milton, and Pope," in *But Vindicate the Ways of God to Man: Literature and Theodicy*, ed. Rudolf Freiburg and Susanne Gruss (Tübingen, Germany: Stauffenburg, 2004), 85–112.

10. William King, *Divine Predestination and Fore-knowledg, Consistent with the Freedom of Man's Will. A Sermon Preach'd at Christ-Church, Dublin, May 15, 1709 Before His Excellency Thomas Earl of Wharton, Lord Lieutenant of Ireland, and the Right Honourable the House of Lords* (Dublin, 1709).

11. Christiaan Huygens, *The Celestial Worlds Discover'd: Or, Conjectures Concerning the Inhabitants, Plants and Productions of the Worlds in the Planets. Written in Latin by Christianus Huygens, Late Secretary to His Majesty K. William* (London, 1698).

astronomers who began to unravel the nature of the rings of Saturn. He also discovered one of its moons, Titan, and became increasingly interested in the plausibility of extraterrestrial life. Separately from the Royal Society's delegation, Huygens conducted his own experiments replicating Van Leeuwenhoek's observations of cellular life.

Literature had long anticipated Derham, Huygens, and the Frenchman Bernard le Bovier de Fontenelle, who wrote *Entretiens sur la pluralité des mondes*—a book King had in his library.[12] Cicero's *De re publica* presents a complex cosmology in book six, *Somnium Scipionis*,[13] wherein Scipio ascends into the heavens and observes, "The earth itself seemed so small to me that I felt ashamed of our empire, whose extent was no more than a dot on its surface."[14] C. S. Lewis reminds us that "this passage was constantly in the minds of succeeding writers. . . . It was part of the moralists' stock-in-trade."[15] Boethius's *Consolation of Philosophy*, Dante's *Divine Comedy*, and John Milton's *Paradise Lost* all depend on a universe far more complex than contemporary astronomy offered them. Milton describes the Earth as "this punctual spot" (8.23) and "of smallest Magnitude" (2.1053).

That the Church of Ireland was as engaged in this same synthesis of faith, reason, and literature as its English counterpart should have come as no surprise. Puritan England had seen a chaotic, largely unfettered argument within a broad, Protestant consensus, but Cromwellian Ireland had been far more alarming for all, with sect after sect taking to print to state its case, often advocating a violent rejection of both "false doctrine"

12. Bernard le Bovier de Fontenelle, *Entretiens sur la pluralité des mondes* (Paris, 1686). The first English edition appeared the following year in Dublin (translated by Sir W. D. Knight) and then in London in 1688 (translated by John Glanvill); also in 1688, two versions of a translation by Aphra Behn appeared. Also in King's library were Derham's *Astro-theology* and his *Physico-theology: Or, a Demonstration of the Being and Attributes of God*, 3rd ed. (London, 1714). For the holdings in King's library, see Robert S. Matteson with Gayle Barton, *A Large Private Park: The Collection of Archbishop William King, 1650–1729*, 2 vols. (Cambridge, UK: LP Publications, 2003).

13. Cicero, *The Republic, The Laws*, trans. Niall Rudd (Oxford: Oxford University Press), 1998.

14. Ibid., 89.

15. C. S. Lewis, *The Discarded Image: An Introduction to Medieval and Renaissance Literature* (Cambridge: Cambridge University Press, 1964), 26.

and civil authority.[16] As far as the Church of Ireland was concerned, matters were little improved after William III's victory re-emboldened the Presbyterians to again espouse their tenets of faith, culminating in John Toland's *Christianity Not Mysterious.*[17] That the Irish parliament ordered the book burned did not, as far as several leading Church of Ireland clerics saw it, lessen the need to answer Toland's claims, and various attacks specifically on Toland appeared in Dublin. Doctrinal assaults aside, the Church of Ireland sought more comprehensive responses to Toland's ideas, recognizing, in part, that appeals to doctrine alone provided a rhetorical framework with its own built-in complications. The Irish layman Robert Boyle had sufficient sense to recognize the practical benefits of trusting that a broader religio-scientific response would be sufficient to answer the claims of Toland and his ilk. Boyle's bequest establishing the lecture series that bore his name stipulated that the series seek "to prove the Christian religion against notorious Infidels, Theists, Pagans, Jews and Mahometans, without descending to any Controversies that are among Christians themselves."[18]

The matter of the size and nature of the universe meshed with microscopic observation to offer a means to address what had hitherto been a conundrum that seemed to preclude rational extrapolation. The argument of the church fathers was that part of God's essence is his creation. It would seem to follow that God, being infinite, must have the capacity to create an infinite range of things, both animate and inanimate. Until recently, however, God's creation had seemed to have been limited to a distinctly human scale, raising the absurd possibility that the power of his creation was, in fact, limited to a particular range of size. Prior to discoveries of microscopic life and increasing evidence

16. Crawford Gibben, *God's Irishmen: Theoretical Debates in Cromwellian Ireland* (Oxford: Oxford University Press, 2007).

17. John Toland, *Christianity Not Mysterious: A Treatise Shewing, That There is Nothing in the Gospel Contrary to Reason, Nor Above It: And that No Christian Doctrine Can Be Properly Called a Mystery* (London, 1696). The subtitle nicely sums up Toland's argument. Helpful notes to the book are available at http://www.alisonmorgan.co.uk/Toland.pdf, accessed July 24, 2013.

18. Robert E. W. Maddison, *The Life of the Honourable Robert Boyle, F. R. S.* (London: Taylor & Francis, 1969), 275, quoted in Jack J. MacIntosh and Peter Anstey, "Robert Boyle," *The Stanford Encyclopedia of Philosophy*, ed. Edward N. Zalta, Fall 2010 edition, accessed September 10, 2010, http://plato.stanford.edu/entries/boyle/index.html#note-15.

of astronomical complexity, the best solution to the argument was that God had created all that was necessary for his own works. However, this suggested some sort of limitation either to God's creative powers or to his ambition, and neither was a particularly satisfactory outcome. This intimation of limitations on God's part played into the traditional paradox that if God were omniscient he would not have created anything that would permit of evil in the world. This left the problem of evil susceptible to claims that evil was in some sense inherent in God's act of creation, that evil was a constituent aspect of God. Various Christian heresies had developed as a result of this line of thought, and until the tail end of the seventeenth century the only possible response to that challenge was the observation that God was unknowable. Recent observations were filling in the void at both micro- and macroscopic levels and seemed increasingly to indicate a dynamic system that offered new ways of understanding old problems. For Anglican theologians and scientists, this relatively sudden and dramatic filling of the void, at both ends of the scale, offered something exhilarating: the opportunity to demonstrate that their faith embraced the idea of a plurality of worlds teeming with life and evidence of God's creation.

The vicar of Laracor and dean of St. Patrick's Dublin, Jonathan Swift, demonstrated one rhetorical approach to combining faith and observation in perhaps his most charming surviving sermon, "On the Trinity," which directly addresses the very first article of religion of the Church of Ireland.[19] He opens with a typically blunt guide to what his sermon is about:

> This day being set apart to acknowledge our Belief in the Eternal TRINITY, I thought it might be proper to employ my present Discourse entirely upon that Subject; and, I hope, to handle it in such a Manner, that the most Ignorant among you

---

19. Article 1, "Of Faith in the Holy Trinity," states, "There is but one living and true God, everlasting, without body, parts, or passions; of infinite power, wisdom, and goodness; the maker and preserver of all things both visible and invisible. And in unity of this Godhead there be three Persons, of one substance, power, and eternity; the Father, the Son, and the Holy Ghost." The Thirty-Nine Articles of Religion of the Church of England (and of the Church of Ireland) can be found at http://www.eskimo.com/~lhowell/bcp1662/articles/articles.html/.

may return home better informed of your Duty in this great
Point, than probably you are at present.[20]

The reason for such ignorance, Swift points out, is that the word
trinity is "not in Scripture, but was a Term of Art invented in the earlier
Times to express the Doctrine by a single Word, for the sake of Brev-
ity and Convenience."[21] For Swift, this is an opportunity to get as close
to theology and philosophy as he ever undertakes, and that he does so
while sailing very close to Toland's waters in his advocacy of the individual's ability to rely on reason to understand the commands of faith
underlines both his skill and confidence:

> It must be allowed that every Man is bound to follow the Rules
> and Directions of that Measure of Reason which God hath given
> him; and indeed he cannot do otherwise, if he will be sincere,
> or act like a Man. For Instance, if I should be commanded by an
> Angel from Heaven to believe it is Midnight at Noon-day; yet I
> could not believe him.[22]

Nonetheless, the "Doctrine . . . as delivered in Holy Scripture . . . is
very short, and amounts only to this, That the Father, the Son, and the
Holy Ghost, are each of the God, and yet there is but one God."[23] That
some people were too obtuse or too willful to accept this led to the
Arian heresy "revived in the World about an hundred Years ago, and
continued ever since; not out of a Zeal to Truth, but to give Loose to
Wickedness, by throwing off all Religion."

The solution, says Swift, is straightforward: Although

> God is [in Holy Scripture] expressed in three different Names,
> as Father, as Son, and as Holy Ghost . . . there is but one

---

20. Jonathan Swift, "On the Trinity" (London, 1744), in *Irish Tracts, 1720–1723, and
Sermons: Prose Works of Jonathan Swift*, vol. 9, ed. Herbert Davis (Oxford, UK: Blackwell,
1948), 159–68, esp. 159. On the dating of Swift's surviving sermons, see Carl P. Daw, "An
Annotated Edition of Five Sermons by Jonathan Swift" (PhD diss., University of Virginia,
1970).
21. Swift, "On the Trinity," 160.
22. Ibid., 161.
23. Ibid., 160.

God. But this Union and Distinction are a Mystery utterly unknown to Mankind.

This is enough for any good Christian to believe on this great Article, without ever inquiring any farther: And this can be contrary to no Man's reason, although the Knowledge of it is hid from him.[24]

Swift seeks to remind his congregation that obedience to God's revealed will is paramount in a world in which, nonetheless, "God did never command us to believe, nor his Ministers to preach, any Doctrine which is contrary to the Reason he hath pleased to endow us with." [25] Reason here serves as a guide to the *via media* between the Marian tendencies of the Roman Catholic Church and the rejection of the Christian Mysteries as espoused by Toland. The argument that reason and faith can be mutually confirming is bolstered if a positive feedback loop can be demonstrated as new discoveries emerge. Swift's explication of the doctrine of the trinity serves as a precise demonstration of an absolutely orthodox approach to the nexus of science and religion rapidly embraced by the Anglican churches. Reason was not paramount, but it was a sufficient guide to understand how the wonders of God's works might be understood in light of what was being revealed by the works of reason through science.

George Berkeley, an Irish cleric more inclined than Swift to philosophical consideration of how to align faith, reason, and science, noted at about the time that Swift was considering the nature of the trinity that

To one who regards things with a Philosophical Eye, and hath a Soul capable of being delighted with the sense that Truth and Knowledge prevail among Men, it must be a grateful Reflection

---

24. Ibid., 162.

25. Ibid., 164–65. For the consequences of taking too drastically the step Swift hopes for, see Jonathan Swift, *An Argument to Prove, That the Abolishing of Christianity in England, May, as Things now Stand, be Attended with Some Inconveniences* (1708), in *Bickerstaff Papers and Pamphlets on the Church: Prose Works of Jonathan Swift*, ed. Herbert Davis, vol. 2 (Oxford, UK: Blackwell, 1940), 26–39.

to think that the sublimest Truths . . . are now grown familiar to
the meanest Inhabitants of these Nations.[26]

Like Swift, Boyle, and Derham, Berkeley rejoiced in the convergence
of Truth (with its implication of the divine) with knowledge derived
from reason. Indeed, the more that knowledge could be disseminated
even to the "meanest inhabitants," and the more it could be shown to
be complementary to truth as revealed by the Bible, the more secure
would be the justification of the two established churches' *via media*.
Berkeley, who would finish his career as bishop of Cloyne, proceeds
to ask whether "the Mind of a Philosopher [can] rise to a more just
and magnificent and at the same time a more amiable Idea of the
Deity. . . . And yet [Jesus's language] is the language of Shepherds and
Fishermen."[27] It was a sentiment Swift echoed in his sermon on the
trinity and wholeheartedly endorsed, most famously in his *Letter to a
Young Gentleman Lately Entered into Holy Orders*, wherein he warns
against the "frequent Use of obscure Terms . . . than which I do not
know a more universal, inexcusable, and unnecessary Mistake among
the Clergy of all Distinctions."[28] Berkeley's own philosophical treatises
would draw heavily on questions of sight and scale, insights Swift would
adopt in determining the relative heights of Gulliver, the Lilliputians,
and the Brobdingnagians.[29] But it was a more senior Irish cleric who
embraced the lessons of the new observational sciences to tackle
head-on a substantive matter so complicated that unraveling the answers
threatened to dismantle the very framework not just of the Thirty-Nine
Articles but of the Christian faith itself.

The question was hardly new: Why is there evil? But the answer
William King, already a prominent member of the Dublin Philosophical
Society, outlined was very much of its time, and almost breathtakingly

26. George Berkeley, *Guardian* 88 (June 22, 1713), in *The Guardian*, ed. John Calhoun
Stephens (Lexington: The University Press of Kentucky, 1982), 318.

27. Ibid., 319.

28. Jonathan, Swift, *Letter to a Young Gentleman Lately Entered into Holy Orders*
(London, 1720), in *Irish Tracts, 1720–1723, and Sermons: Prose Works of Jonathan
Swift*, ed. Herbert Davis, vol. 9 (Oxford, UK: Blackwell, 1948), 61–81, esp. 65.

29. See William A. Eddy, *Gulliver's Travels: A Critical Study* (New York: Russell &
Russell, 1963).

so.[30] Indeed, in answering the question of the origin of evil King wrote himself into a position that required him also to consider the question of predestination and free will in light of Church of Ireland doctrine that had a stronger Calvinist streak than its English counterpart. Although the Church of Ireland took the predestination aspects of article 17 seriously, it had also to admit the existence of free will in order to distinguish itself from various Protestant sects.[31] Both treatises rely on traditional theological tropes while drawing on recent scientific developments to justify church doctrine and seek to demonstrate that recent discoveries underscore the foundational strength of the Anglican churches.

King's remarkably generous theodicy, *De origine mali*, earned extensive commentary from Pierre Bayle and high praise from Gottfried Leibniz and directly influenced Alexander Pope's *Essay on Man*. New discoveries enabled by improvements in optics offered the possibility of an answer to that old puzzle of why there was so much "nothingness" in a cosmos created by an all-powerful divinity. It was an answer King seized on. Politically conservative and naturally cautious, King, in his analysis, is surprisingly optimistic. While acknowledging that part of the challenge confronting any theodicist is that God's nature cannot, by definition, be known, King argues at some length that our God-given faculties are making the world increasingly

---

30. See K. Theodore Hoppen, *The Common Scientist in the Seventeenth Century: A Study of the Dublin Philosophical Society* (Charlottesville: University Press of Virginia, 1970). In the context of this paper, it is worth noting that King's interest in applied science lasted throughout his life. An early publication of his was *A Discourse Concerning the Bogs and Loughs of Ireland* (London, 1686), an edition of "A Discourse Concerning the Bogs, and Loughs of Ireland as it was presented to the Dublin Society by Mr William King, Fellow of that Society," in Dublin in 1685. One of King's last published works was "An Account of the Manner of Manuring Lands by Sea-shells, as Practised in the Counties of Londonderry and Donegall in Ireland. By His Grace the Lord Archbishop of Dublin. Communicated by Samuel Molyneux Esq.," *Philosophical Transactions 1708–1709* 26 (1708): 59–64, accessed April 11, 2013, http://rstl.royalsocietypublishing.org/content/26/313-324/59.full.pdf+html.

31. For the historical background, see Alan Ford, "Dependent or Independent? The Church of Ireland and Its Colonial Context, 1536–1649," *The Seventeenth Century* 10, no. 2 (1995), 163–87.

comprehensible and that it will, in time, be possible to know not the nature of God but the nature of God's creation.

An Essay on the Origin of Evil was very much of its time; indeed, in his 1731 English translation of King's work, Edward Law, later bishop of Carlisle, adds a lengthy note referring the reader to *Spectator* 519 (October 25, 1712), in which Joseph Addison reflects, after reading de Fontenelle, that "[t]he Material World is only the Shell of the Universe . . . [and] it is amazing to consider the Infinity of Animals" now revealed on the micro level. "Infinite Goodness," Addison suggests, "is of so communicative a nature that it seems to delight in the conferring of Existence upon every Degree of Perceptive Being."[32] Having read King and, of course, the various literary lights of his acquaintance, Pope reflects in his first epistle of the *Essay on Man* on "The Nature and State of Man with Respect to the Universe," that "worlds on worlds compose one universe," and asks us to

> Observe how system into system runs,
> What other planets circle other suns,
> What vary'd being peoples every star.[33] (24–27)

That existence had now been identified on previously unimaginable scales and that deductive reasoning suggested it might yet be found to be "conferred . . . upon every degree of perceptive being" solved the problem of the apparent void in the creation of God. It was becoming clear through the microscope and the telescope that an infinitely powerful God had created an infinitely physical world. This was critical to King.

Early in the *Essay*, King spends some time exploring the connection between God's nature and his creation. From this, King concludes that the scale between perfection and nonexistence is infinite and populated at all degrees by created things. Indeed, King would seem to take to heart the implications of an infinite scale when he acknowledges the profoundly humbling probability, if not the certainty, that life is not anthropocentric: "Those . . . who urge the Unfitness of

32. Joseph Addison, *Spectator* no. 519 (October 25, 1712), accessed June 2, 2010, http://www.gutenberg.org/files/12030/12030-h/SV3/Spectator3.html#section519.

33. Alexander Pope, *Essay on Man* (London, 1732).

certain parts of the Earth for the Sustenance of Man . . . are oblig'd to prove that the Earth was made for the sake of Mankind only, and not of the Universe. . . . But this is absurd."[34] Addison would reflect on de Fontenelle's suggestion that such is the overwhelming abundance of life it is likely all other planets have life on them. Addison was not particularly interested in exobiology, but his suggestion that distant planets "should be furnished with Beings adapted to their respective Situations" leads him to reflect, as King had noted, that "there is an infinitely greater space and room for different Degrees of Perfection, between the Supreme Being and Man, than between Man and the most despicable Insect."[35]

In both King and Addison, we see the last vestiges of the traditional "Great Chain of Being" argument about the relationship between God and man.[36] They were not alone, however, in rejecting the "chain" concept and preferring an image closer to something approximating a web of infinite gradation from the perfect center (God) to an infinite variety of life spread out across the vastness of space. Diverse and unimaginably variegated on both a micro- and a macroscopic level though life might be, God is not arbitrary, and "since it is proper that matter should be put into Motion, 'tis better that this should be done according to some certain Laws."[37] King's framing introduction to the *Essay* explicitly shares the motives of Newton and Boyle. Newton's laws of motion, the practicalities of which had been known for millennia, were not explained until the 1687 *Philosophiae naturalis principia mathematica*, wherein he observes that "Geometry does not teach us to draw . . . lines, but requires them to be drawn. For it requires that the learner should first be taught to describe these [lines] accurately, before he enters upon Geometry."[38] Newton makes

---

34. King, *Essay*, 106.

35. Addison, *Spectator* no. 519. He is paraphrasing John Locke's *Essay Concerning Human Understanding* (London, 1690), 3:vi,12, 213.

36. For a full discussion on this topic, see the still-relevant Arthur O. Lovejoy, *The Great Chain of Being: A Study of the History of an Idea* (Cambridge, MA: Harvard University Press, 1936).

37. King, *Essay*, 99.

38. Isaac Newton, *The Mathematical Principles of Natural Philosophy By Sir Isaac Newton. Translated into English by Andrew Motte* (London, 1729), 8. All references are to

it clear in his preface that he considers his work philosophy rather than mechanics, expressing the

> wish [that] we could derive the rest of the phenomena of Nature by the same kind of reasoning from mechanical principles. For I am induced by many reasons to suspect that they may all depend upon certain forces by which the particles of bodies, by some causes hitherto unknown, are either mutually impelled towards each other . . . or are repelled and recede from each other.[39]

He asserts that his intention is that where "philosophers have hitherto attempted the search of Nature in vain . . . I hope the principles here laid down will afford some light to that, or some truer, method of Philosophy."[40]

It was a challenge to which King would rise. To prove his point, King would draw not only on Newton but also on his Irish compatriot and a sometime collaborator with Newton, Boyle, who had relocated to England after declaring Ireland "a barbarous country, where chemical spirits are so misunderstood, and chemical instruments so unprocurable, that it is hard to have any Hermetic thoughts in it."[41] However that might have been, Boyle coined the term "chemical analysis" as we now use it while in Ireland and compensated for the lack of chemical instruments by studying anatomy with his friend Sir William Petty, who had his own remarkable impact on Ireland—and on cartography and surveying in general—by overseeing the Down Survey.[42] Settled in Oxford, Boyle grew fascinated with the air pump and in 1660 published

---

this first English-language edition of the *Principia*. King owned the Latin original.

39. Ibid., 10.

40. Ibid.

41. Robert Boyle to Frederick Clodius (undated, likely between April and May 1654), qtd. in *The Correspondence of Robert Boyle*, ed. Michael Hunter, Antonio Clericuzio, and Lawrence M. Principe, vol. 1, *Introduction and Letters from 1636 to 1661* (London: Pickering and Chatto, 2001), 165. Boyle continued throughout his life to derive significant income from his Irish estates. The list of Boyle's works in King's library is extensive, running to at least nineteen different titles. See Matteson with Barton, *A Large Private Park*.

42. For more on Petty, see Ted McCormick, *William Petty and the Ambitions of Political Arithmetic* (Oxford: Oxford University Press, 2010).

New Experiments Physico-Mechanicall.[43] Even such an apparently mundane topic had religious implications, and it was while answering Francis Line, a Jesuit critic of the *New Experiments*, that Boyle made his first mention of the law that states that at constant temperature the product of the pressure and volume of an ideal gas is always constant; that is, that PV = K. Boyle's and Newton's laws offered precisely the type of evidence that underscored King's dictum that if "matter should be put into Motion, 'tis better that this should be done according to some certain Laws,"[44] a dictum that permitted the reassertion of theological "laws" delineated in the manner of Boyle and Newton.

Newton's "truer philosophy," and hence King's work, had, of course, a predecessor in Francis Bacon. Time and again, Bacon makes a connection between natural philosophy and theology. In *De augmentis scientiarum* he observes that "Sacred Theology is grounded on, and must be deduced from the Oracles of God; not from the light of Nature, or the Dictates of Reason,"[45] noting that

> the use of humane Reason in matters pertaining to Religion is of two sorts; the one in the explication and conception of the Mystery; the other in ill[umin]ations and Inferences derived from thence. . . . [For] God vouchsafeth to descend to the weaknesse of our capacity, so expressing and unfolding his Mysteries as they may be best comprehended by us.[46]

What Bacon brought to English religious discourse was the idea that "nature should be established as divine instead of satanic . . . that God has revealed himself . . . by means of two scriptures: . . . the written word . . . [and] through his handiwork, the created universe."[47] Part of King's

---

43. Robert Boyle, *New Experiments Physico-Mechanicall, Touching the Spring of the Air, and its Effects: Made for the Most Part in a New Pneumatical Engine* (London, 1660).

44. King, *Essay*, 99.

45. Francis Bacon, *Of the Advancement and Proficience of Learning; or, the Partitions of Sciences. Nine Books. Written in Latin [De Augmentis Scientiarum] by the Most Eminent, Illustrious, and Famous Lord Francis Bacon, Baron of Verulam, Viscount St. Alban, Councellor of Estate, and Lord Chancellor of England. Interpreted by Gilbert Watts* (Oxford, 1640), 474–5, esp. 474.

46. Ibid., 470–1.

47. Basil Willey, *The Seventeenth-Century Background: Studies in the Thought of the Age in Relation to Poetry and Religion* (New York: Doubleday, 1953), 42.

solution to the problem of evil lay in developing this idea of the divine in nature.[48]

King's *Essay* itemizes the varieties of natural evil, just as Bacon had done for the varieties of the sciences in *De augmentis scientiarum*. King's list of subheads that he will consider in turn offers a list that reads almost as a catalog of human inquiry as it stood at that time, albeit in an order that appears to defy logical sequencing: "generation and corruption," "animals and the variety of them," "death," "hunger, thirst, and labour," "propagation of the species, childhood, and old-age," "diseases, wild-beasts, and venomous creatures." In part, it is King's ability to develop the ideas implicit in recent discoveries of the vast "variety" of animals that permits him to do more than reiterate a version of the great chain of being. Instead, he draws on the increasing evidence of an infinite scale of existence to confirm through deduction ideas that had previously had to be accepted on faith alone. But King is careful, too, to warn against ignoring the guidance offered by faith, a not-so-veiled attack on Toland's recognition of a Christianity not mysterious. Such considerations lead King to the final substantive section, "concerning the errors and ignorance of man,"[49] which builds on the preceding exploration of the connection between nature, understood through science and human insight, and God, understood through theology informing science and human insight.

To address the question of moral evil, King returns to the wax problem of René Descartes, which he had earlier considered in his opening section. Admitting once again that "we acquire [knowledge] by the Senses" and reminding the reader that as "things [can be] very different internally [yet] have sometimes the same external marks," King acknowledges that "we must of necessity be often doubtful" of our perceptions.[50] Nonetheless, such sensory perception is "no more to be avoided than [any] other kind of *Imperfection*," even though "an

---

48. Among the works of Bacon in his library, King had a copy of *Opera omnia* (Frankfurt, 1665). For more on the range of King's intellectual reach and curiosity, see Joseph Richardson, "William King—European Man of Letters," in *Archbishop William King and the Anglican Irish Context*, 1688–1729, ed. Christopher Fauske (Dublin: Four Courts Press, 2004), 106–22.

49. King, *Essay*, 135–41.

50. Ibid., 135.

imperfect Nature . . . understands also imperfectly."[51] This interpretation permits the possibility of a Baconian gambit and, indeed, might even be said to require such a move. King answers the objection that, if he wanted to, God could make everything clear to humankind with the caveat that this would be an "interruption of the course of Nature" and reduce his creation to nothing more than random chance, a logical impossibility.[52] King reiterates the central significance of "the course of Nature" as proof of the coherence of God's design—a coherence required if one is to privilege the ability of human reason to be a guide to divine will—because he was writing at a time when science was "making clear" much of God's creation that until then had been hidden. True, such discoveries ran the risk of misinterpretation, but it was possible to "distinguish between those Errors which we fall into after our utmost diligence and application, and such as we are led into by carelessness, negligence, and a depraved Will."[53] Errors of understanding "are to be reckon'd among Natural Evils, and [are] not imputable to us: for they arise from the very State and Condition of the Mind of Man, and are not to be avoided."[54] Such an interpretation allowed for the continuing work of science precisely because any errors of understanding were neither moral failings nor necessarily a challenge to the moral underpinnings of society. Scientific experiment and observation, said King, served the religious purpose sought by Bacon and Newton, and there was nothing that had been discovered that fell afoul of Swift's admonition that "God did never command us to believe, nor his Ministers to preach, any Doctrine which is contrary to the Reason he hath pleased to endow us with."[55] Indeed, precisely because "an imperfect Nature . . . understands also imperfectly" but could be informed by rational consideration, appropriateness of religious doctrine could be determined by its ability to mediate the twin poles of faith and observation.

Having addressed natural evil, King extends his consideration of the possibilities provided by experimental observation, reason, and

---

51. Ibid., 135.
52. Ibid., 136.
53. Ibid.
54. Ibid.
55. Swift, "On the Trinity," 164–65.

conscience to address the question of moral evil. Moral evils, he says, "are to be reckon'd among" those which "come upon us knowingly and in a manner within our Consent," and "he must be esteem'd the cause of them, who knowingly and of his own accord, brings them either upon himself or others by a depraved or foolish choice."[56] King begins his analysis of moral evil by considering the matter of "election"—that is, the matter of an individual's ability to choose to act. Here, King returns to the ideas of John Locke, who had argued that "moral actions are only those that depend upon the choice of an understanding and free agent."[57] Or, as Milton put it in *Paradise Lost*, even if God "foreknew, / Foreknowledge had no influence on their fault / Which had no less prov'd certain unforeknown,"[58] which has the useful benefit of suggesting that free will is not at odds with God's foreknowledge. Moral evil, ultimately, is a matter of choice, made in rejection of the laws of God and of nature as understood by us. What makes *De origine mali* ultimately so optimistic a work is its insistence that evil is not inherent in the universe; rather, as the increasing evidence of science illuminates, the nature of the universe so broadens our ability to know and understand the full tapestry of creation that it will be ever less likely that we might act in violation of the morally appropriate, just as the better ordered, and hence understood, a civic society becomes, so the less likely one is to want to act in violation of its laws.

In proposing his solution to the problem of reconciling free will and an omniscient creator, required if there is to be such a thing as "moral evil" rather than divine caprice, King asserts that "there are certain Powers, faculties and Appetites implanted in us by Nature, which are directed to certain Actions."[59] These "faculties and appetites" are the ones in which "our Happiness, if we have any, seems to consist" if we "proper[ly] exercise" them.[60] What follows draws on that great question of early-eighteenth-century Irish philosophy, "Molyneux's problem,"

---

56. King, *Essay*, 149.
57. John Locke, "Of Ethic in General," in *Locke: Political Essays*, ed. Mark Goldie (Cambridge: Cambridge University Press, 2004), 300.
58. John Milton, *Paradise Lost: A Poem in Three Books* (London, 1667), bk. 3, lines 117–19.
59. King, *Essay*, 172.
60. Ibid.

in which a blind man suddenly sees,[61] a problem posed in response to Locke's explanation of various recent discoveries in the field of optics. Sight does nothing, says King, but "perceive . . . Light, Colours, &c. and, upon the Removal of these, its Action ceases."[62] It has, therefore, no intrinsic benefit, and reason, not sight itself, is the appropriate means by which to understand what we see.

King developed the consequences of this insight by drawing on an example straight out of Molyneux's other great preoccupation, the legal status of Ireland, an issue of great import, in particular, to the Church of Ireland, which claimed a national as well as theological justification for its position in Irish society. "It does not seem any more absurd for a Power to create an Agreeableness between itself and an Object, by applying itself to that Object," King writes, "than for a Man to acquire a Right to a thing by occupying it,"[63] underscoring the very practical connections men such as King sought to make between religion, science, and policy. Just as claims to the land by right of occupation, if held in accordance with the moral requirements identified by authors such as Hugo Grotius and Samuel von Pufendorf,[64] enable one to better identify with and delineate the nature of that country, so we acquire "rights" to nature by discovering, identifying, and naming its increasingly varied parts. Thus does the toolbox grow by which humankind can better understand the relationship between God and

---

61. "A Man, being born blind, and having a Globe and a Cube, nigh of the same bignes, Committed into his Hands, and being taught or Told, which is Called the Globe, and which the Cube, so as easily to distinguish them by his Touch or Feeling; Then both being taken from Him, and Laid on a Table, Let us Suppose his Sight Restored to Him; Whether he Could, by his Sight, and before he touch them, know which is the Globe and which the Cube? Or Whether he Could know by his Sight, before he stretch'd out his Hand, whether he Could not Reach them, tho they were Removed 20 or 1000 feet from Him?" William Molyneux to John Locke, July 7, 1688, quoted in Marjolein Degenaar and Gert-Jan Lokhorst, "Molyneux's Problem," The *Stanford Encyclopedia of Philosophy*, accessed October 27, 2011, http://plato.stanford.edu/entries/molyneux-problem/#1.

62. King, *Essay*, 172–73.

63. Ibid., 174.

64. For more on the links between King, Molyneux, and national identity, see Christopher Fauske, "The 'Good Irishmen': William Molyneux, Archbishop King, and the Poverty of a Nation," American Society for Eighteenth-Century Studies 2011 Annual Meeting, Vancouver, British Columbia, Canada, March 19, 2011, available at http://www.academia.edu/1678230/The_good_Irishmen_William_Molyneux_Archbishop_King_and_the_poverty_of_a_nation.

man: the greater the variety of experiences, the greater the ways of understanding God's creation.

King's many publications and his correspondence all indicate that narrative was a concept largely alien to him. During the debate over the plan to introduce a half-pence coin into Ireland (made famous by Swift's series of Drapier's Letters on the subject), King praised two treatises opposing the plan but reported not being impressed by those "printed before by some body, that calleth himself a Drapier, which were in a ludicrous and Satyrical Style."[65] It is possible King's comments to Samuel Molyneux were designed to protect Swift, the person then calling "himself a Drapier"; but it is at least as likely that they reflect his genuine opinion of the author's talents. Admiring Addison's *Cato*, King admitted he had little to judge it against as he had read no other English play "this thirty years" past.[66] It is a testament to the importance of its argument, then, rather than to its literary elegance, that *De origine mali* would not only receive attention from philosophers such as Berkeley, Bayle, and Leibniz but would also influence the philosopher Francis Hutcheson and thus inform the development of the sentimental school of philosophy and the flourishing of a later-eighteenth-century British literature of sentiment and sensibility.[67]

Berkeley identified in King's interest in questions of perception and scale the inherent problem in relying on the material world, which must be known through perception, to provide insight into the actual state of the universe. Molyneux's problem and King's use of it further underscored the problematic matter of material that could only be known through perception. In the discourse between King and other theologians, Berkeley recognized that in failing to follow his logic to

65. William King to Samuel Molyneux, November 24, 1724, quoted in Matteson with Barton, *A Large Private Park*, xxxiv.

66. William King to R. Daniel (n.d.), quoted in Matteson with Barton, *A Large Private Park*, xxxiv.

67. For the surprising relationship between King and Hutcheson, see Michael Brown, "The Strange Case of Dr. King and Mr. Hutcheson," in *Archbishop William King and the Anglican Irish Context, 1688–1729*, ed. Christopher Fauske (Dublin: Four Courts Press, 2004), 135–47. For the connection between early-eighteenth-century Irish philosophy and later Scottish philosophy, see David Berman, "The Birth of Scottish Philosophy from the Golden Age of Irish Philosophy," *Eighteenth-Century Studies* 45, no. 3 (2012): 379–92.

its conclusion, namely, that "things" are dependent on perception, King had left his work subject to attack from those who would quibble with the specifics of his examples without regard for the validity of his conclusions.[68] Berkeley's solution was to demonstrate that "material things [are] *mind-independent things or substances*" and that, therefore, as *esse est percipi*, it follows that "there are no such mind-independent things" we can perceive.[69]

Perhaps underscoring the reasons for Berkeley's rejection of materialism, Hutcheson, who despite his dissenter credentials had received some protection from King in Dublin, bases his argument in *An Essay on the Nature and Conduct of the Passions and Affections* in part on King's use of the infinite scale of creation to support his assertion that

> our State is absolutely Good, notwithstanding a considerable Mixture of Evil. The Goodness of the great Author of Nature appears even in producing the inferior Natures, provided their State in the whole be absolutely Good: Since we may probably conclude that there are in the Universe as many Species of superior Natures, as was consistent with the most perfect State of the whole.[70]

---

68. In particular, the debate between King and Peter Browne underscored for Berkeley the inherent failings of a materialist foundation. King and Browne agreed on the conclusion but differed bitterly about the nature of the evidence. Berkeley, who likewise shared their conclusion, recognized that their dispute arose from a mutual failure to grasp the immaterial nature of the world. For more on King, Berkeley, and Browne, see David Berman, *George Berkeley: Idealism and the Man* (Oxford: Oxford University Press, 1994), esp. 147–52; see also Paul J. Olscamp, "Peter Browne, Berkeley and the Deists," in *The Moral Philosophy of George Berkeley*, International Archives of the History of Ideas, vol. 33 (The Hague: Nijhoff, 1970), 204–22.

69. Lisa Downing, "George Berkeley," *The Stanford Encyclopedia of Philosophy* (Spring 2013 Edition), ed. Edward N. Zalta, accessed March 4, 2013, http://plato.stanford.edu/archives/spr2013/entries/berkeley/.

70. Francis Hutcheson, *An Essay on the Nature and Conduct of the Passions and Affections, with Illustrations on the Moral Sense*, ed. Aaron Garrett (Indianapolis, IN: Liberty Fund, 2002). Treatise 1, *An Essay on the Nature and Conduct of the Passions and Affections*, section ii: "Of the Affections and Passions: The Natural Laws of Pure Affection: The Confused Sensations of the Passions, with their Final Causes," accessed March 23, 2013, http://oll.libertyfund.org/titles/885/65924#a_1605736.

De origine mali provided the foundational work for a distinctly Anglophone eighteenth-century political and moral science based on the juncture through perception of a divinely inspired moral sentiment and an experiential worldview. Another influential British reaction to King's work would come from John Wesley, who misinterpreted King's understanding of the role of observational science in developing his own, perhaps less optimistic, explanation of the origin of evil, but who came over time to appreciate the distinction between natural and moral evils.[71]

While the work of Hutcheson and like-minded philosophers became the dominant perspective of mid-eighteenth-century Britain, literature, too, began to explore the implications of the worldview of *De origine mali*. One clear example can be seen in the work of Laurence Sterne, a native Irishman; long-serving vicar of Sutton-in-the-Forest, Yorkshire; and sometime preacher at York Minster, the very title of whose *A Sentimental Journey Through France and Italy* speaks to its ethos. In his great novelistic exposition of sentiment, *Tristram Shandy*, Sterne offers an extensive demonstration of the connections between sentiment, perception, and morality, including a sermon on the subject of trust. The sermon takes as its theme Hebrews 13:18: "Pray for us: for we trust we have a good conscience, in all things willing to live honestly." Yorick, speaking for Sterne,[72] argues that

> [i]f a man thinks at all, he cannot well be a stranger to the true state of this account;—he must be privy to his own thoughts and desires;—he must remember his past pursuits, and know certainly the true springs and motives, which, in general, have governed the actions of his life. . . . In other matters, we may be deceived by false appearances; and as the wise man complains,

---

71. For an explanation of Wesley's use of observational science and an account of his apparent misunderstanding of King's essay on evil, see Barry E. Bryant, "John Wesley On the Origins of Evil," *Wesleyan Theological Journal* 30, no. 1 (1995): 111–33.

72. For more on Sterne's sermons, see *Divine Rhetoric: Essays on the Sermons of Laurence Sterne*, ed. William B. Gerard (Newark: University of Delaware Press, 2010). For Sterne's doctrinal orthodoxy, see Christopher Fauske, "On Being Orthodox: The Sermons of Laurence Sterne and the Church of England Context," in *Divine Rhetoric*, 45–62.

hardly do we guess aright at the things that are upon earth, and with labour do we find the things that are before us.[73] But here the mind has all the evidence & facts within herself.[74]

Even if, as Yorick suggests, "the mind has all the evidence . . . [about herself] within herself," there remains the problem that while "one can be mistaken in one's beliefs," the really important question, as a late-twentieth-century novelist puts it, is whether it is

> possible to be mistaken *about* one's beliefs. If a person believes himself to exist, then he cannot be mistaken. But if a person claims not to believe in his own existence, how are we to respond to this? . . . Is he wrong in imagining himself to have such a belief?[75]

King had identified the solution to this problem by seeking to connect ideas of moral conduct with experiential evidence. It is this reliance on thought and perception that underscores Berkeley's concerns about the materialist underpinnings of King's work, but at the same time, Yorick, perhaps anticipating such a query about the individual understanding of one's own ideas, admonishes his congregation to focus on practical matters and

> remember this plain distinction, a mistake in which has ruined thousands,—that your conscience is not a law:—No, God and reason made the law, & have placed conscience within you to determine [it].[76]

---

73. Wisdom 9:16—an interesting choice as the Book of Wisdom (or the Wisdom of Solomon) is extracanonical and more often cited in Roman Catholic than in Anglican tracts.

74. Laurence Sterne, *The Life and Opinions of Tristram Shandy, Gentleman* (New York: Knopf, 1991), 136.

75. Andrew Crumey, *Pfitz* (Sawtry, UK: Dedalus, 1995), 85. This is a question that underpins the subsidiary plot in the episode "My Lucky Charm" of the television show *Scrubs*. Jerry is a patient with Cotard Delusion, or walking-corpse syndrome, who believes he is dead even though he is walking around and talking to patients and doctors. Mike Schwartz, "My Lucky Charm," in *Scrubs*, season 4, episode 14, directed by Chris Koch, aired January 25, 2005, (New York: NBC).

76. Sterne, *Tristram Shandy*, 155.

Sterne here seeks to ignore the argument between King and Berkeley, preferring to focus on the point King had made in distinguishing natural and moral evil in his admonition that "God *and* reason" together provide the means for recognizing the moral choices that must be made. While one component in that duality is ineffable, the other is eminently testable through observation and experimentation. Together, as for Bacon and King, they make the law that conscience helps us live by. The test of reason is its compatibility with faith; the test of faith is that its parameters can be extrapolated from reason. The role of conscience is to check that neither faith nor reason is advanced at the expense of the other.

Although the *Essay* attracted significant attention on its own merits, King did not find it necessary to answer his critics, at least in part because he was aware that, having addressed the problem of evil with a solution that posited the existence of free will, he had obliged himself to address the problem of salvation, which the Church of Ireland identified as essentially predestined. King would offer his solution in a sermon preached before the Lord Lieutenant of Ireland and the members of the Irish House of Lords in 1709 and published immediately thereafter as *Divine Predestination and Fore-knowledg, Consistent with the Freedom of Man's Will*. In this companion piece to *De origine mali*, we can see further demonstrations of King's enthusiastic and reassured embrace of science to underscore the validity of his faith. What King intended to do, he told his audience, was

> to lay before you that which I take to be the edifying part of the Doctrine of *Predestination*; and in such a manner . . . as to avoid every thing, that may give occasion to ignorant or corrupt Men to make an ill use of it.[77]

This admonition against "ignorant or corrupt Men" who might "make an ill use" of King's doctrine harks back to the definition of moral evil as an action deliberately chosen. King undertook his examination of free will in the same spirit as he had *De origine mali*, sure that we could deduce something of God from "Observations we have made of his

---

77. King, *Divine Predestination*, 4.

Works, and from the Consideration of those Qualifications, that we conceive would enable us to perform the like."[78]

The sermon's rhetorical style adheres to an Anglican tradition exemplified by the advice of John Wilkins, bishop of Chester, who had called in his 1646 treatise *Ecclesiastes, or, A Discourse Concerning the Gift of Preaching* for a style "plain and without rhetorical flourishes."[79] Dense though King's work can at times appear, the archbishop would seem to have been striving to honor his own admonition against those

> Philosophers [who] . . . being either puff'd up with the Vanity of appearing wise above the Vulgar, or impos'd upon by their own Subtilty, often frame Monsters of their own . . . : while they are striving to pursue Truth thro' Coverts impervious and inaccessible to human Wit, they leave her behind their Backs, and are blind in full Light.[80]

Wilkins's example might well have appealed to King for one other reason: he had been instrumental in the founding of the Royal Society and had been its first secretary. In that capacity, Wilkins had encouraged the work of a young graduate of Leiden University, Nehemiah Grew, son of a Nonconformist minister and the author in 1670 of a work made possible only because of the microscope, *The Anatomy of Vegetables Begun,*[81] which Wilkins brought to the Society's notice and to whom it was dedicated. The next year, at Wilkins's recommendation, Grew was elected a fellow. It was Grew who was asked by the Society to replicate Van Leeuwenhoek's discovery of cells. Wilkins himself had been pondering the implications of the discoveries being made through the telescope as early as his 1640 treatise *A Discourse Concerning a New World and Another Planet*, in which he observes that

---

78. Ibid., 5.

79. Arthur A. Tilley, "The Essay and the Beginning of Modern English Prose," in *The Cambridge History of English Literature*, vol. 8, *The Age of Dryden*, ed. Adolphus W. Ward and Alfred R. Waller (Cambridge: Cambridge University Press, 1912), 423.

80. King , *Essay*, 198.

81. Nehemiah Grew, *The Anatomy of Vegetables Begun, with a General Account of Vegetables Thereon* (London, 1672).

it were happy for us if we could exempt Scripture from Philosophicall controversies: if we could bee content to let it bee perfect for that end unto which it was intended, for a rule of our Faith and Obedience; and not stretch it also to be a judge of such naturall truths, as are to be found out by our owne industry and experience.[82]

What could be found out by human endeavor could still be wonderful, as Van Leeuwenhoek's work had demonstrated. "Indeed," wrote Samuel Hoole in his introduction to his translation of many of Van Leeuwenhoek's papers, "the extreme minuteness of many of the subjects on which he treats, is in some instances beyond the reach of our capacities to comprehend, although we may be fully assured of their existence."[83] Hoole then makes a reference to the *Spectator*, in this case number 420, which was itself adapted from a longer essay of Addison's "On the Pleasures of the Imagination," in which it was observed that "we may yet . . . discover in the smallest particle of this little world, a new inexhausted fund of matter, capable of being spun out into another universe."[84]

Wilkins's sentiments are echoed by King near the opening of the sermon, where he acknowledges that on the subject of free will and predestination "Learned Men have engag'd with the greatest Zeal and Fierceness . . . and the Disputes have prov'd so intricate, that the most diligent Reader will perhaps . . . be but little satisfy'd, and less edify'd, by the greatest part of all that has been written."[85] For King, as for Wilkins, Derham, and other scientists and philosophers who were also clerics, all these troubles could be reconciled if only people would recognize that faith without reason was at best ill informed and that reason without faith was morally enervating. Justification of either lay in the evidence of the other. In explicating the means by which free

82. John Wilkins, *A Discourse Concerning a New World and Another Planet* (London, 1640), 19–20.

83. Antony Van Leeuwenhoek, *The Select Works of Antony Van Leeuwenhoek, Containing his Microscopical Discoveries in Many of the Works of Nature. Translated from the Dutch and Latin Editions Published by the Author, by Samuel Hoole. Part the First* (London, 1798), iii–iv.

84. Joseph Addison, *Spectator* no. 420 (July 2, 1712), accessed April 11, 2013, http://www.gutenberg.org/files/12030/12030-h/SV3/Spectator3.html#section420.

85. King, *Divine Predestination*, 3.

will and predestination can be shown to be compatible, King this time looks not at the microscopic but instead to the vastness of the universe, which allows him to base his argument on a consideration of the smallness of humanity's grasp of the whole. In deploying what David Berman identifies as "the representative theory of perception," King

> supposes that our perception of the physical world involves three terms: (1) the mind, (2) its immediate experiences, called ideas or perceptions, and (3) the physical object and its qualities.[86]

He reiterates an argument made in *De origine mali* that an object does not necessarily contain the experience that it triggers: ice makes us feel cold not because it is cold per se but because of the experience—the perception—that our mind interprets as "cold." Perception tells us only a very small thing about the object being experienced, perhaps enough to react intelligently to the presence of the object as we should. A tiger charging toward us does not itself contain fear; we experience fear within ourselves and so flee (if all goes well) before the attributes inherent in the tiger cause us to be eaten.

Although the representative theory of perception offers a strategy to help understand the physical world, unless one sides with Berkeley in rejecting materialism as mistaking perception of a thing for knowing the thing, King also uses it as an analogy for how we might grasp at least the edges of the divine, equating the three terms identified earlier with their religious counterparts:

> (1) the mind, (2) what it knows of God's attributes, and (3) God's attributes as they are in God. . . . King supposes that (3) is known through (2) and that (2) represents (3). And King also tends to see a causal relationship between (3) and (1), which is productive of (2).[87]

The challenges provided by the potential lack of relationship between what is sensed and the thing sensed underscore that

---

86. David Berman, "The Irish Pragmatist," in *Archbishop William King and the Anglican Irish Context, 1688–1729,* ed. Christopher Fauske (Dublin: Four Courts Press, 2004), 123–34, esp. 125.

87. Ibid., 126.

the Nature and Perfections of God, as he is in himself, are such, that it is impossible we should comprehend them, especially in the present State of Imperfection, Ignorance and Corruption, in which this World lies. He is the Object of none of our Senses, by which we received all our direct and immediate perceptions of things; and therefore if we know any thing of him at all, it must be by Deductions of Reasons, by Analog and Comparison.[88]

So it is, says King, that to assume foreknowledge is "inconsistent with . . . Free-Will . . . is the same Absurdity as it is to conclude, that *China* is no bigger than a Sheet of Paper, because the Map, that represents it, is contain'd in that Compass."[89] "All maps are imperfect; this is the sadness of maps,"[90] but this sadness is critical for King because it once again allows him to draw on Molyneux's problem. For all our knowledge, deductive reasoning, and analytic skills, we have, in effect, the same relationship to God as a blind man has to color, and yet, like the blind man, we can make sense of the ideas that

> *Light* and *Colours* are but Effects . . . and that there are no such Things at all in Nature, but only in our Minds; of this at least we may be sure, that *Light* in the *Sun* or *Air*, are very different Things from what they are in our Sensations of them, yet we call them both by the same Names. . . . And yet strictly speaking, it is certain, that which in the *Sun* causes the Conception of *Light* in us, is as truly different in Nature from the Representation we have of it in our Mind, as our *Fore-knowledge*, is from what we call so in God.[91]

Aware that "there is [a] great difference between the Analogical Representations of God" and comparable analogies of the natural world, King reflects that this need not obviate his methodology:

> Whereas in ordinary figurative Representations, the thing express'd by the Figure, is commonly of much less moment

---

88. King, *Divine Predestination*, 10.

89. Ibid., 11.

90. Timothy Ferris, *The Whole Shebang: A State-of-the-Universe(s) Report* (New York: Simon & Schuster, 1997), 70.

91. King, *Divine Predestination*, 18.

than that to which it is compar'd, in these Analogies the Case is otherwise, and the things represented by them, have much more Reality and Perfection in them, than the things by which we represent them. Thus weighing a thing in our Minds, is a much more noble and perfect Action, than examining the Gravity of a Body by Scale and Balance . . . and yet if we reason from them by Analogy and Proportion, they are sufficient to give us such a Notion of God's Attributes, as will oblige us to fear, love, obey, and adore him.[92]

To underscore his point as the sermon nears its conclusion, King revisits mathematics and reflects on the fact that although it "seems inconceivable" that a negative integer multiplied by a negative integer

should be positive . . . yet if the most Ignorant will but have patience, and apply themselves for Instruction to the Skilful in these matters, they will soon find all the seeming Contradictions vanish . . . [and see] that the Assertions are . . . plain and easy Truths. . . .

Ought we not then to suspect our own Ignorance, when we fancy Contradictions in the descriptions given us of the Mysteries of our Faith and Religion?[93]

Perhaps we should, but we ought not, says King, deny the evidence of such "plain and easy Truths" as can be made out with the aid of a microscope, a telescope, and God-given reason.

The discovery of teeming multitudes of life at the microscopic and macroscopic levels and an expanding universe had excited the minds of more people than Derham, Addison, and de Fontenelle. As King demonstrated in his two monumental works of theology, reasonable deduction from the mass of newly discovered evidence could help secure faith. More than that, the compatibility of science and faith—the ability of each to reinforce the logical and empirical foundations of the other—underscored the claims that the Churches of Ireland and England were more than mere political creations.

92. Ibid., 22–23.
93. Ibid., 29–30.

Anglican laymen and clerics could look to science to justify their faith and to their faith to justify their scientific endeavors.

Equal Portions of Heavenly Fire: Mary Wollstonecraft and the Sexless Soul

Rachael Givens Johnson
University of Virginia

"This female philosopher indignantly rejects the idea of a sex in the soul, pronouncing the sensibility, timidity and tenderness of women, to be merely artificial refinements of character, introduced and fostered by men," writes the appalled (and fictional) Hindu philosopher Shahcoolen in Benjamin Silliman's series *The Letters of Shahcoolen* (1802).[1] Published not long after Mary Wollstonecraft's manifesto, *A Vindication of the Rights of Woman* (1796), Silliman's series dedicates four epistles to detailing the nature and influence of the "re-generating system of this female lunatic."[2] Another detractor brands Wollstonecraft "an unsex'd female" in a poetic satire on the author's manifesto and her fellow female "combatants" in "the new field of the Rights of Woman."[3]

---

1. Benjamin Silliman, *Letters of Shahcoolen, A Hindu Philosopher, Residing in Philadelphia: To His Friend El Hassan, an Inhabitant of Delhi* (Boston: Russell and Cutler, 1802), 22–23. *Letters* was originally published anonymously in the New York paper *Commericial Advertiser* and then compiled and published under Silliman's name (see preface). Four out of fourteen "letters" were on Wollstonecraft.

2. Ibid., 24.

3. *Critical Review*, n.s., 4, (April 1792): 389–98, and n.s., 5, (June 1792): 13–41, as compiled in Harriet Devine Jump, *Mary Wollstonecraft and the Critics, 1788–2001* (New York: Routledge, 2003), 50–51.

No greater compliments could have been paid to the pioneering, eighteenth-century feminist Mary Wollstonecraft than to have been considered "unsexed" and recognized for her rejection of the "sexed soul," notwithstanding the harsh indictment such ideas elicited from many of her contemporaries. Indeed, she insists in *Vindication*, "A wild wish has just flown from my heart to my head, and I will not stifle it, though it may excite a horse-laugh. I do earnestly wish to see the distinction of sex confounded in society . . . for this distinction is, I am firmly persuaded, the foundation of the weakness of character ascribed to woman."[4]

Amid the social reforms and political revolutions that would fuel Enlightenment philosophes, Wollstonecreaft would see the very categories of male and female as hindering women from achieving the progress that men were enjoying in intellectual, political, and moral spheres.[5] Mary Wollstonecraft recoils at the increasingly essentialist paradigms that would define women by their sex instead of their humanity—or, more significantly, their divinity. For, she asks, are not men and women both "children of the same parent?"—God?[6] Are they not, she insists, given "heavenly fire" in "equal portions"?[7]

By delving straight into the locus of human identity—the soul—and desexualizing it, Wollstonecraft upsets the sexual categories that continue to cripple women and "stop the progress of knowledge and virtue" throughout society.[8] Through destabilizing gender categories, Wollstonecraft seeks to reconstruct human identity on the basis of humanity's true identity as sexless souls, unencumbered from the socially constructed and biologically trivial distinctions that have made

---

4. Mary Wollstonecraft, *A Vindication of the Rights of Woman: With Strictures on Political and Moral Subjects* (London: J. Johnson, 1796), 121 (hereafter cited as *Vindication*).

5. Some scholars have judged Wollstonecraft's ideas as being directed at the bourgeois only. Yet Barbara Taylor argues that, while certain passages "certainly seem to support the interpretations of Wollstonecraft as a bourgeois thinker," her ideas on the whole reflect a more utopian eradication of such "partial interests and sectional loyalties"; *Mary Wollstonecraft and the Feminist Imagination* (Cambridge: Cambridge University Press, 2003), 168..

6. Wollstonecraft, *Vindication*, 225.

7. Ibid., 68.

8. Ibid., vi.

humanity "forget their grand destination" as souls "capable of rising to [God]."[9]

In Wollstonecraft's envisioned social utopia, the recognition of men and women's shared identity as equal, rational, sexless souls is an essential prerequisite. Wollstonecraft argues that women must help construct this utopia through the exercise of reason, virtue, and universal benevolence, not only because society needs such women, but also because women are designed to do so in light of their spiritual and intellectual identities as sexless souls made in the *imago Dei* (image of God).[10] As historian Barbara Taylor has aptly argued, this religious vision, and the utopia it would facilitate, is the defining element of Wollstonecraft's *Vindication*.[11] The only obstacles for women who fully exercise their divine gifts of reason and virtue are the socialization and the lack of education that train women to "please, and . . . live only to please" rather than to

---

9. Ibid., 135, 146.

10. The soul was then understood to encompass both meanings simultaneously, given the long-standing connection in Western Christian theology and philosophy between the mind and the soul. Both spiritual and intellectual identities were then understood to be the eternal element of humankind, the *imago Dei*, the innermost identity, and the seat of reason (humankind's defining attribute). In this article (unless otherwise noted), the concepts of mind and soul are equivalent.

11. Barbara Taylor has pioneered a new treatment of Wollstonecraft as a profoundly religious thinker in *Mary Wollstonecraft and the Feminist Imagination* and in several smaller articles and anthology chapters. Although Taylor's is the most comprehensive account of Wollstonecraft's religious consciousness, other articles treat Wollstonecraft's spiritual themes and influences as well. Complementing Taylor's analysis is Arleen Ingham's *Women and Spirituality in the Writing of More, Wollstonecraft, Stanton, and Eddy* (New York: Palgrave Macmillan, 2010), which compares the literary works of key eighteenth- and nineteenth-century feminists and highlights commonalities and differences in their religious thought. Historian Gregory Claeys has authored a chapter titled "The Divine Creature and the Female Citizen," which revisits Wollstonecraft's concepts of rights "in the context of her much-neglected religious beliefs"; *English Radicalism, 1550–1850*, ed. Glenn Burgess and Matthew Festenstein (Cambridge: Cambridge University Press, 2007), 115–34. Patricia Michaelson has also written of Wollstonecraft's feminism as "very much an expression of religious belief"; "Religious Basis of Eighteenth-Century Feminism: Mary Wollstonecraft and the Quakers," *Women's Studies* 22 (1993): 282. Other scholars such as Mervyn Nicholson have found in *Vindication* an "unbroken chain of deductions" leading from the just nature of God to the emancipation of women and equality of the sexes; "The Eleventh Commandment: Sex and Spirit in Wollstonecraft and Malthus," *Journal of the History of Ideas* 51, no. 3 (1990): 418.

be "rational creatures."[12] Thus Wollstonecraft's *Vindication* is not merely
an educational or philosophical treaty, as many of her contemporaries
would view it; instead, it is also a synthesis of theological and philosophical ideas that attempts to re-conceptualize human identity beyond
sexual categories and within a realm where religious devotion and
rational thought meet. The rational, sexless soul—a concept with a rich
history in Western philosophy and Christianity—provides the platform
for this reformulation.

Wollstonecraft was not the first to recognize the emancipating
and equalizing potential of the sexless soul. Many of Wollstonecraft's
defenses of the sexless soul, as well as her criticisms of the socialization
obscuring it, had been articulated a century before by other women's
advocates who rallied around the idea of the sexless soul. What makes
Wollstonecraft's arguments different? How exactly does she define
the sexless soul? And what happens to the notion after the turn of the
century, when a new wave of women's advocates takes to the press,
particularly in America?

To address these questions, this article analyzes Wollstonecraft's
use of the sexless soul in the context of its broader philosophical and
religious history as well as in particular passages of *Vindication* itself.
Although the notion of the sexless soul hearkens back to Pythagorean philosophers in the sixth century BC and flourishes well into AD
seventeenth century, Wollstonecraft's eighteenth-century manifesto
is arguably the first time the idea is politicized; its implications are
intended to have direct bearing on women's social, intellectual, and
political position. The strong reactions that Wollstonecraft's manifesto
would provoke as well as the variations on the sexless soul that would
develop among Wollstonecraft's successors illuminate the different
ways in which the sex of the soul served as a lightning rod for other
social, political, and religious concerns. This contextualization will help
elucidate the significant and unique cultural work that Wollstonecraft's
Vindication performs as well as the significant religious undercurrents
in Wollstonecraft's thought and in early modern feminism as manifest
in the heated debates surrounding the sex of the soul.

---

12. Wollstonecraft, *Vindication*, 43, 108.

Sex and Gender

"Sex" and "gender" are difficult to untangle in the concept of the sexless soul. Post-1970s scholars have generally understood "gender" as referring to socially constructed behaviors, attributes, and norms that signal masculinity or femininity within a particular cultural context and "sex" as referring to the biological status of male or female as determined by chromosomes, hormones, or anatomical differences. This bifurcation is difficult to apply in periods during which no such distinguishing vocabulary was used. However, for the purposes of this article, I claim that Wollstonecraft operates roughly within this dichotomy. Wollstonecraft views sex (maleness and femaleness) as a biological fact, pertinent primarily for "produc[ing] the fruit of life" (procreation) and fulfilling particular (and ultimately secondary) duties that arise from those procreative roles.[13] Biological differences of sex also matter, however, in that a man's superior physical faculties enable him "from the remotest antiquity . . . to exert his strength to subjugate his companion [woman]."[14] Men often exploit the physical difference that Providence has granted them in order to subject women to duties, norms, attributes, and distinctions (in which women are far too complicit, Wollstonecraft seethes) that satisfies men's own sexual needs and vanity. In other words, men have manipulated the biological consequences of being sexed male to produce a social condition—or "gender"—in which women are oppressed, in spite of the common material God has used to design their (equal) souls. Overturning the unnatural, constructed roles of gender would emancipate men as well as women from the moral shackles that have

---

13. See, for example, this excerpt from Wollstonecraft's *Vindication*: "Women, I allow, may have different duties to fulfill . . . but they are *human* duties" (106, emphasis in the original). While Wollstonecraft refers to the roles of wife and mother as "the proper places" (xii) for women, she depicts these as only educational, temporary roles that render the "road more pleasant" (48) and serve as useful lessons in this school during the soul's "infancy" (245), or mortality's "education" (245). Wollstonecraft acknowledges that men and women typically inherit different duties in life but argues that exacerbating and crystallizing those differences with socially constructed gender norms misconstrues the intention of those different duties as a divinely ordered method to develop virtue.

14. Wollstonecraft, *Vindication*, 49.

hindered them from "the grand purpose of life, that of rendering human creatures wise and virtuous."[15]

Thus Wollstonecraft could be said to be operating with an understanding of "sex" (biological, given) and "gender" (social, constructed), terms that had not been semantically differentiated at the time. Indeed, for much of Western philosophical history, Aristotelian body–mind unity had rendered sex and gender interchangeable concepts, with the biological and the social (and intellectual, moral, spiritual, and so on) elements of human nature fused together. The relationship of biological sex and social roles (maleness and masculinity versus femaleness and femininity) began to be more problematized around the thirteenth century.[16] By the eighteenth century, the relationship had grown complicated to a degree that would permit Wollstonecraft and her contemporaries to describe some women as masculine and some men as feminine (although the latter expressions are intended, more often than not, to be derogatory).[17] This paradoxical behavior of Wollstonecraft's—wishing to eradicate sexual distinctions while negatively affirming them—is explored at a later point. For this article's purposes, the term *sexless soul* indicates a soul without a moral, spiritual, or intellectual nature that could be identified with cultural understandings of "feminine" or "masculine" (which, in virtually all cases, unless otherwise noted, is synonymous with or inclusive of "male" or "female").

---

15. Ibid., 418.

16. Prudence Allen argues that "in the thirteenth century we begin to find more and more philosophers recognizing that men and women are slightly more complicated than simply male beings with masculine characteristics and female beings with feminine characteristics," although it would take "six more centuries" to "articulate theories about this complex fact of human existence"; *The Concept of Woman: The Early Humanist Reformation, 1250–1500* (Grand Rapids, MI: W. B. Eerdmans, 2002), 320.

17. Wollstonecraft and her radical contemporaries had excoriated the conservative philosopher Edmund Burke for being feminine, for example, and others had accused French aristocratic elites of being effeminate and responsible for the corruption of political and social order. See Wollstonecraft, *Vindication of the Rights of Men in a Letter to the Right Honourable Edmund Burke; Occasioned by His Reflections on the Revolution in France* (London: J. Johnson, 1790).

Origins of the Sexless Soul

The sexless soul has a long and ambivalent history in Western philosophy and religion, through its initial development in the writings of Pythagoras, Plato, and Aristotle and its contentious incorporation into Christian theology. The following précis provided a sense of the key figures in the history of the sex of the soul—a history into which Wollstonecraft and her fellow advocates and dectractors enter.

The concept of the sexless soul had existed uneasily, for the most part, alongside a belief in the female's physical inferiority—a being defined in contrast to or as a privation of the male's superior physical nature. Pythagoras first articulates the belief in a sexless, immaterial identity housed within a series of reincarnated, sexed, material bodies (with the male body superior to the female).[18] Plato later elaborates on Pythagorean beliefs, holding that immortal and sexless souls, once dethroned from their place among the perfect, immaterial world of forms, fall into a series of reincarnations in the inferior, material realm until they are able to free themselves of the bodily reincarnations, through wisdom and virtue, and reunite with the immaterial forms. Like the Pythagoreans, Plato believes female bodies are inferior (and that female reincarnation is a punishment), but as Prudence Allen puts it, Plato allows that, given humankind's *true* identity as sexless souls, "from the perspective of their real nature, [men and women] are the same."[19] Yet Plato's successor, Aristotle, would reject Plato's influential metaphysical dualism (the imperfect, material world and the perfect, immaterial

---

18. Allen, *The Concept of Woman*, 20–21. Although Pythagoras opposed and hierarchized the feminine and masculine elements in his Table of Opposites, he believed that reason was the superior part of humankind's identity and had no sexual nature, rendering men and women essentially the same in their core personal identity.

19. Ibid., 61. See also 60–62, 88. Note that Plato's conception of sexual distinction was more complicated; Plato believed in a cosmic sex polarity of a superior, masculine force of activity and an inferior feminine force of passivity. However, pertaining to individuals rather than cosmic forces, the "identity of a woman or man comes from their mind (or soul) and not from their body," and thus, "the material aspects of generation, which played such a crucial role on the cosmic level of male and female identity, have no role at all on the level of actual human existence"; it is, in fact, "the sexless soul and not the material body that determines the identity of the woman or man"; Ibid., 61.

world of forms) as well as Plato's belief in a rational, immortal, sexless soul as ontologically separate from the material body.

Aristotle propounds the unity of soul and body, with the implication that physical distinctions reflect internal ones; therefore, men and women's differing physical nature reflect an internal difference—and not one that is favorable to women. The female is, as it were, a deformed male, Aristotle surmises, setting in motion a paradigm in which females would long remain at the underdeveloped end of the male continuum.[20] Aristotle also believes the male has the creative capacity to give life and shape to the body—the "soul," as he terms this animated essence—whereas the female is merely the passive receptacle or source of raw material for new life; women are the wood, men are the carpenters. "Thus," he summarizes, "the physical part, the body, comes from the female, and the Soul from the male, since the Soul is the essence of a particular body."[21] Aristotle's decidedly unfavorable perception of women as the privation of maleness, both physically and intellectually, would become deeply influential for centuries in the scholarly understanding of the human body.

This dual inheritance—Aristotle's identification of women with matter, and Plato's demotion of the material—would shape the development of early Christian theological attempts to reconcile Greek philosophy with Christianity regarding gender. The addition of Christian theological elements such as the creation and fall of man and woman, the resurrection of the physical body, and the nature of God would produce new and often ambiguous variations on the concept of the sexless soul.

The first four centuries of Christianity largely upheld a male Godhead, leaving only men created in the *imago Dei*; according to several early church fathers, women could achieve salvation by becoming desexed or "male" in Christ through grace and the resurrection.[22] The shift toward Platonized Christianity, centering on an asexual

---

20. Thomas Laqueur, *Making Sex: Body and Gender from the Greeks to Freud* (Cambridge, MA: Harvard University Press, 1990), 28.

21. Aristotle, "On the Generation of Animals," quoted in Mary Briody Mahowald, ed., "Aristotle," in *Philosophy of Woman: An Anthology of Classic to Current Concepts* (Indianapolis, IN: Hackett Publishing, 1994), 25.

22. Christopher Roberts, *Creation and Covenant* (New York: T&T Clark International, 2007), 13–38. Several prominent early church fathers such as Tertullian, Clement, Tatian,

Godhead, would rekindle the belief in a sexless, rational soul (having been made in the sexless, rational *imago Dei*) encapsulated in both male and female bodies.[23] This dualistic concept dominates theology and philosophy from late antiquity until the nineteenth century and is aided particularly in the fifteenth and sixteenth centuries by the widespread accessibility of Latin translations of Plato's dialogues.[24] The sex of the soul would be tangled in centuries-long debates among theologians over whether sexual differentiation had resulted from the Fall or from divine design, whether women could independently represent the *imago Dei*, whether sex extends to the soul or simply the mortal body, whether it would be eliminated or preserved after the resurrection, and what it would mean if it were preserved.[25] Their conclusions typically correlated with their beliefs about the materialism and gender of God— issues that eluded unanimity in this period.

Two of the most influential Christian theologians, Augustine and Aquinas, established two predominant ways of thinking about the sex of the soul among later Western Christian philosophers that reflected the fundamental distinctions between Platonic and Aristotelian tenets. Augustine promoted the Neoplatonic adoption of a rational, sexless soul

Greory of Nyssa, and others believed that God, in creating male and female, established a sexual differentiation that served some broader, providential purpose in mortality, but would be overcome through spiritual transcendence and ultimately, the resurrection, where the soul would rise as either sexless or male. See also Benjamin Dunning, *Specters of Paul: Sexual Difference in Early Christian Thought* (Philadelphia: University of Pennsylvania Press, 2011). In chapter 2, Dunning examines Clement's seemingly contradictory views on gender and eschatology; while Clement believed the soul was rational and sexless, for both men and women, the latter must shed the particularities of female sexual difference in a "redemptive translation into the male" (32).

23. Origen's views are one such example of this Platonic bent; he believed that God created only men and women's sexless souls; the Fall and its corrupting effects introduced sexual differentiation, a condition that would be overcome through spiritual mastery and the resurrection. See Peter Brown, *The Body and Society* (New York: Columbia University Press, 1998), 163–68.

24. Kari Elisabeth Børresen, "Recent and Current Research on Women in the Christian Tradition," in *Studia Patristica*, ed. Elizabeth Livingstone (Leuven, Belgium: Peeters, 1997), 224–27.

25. See Roberts, *Creation and Covenant*; Dunning, *Specters of Paul: Sexual Difference in Early Christian Thought*; Jacqueline Murray, *Handling Sin: Confession in the Middle Ages*, ed. Peter Biller and A. J. Minnis (York, England: York Medieval Press, 1998); Brown, *The Body and Society*; and Allen, *The Aristotelian Revolution*, 218–21.

in the image of a transcendent, immaterial God. He believed that woman, not having been made temporally in the image of God like Adam, was therefore incomplete and imperfect in the mortal world. However, the intellect or the soul of a woman was in the image of God, ensuring an equality between man and woman in their core identity: "man is made there in the image of God, where there is no sex, namely, in the spirit of his mind."[26] Aquinas, with his appropriation of the Aristotelian unity of body and soul (including the perception of female inferiority), perpetuated the idea, in the words of Prudence Allen, that "sex identity would always be an essential part of personal identity."[27] Although both were equally capable of being perfected by grace, woman (in classic Aristotelian terms) was the passive sex providing raw material for new souls through procreation, and was less capable of intellectual virtues.[28]

There were exceptions to these Augustinian-Neoplatonic and Thomistic Aristotelian trends, of course. Some Christian sects would utilize the sexless soul as a platform from which they could acceptably transcend or transgress their own material sex in spiritual encounters with a maternal or erotic Jesus.[29] Others like Bernard

---

26. Augustine, *The Trinity* (Washington, DC: The Catholic University of America Press, 1963), XII:354, quoted in Allen, *The Aristotelian Revolution*, 221. See also 222–24 and 301. Augustine, like Plato, requires some work to untangle his thoughts on the sex of the soul. Allen argues that Augustine's views fall along fragmented lines. While Augustine asserts that the mind has no sex and therefore that men and women were equally divine when acting according to their highest functions, he also argues that, on a temporal level, women were inferior to men, since only man could be properly described as being "in the image of God" (given Eve's creation from Adam's rib). Notwithstanding this, Augustine also believes that sexual differentiation would persist after the resurrection, for "God . . . who made us man and woman will raise us up as man and woman"; however, this would not detract from their true identity as sexless souls; Augustine, *The City of God Against the Pagans*, book XII (Cambridge, MA: Harvard University Press, 1966), 17, quoted in Allen, *The Aristotelian Revolution*, 226.

27. Allen, *The Aristotelian Revolution*, 385. Aquinas resolves the conundrum of permitting inferior females into heaven by claiming that, while women would require more grace to perfect their inferior natures, they would end up in an equal state of perfection with men in the afterlife.

28. Ibid., 386.

29. See Kathleen Crowther, *Adam and Eve in the Protestant Reformation* (Cambridge: Cambridge University Press, 2013), 132; Katharine Hodgkin, ed., *Women, Madness and Sin in Early Modern England: The Autobiographical Writings of Dionys Fitzherbert* (Burlington, VT: Ashgate, 2010), 70; Gosta Hallonsten, "The New Catholic Feminism: Tradition

of Clairvaux (twelfth century AD) would cast the soul as a female wooed and pursued by a masculine Christ.[30] Although in the minority, a few Christian thinkers—particularly the church mothers Julian of Norwich, Hildegard von Bingen, and other mystics—would celebrate a God with feminine attributes. Hildegard believed God possessed a perfection of both masculine and feminine elements that men and women were to emulate in order to become wholly integrated.[31] In addition to their perfected bisexual divine nature, men and women would rise in the resurrection "in the integrity of their bodies and their sex"—that is, as males and females.[32] In the following century, the mystic Julian of Norwich recorded a series of visions that celebrated the "motherhood" of God and Christ in a radically feminized Godhead.[33] For the most part, however, the Platonic sexless soul would dominate the *querelle des femmes* of the seventeenth century.

The Sexless Soul in the Age of Reason

The debates over the sex of the soul and the equality of women would proliferate dramatically during the Renaissance's *querelle des femmes* at a primarily polemical level. During the seventeenth-century Age of

and Renewal in Catholic Gender Theology," in *Christian Masculinity*, ed. Yvonne M. Werner (Leuven, Belgium: Leuven University Press, 2011), 275; Ivy Schweitzer, *The Work of Self-Representation: Lyric Poetry in Colonial New England* (Chapel Hill: University of North Carolina Press, 1991), 4; and Catherine Brekus, *Strangers and Pilgrims* (Chapel Hill: University of North Carolina Press, 1998), 38.

30. Roberts, 79–98. See also Brekus, *Strangers and Pilgrims* for a discussion of soul-as-female imagery among nineteenth-century "New Light" Christians and other Evangelicals. See also Schweitzer, *Lyric Poetry in Colonial New England* for similar discourse among seventeenth-century Puritans.

31. Allen, *The Aristotelian Revolution*, 297–98.

32. Francesca Maria Steele, *The Life and Visions of St. Hildegard* (London: Heath, Cranton and Ousely, Ltd., 1914), 176, quoted in Allen, *The Aristotelian Revolution*, 301.

33. For example, see: "God is as truly our mother as he is our father . . . Jesus is our mother in nature by our first creation, and he is our true mother in grace by his assumption of our sensual being," and "our heavenly mother Jesus will not allow those of us who are his children to perish—for he alone is almighty, all wisdom and all love." See Julian of Norwich, *Revelations of Divine Love*, trans. by Frances Beer (Cambridge, UK: D.S. Brewer, 1998), 64, 68.

Reason, more women would join in the debate and use scripture, theology, and logic to extend the implications regarding a sexless soul in
the image of a rational, asexual God toward a greater recognition of
women's equality, the instability of gender categories, and the need for
improving women's education.

For example, Marie de Gournay, the well-known French author of
various works on aesthetics, ethics, and social criticism (and friend and
editor of Montaigne's *Essais*), penned *Égalité des hommes et des femmes*
(*The Equality of Men and Women*) in 1622, two decades before René
Descartes's influential *Meditations* (1641).[34] An admirer of Plato, Marie
de Gournay looks not only to Plato's egalitarian depiction of women
in *The Republic* (380 BC) for support of gender equality but also to
Plato's identification of humankind's defining essence as the rational,
sexless soul. "The human animal," she explains, "taken rightly, is neither
man nor woman, the sexes having been made double, not so as to constitute a difference in species, but for the sake of propagation alone.
The unique form and distinction of that animal consists only in its
rational soul."[35] Like Plato, she claims that sexual difference exists not to
indelibly bifurcate the human species but simply to enable procreation.
The "rational soul" is a reflection of a God without sex; and "if anyone is
so dull as to imagine masculine or feminine in God," she quips, "such a
person shows in a plain light that he is just as bad a philosopher as he is
a theologian."[36] According to de Gournay, sexual categories do not work
for the Divine or his creations. However, this does not prevent her from
advocating for women as a social class to receive more privileges, like
improved education. After all, she argues, "If, therefore, women attain
less often than men to the heights of excellence," it is only for "lack

---

34. Marie le Jars de Gournay, *Apology for the Woman Writing and Other Works*, ed.
and trans. Richard Hillman and Colette Quesnel (Chicago: The University of Chicago
Press, 2002); and René Descartes, *Meditations on First Philosophy*, trans. Michael Moriarty
(New York: Oxford University Press, 2008).

35. de Gournay, "Equality" in *Apology*, 86–87, quoted in Dorothea Heitsch, "Cats
on a Windowsill: An Alchemical Study of Marie de Gournay," in *Gender and Scientific
Discourse in Early Modern European Culture*, ed. Kathleen Long (Burlington, VT: Ashgate,
2010), 228.

36. de Gournay, "Equality" in *Apology*, 94, quoted in Heitsch, "Alcehmical Study of
Marie de Gournay," 229n62.

of good education."[37] Yet, to Marie de Gournay, the battle for women's improved condition and acknowledged equality would remain on primarily a theoretical level; aside from encouraging better education and lamenting the lack of public offices, titles, or responsibilities for women, she does not explicitly utilize the sexless soul to advocate particular political changes.

Some of her main arguments are closely mirrored by the popular and respected Spanish writer María de Zayas. In the preface to her first publication, *Exemplary Tales of Love and Tales of Disillusion* (1637), María de Zayas feels it necessary to defend her authorship as a woman to her male readers, since many would be "amazed that a woman has the audacity not only to write a book, but to send it for printing."[38] Yet, she continues, anyone with good sense should not be astonished, given that no reason exists for "why we [women] would not have aptitude for books."[39] For, she asks her female readers rhetorically, "If this material of which men and women are made . . . is no more noble in them than in us, if our blood is the same thing . . . the soul the same as theirs—since souls are neither male nor female—what reason is there that they would be wise and presume we cannot be so?"[40] Blood, sense, faculties, organs, and, most importantly the soul, admit no sexual distinctions, she claims; men and women are virtually the same.

The only difference she acknowledges between men and women— besides the differences in humors and temperatures, an Aristotelian concept that still held sway in Spain—is women's lack of education and different upbringing. If, she argues, "they were to provide us with books and preceptors, we would prove as apt for posts and professorships as men."[41] Wryly, she concludes that she is "confident" in the "gallantry" of her male reader, who, if he should find her work displeasing, "will be able to pardon me because I was born a woman."[42] The implicit

37. de Gournay, "Equality," in *Apology*, 81.
38. María de Zayas y Sotomayor, *Exemplary Tales of Love and Tales of Disillusion*, ed. and trans. Margaret R. Greer and Elizabeth Rhodes (Chicago, IL: University of Chicago Press, 2009), 47.
39. de Zayas, 51.
40. Ibid., 47; emphasis added.
41. Ibid., 48.
42. Ibid., 51.

emphasis on the incidental nature of her female embodiment throws into relief María de Zayas's defense of the intellectual product of her rational, sexless soul.

Sor Juana Inés de la Cruz, an extraordinarily well-read nun in New Spain, echoes the Neoplatonic notion that the soul is without sex in many of her personal writings and poems near the turn of the seventeenth century. To her, the body is only the "neuter . . . dwelling of [her] soul."[43] She would pursue intellectual interests within the walls of a convent so that, as she says, "if in fact I am a woman, no one could find it out."[44] In a poem to the Countess de Paredes, she reminds the countess that "souls are ignorant of distance and gender."[45] Although Sor Juana certainly does not position herself to argue for women's rights, she feels her personal life of the mind—one usually reserved for men—is justified by her belief in the sexless soul and the universal call to learning.

About the same time, Anna Maria van Schurman, the celebrated Dutch linguist, philosopher, and correspondent of Marie de Gournay, would add her voice to the support of the sexless soul—although via medieval forms of scholastic argumentation. In "Whether the Study of Letters Is Fitting to a Christian Woman" (1646), her defense of women enjoying the life of the mind, Schurman affirms that "whatever leads to true greatness of the soul" is fit for the Christian woman, regardless of gender.[46] According to one scholar, Schurman's theology "did not allow for distinctions of sex in regard to the human mind or soul."[47] Schurman's own mentor, Gisbertus Voetius (a devotee of Aristotle who gets into sharp disputes with Descartes) defends the spiritual equality of

43. Sor Juana Inés de la Cruz, prefatory material in *Obras selectas*, ed. Georgina Sabat de Rivers and Elias L. Rivers (Barcelona: Noguer, 1976), quoted in Georgina Sabat-Rivers, "A Feminist Rereading of Sor Juana's Dream," in *Feminist Perspectives on Sor Juana Ines de la Cruz* (Detroit, MI: Wayne State University Press, 1991), 143.

44. Ibid.

45. de la Cruz, "No. 403" in *Obras selectas*, quoted in Sabat-Rivers, "A Feminist Rereading," 144.

46. Anna Maria van Schurman, "Whether the Study of Letters Is Fitting to a Christian Woman," in *Whether a Christian Woman Should Be Educated and Other Writings from Her Intellectual Circle*, ed. and trans. Joyce Irwin (Chicago: The University of Chicago Press, 1998), 32.

47. Gerda Lerner, *The Creation of Feminist Consciousness: From the Middle Ages to Eighteen-Seventy* (New York: Oxford University Press, 1993), 155–56.

women in his own essay "Concerning Women" (part of his major work, *Politica Ecclesiastica*, 1663–76), by arguing that "the same essential parts constitute a woman as well as a man, namely a human soul and a human body."[48] The soul is not gendered male or female but is simply a "human soul" present in male and female bodies alike. As Voetius puts it, a woman "essentially has the same human body as that of a man" with only minor differences necessary for procreation; the most important thing, however, he argues, is that women's souls, as men's, are made in the image of God.[49]

After mid-seventeenth century, new modes of discourse would set the stage for more sophisticated defenses of the sexless soul and its implications of equality for women and men. As one scholar summarizes, "[John] Locke's empiricism enabled men and women to argue for the importance of nurture against essentialist notions of female inferiority, while [René] Descartes' mind-body dualism facilitated the argument that the mind has no sex."[50] Indeed, the Cartesian divide between the immaterial mind and the corporeal body would enable future feminists to claim with more philosophical rigor that the soul and mind have no sex and that women, too, are defined by their capacity to think. Locke's tabula rasa notion, on the other hand, would allow feminists to throw into relief the deeply informative influence of socialization and education on individual character.

French philosopher François Poulain de la Barre would be the first to recognize the potential for a Cartesian case for feminism because, interestingly, Descartes himself had forged no direct link between his metaphysical dualism and the question of gender. A few decades after Descartes's *Mediations*, Poulain would write a succession of books arguing for women's equality, starting with *De l'égalité des deux sexes* (*Equality of*

---

48. Gisbertus Voetius, "Concerning Women," in *Whether a Christian Woman Should Be Educated and Other Writings from Her Intellectual Circle*, trans. Joyce Irwin (Chicago: University of Chicago Press, 2007), 99.

49. Ibid.

50. Clarissa Campbell Orr, "Championing Women: Early Enlightenment Feminisms," in *Women, Gender, and Enlightenment*, ed. Barbara Taylor and Sarah Knott (New York: Palgrave Macmillan, 2005), 352.

the Two Sexes) in 1673.[51] In it, he pens the famous phrase "the mind has
no sex,"[52] in what one scholar describes as a feminist philosophy of social
Cartesianism that extends the argument for the equality of the sexes to
all fields of social life.[53] Although the book (and Poulain's authorship of
it) received nominal attention in France, one scholar notes that it had a
"significant influence in England following its translation in 1677 as *The
Woman as Good as the Man*."[54] A spate of essays followed in its wake,
defending the equality and sexlessness of men's and women's minds.

One prominent essay within this group combines Poulain's belief in
the sexless mind and soul with Locke's empirical methods: *In Defense
of the Female Sex*, published anonymously in 1696 by Judith Drake.[55]
One of the first sections in the book is titled "No Distinction of Sexes
in Souls." In it, she challenges her readers (in a passage uncannily
similar to one in Wollstonecraft's future *Vindication*) that if women
"be naturally defective, the Defect must be either in Soul or Body";
but in the "Soul it can't be, if what I have heard some learned Men
maintain to be true, that all Souls are equal, and alike, and that consequently there is no such Distinction as Male and Female Souls."[56] In a
markedly Lockean line of thinking, she continues, "there are no innate
Ideas, but that all the Notions we have are deriv'd from our external
Senses."[57] But since she sees "no Difference in the Organization of those
Parts which have any Relation to, or Influence over, the Mind" and sees
"no natural Impediment in the Structure of our Bodies," the difference
between men and women must reside in the "disparity [between men's

---

51. François Poulain de la Barre, *De l'Égalité des deux sexes, discours physique et moral
où l'on voit l'importance de se défaire des préjugés* (Paris: Chez Jean du Puis, 1673).
52. Ibid., 109.
53. Siep Stuurman, "Feminism in the Seventeenth Century," in *Perspectives on Feminist
Political Thought in European History: From the Middle Ages to the Present*, ed. Tjitske
Akkerman and Siep Stuurman (New York: Routledge, 1998), 76.
54. Desmond Clarke, "François Poulain de la Barre," in *The Stanford Encyclopedia of
Philosophy* (Summer 2013 ed.), ed. Edward N. Zalta, accessed June 2, 2013, http://plato.
stanford.edu/archives/sum2013/entries/francois-barre/.
55. Siep Stuurman, *François Poulain de la Barre and the Invention of Modern Equality*
(Cambridge, MA: Harvard University Press, 2004), 281.
56. Judith Drake, *In Defense of the Female Sex* (London: S. Butler, 1721), 10.
57. Ibid.

and women's] customary education."[58] On the other hand, women's less robust physicality—"the very make and temper of our bodies"— could indicate that women are, in fact, "chiefly intended for thought, and the exercise of the mind."[59] Given women's fundamental intellectual aptitude, which is equal (if not superior) to men, no reason exists, the author argues, for women to be barred from civic involvement and improved education.

As Desmond Clarke explains,[60] other contemporary works also borrow from Poulain's Cartesian ideas, with phrases plagiarized and pirated by other various English defenders of women's equality. Such works include *Woman Not Inferior to Man* (1739) by the pseudonymous "Sophia"; the expanded edition of that book, retitled *Beauty's Triumph* (1751); and *Female Rights Vindicated* (1758) by the pseudonymous "Lady," which was republished as *Female Restoration* (1780) and *Female Rights Vindicated* (1833).[61] Another anonymously written text, the 1766 *Biographium Faemineum: The Female Worthies*, also affirms that "souls are of no sex, any more than wit, genius, or any other of the intellectual faculties."[62] Yet, while these philosophical and epistemological tools would prove highly useful to advocates of women's innate equality in the next century, other trends would develop as the Enlightenment project gained momentum throughout Europe, complicating the defense of women's equality.

58. Ibid., 11, 23.

59. Ibid., 23.

60. Clarke, "François Poulain de la Barre."

61. Sophia [pseud.], *Woman Not Inferior to Man, or A Short and Modest Vindication of the Natural Right of the Fair-Sex to a Perfect Equality of Power, Dignity, and Esteem, with the Men* (London: John Hawkins, 1739); Sophia [pseud.], *Beauty's Triumph, or The Superiority of the Fair Sex Invincibly Proved,* (London: J. Robinson, 1751); A Lady [pseud.], *Female Rights Vindicated, or The Equality of the Sexes Morally and Physically Proved* (London: G. Burnet, 1758); A Lady [pseud.], *Female Restoration, by a Physical and Moral Vindication of Female Talents, in Opposition to All Dogmatical Assertions Relative to Disparity in the Sexes* (London: Free-Masons Coffee-House and J. MacGowan's, 1780); and A Lady [pseud.], *Female Rights Vindicated, or the Equality of the Sexes Proved* (South Shields, England: James Jollie, 1833). For a discussion of these works, see Clarke, "François Poulain de la Barre."

62. *Biographium Faemineum: The Female Worthies* (London: S. Crowder and J. Payne, 1766), vii, quoted in Susan Wolfson, *Borderlines: The Shiftings of Gender in British Romanticism* (Stanford, CA: Stanford University Press, 2006), 285.

The Age of Enlightenment's preoccupation with championing natural rights, universalizing schemes of reason and moral virtues, and identifying and moralizing the "natural order"[63] had developed in tandem with an increasing emphasis on women as biologically, intellectually, and morally "other."[64] The tensions and paradoxes of the Enlightenment's universalizing project that had coexisted with the crystallization of gender roles and sexual categories would create, as one scholar dubs it, a "watershed in European culture's attempts to define difference between the sexes."[65]

A contextualizing summary from Thomas Laqueur captures the variety of forces that would fortify perceptions of women as inherently different and inferior throughout the eighteenth century:

> Social and political changes are not, in themselves, explanations for the reinterpretation of bodies. The rise of Evangelical religion, Enlightenment political theory, the development of new sorts of public spaces in the eighteenth century, Lockean ideas of marriage as a contract, the cataclysmic possibilities for social change wrought by the French revolution, postrevolutionary conservatism, postrevolutionary feminism, the factory system with its restructuring of the sexual division of labor, the rise of a free market economy in services and commodities, the birth of classes, singly or in combination—none of these things caused the making of a new sexed body. Instead, the remaking of the body is itself intrinsic to each of these developments.[66]

In other words, all the following forces combined to add great weight to the notion of a sexed body and, increasingly, a sexed soul in mainstream culture: the conservative forces in religious and political spheres, industrial trends more clearly delineating the public and private spheres, and

---

63. Dorinda Outram, "Gender," in *The Cambridge History of Science: Volume 3, Early Modern Science*, ed. Roy Porter, Katharine Park, and Lorraine Daston (Cambridge: Cambridge University Press, 2006), 814.

64. Dorinda Outram, *The Enlightenment* (Cambridge: Cambridge University Press, 1995), 77–78.

65. Ibid., 77.

66. Thomas Laqueur, *Making Sex: Body and Gender from the Greeks to Freud* (Cambridge, MA: Harvard University Press, 1990), 11.

a medical discourse increasingly linking the distinctive "biological" differences of men and women to their "moral and ... social differences."[67] Because of these polarizing forces, Laqueur argues that the dimorphic understanding of sex had, in fact, been "invented" in the eighteenth century. Political, social, religious, and economic forces would enable a two-sex model—one which defines men and women as biologically incommensurable creatures—to overturn the centuries-long one-sex model that had placed men and women on a single spectrum, with the female being the underdeveloped version of the male. With a two-sex model, in which men and women are completely opposite or "other," social boundaries and gender hierarchies receive stronger justification.[68]

This would not sit well with radical progressives and intellectuals like Wollstonecraft who were alert to the ways in which women had been excluded from the Enlightenment project. While Wollstonecraft's first philosophical and political foray in print, *Rights of Men*, defends the overturning of aristocratic and monarchic institutions in the context of the French Revolution, her *Vindication* is even more passionate about the "revolution in manners" that would be needed to bring down the social institutions oppressing women and corrupting society.[69] Questions of sex became a litmus test for how far Wollstonecraft's contemporaries would be willing to go in their embrace of Lockean psychology, Cartesian dualism, and rational scrutiny and in their belief that all human beings are perfectible, virtuous, and rational and are in possession of natural, inalienable rights.

Mary Wollstonecraft's *Vindication* and the Sexless Soul

Mary Wollstonecraft's social circle had prepared her well to issue a revolutionary manifesto. Wollstonecraft had surrounded herself with an "eclectic circle of artists, poets, and revolutionaries" and Rational Dissenters, including the influential publisher Joseph Johnson, Joseph

---

67. Londa Scheibinger, *The Mind Has No Sex?: Women in the Origins of Modern Science* (Cambridge, MA: Harvard University Press, 1989), 222.

68. Laqueur, *Making Sex*.

69. Wollstonecraft, *Vindication*, xix.

Priestly, Richard Price, Thomas Paine, and others.[70] Rational Dissent—a highly cerebral, liberal, and "very reform-minded creed" that would eventually become known as Unitarianism—was a brand of Protestant Nonconformity created essentially by and for the avant-garde, educated middle class.[71] It embraced "Lockean psychology, Newtonian cosmology, rationalist morality and reform politics" in a profoundly optimistic teleology.[72] In contrast to the Calvinist preoccupation with humankind's sinful nature, Rational Dissent dismissed the concept of original sin[73] and focused on humanity's inherently good nature; its capacity for personal judgment, authority, and revelation; and its potential for progress and perfectibility.

Wollstonecraft's social circle had certainly been key in propelling Wollstonecraft into public discourse; the timing was also fortuitous, for it was a time of revolution. With the still-lingering success of the American Revolution's republican project, the exhilarating dawning of the French Revolution, and vindications of human rights dripping ink all over Europe and the Americas,[74] the stage had been set for

_____

70. Adriana Craciun, *Mary Wollstonecraft's* A Vindication of the Rights of Woman: *A Sourcebook* (New York: Routledge, 2002), 10. For a good discussion on the role of Radical Dissent in eighteenth-century England, see Knud Haakonssen, ed., *Enlightenment and Religion: Rational Dissent in Eighteenth-Century Britain* (Cambridge, MA: Cambridge University Press, 1996).

71. Taylor, *Feminist Imagination*, 7. Also see Barbara Taylor, "The Religious Foundations of Mary Wollstonecraft's Feminism" in *A Cambridge Companion*, ed. Claudia Johnson (Cambridge, MA: Cambridge University Press, 2002), 107–9.

72. Taylor, *Feminist Imagination*, 103.

73. Wollstonecraft would go so far as to say this in another text: "We must get entirely clear of all the notions drawn from the wild traditions of original sin: the eating of the apple, the theft of Prometheus, the opening of Pandora's box, and the other fables, too tedious to enumerate, on which priests have erected their tremendous structures of imposition, to persuade us, that we are naturally inclined to evil: we shall then leave room for the expansion of the human heart, and, I trust, find, that men will insensibly render each other happier as they grow wiser"; *An Historical and Moral View of the Origin and Progress of the French Revolution* (London: Joseph Johnson, 1794), 17.

74. The era's most well-known works promoting human rights are Thomas Paine's *Rights of Man: Answer to Mr. Burke's Attack on the French Revolution* (London: J. S. Jordan, 1792), Edmund Burke's *Reflections on the Revolution in France and on the Proceedings in Certain Societies in London* (London: J. Dodsley, 1790), and Wollstonecraft's *Vindication of the Rights of Men* (1790), which was her response to Burke's criticism in *Reflections* of her mentor Richard Price's pro–French Revolution sermons. Vindications of human rights also date decades back, from Edmund Burke's *Vindication of Natural Society: A View of*

Wollstonecraft to make a fresh case for a "revolution in manners" through the reconstruction of human identity based on the sexless soul.

It would be an uphill battle for Wollstonecraft because Enlightenment thinkers—radicals and conservatives alike—had been intensely occupied with the "natural order" and had appealed to nature as the blueprint of the divine will, the source of morality, and "the arbiter of everything from aesthetics to the political order."[75] Unfortunately for Wollstonecraft, the distinctions of sex and the hierarchy they had long entailed were becoming increasingly naturalized, accumulating the moral weight of religious tradition and the intellectual authority of natural economy and scientific proofs.[76] Even her own French radical allies would hedge reforms for women because, in the words of Charles Maurice de Talleyrand-Périgord, the "will of nature" dictates that women "do not aspire to exercise rights and political functions."[77] Talleyrand-Périgord is, notably, the French politician to whom Wollstonecraft dedicates Vindication.[78] Yet it is this interpretation of "the will of nature" that Wollstonecraft seeks to overturn in order to secure women full participation in the "natural rights of mankind."[79] Her use of the sexless soul as an underlying defense for women to "share the advantages of education and government with man" is far more developed, far-reaching, politicized, and subversive than anything her seventeenth-century predecessors had dared.

What exactly does the "soul" mean to Wollstonecraft? Wollstonecraft avoids the convoluted and contested interpretations that try to utilize the Genesis creation account to answer the question "from whence the soul?" and thus dismisses the whole account as "Moses' poetical story"

---

the Miseries and Evils Arising to Mankind from Every Species of Artificial Society (London: M. Cooper, 1756) to numerous vindications of other issues during the eighteenth century, such as tithes, the House of Lords, the right of kings, the divinity of Christ, and so on.

75. Outram, Cambridge History of Science, 814.

76. See Laqueur's Making Sex for an in-depth discussion regarding the medicalization of sexual difference and the two-sex model.

77. Charles-Maurice de Talleyrand-Périgord, Rapport sur l'instruction publique, fait au nom du Comité de constitution, á l'Asemblée nationale, les 10, 11, et 19 septembre 1791 (Paris, 1791), 120, quoted in Janet Todd, Mary Wollstonecraft: A Revolutionary Life (London: Weidenfeld and Nicolson, 2000), 179.

78. Todd, Mary Wollstonecraft: A Revolutionary Life, 179.

79. Wollstonecraft, Vindication, x.

(in true Rational Dissenting fashion).[80] Instead, Wollstonecraft claims straightforwardly that the soul is the source of each individual's true, immutable identity and the locus of both reason and virtue—the two defining attributes of the typical rational believer's Creator-God—on which are "stamped the heavenly image."[81] Reason is the "emanation of divinity, the tie that connects the creature with the Creator," and the means for developing virtue.[82] Appealing both to the Enlightenment belief in a "universal value system based on reason and virtue"[83] and to the theological axiom that God, the author of that universal system, is rational, eternal, immutable, and one, Wollstonecraft argues that all of humanity can have only one standard of virtue. And since virtue is a function of the soul, it follows that only one type of soul exists—a single, rational soul, not two sexually differentiated ones. Both men and women, "having an immortal soul," will find that their "employment of life [is] to improve," she declares.[84]

Elsewhere, she again emphasizes the uniformity of the soul vis-à-vis the uniformity of virtue. Although "many ingenious arguments have

---

80. In case her feelings about the creation account are in any doubt, she writes, "I will simply declare, that were an angel from heaven to tell me that Moses' beautiful, poetical cosmogony, and the account of the fall of man, were literally true, I could not believe what my reason told me was derogatory to the character of the Supreme Being"; Wollstonecraft, *Vindication*, 173. Such freedom with scriptural texts was common to many Enlightenment philosophes, including Thomas Jefferson, Joseph Priestley, and others.

81. Wollstonecraft, *Vindication*, 111.

82. Ibid. Because of this close connection, Wollstonecraft uses *soul* and *mind* interchangeably, perhaps due to René Descartes's conflation of the soul and the mind. As one scholar explains, "Descartes did not deny the distinction between animate and inanimate, but he redrew the line between ensouled and unensouled beings. In his view, among earthly beings only humans have souls. He thus equated soul with mind: souls account for intellection and volition, including conscious sensory experiences, conscious experience of images, and consciously experienced memories"; Gary Hatfield, "René Descartes," in *The Stanford Encyclopedia of Philosophy* (Winter 2014 ed.), ed. Edward N. Zalta, accessed May 10, 2013, http://plato.stanford.edu/archives/sum2011/entries/descartes/. See also James Byrne, *Religion and the Enlightenment: From Descartes to Kant* (Louisville, KY: Westminster John Knox Press, 1996), 68. The interchangeability of these terms is evident in one of Wollstonecraft's scathing passages directed at the contemporary philosopher Jean-Jacques Rousseau, who, by giving "a sex to *mind*" was "not very consistent with the principles of a man who argued so warmly, and so well, for the immortality of the *soul*"; Wollstonecraft, *Vindication*, 85.

83. Outram, *Enlightenment*, 79.

84. Wollstonecraft, *Vindication*, 135, emphasis added.

been brought forward to prove, that the two sexes, in the acquirement of virtue, ought to aim at attaining a very different character," Wollstonecraft argues, "it should seem, *allowing them to have souls,* that there is but one way appointed by Providence to lead mankind to either virtue or happiness."[85] If men are to "give sex a virtue,"[86] then not only would God's oneness and consistency be undermined, but, as Dorinda Outram points out, the entire "Enlightenment project of emancipation" through a universally applicable, "non-gendered standard of morals and rationality" would also be delegitimized.[87]

And what of the soul's relationship to the body? While her predecessors had comfortably accepted the Cartesian division between the rational, immortal soul/mind and the irrational, corruptible body, Wollstonecraft had seen a more complicated relationship. After all, if women's souls were completely removed from and unaffected by bodily conditions and physical experiences, then women would have no need to be educated or politically and civically involved. Wollstonecraft's whole argument for women's education and empowerment rests on the mutual permeability of the soul and the body.

So even as the immortal soul is platonically "struggling to free itself from the shackles of matter,"[88] Wollstonecraft believes that the feelings and passions are "set in motion to improve our nature," "unfold our reason," and prompt the soul toward "the heavenly."[89] She chastises her sex (and the rich, whom she and other radicals blisteringly feminize) for allowing reason to be subsumed by "senses [that] are inflamed," becoming "prey of their senses . . . [and] blown about by every momentary gust of feeling."[90] Yet the passions are only detrimental insofar as they upset the dominance of reason and prevent the cultivation of virtue; Wollstonecraft does not wish to "guard the female

---

85. Ibid., 32.
86. Ibid., 10.
87. Outram, *Enlightenment*, 79.
88. Wollstonecraft, *Vindication*, 98.
89. Ibid., 22, 20, 162, respectively. It is worth noting that a few scholars such as Ann Curthoy and Susan James have noted the resemblance between Wollstonecraft's and Spinoza's attitudes toward the passions in that reason and passion can, and should, work harmoniously together and are mutually necessary for human happiness and growth.
90. Wollstonecraft, *Vindication*, 129.

heart" against "strong, persevering passions" but only against "romantic wavering feelings" that lead to idle reveries and indulgent fancies.[91] Even if women have a tendency to be dominated by such instable feelings, she counters, the tendency would not "prove that there is a sex in souls," for "fatal passions" have "ever domineered over the *whole* race."[92]

Wollstonecraft carefully grants that the sexless souls of both men and women are not impervious to bodily passions—on the contrary, they are dependent, to a degree, on them—but she is straightforward about the influence of the physical faculties themselves on the soul. In one passage, she posits that women's "want of understanding" may have arisen from "physical or accidental weakness of faculties."[93] Not only did physical strength affect the intellect; it correlated with the soul's other twin function: virtue.[94] In one docile passage, Wollstonecraft reassures her readers: "Let it not be concluded that I wish to invert the order of things; I have already granted, that, from the constitution of their bodies, men seem to be designed by Providence to attain a greater degree of virtue."[95] Indeed, when facing the dismal record of truly emancipated women, Wollstonecraft peevishly wonders if the "few extraordinary women who have rushed in eccentrical directions out of the orbit prescribed to their sex" are actually "*male* spirits" trapped in female bodies.[96] She then surmises, however, that "if it be not philosophical to think of sex when the soul is mentioned, the inferiority must depend on the organs."[97] To remedy women's physically inferior condition (and consequently, their morally and intellectually inferior condition), Wollstonecraft urges Locke's prescription of physical exercise for young girls, for the "most perfect education . . . is best calculated to strengthen the body and form the heart."[98] Women's

---

91. Ibid., 163.

92. Ibid., 128.

93. Ibid., 168.

94. See the unpublished dissertation by Chloe Louise Underwood, "Exercising Virtue: The Physical Reform of the Lesiured Elite in Eighteenth-century France" (PhD diss., University of Warwick, 2001) for a discussion on the relationship between physical health and moral virtue in Enlightenment France.

95. Wollstonecraft, *Vindication*, 49.

96. Ibid., 68.

97. Ibid.

98. Ibid., 37.

socially prescribed sedentary lifestyle "weakens the muscles and relaxes the nerves" and, presumably, prevents women from attaining virtue.[99] In short, although the soul could inspire and refine bodily passions, the soul could also be conditioned or crippled by the education and experiences that the body encounters—and even by the inferior physical faculties the body itself might possess.

Acknowledging this connection was risky but necessary for Wollstonecraft's defense of women's right to equal and unfettered education. Yet, even while implicitly admitting the permeability between the soul and body, Wollstonecraft tries to maintain careful boundaries between the two. As one scholar notes, "[t]o make her protest Wollstonecraft had to shy away from her own occasional sense that the unsatisfactory body controlled the brain and disturbed reason. If the female body were emphasized, woman would be omitted from the Enlightenment experiment and perhaps suffer another millennium of oppression."[100] This "Enlightenment experiment," or the audacious belief in universal reason, would be jeopardized for women so long as women would continue being defined as creatures of passion, nerves, hysterics, and other weaknesses that are seen as inherently feminine and irrational. Wollstonecraft had to tread the line uniting body and soul very carefully.

Even when that relationship between the body and soul grows hazy, Wollstonecraft refuses the incursion of sex into the soul. After all, she is "firmly persuaded" that "the distinction of sex" lies at the root of all inequalities and that "the desire of being always a woman is the very consciousness that degrades the sex."[101] Maintaining the sexlessness of the locus for human identity and divinity—the soul—is imperative to Wollstonecraft's equalizing intentions, and the notion is often repeated throughout the text. Indeed, one scholar observes that "so repeatedly does *A Vindication of the Rights of Woman* refer to a notion of soul that is not sex-differentiated that it seems to authorize its case on this ground

99. Ibid., 84. See also Natalie Taylor, *The Rights of Woman as Chimera* (New York: Routledge, 2007), 78.

100. Todd, *Revolutionary Life*, 186.

101. Wollstonecraft, *Vindication*, 121, 221.

alone."[102] Given the ample historical precedents we have reviewed for the philosophy and religious belief of a sexless soul, Wollstonecraft may not have felt the need for much authorization; as she says, it is "not philosophical to speak of sex when the soul is mentioned."[103] She recognizes, however, the shifting tides; in light of the growing tendencies in the eighteenth century to extend the sexual differentiation of men and women's biology into the moral and spiritual spheres, the attempt to eradicate this increasingly entrenched distinction is, she acknowledges rather desperately, a "wild wish."[104] She realizes that, although most of her intellectual peers do not seem to agree with the medical claims for the innate incommensurability of men and women, they do seem to agree at least with Rousseau's popular belief that sexual distinction is nature's way of ensuring social stability and order.[105]

However, one tendency of Wollstonecraft's threatens to mar her commitment to the complete eradication of the soul's sexual distinction. Throughout *Vindication*, Wollstonecraft reinforces, in some ways, sexed associations with her ideals of humanity. The words *feminine* and *masculine* are morally laden and rhetorically useful to Wollstonecraft. So while Wollstonecraft may have appealed to the sexless soul to argue for women's education and eventual liberation, she holds up "masculine" virtues as the ideals that men and women should seek. Virtually all

---

102. Susan Wolfson, "Gendering the Soul," in *Romantic Women Writers: Voices and Countervoices*, ed. Paula Feldman and Theresa Kelley (Hanover, NH: University Press of New England, 1995), 33.

103. Wollstonecraft, *Vindication*, 68.

104. Ibid., 121.

105. Londa Schiebinger, "Social Inequality as Natural Law," in *The Making of the Modern Body: Sexuality and Society in the Nineteenth Century*, ed. Catherine Gallgaher and Thomas Laqueur (Los Angeles: University of California Press, 1987), 67. Interestingly, one passage in Rousseau's novel *Heloise* depicts a character saying, "You pleasantly asked me once, if souls were of a different sex. No, my dear, the soul is of no sex; but its affections make that distinction, and you begin to be too sensible of it"; Jean-Jacque Rousseau, *Eloisa: Or, a Series of Original Letters*, vol IV (London: R. Griffiths, 1761), 70. Rousseau seems to have represented an ambiguous gray area in which the soul may have no sex, but for all intents and purposes, nature had established sexual distinctions that eclipsed it. It should be noted that a few of the more radical Enlightenment philosophers, particularly Voltaire, Montesquieu, and Diderot, had held more egalitarian views on women that minimize or trivialize differences between the sexes. See Outram, *Enlightenment*, 91.

the terms Wollstonecraft uses for femininity connote vices (vanity, weakness, sentimentality, indulgence), whereas the terms she uses for masculinity represent a monopoly on celebrated, eighteenth-century virtues (reason, judgment, and independence). This pattern reflects the broader "classical republican language of politics," which "associate[s] 'manly' virtues with patriot activism and tend[s] to identify aristocracy with a feminized sensibility."[106] For all Wollstonecraft's insistence that there "[is] no sex in virtue," masculinity certainly seems synonymous with virtue in many instances within her text. "All those who view [manly virtues] with a philosophical eye must, I should think, wish with me that [women] may every day grow more and more *masculine*," she writes dryly in her introduction; a few pages later, she retorts, "I presume that rational men will excuse me for endeavoring to persuade [women] to be more *masculine* and respectable."[107] At times, she attempts to recast these traditionally masculine virtues as more gender neutral; some examples include her refusal to call the admired Catherine Macaulay's intelligence "a masculine understanding, because I admit not of such an arrogant assumption of reason"[108] and her correction that "manly virtues [are], more properly speaking, the attainment of those talents and virtues, the exercise of which ennobles the human character."[109] Whether explicitly appealing to masculine traits or trying to recast them as more universal virtues, Wollstonecraft still reaffirms the superiority of what society has deemed the "masculine" virtues.

Various scholars have interpreted this discursive inconsistency in different ways, positing that Wollstonecraft may have been imbuing the sexless soul with Western rational maleness, attempting a fully masculine makeover of women, trying to show the constructed nature of both masculinity and femininity, or simply working within the semantic discourse available to her.[110] Given her commitment to the

---

106. Jon Mee and David Fallon, eds., *Romanticism and Revolution: A Reader* (Malden, MA: Wiley-Blackwell, 2011), 92.

107. Wollstonecraft, *Vindication*, 4, 10, emphasis added.

108. Ibid., 235.

109. Ibid., 4.

110. Genevieve Lloyd, in her influential monograph *Man of Reason*, argues that "sexlessness" is often a "covert way of privileging maleness," given the implicit and indelible association in Western thought of the material (including bodily passions) with

sexless soul as a platform from which she could logically argue the constructed nature of sexual identity (and thus, the need for reform), it is most likely that she resorts to masculine identification because, as one historian notes, both the realm of citizenship itself and "the attainment of those talents and virtues, the exercise of which ennobles the human character, had been largely confined to men."[111] Men had appropriated the realm of virtues that Wollstonecraft believes belonged to humanity. Therefore, Wollstonecraft's appeal to masculinity does not, in fact, undercut her commitment to the sexless soul; it simply manifests the social context within which Wollstonecraft is forced to communicate.

Ultimately, occasional regression in her terminology notwithstanding, Wollstonecraft's reliance on a sexless soul holds the promise

---

the feminine and the immaterial (including incorporeal reason) with the masculine; *The Man of Reason: "Male" and "Female" in Western Philosophy* (London: Routledge, 1993), xiii. Thus, given the "complex configuration of sexual symbolism with ideas of reason," the sexless soul inevitably "takes on a shadowy maleness"; Lloyd, *Man of Reason*, xiii. Other scholars go further, arguing that Wollstonecraft encourages more than a "shadowy maleness"; rather, they argue, she encourages a full identification with the masculine (deliberately or not). Leanne Maunu argues that "although [Wollstonecraft] claims otherwise, I suggest that the standard of morality Wollstonecraft believes in is essentially a 'masculine' and British one"; *Women Writing the Nation* (Cranbury, NJ: Rosemont Publishing, 2007), 162. And Steven Blakemore says that Wollstonecraft "actually aspires to *be* a man, for she suspects the shortest way to success and equality is to join the cultural myth-makers, to hide what seemed to her a fatal female flaw beneath the mask of male discourse"; *Intertextual War: Edmund Burke and the French Revolution in the Writings of Mary Wollstonecraft, Thomas Paine, and James Mackintosh* (Cranbury, NJ: Associated University Press, 1997), 50. Adriana Craciun resolves the conundrum by claiming Wollstonecraft recognized both masculinity and femininity to be constructions; for if "sex can be separated from gender in women's case [as Wollstonecraft vehemently argues], it can in men's as well"; *Fatal Women of Romanticism* (Cambridge, MA: Cambridge University Press, 2003), 69. Seeing "natural 'manliness' . . . as a construction"enables Wollstonecraft to appeal to masculine virtues without privileging *men* themselves; ibid., 69. Masculinity is simply the social construction, or amalgamation of virtues, that happens to capture the right ideals. Barbara Taylor offers what seems to be the most compelling explanation: Wollstonecraft is not appealing to constructions but shattering them. Wollstonecraft's "wild hope" is, ultimately, "for a revolution of sexual subjectivity which will transform—at times she even hints supersede—gender as a psychological reality as well as a cultural force"; Barbara Taylor, "Mary Wollstonecraft and the Wild Wish of Feminism," *History Workshop* 33 (Spring 1992): 213, http://www.jstor.org/stable/4289149.

111. Taylor, "Wild Wish of Feminism," 206.

of escaping the binaries responsible for the inequalities that prevent women—and society—from achieving the wisdom and virtue for which they, as God's children, are destined. Sexual distinction is the last terrain to overcome—the "*ne plus ultra* [highest point] of democratic leveling," as Taylor puts it.[112] However, if the sexless soul had been a fairly common thesis in the seventeenth century and, according to Wollstonecraft, was a philosophical given in at least a few intellectual circles of the eighteenth century ("if it be not philosophical to think of sex when the soul is mentioned . . ."), it certainly would not be by the turn of the century. The controversy this radical egalitarianism would stir, and the few radical supporters it would gain, illuminates a culminating point in a debate that had been brewing for centuries. Wollstonecraft's radical politicization of the concept, combined with shifting intellectual, social, economic, and scientific tides that increasingly promoted a two-sex model of the human body and human nature would contaminate the soil necessary for the idea to flourish.

Contemporary Responses to Wollstonecraft's "Sexless Soul"

If a poem of Susanna Wright, the Quaker poetess, could be used as a gauge, the decline of the sexless soul's legitimacy would not take long; in 1750, she could write that "No right has man his equal to control, / Since, *all agree*, there is no sex in soul."[113] But by 1792, when Wollstonecraft would publish *Vindication*, the agreement would seem anything but unanimous. The backlash against the French Revolution (including, in particular, the sexual radicalism and social subversion it had promoted) would make the idea increasingly suspect toward the end of the eighteenth century. Of course, Wollstonecraft's own sexually radical reputation would not help. *Vindication* had only a few short years to be attacked or defended on its own merits before the book and its author's

---

112. Taylor, *Feminist Imagination*, 3.
113. Susana Wright, "To Eliza Norris—at Fairhill" (1750), in *Transatlantic Feminisms in the Age of Revolutions*, ed. Lisa L. Moore, Joanna Brooks, and Caroline Wiggington (New York: Oxford University Press, 2012), 131, emphasis added.

reputation would be sabotaged in the scandalous *Memoir* (1798) written by William Godwin, her husband, who would publish it a year after Wollstonecraft died from a childbirth-related infection. After *Memoir*, it would be difficult for people to untangle Wollstonecraft's ideas from her shockingly liberal sexual lifestyle that the book exposes (including illegitimate children, sexual affairs, and her initially unwed cohabitation with the political radical and Dissenter-turned-atheist Godwin himself).

Nonetheless, Wollstonecraft's widely read *Vindication* seems to have marked her as the sexless soul's most vocal champion, and the idea garnered a smattering of ardent support from Wollstonecraft's contemporaries at home and abroad. One early review of Wollstonecraft's *Vindication* from Dissenting minister William Enfield in the radical *Monthly Review* heartily endorses Wollstonecraft's argument that the "mind is of no sex" and urged "both men and women . . . to regard themselves, and . . . be treated by each other, as human beings."[114]

American advocate for women's rights Judith Sargent Murray had defended the idea in print two years before Wollstonecraft's *Vindication*, though, according to Marion Rust, their arguments anticipated each other on certain issues.[115] Murray's 1790 essay "On the Equality of the Sexes" opens with a poetic verse that presages the vision of Wollstonecraft's sexless utopia: "Yet haste the era, when the world shall know / That such [sexual] distinctions only dwell below; / The soul unfetter'd, to no sex confin'd / Was for the abodes of cloudless day design'd."[116] Rust opines that Murray's "single greatest contribution to female equality" is the "popularization of the concept of the sexless soul" with which she "was able not only to defend the disgraced Wollstonecraft and preach the merits of female self-regard but also to advise her readers that

---

114. William Enfield, "Review," in *Monthly Review* 8, ed. Ralph Griffiths (1792), 198, 209, quoted in R. M. Janes, "On the Reception of Mary Wollstonecraft's: *A Vindication of the Rights of Woman*," *Journal of the History of Ideas* 39, no. 2 (April–June, 1978): 295.

115. Marion Rust, *Prodigal Daughters: Susanna Rowson's Early American Women* (Chapel Hill: The University of North Carolina Press, 2008), 101n73.

116. Judith Sargent Murray, "On the Equality of the Sexes," in *Selected Writings of Judith Sargent Murray*, ed. Sharon Harris (New York: Oxford University Press, 1995), 3–4, quoted in Rust, *Prodigal Daughters*, 100.

gender itself . . . did not survive into the afterlife."[117] On the other hand, perhaps she had been in a position to defend Wollstonecraft because her treatment of the sexless soul had been more socially palatable thanks to Murray's endorsement of profound differences in the aptitudes and gifts between men and women. For instance, she writes to her friend John Winthrop, explaining why a widowed father is not equipped to raise a daughter: "Nature, although equal in her distribution is nevertheless various in her gifts, and her discriminating lines are perfectly obvious."[118] Those lines are not so obvious—or perhaps so significant— to Wollstonecraft.

One of Murray's peers, Annis Boudinot Stockton, poet and hostess for one of the most famous literary salons of the American colonies, would discuss Wollstonecraft's advocacy of the sexless soul in an exchange of letters with her daughter. She summarizes, "You know it is a favorite tenet with me that there is no sex in Soul—I believe it as firmly as I do my existence."[119] But, like Murray, she moderates her position: "but at the same time, I do not think that the sexes were made to be independent of each other . . . if our education [were] the same, our improvement would be the same—*but there is no occasion for exactly the same education.*"[120] Stockton's reticence signals the discomfort even supporters of the sexless soul felt toward upsetting the status quo or dismissing the sexual distinctions that render men and women less autonomous than what Wollstonecraft idealized.

English historian and feminist Lucy Aikin is more straightforward about the sexless soul in her own feminist history of Western culture in *Epistles on Women* (1810).[121] One scholar notes her usage of the

---

117. Rust, *Prodigal Daughters*, 100–101.

118. Judith Sargent Murray to Winthrop Sargent, 1 Nov. 1796, Letterbook, 9:598, quoted in Sheila Skemp, *Judith Sargent Murray: A Brief Biography with Documents* (Boston: Bedford Books, 1998), 82.

119. Annis Boudinot Stockton to Juliet, March 1793, quoted in Rust, *Prodigal Daughters*, 102.

120. Ibid.

121. Lucy Aikin, *Epistles on Women: Exemplifying their Character and Condition in Various Ages and Nations, with Miscellaneous Poems* (London: J. Johnson, 1810). Aikin was the niece of the notable British poet and pro-revisionary Dissenter Anna Laetitia Barbauld, whose essentialist views Wollstonecraft criticizes in *Vindication*.

"Wollstonecrafted claim"[122] of the sexless soul in a poetic verse of her text: "Souls have no sex; sublimed by Virtue's lore / Alike they scorn the earth and try to soar."[123] By the time Samuel Taylor Coleridge, the Romantic poet and former peer of Wollstonecraft, starts writing his *Notebooks, 1808–1819*, he apparently sees enough supporters of the idea for him to wonder, "Is it true what is so *constantly affirmed*, that there is no Sex in Souls?"; yet he himself is not convinced: "I doubt it—I doubt it exceedingly."[124]

Coleridge is not the only one unconvinced. Judging by the "flood of didactic literature" that "poured from the pens of popular writers advocating a style of womanhood so steeped in the feminine, so excessively assertive of sexual difference, that to the modern reader it smacks of parody," cultural tides favored the sexed soul and the social stability it secures.[125] Social harmony and "nature's order" became paramount, making Wollstonecraft's advocacy of the sexless soul all the more distasteful to those in conservative circles who associated such radical egalitarianism with the alarming trajectory of French Revolution politics. According to Edmund Burke, the blurring of gender distinctions had fostered "domineering," shameless women who are mixing with ferocious men in an "inverted order in all things."[126] Rousseau had felt similar alarm at the chaos that would result from eradicating sexual roles and identities, as women, "unable to make themselves into men . . . make us into women."[127] Taylor summarizes Rousseau's anxieties

---

122. Wolfson, *Borderlines*, 310.

123. Lucy Aikin, Epistle III, *Epistles 57*, quoted in Wolfson, *Borderlines*, 310.

124. Coleridge, *Notebooks, 1808–1819*, quoted as epigraph in Wolfson, "Gendering the Soul," 33; emphasis added. Coleridge would follow up with a more emphatic disagreement as he develops his philosophy of the "union of difference": "I would hazard the impeachment of heresy, rather than abandon my belief that there is a sex in our SOULS"; Coleridge, Letter (to a Lady), *The Friend*, 7 December 1809, quoted as epigraph in Wolfson, "Gendering the Soul," 33.

125. Taylor, "Wild Wish," 26.

126. Edmund Burke, *French Revolution*, 63.

127. Jean-Jacques Rousseau, *Politics and the Arts: Letter to M. D'Alembert*, trans. Allan Bloom (Ithaca, NY: Cornell University Press, Agora Editions, 1960), 100, quoted in Joel Schwartz, *The Sexual Politics of Jean-Jacques Rousseau* (Chicago: The University of Chicago Press, 1984), 62.

thusly: "Women will become men; men will become women; paternity will be uncertain; society's moral structure will disintegrate."[128]

In light of the threat that such leveling would pose to the division of labor and social hierarchy, the authors of another review conclude that they are "infinitely better pleased with the present system" and that women themselves would be happier too.[129] Thomas Hearn also urges the eschewal of the "miserable phantoms of metaphysical equality" in his *Short View of the Rise and Progress of Freedom in Modern Europe* (1793).[130] The *English Review* opines, "Miss Wollstonecraft, if she were to be appointed AUTOCRATIX over all the human species, in arranging the affairs of nations, as well as those of the different sexes, would really, in many points, *'turn the world upside down.'*"[131] "Let all things be done in order," the review concludes piously, because "this is the precept of grace."[132] The sexless soul, and all the "metaphysical equality" it entailed, imperiled the delicate social order whose harmony depended, in large part, on sexual distinctions.

In typical Enlightenment fashion, other reviewers appeal to the divine will as manifest in nature's patterns. Laetitia Hawkins reflects this mentality in a direct response to Wollstonecraft's *Vindication* with her *Letters on the Female Mind* (1792), arguing that "it cannot, I think, be truly asserted, that the intellectual powers know no difference of sex. Nature certainly intended a distinction."[133] Also concurring with this opinion is Benjamin Rush, the famous American physician whose medical lectures would do much to forward the notion of the male and female difference. Responding to "the ingenious and eloquent female author of the *Rights of Women*," Rush argues, "There is an original

---

128. Taylor, *Feminist Imagination*, 83.

129. *Critical Review*, n.s., 4, (April 1792): 389–98, as compiled in Jump, *Critics*, 50–51.

130. Thomas Hearn, *Short View of the Rise and Progress of Freedom in Modern Europe as connected with the causes which led to the French Revolution* (London: W. Richardson, 1793), 23, quoted in Taylor, *Feminist Imagination*, 3.

131. "Wollstonecraft's *Historical and Moral View of the Origin and Progress of the French Revolution*," Article VI, in *English Review, or An Abstract of English and Foreign Literature*, vol. 25 (London: H. Murray, 1795), 349–50.

132. Ibid., 352.

133. Laetitia Hawkins, *Letters on the Female Mind, Its Powers and Pursuits, Addressed to Miss H. M. Williams*, vol 1 (London: Hookman and Carpenter, 1792), 6, quoted in Outram, *Enlightenment*, 82.

difference in the bodies and minds of men and women, stamped upon both in the womb by the hand of nature," with a clear "line between male and female."[134] This is not to say that oddities could not occur; he admits that doctors found "as many female minds and bodies among men as [they find] masculine minds and bodies among women."[135] Hannah More, a staunchly conservative Evangelical moralist and one of the era's most prolific British female authors, may have agreed with many of Wollstonecraft's opinions on improving girls' education, but she had refused to read Wollstonecraft's *Vindication*.[136] She, for one, is convinced that the "preservation and observance" of the distinction and "natural bias" in the "mind [of] each sex" is necessary for men's and women's happiness.[137]

In addition, at the turn of the eighteenth century, evangelical Christianity's "ideological shift of stunning proportions" would recast women from their former roles as inferior, weak, and sensual creatures to "apostles of virtue," capable of exerting a redemptive moral influence on society.[138] With the increased reliance on sexual difference being heightened, the threatening implications of the sexless soul would play a pivotal role in how Susan Rowson would craft her image as an author. Notably, Rowson is the British-American author of America's first best seller, *Charlotte Temple*, originally published in England in 1791. According to one scholar, Rowson's contemporaries would seek to "keep Rowson from suffering the fate of a Wollstonecraft" in urging her not to invoke the radical idea of "her fitness as a sexless soul."[139] Instead, her publishers use Rowson to "feminize the novelistic enterprise," in

---

134. Benjamin Rush, *Benjamin Rush's Lectures on the Mind*, ed. Eric T. Carlson, Jeffrey L. Wollock and Patricia S. Noel (Philadelphia: American Philosophical Society, 1981), 697, quoted in Sarah Knott, "Enlightenment Medicine and Female Citizenship," in *Women, Gender, and Enlightenment*, 659.

135. Ibid., 659–60.

136. Janet Todd, *The Sign of Angellica: Women, Writing, and Fiction, 1660–1800* (New York: Columbia University Press, 1989), 214.

137. Hannah More, *Essays for Young Ladies* (London: J. Wilkie, 1777), 266, quoted in Wolfson, *Borderlines*, 290.

138. Bridget Ford, review of *Strangers and Pilgrims: Female Preaching in America, 1740–1845* by Catherine A. Brekus, Humanities and Social Sciences Online, H-Net Reviews, May 1999, http://www.h-net.org/reviews/showrev.php?id=3092.

139. Rust, *Prodigal Daughters*, 115.

order for her "womanly capacity to remain above grubby considerations of profit, fame and fortune."[140] As Wollstonecraft's reputation had
continued to deteriorate in the onslaught of vicious attacks in the wake
of Godwin's *Memoir*, critics like Richard Polwhele would make any association with the sexless soul and Wollstonecraft's other radical ideas
even more hazardous. In a particularly vicious passage of his poem, *The
Unsex'd Females* (1798), Polwhele insinuates that "[Wollstonecraft] died
a death that strongly marked the distinction of the sexes, by pointing
out the destiny of women, and the diseases to which they are liable"
(in this case, infection from giving birth) and hopes that, with her
ignoble death, "the fallacy of her doctrines and the effects of an irreli-
gious conduct, might be manifested to the world."[141] It is, in Polwhele's
eyes, an inexorable lesson that women should learn: the distinction of
the sexes will be preserved in life-and-death situations, radical philosophies notwithstanding.

Even Wollstonecraft's daughter, Mary Shelley, would muse decades
later in an 1835 letter about her mother's belief in a sexless soul: "In
short my belief is—whether there be sex in souls or not—that the sex
of our material mechanism makes us quite different creatures—better
though weaker but wanting in the higher grades of intellect."[142] One
scholar interprets Shelley's own famous work, *Frankenstein*, as a manifestation of "one of Shelley's central tenets... that her mother's feminism
reduces the human to a rational corpse."[143] Shelley's admission of the
overpowering—and even enriching—influence of the sexed, material
body captures what appears to be the late eighteenth and early nineteenth centuries' dominant sentiment, as Taylor aptly summarizes: "the
soul may be sexless, but its earthly vehicles patently are not: a fact that
acquired increasing weight over the course of the eighteenth century"
and beyond.[144]

140. Ibid., 139, 115, respectively.
141. Richard Polwhele, *The Unsex'd Females: A Poem* (New York: Garland Publishing, 1974), 29–30.
142. Mary Shelly to Maria Gisborn, June 11, 1835, quoted in Wolfson, "Gendering the Soul," 33.
143. Paul Youngquist, "Frankenstein: The Mother, the Daughter, and the Monster," *Philological Quarterly* 70, no. 3 (Summer 1991): 342.
144. Taylor, *Feminist Imagination*, 101.

Early- to Mid-Nineteenth-Century Permutations of the Sexless Soul

As the Enlightenment project withered in the wake of the guillotines and gunpowder of France's Reign of Terror, a reinvigorated conservatism and middle-class reformism would sweep through England, extending across the Atlantic to America. With the rise of an "overtly utilitarian discipline of political economy" and the "triumph of anti-intellectual Evangelicalism," women's place in the private, domestic, and wholly feminine sphere became more entrenched.[145] Romantic ideals would also play a role in reinforcing sexual distinctions, as both Philip Shaw and Susan Wolfson demonstrate.[146] According to these scholars, some male romantic poets—including William Wordsworth, Percy Bysshe Shelley, Samuel Taylor Coleridge, John Keats, and William Blake—often portray the feminine as other, alien, and, in some instances, dangerous. However, more positive portrayals of sexual difference exist in romantic literature as well, typified in Coleridge's approving affirmation that "there is a Sex in our Souls as well as in our perishable garments."[147] Another example is Alfred Lord Tennyson's poetic claim that "Woman is not undeveloped Man, / But diverse; could we make her as the Man, / Sweet love were slain; whose dearest bond is this, / Not like to like, but like in difference."[148]

---

145. John Robertson, "Women and Enlightenment: A Historiographical Conclusion," in *Women, Gender, and Enlightenment*, 702. See also Brekus, *Strangers and Pilgrims*, which locates the history of America's nineteenth-century female religious leaders during the final eclipse of, to use Laqueur's terminology, the one-sex model by the two-sex model, in which men and women are biologically incommensurate creatures.

146. See Philip Shaw, *The Sublime* (New York: Routledge, 2006); and Wolfson, *Borderlines*.

147. Samuel Taylor Coleridge, "Letter II: To a Lady," in *Biographia Literaria, or Biographical Sketches of My Literary Life and Opinions*, vol. 2 (London: Rest Fenner, 1817), 206. This verse is quoted in two nineteenth-century authors' discussions of sexual difference. See Leopold Hartley Grindon, *The Sexuality of Nature: An Essay* (Boston: Nichols and Noyes, 1868); and Elizabeth Strutt, *The Feminine Soul: Its Nature and Attributes* (London: J. S. Hodson, 1857).

148. Alfred Lord Tennyson, "The Woman's Cause is Man's," from *The Princess*, canto vii (London: E. Moxen, 1847). This verse is also quoted and discussed in Grindon's *Sexuality of Nature* and Strutt's *Feminine Soul*.

Although these trends diverged from Wollstonecraft's efforts to champion the sexless soul and secure social and intellectual equality for women, the increased emphasis on sexual differentiation also opened up different possibilities for advocates of women's rights. One scholar has surmised that "[feminists] either had to argue that women were the same as men, and therefore deserved equal treatment; or that women were essentially different from men but on those grounds 'womanly' qualities should be brought to the public spheres of education, politics, and religion."[149] While it risks oversimplification, this formulation is helpful in describing the orientation that many nineteenth-century feminists would adopt in their advocacy of women's rights. The permutations resulting from the combination of a sexless soul and sexed body would create more varied understandings of human nature and spiritual identity.

Indeed, the debate over the sex of the soul would not end with Wollstonecraft's death. As Eileen Botting and Christine Carey have shown, women's rights advocates across the Atlantic would pick up Wollstonecraft's *Vindication*, engaging with and incorporating many of Wollstonecraft's ideas into their own philosophies and political platforms.[150] Margaret Fuller, Elizabeth Cady Stanton, and Sarah Grimké, as well as other intellectuals from major literary journals and magazines, would continue debating over the extent to which sexual differentiation affects man's and woman's innermost locus of identity. No one would advocate for the sexless soul and the eradication of sexual distinctions in society to the extent that Wollstonecraft did, although Grimké would lean in that Plato-inspired direction. Others, such as Stanton, would find the surest guarantee for women's equality by arguing the opposite—that women were intellectually and spiritually distinct, their particular genius not replicable by men. Still others, like Fuller, would blend both strands in a Hildegardian model that upheld an androgynous human nature in which both the male and female elements were essential. The

---

149. Jane Shaw, "Reformed and Enlightened Church," in *Queer Theology: Rethinking the Western Body*, ed. Gerard Loughlin (Malden, MA: Blackwell Publishing, 2007), 224.

150. Eileen Botting and Christine Carey, "Wollstonecraft's Philosophical Impact on Nineteenth-Century American Women's Advocates," *American Journal of Political Science* 48, no. 4 (2004): 707–22.

sex of the soul represented the key for many feminists and intellectuals striving to advance women's rights, although consensus was no closer than it had been in the debates of the early church fathers.

A well-known antislavery and women's rights activist, Sarah Grimké would become both a convert to Quakerism and, thanks to feminist Lucretia Mott, to Wollstonecraftian philosophy.[151] In her 1838 *Letters on the Equality of the Sexes, and the Condition of Woman*, Grimké claims that men and women's moral and intellectual equality stems from their shared spiritual pedigree, having been created jointly "in the image of God."[152] As dual inheritors of the heavenly image, she writes, "not one particle of difference [is] intimated as existing between them"; woman is "clothed by her Maker with the same rights, and of course . . . the same duties" as man.[153] The well-known American author and journalist Edward D. Mansfield concurs in his treatise on education a few years later, stating as a "broad fact" that "the human soul has no sex," for it is the "consciousness that the original and distinctive attributes of spirit are the same in men and women, and among all nations," affirming that "human nature is not two."[154] The pseudonymous male author "G," in the well-respected literary journal *New England Magazine*, offers a slightly moderated view of the soul that, while sexless, still takes on "a tinge from [one's] sex" by virtue of its embodied state and consequent stations and duties.[155] Although the author emphatically argues that "there is no sex in the soul" and that "their [men and women's] abilities, their capacities, their affections, are equal," the "original texture" of the sexless soul is nonetheless "lost in the thousand webs, which custom, education and society has woven around them."[156] The author articulates the permeability of soul and body that Wollstonecraft had reluctantly implied;

151. Ibid., 713.

152. Sarah Grimké, *Letters on the Equality of the Sexes*, ed. Elizabeth Ann Bartlett (New Haven: Yale University Press, 1988), 32, as quoted in Botting and Carey, "Wollstonecraf's Philosophical Impact," 714.

153. Sarah Grimké, *Letters on the Equality of the Sexes* (Boston: Isaac Knapp, 1838), 4, 122–123.

154. Edward D. Mansfield, *American Education, its Principles, and Elements* (New York: A. S. Barnes, 1851), 297–98.

155. "G" [pseud.], "Female Education," *New England Magazine* (July–December 1832): 283.

156. Ibid., 280.

while urging his readers to "remember, that spirits have no sex," he also reminds women to recognize that souls are nonetheless "formed by their interests and objects."[157] "Whilst you feel that you are intellectual beings," he concludes, "never forget that you are women. That is your station; there you are to act; there you must be useful; there you must find your happiness."[158]

Elizabeth Cady Stanton, staunch feminist and co-organizer of the first women's rights convention at Seneca Falls in 1848, would fully embrace and propound the sexed nature of the soul. As much as she openly admires and champions Wollstonecraft, their objectives would part ways at a crucial point.[159] The liberation of women, according to Stanton, depends on recognizing the distinctiveness and otherness of both sexes, rather than trying to mask or expunge their sexual differences. "No doubt there is sex in the mortal and spiritual world," she argues emphatically, asserting that the complementary nature of "the masculine and female elements" is vital to ensuring that humankind "reach the divinest heights of which he is capable."[160] Both man's and woman's potential could only be realized through a full recognition and uniting of their true natures as harmonized sexed souls. In later correspondence with a friend about the flagging suffrage movement, Stanton marvels at the "indifference and apathy of our women" regarding this truth: "When philosophers come to see that ideas as well as babies need the mother soul for their growth and perfection, that there is sex in mind and spirit, as well as body, they will appreciate the necessity of a full recognition of womanhood in every department of life."[161] The surest way to emancipate women, she says, is to remind

157. Ibid.

158. Ibid., 283.

159. Stanton's ideological parting of ways with Wollstonecraft is evident in her correspondence with Lucretia Mott, and in the articles she would publish about Wollstonecraft's life and philosophy in her weekly newspaper *The Revolution*.

160. Elizabeth Cady Stanton, "Co-Education" (speech to the United States Senate Judiciary Committee, Washington, DC, January 10, 1872), quoted in Beth Waggenspack, ed., *The Search for Self-Sovereignty: The Oratory of Elizabeth Cady Stanton* (New York: Greenwood Press, 1989), 132.

161. Stanton, Letter (1867), Dickinson Papers, Library of Congress, as quoted in William Leach, *True Love and Perfect Union: The Feminist Reform of Sex and Society*, 2nd ed. (Middletown, CT: Wesleyan University Press, 1980), 388n72, quoted in Sue Davis, *The*

them of the unique nature of their "mother soul" and prove their indis-
pensability as women to the civic world. Women must, Stanton stoutly
urges, unite in solidarity to "stand by womanhood."[162] Wollstonecraft,
on the other hand, believed that dissolving "womanhood" in the
broader ocean of humanity was the way to liberate women; rather than
fighting for "womanhood," women were to "obtain a character as *a
human being*, regardless of the distinction of sex."[163]

The gifted transcendentalist Margaret Fuller had been a fellow
admirer and defender of Wollstonecraft who engaged directly with Wollstonecraft's ideas in her own landmark work *Woman in the Nineteenth
Century* (1843). Fuller represents a middle ground in which the soul has
both masculine and feminine elements. Like Stanton, Fuller believes that
sexual distinctions should be celebrated, not erased; unlike Stanton or
Wollstonecraft, Fuller believes that such dualism is housed within the
soul of each man and woman. "Male and female represent the two sides of
the great radical dualism . . . there is no wholly masculine man, no purely
feminine woman," she explains; hence, masculine and feminine qualities
intermingle in the human soul like fluids.[164] The difference between men
and women is merely a matter of emphasis; women are characterized
by a greater degree of "femality," or the "especial genius of woman," and
vice versa for men.[165] Only when the soul has completely developed both
aspects of its nature could one claim that "all soul is the same" in the
"totality or wholeness of the animating powers."[166] *The Sexuality of Nature*
(1853), a book published a few years later by the educator and botanist
Leopold Hartley Grindon, closely reflects this commingling duality of
the soul: "For just as mankind in general is of twofold composition,
consisting of both men and women," he explains, "so is there a duality

---

*Political Thought of Elizabeth Cady Stanton: Women's Rights and the American Political
Tradition* (New York: New York University Press, 2008), 153.

162. Stanton, Letter to Martha Coffin Wright, Highwood Park, March 21, 1871,
quoted in Ann D. Gordon, ed., *The Selected Papers of Elizabeth Cady Stanton and Susan
B. Anthony: Against an Aristocracy of Sex, 1866 to 1873* (New Brunswick, Canada: Rutgers
University Press, 2000), 428, quoted in Botting and Carey, "Wollstonecraft's Philosophical
Impact," 717.

163. Wollstonecraft, *Vindication*, 7, emphasis added.

164. Margaret Fuller, *Woman in the Nineteenth Century* (London: H. G. Clark, 1845), 108.

165. Ibid., 107.

166. Ibid., 108.

in the soul of every individual . . . a blended male and female."[167] Like Fuller (and Stanton, on an individuated level), Grindon claims that the "healthiest and comeliest condition of the soul is when these two great principles of its being, or its masculine and feminine, are well adjusted; when they are married."[168] By and large, the most common "marriage" in this era, however, would remain between emphatically sexually differentiated beings—not the androgynous elements of the individual soul.

Conclusion

The debate over the sex of the soul would remain alive and well throughout the nineteenth century. As this sampling of commentaries throughout the seventeenth, eighteenth, and nineteenth centuries shows, the debate's terrain is broad and complex. The sex of the soul would remain entangled in related debates over the "natural" order, the nature of embodiment, the influences of society and culture, the nature of God, and other key issues of the time. Advocates defended women's equality from the point of view of the sexless soul as well as the sexed, just as did critics of feminist thought. Although defenses of the sexless soul would not lead directly to any of the radical reforms or "Utopian dreams"[169] that Wollstonecraft had wistfully envisioned, the debate over the sex and nature of the soul continue to both shape and mirror opinions about the social order and the "woman's question."

For Wollstonecraft, at least, her feminist aims were closely tied with—if not subsumed in—a utopian vision in which all human beings would be restored to their rational and spiritual identity as sexless souls pursuing virtue and wisdom. As Taylor points out in her seminal study on Wollstonecraft's religious influences, it is impossible to understand Wollstonecraft's thoughts without taking into account the religious consciousness that animates her work. Given Wollstonecraft's centrality to the development of feminism, Taylor explains, analyses of Wollstonecraft's particular religious understanding can "give us more than

---

167. Grindon, *Sexuality of Nature*, 29.
168. Ibid., 29–30.
169. Wollstonecraft, *Vindication*, 72.

local insights into the religious impulse as it has operated across the feminist tradition."[170] Indeed, it is impossible to understand the history of feminism without discussing the religious ideas that undergirded early discourse. After all, as Sarah Apetrei notes, religion is "not just the envelope for an unconsciously secular or self-serving agenda: it [is] the very origin and goal of feminism."[171] Of course, debates over the sex of the soul would not have been labeled or compartmentalized as "religious" by such women in the past; the sex of the soul was no mere social, political, or philosophical idea but was a question of spiritual, moral, and even eschatological proportions.

Wollstonecraft's wild wish to eradicate sexual distinctions vis-à-vis a sexless soul shorn from earthly baggage still persists as a logical conclusion, fanciful chimera, or misguided aim to many feminists today. In chasing after her own utopian dream, Wollstonecraft crystalizes one of the enduring dilemmas of feminism. Does the liberation of women necessitate the erasure of the feminine? Or is this erasure simply an oppression of another kind? Judging by the responses of her contemporaries, her successors, and today's ongoing debates, neither side of the controversy is without its inherent perils.

170. Taylor, "Religious Foundations," 103.
171. Sarah Apetrei, *Women, Feminism and Religion in Early Enlightenment England* (Cambridge: Cambridge University Press, 2010), 36.

Providential Empiricism: Suffering and Shaping the Self in Eighteenth-Century British Children's Literature[1]

Adrianne Wadewitz
Occidental College

In Heav'n he shines with Beams of Love,
With Wrath in Hell beneath!
'Tis on his Earth I stand or move,
And 'tis his air I breathe.

His Hand is my perpetual Guard;
He keeps me with his Eye:
Why should I then forget the Lord,
Who is for ever nigh?
—Isaac Watts[2]

In "Praise for Creation and Providence" eighteenth-century Dissenting cleric Isaac Watts conveys God's encompassing presence—not only is he in heaven and hell, but he also inhabits (and owns) Earth and everything in it. This poem was reprinted for more than 150 years

---

1. I would like to thank Deidre Lynch, Nicholas Williams, Sarah Knott, Mary Favret, Jesse Molesworth, Mica Hilson, and the anonymous readers for their invaluable feedback on various iterations of this essay.

2. Isaac Watts, "Praise for Creation and Providence," in *Divine Songs: Attempted in Easy Language for the Use of Children* (London: J. Buckland, J. and F. Rivington, T. Longman, W. Fenner, T. Field, and E. and C. Dilly, 1775), 3–4.

in Watts's *Divine Songs: Attempted in Easy Language for the Use of Children* (1775). A child reciting this poem is made keenly aware of how much he or she owes to God—soul, planet, and life. Watts emphasizes how one senses God's physical presence ("Beams of love," "His Hand," and "his Eye") with the body ("I stand or move" and "I breathe") in order to understand his transcendence and judgment. Watts continues this theme in his "Discourse on the Education of Children and Youth" (1753), advising parents and teachers to expose children to nature and encouraging them to instruct their charges "that the Great God made all these Things" and that "his Providence governs them all."[3] Watts argues that experiential learning demonstrates both God's existence and magnificence—it allows children to see God in nature. Importantly, to grasp the role of providence, both the child in the hymn and the reader suffer in order to gain experience that ultimately constitutes the self.

This vision of God—an active, involved God who is committed to human affairs on the individual level—pervades eighteenth-century British children's literature and determines the construction of the self; sensory perceptions are providential and experiences are God given. Rather than seeing the child solely as a blank slate, as John Locke does, many eighteenth-century British children's texts portray the child as a supplicant or a penitent awaiting discipline and fulfillment from God. In highlighting providence's role in the formation of the self, these writers encourage their readers to develop a specifically Christian subjectivity. They integrate Locke's newly popularized idea of the tabula rasa with older forms of Christian subjectivity, specifically the role of suffering in forming character.

In exploring this "providential empiricism," I demonstrate the deeply religious underpinnings of Enlightenment education. Whereas we in the early twenty-first century instinctively see a paradox between Christian providential thinking and Lockean empirical thinking, eighteenth-century children's writers seamlessly meld the two, particularly when it comes to how experience forms the self. As Patricia Demers has written in her study of eighteenth- and early nineteenth-century

---

3. Isaac Watts, *The Improvement of the Mind: Second Part. With Various Remarks and Rules about the Communication of Useful Knowledge. Also a Discourse on the Education of Children and Youth* (London: J. Buckland, T. Longman, T. Field, and C. Dilly, 1782), 110.

British religious and moral children's literature, "what was once so straightforward and logical is now for us embroiling, coercive, and uniformly unsatisfying."[4] In the last twenty years, scholarship about the Enlightenment has expanded to challenge the traditional narrative that it had been a movement rooted solely in reason. This new scholarship explains that the Enlightenment is not necessarily the root of modern secularism as previously thought and that modernity and secularism are not necessarily tied together (offering an explanation for why it is hard for us in our historical moment, for example, to reconcile providentialism with empiricism).[5] In this article, I would like to build on this recent work of Enlightenment historians, applying it to the case of Enlightenment education, specifically eighteenth-century British children's literature.

Recent scholarship about the history of education in eighteenth-century Britain has followed the larger trends of Enlightenment historiography, taking into account religious impulses and asking how they relate to questions of the Enlightenment. For example, Mary Hilton and Jill Shefrin's *Educating the Child in Enlightenment Britain* (2009) includes several essays that discuss the role of religion in Enlightenment education.[6] Anne Stott's insightful contribution, "Evangelicalism and Enlightenment: The Educational Agenda of Hannah More" (2009), asks the question, "How does More's apparent indebtedness to Locke square with her Evangelicalism?"[7] Her answer is that More had been part of a "Christian Enlightenment tradition of rational and humane education, designed to produce a piety that was sober as

---

4. Patricia Demers, *Heaven upon Earth: The Form of Moral and Religious Children's Literature, to 1850* (Knoxville: University of Tennessee Press, 1993), 2.

5. For example, see Jonathan Sheehan, "Enlightenment, Religion, and the Enigma of Secularization: A Review Essay," *American Historical Review* 108, no. 4 (2003): 1061–80; S. J. Barnett, *The Enlightenment and Religion: The Myths of Modernity* (Manchester: Manchester University Press, 2003); J. C. D. Clark, *English Society 1660–1832: Religion, Ideology and Politics during the Ancient Regime*, 2nd ed. (Cambridge: Cambridge University Press, 2000); and J. G. A. Pocock, *Barbarism and Religion: The Enlightenments of Edward Gibbon, 1737–1764* (Cambridge: Cambridge University Press, 2003).

6. Mary Hilton and Jill Shefrin, eds., *Educating the Child in Britain: Beliefs, Cultures, Practices* (Burlington, VT: Ashgate, 2009).

7. Anne Stott, "Evangelicalism and Enlightenment: The Educational Agenda of Hannah More," in *Educating the Child in Britain*, ed. Mary Hilton and Jill Shefrin, 42.

well as heartfelt: a religion of the heart but one that also recognized the importance of reason."[8] However, within recent eighteenth-century British children's literature scholarship, scholars tend to focus on the Enlightenment legacy of writers such as Anna Laetitia Barbauld, Maria Edgeworth, Madame de Beaumont, and even Sarah Trimmer without seriously considering the religious motifs in their work.[9] As Demers wrote in 1993, "what still seems lacking, to me, is any sustained reading of the variety of genres that constitute the moral tradition in light of the religious beliefs underpinning it. When they are not designed to avoid it altogether, most histories try to make this material as painless and deal with it as hurriedly as possible."[10] Despite the contributions of Seth Lerer and Mary Jackson, this remains just as much of a problem today.[11] Besides Patricia Demers's discussion, the best readings of these genres are J. Paul Hunter's analysis of didactic genres in his discussion of the rise of the novel and William Sloane's history of seventeenth-century British and American children's literature.[12]

British children's literature of the eighteenth century had grown out of Puritan books for children and thus had retained a strong Christian, even Dissenting, element that is usually passed over quickly in histories of children's literature. In her history of early British children's literature,

---

8. Ibid.

9. See, for example, Mitzi Myers, "Impeccable Governesses, Rational Dames, and Moral Mothers: Mary Wollstonecraft and the Female Tradition in Georgian Children's Books," *Children's Literature* 14 (1986): 31–59; Mitzi Myers, "*Aufklärung für Kinder*? Maria Edgeworth and the Genders of Knowledge Genres; or, 'The Genius of Nonsense' and 'The Grand Panjandrum Himself,'" *Women's Writing* 2, no. 2 (1995): 113–40; William McCarthy, "Mother of All Discourses: Anna Barbauld's *Lessons for Children*," in *Culturing the Child, 1690–1914: Essays in Memory of Mitzi Myers*, ed. Donelle Ruwe (Lanham, MD: The Children's Literature Association and the Scarecrow Press, 2005); M. O. Grenby, "'A Conservative Woman Doing Radical Things': Sarah Trimmer and *The Guardian of Education*," in *Culturing the Child*; and Andrea Immel and Michael Witmore, eds., *Childhood and Children's Books in Early Modern Europe, 1550–1800* (New York: Routledge, 2006).

10. Demers, *Heaven upon Earth*, 6.

11. Mary V. Jackson, *Engines of Instruction, Mischief, and Magic: Children's Literature in England from Its Beginnings to 1839* (Lincoln: University of Nebraska Press, 1989); and Seth Lerer, *Children's Literature: A Reader's History, from Aesop to Harry Potter* (Chicago: University of Chicago Press, 2008).

12. J. Paul Hunter, *Before Novels: The Cultural Contexts of Eighteenth Century English Fiction* (New York: W. W. Norton, 1990); and William Sloane, *Children's Books in England and America in the Seventeenth Century* (New York: King's Crown Press, 1955).

for example, Jackson claims that "most of what was written after the 1740s reveals a continued lightening of mood and, after the 1770s, a growing secularism." Moreover, she draws a division between Locke's pedagogy and that held by the "very devout."[13] This strong impetus to interpret Lockean ideas as secular and to tie them to a secular Enlightenment has led children's literature scholars to ignore the very real way in which Lockean ideas had been interpreted within a Christian framework by pedagogues and children's authors at the time. In focusing on providence in this article, I show how self-discovery through suffering—one aspect of the lingering Puritan and Dissenting tradition in British children's literature—had profoundly shaped the eighteenth century's understanding of how to educate the self.

The Puritans wrote some of the earliest children's literature in England.[14] These "godly books"—such as James Janeway's *A Token for Children, Being An Exact Account of the Conversion, Holy and Exemplary Lives, and Joyful Deaths of Several Young Children* (1672)[15]—are not necessarily designed for early readers in terms of their vocabulary and syntax, but they are nevertheless aimed at children. It is not until the early eighteenth century that publishers in England, such as Thomas Boreman and Mary Cooper, would begin issuing what is more recognizable to modern readers as children's literature. This includes texts such as *A Description of Three Hundred Animals* (1730) and *The Child's New Play-Thing* (1743).[16] During the middle of the eighteenth century, John Newbery would make children's literature into a viable and sustainable publishing enterprise in England for the first time.[17]

---

13. Jackson, *Engines of Instruction, Mischief, and Magic*, 29.

14. The only children's books routinely printed in England before the late seventeenth century were hornbooks (simple primers), language textbooks such as *Orbis Sensualium Pictus* (1658), religious tracts, and chapbooks (which were not written exclusively or even primarily for children).

15. James Janeway, *A Token for Children, Being An Exact Account of the Conversion, Holy and Exemplary Lives, and Joyful Deaths of Several Young Children* (London: Soli Deo Gloria, 1672).

16. *A Description of Three Hundred Animals* (London: Thomas Boreman, 1730); and *The Child's New Play-Thing* (London: Mary Cooper, 1743).

17. For a history of eighteenth-century children's literature, see the following: Jackson, *Engines of Instruction, Mischief, and Magic*; F. J. Harvey Darton, *Children's Books in England: Five Centuries of Social Life*, 3rd ed. (Cambridge: Cambridge University Press,

A scant thirty to forty years after Boreman's, Cooper's, and Newbery's initial successes, children's books had become an accepted genre of literature. British women such as Charlotte Smith, Maria Edgeworth, Lady Ellenor Fenn, and Dorothy Kilner would devote substantial time to composing texts for children. By the 1780s and 1790s, the prestigious *Analytical Review, Critical Review,* and *Monthly Review* would be reviewing major children-oriented works such as Anna Barbauld and John Aikin's *Evenings at Home* (1793–96). With an overwhelming quantity of children's literature fast becoming available to the consumer, Sarah Trimmer had been prompted to found her periodical the *Guardian of Education* in 1802.[18] She announces in the first issue that "under the idea, therefore, that we might render acceptable service to mothers who wish to train up their children in the ways of piety and virtue, and secure them from the corruptions of the age, we have been induced to offer our assistance, as the examiners of books of education, and children's books."[19]

Whereas eighteenth-century British children's books are no longer familiar children's books today, of all the literature published during this period, children's literature almost certainly endured the longest. Even after Henry Fielding, Alexander Pope, and Samuel Johnson had been replaced by Charles Dickens and Alfred Tennyson in the hearts and minds of readers, Isaac Watts's *Divine Songs* (1715), Thomas Day's *Sandford and Merton* (1783–89), and Anna Laetitia Barbauld's *Hymns in Prose for Children* (1781) are still being published and are selling well.[20] Millions of children grew up reading these texts in the English-speaking world. As Seth Lerer points out in his history of children's

1982); Geoffrey Summerfield, *Fantasy and Reason: Children's Literature in the Eighteenth Century* (Athens: University of Georgia Press, 1984); Samuel F. Pickering Jr., *John Locke and Children's Books in Eighteenth-Century England* (Knoxville: University of Tennessee Press, 1981); Alan Richardson, *Literature, Education, and Romanticism: Reading as Social Practice, 1780–1832* (Cambridge: Cambridge University Press, 1994); and Andrew O'Malley, *The Making of the Modern Child: Children's Literature and Childhood in the Late Eighteenth Century* (New York: Routledge, 2003).

18. Matthew Grenby, introduction to *The Guardian of Education* (Bristol, UK: Thoemmes Press, 2002), xiv.

19. Sarah Trimmer, *The Guardian of Education* 1 (2002): 15–16.

20. Thomas Day, *Sandford and Merton* (1783–89); and Anna Laetitia Barbauld, *Hymns in Prose for Children* (London: J. Johnson, 1781).

literature, "Watts'[s] *Divine Songs* . . . was undeniably the most popular book of children's verse ever published. . . . Quite simply, [it] defined, for generations of parents and children, just what verse *was*."[21] His poetry would influence writers such as Benjamin Franklin, Lewis Carroll, and Emily Dickinson.

With the advent of children's literature in the eighteenth century, children would be envisioned as a distinctive readership for the first time, and children's writers would conceive of their readers as having a rich sense of personhood. Ever since the publication of Philippe Ariès's *Centuries of Childhood* in 1962, historians have extensively debated the point at which "childhood" had become a distinctive concept.[22] Because specialized children's publishing had increased dramatically during this period and the child reader had become an important segment of the market, fierce debates about pedagogy had arisen in British philosophical, political, and domestic circles. Some of the first "culture wars" over reading pedagogy had broken out; widespread controversy had arisen about the value of fairy tales; Hannah More had begun publishing her *Cheap Repository Tracts* aimed at teaching the poor to read; and Andrew Bell and Joseph Lancaster had developed competing mass education systems.[23] The participants in these discussions had grasped that these

---

21. Lerer, *Children's Literature*, 90.

22. For more information on this debate, see the following: Philippe Ariès, *Centuries of Childhood: A Social History of Family Life* (New York: Vintage Books, 1960); Lawrence Stone, *The Family, Sex and Marriage in England 1500–1800* (New York: Harper and Row, 1977); George Boas, *The Cult of Childhood* (London: Warburg, 1966); Marilyn R. Brown, ed., *Picturing Children: Constructions of Childhood between Rousseau and Freud* (Aldershot, UK: Ashgate, 2002); Hugh Cunningham, *Children and Childhood in Western Society since 1500* (London: Longman, 1995); Lloyd de Mause, ed., *The History of Childhood* (New York: Psychohistory Press, 1974); Anne Higonnet, *Pictures of Innocence: The History and Crisis of Ideal Childhood* (London: Thomas and Hudson Ltd., 1998); Ludmilla Jordanova, "New Worlds for Children in the Eighteenth Century: Problems of Historical Interpretation," *History of the Human Sciences* 3, no. 1 (1990): 69–83; J. H. Plumb, "The New World of Children in Eighteenth-Century England," *Past and Present* 67 (1975): 64–95; and Neil Postman, *The Disappearance of Childhood* (New York: Vintage, 1994).

23. Nicholas Tucker, "Fairy Tales and Their Early Opponents: In Defence of Mrs. Trimmer," in *Opening the Nursery Door: Reading, Writing and Childhood 1600–1900*, ed. Mary Hilton, Morag Styles, and Victor Watson (New York: Routledge, 1997); Susan Pedersen, "Hannah More Meets Simple Simon: Tracts, Chapbooks, and Popular Culture in Late Eighteenth-Century England," *Journal of British Studies* 25, no. 1 (1986): 84–113; and

new children's texts would be shaping generations to come and, hence, had subjected them to intense scrutiny. Although it has been traditional to read educational philosophy and then look for its impact on children's literature—such as finding Locke in Newbery—early children's writers were independent and responded to educational philosophy not only by incorporating it but also by revising it. They are part of large, ongoing shifts in how childhood would be perceived and in discussions about how education should be shaped.

While scholars have generated excellent work showing how Locke's educational philosophy had influenced eighteenth-century British children's literature, scholars tend to mimic the older model of Enlightenment intellectual history, following a trail of ideas from philosophers to "lesser" writers, who are, in this context, often women. This model assumes that ideas only flow in one direction—from male philosophers to female writers of children's literature, privileging philosophical discourse above the literature that thousands encountered on a daily basis. Moreover, looking only for Locke's ideas restricts the concepts we see as central to eighteenth-century pedagogy: writers of eighteenth-century British children's literature have created their own pedagogies that deserve to be explored.

To give one recent example, while Heather Klemann's article "The Matter of Moral Education: Locke, Newbery, and the Didactic Book-Toy Hybrid"[24] is a wonderful explanation of how thing theory can be applied to Newbery's texts—an important contribution to the scholarship on eighteenth-century British children's literature—it shows only that Locke's pedagogical ideas appear in Newbery's texts. Klemann does not consider who the authors of Newbery's texts might have been or how they may have been reshaping pedagogy outside of the Lockean model. And although her article does an excellent job in bringing the commercial and physical elements of Newbery's production to the fore, she does so at the expense of his authors' complex religious heritage. For example, she contrasts Puritan children's texts with Newbery's,

---

Andrew O'Malley, "Toward the Self-Regulating Subject: Teaching Discipline in Pedagogical Systems and Children's Books," in *The Making of the Modern Child*, 86–101.

24. Heather Klemann, "The Matter of Moral Education: Locke, Newbery, and the Didactic Book-Toy Hybrid," *Eighteenth-Century Studies* 44, no. 2 (2011): 223–44.

arguing, "In contrast to the juvenile texts of the late seventeenth-century Puritanical tradition, which guide readers toward the immaterial religious afterlife, Newbery's incorporation of objects with texts prepares children for adult life in commercial society."[25] But, in fact, it is not as simple as this because the Puritans had been some of the first to commercialize the language of the soul.[26] Her analysis claims a deep divide between the religious instruction of earlier children's literature and the moral instruction of Newbery's children's literature, which is hard to see on close examination of the stories.[27] Without placing Newbery's works in a larger context of eighteenth-century British children's literature, it is perhaps easier to make this distinction, but as will be seen, the texts of the period have a strong and continuing Christian, even Dissenting, flavor.

Although scholars who trace the influence of Locke have long acknowledged the central role of empirical thought in eighteenth-century British children's literature, scholars have yet to really study the importance of providential thinking, partially because of the insistence on seeing secular Lockean thinking as central to the narrative of the genre's development.[28] However, in his exploration of the rise of the educational novel, Richard Barney provides one of the more sophisticated analyses regarding the role of providential themes in didactic texts.[29] Exploring the generic impact of providential motifs in Daniel Defoe's *Robinson Crusoe* (1719), he argues that "Defoe's combination of the Puritan and empiricist paradigms results in such a violent narrative ebb and flow that Crusoe—as both protagonist and narrator—often comes close to being overwhelmed. These contrary currents, in fact,

---

25. Ibid., 225.

26. For more information, see Max Weber, *The Protestant Ethic and the Spirit of Capitalism* (New York: Routledge, 1905; 1997); Christopher Hill, *A Turbulent, Seditious, and Factitious People: John Bunyan and His Church 1628–1688* (Oxford, UK: Clarendon, 1988); David Zaret, *The Heavenly Contract: Ideology and Organization in Pre-Revolutionary Puritanism* (Chicago: University of Chicago Press, 1985); and Lori Branch, "'As Blood is Forced out of Flesh': Spontaneity and the Wounds of Exchange in Grace Abounding and The Pilgrim's Progress" *English Literary History* 74, no.2 (Summer 2007): 271–99.

27. Klemann, "Moral Education," 237.

28. Pickering Jr., *John Locke and Children's Books.*.

29. Richard Barney, *Plots of Enlightenment: Education in Eighteenth-Century England* (Stanford, CA: Stanford University Press, 1999).

threaten Crusoe's story with a kind of narrative schizophrenia."[30] Unlike
Barney, however, I posit that the writers of eighteenth-century British
children's literature try to present their readers with a coherent understanding of how providential experience and empirical experience
operate in harmony; hence, the children's texts I analyze show little of
the "schizophrenia" that Barney finds in *Crusoe*.

In order to explain fully how the two discourses of providence and
empiricism can work together harmoniously in eighteenth-century
British literature to present a model of selfhood, I first explain Locke's
theory of the self. Then I explore how eighteenth-century British children's writers had both adhered to and challenged it; how authors had
understood and integrated providence into children's literature, particularly through the role of suffering; and, finally, how children's writers
had communicated their version of providential empiricism. To illustrate not only the existence and persistence of providential empiricism
across a wide range of eighteenth-century British children's literature,
but also the different ways in which it is represented, I compare and
contrast representative works of Anna Laetitia Barbauld, Mary Wollstonecraft, and Mary Martha Sherwood.[31] Wollstonecraft and Barbauld
are generally viewed as progressive writers because they support the
ideals of the French Revolution. Wollstonecraft, while part of a Dissenting circle, is Anglican and eventually much less religious, yet Barbauld
is a strong Dissenter. Generally, Sherwood is viewed as conservative and
is evaluated almost solely through the lens of her evangelicalism.[32] But

---

30. Ibid., 228.

31. Regarding Barbauld, see Daniel White, "The 'Joineriana': Anna Barbauld, the Aikin
Family Circle, and the Dissenting Public Sphere," *Eighteenth-Century Studies* 32, no. 4 (1999):
511–33; and Norma Clarke, "'The Cursed Barbauld Crew': Women Writers and Writing for
Children in the Late Eighteenth Century," in *Opening the Nursery Door: Reading, Writing
and Childhood 1600–1900*, ed. Mary Hilton, Morag Styles, and Victor Watson (New York:
Routledge, 1997). Regarding Wollstonecraft, see Claire Tomlin, *The Life and Death of Mary
Wollstonecraft* (New York: Routledge, 1992). Regarding Sherwood, see Patricia Demers,
"Mrs. Sherwood and Hesba Stratton: The Letter and Spirit of Evangelical Writing of and
for Children," in *Romanticism and Children's Literature in Nineteenth-Century England*, ed.
James Holt McGavran Jr. (Athens: University of Georgia Press, 1991).

32. Even Patricia Demers, who has greatly expanded the discussion of didactic writing
for children, considers Sherwood almost solely as an evangelical writer. For her exploration of Sherwood and Romanticism, see Demers, "Mrs. Sherwood and Hesba Stratton."

these easy political and religious labels do not convey the complexity of the children's literature that these three women have produced. The children's writings of Barbauld, Wollstonecraft, and Sherwood evince a skepticism regarding Locke's theory of the self and a reliance on providence to shape the self. Moreover, all three writers portray the efficacy of God-given suffering to shape the self. In replicating traditional political alliances in modern scholarship, we run the risk of missing similarities that pervade eighteenth-century British children's literature and of misunderstanding what had been central to the genre at the time.

Locke's *Essay Concerning Human Understanding* (1690) would set the terms for the eighteenth-century debate about the self.[33] Because his ideas are still so familiar to us today—describing the mind as a blank slate and associating personal identity with consciousness—we do not often pause to consider how radical and even heretical Locke's arguments appeared at the time. In fact, a discussion revolving around "matters of morality and revealed religion" is what prompted Locke to write *Essay* in the first place.[34] Locke argues that what constitutes a "self" is, very broadly, a "consciousness" seated in a human body.[35] This definition breaks with two important traditions. First, it breaks with those who assert that the self is located in an invisible and immaterial soul.[36]

33. John Locke, *Essay Concerning Human Understanding*, ed. Roger Woolhouse (New York: Penguin, 1997).

34. Nicholas Wolterstorff, "Locke's Philosophy of Religion," in *The Cambridge Companion to Locke*, ed. Vere Chappell (Cambridge: Cambridge University Press, 1994), 174.

35. Granted, this is clearly a reductive definition of the Lockean self. Also, although many commentators have emphasized consciousness over the body in Locke's definition of the self, Jerrold Siegel reminds us that, for Locke, they are tied together: "The personal identity established by consciousness existed together with the organic identity every individual possessed as 'man'; however reflective the first became it never substituted for the corporeal identity of the second. Moreover, the body was an important part, not just of an individual's identity as a 'man,' but of personhood too. As John Yolton has emphasized, the body was the instrument by which any individual performed those actions for which he or she was responsible: Lockean selfhood was always embodied, never disembodied. What memory tied together was not merely a series of states of consciousness, but a range of actions carried out by bodily means"; *The Idea of the Self: Thought and Experience in Western Europe since the Seventeenth Century*, reprint (Cambridge: Cambridge University Press, 2005), 99.

36. For further discussion, see Raymond Martin and John Barresi, *Naturalization of the Soul: Self and Personal Identity in the Eighteenth Century* (London: Routledge, 2000), 1–7.

Locke claims, shockingly, that God's judgment "shall be justified by the consciousness all persons shall have, that they *themselves*, in what bodies 'soever they appear, or what substance 'soever that consciousness adheres to."[37] For Locke, it is not the soul, therefore, that would be judged, but rather the consciousness or mind. Furthermore, he does not agree with many of his contemporaries that the self must be located in the soul for resurrection to occur at the Last Judgment or that the soul would necessarily be reunited with the body.[38] Second, and more important, "by locating personal identity in consciousness and making both distinct from spiritual substance, Locke had opened the door to a materialistic interpretation of the self."[39] If God does not endow humans with innate ideas and if the self is a material invention—that is, if it consists of "thinking matter" as Locke maintains[40]—would grave doubts arise regarding the ability of such a self to recognize moral truth and thus to be saved through traditional Christian theology?

Most eighteenth-century British children's authors had accepted the general outlines of the Lockean self; that is, most had accepted that the child is a tabula rasa and that associationism is crucial to constructing the self. However, they do not agree with Locke on the source of experience. They solve the problem of the self's moral responsibility with an overtly Christian solution. To avoid the materialistic consequences of defining a self conceived of only as an amalgam of transient sensations, writers such as Barbauld, Wollstonecraft, and Sherwood argue that God controls life experiences—the stuff of which the mind is formed. This claim emerges even more strongly in Evangelical writings like Sherwood's, which speak of "God's plan" for each person and question "if accidental is [even] a word allowed to a Christian."[41] Altogether, these texts embrace Locke's theory of the "association of ideas"; but rather than emphasizing the formation of "ideas wholly owing to chance or

---

37. Locke, *Essay*, 312.

38. John Yolton, *A Locke Dictionary* (Oxford: Blackwell, 1993), 268–71.

39. Christopher Fox, *Locke and the Scriblerians: Identity and Consciousness in Early Eighteenth-Century Britain* (Berkeley: University of California Press, 1988), 48.

40. Locke, *Essay*, 312.

41. Mary Martha Sherwood, "Le Fevre," in *The Works of Mrs. Sherwood*, vol. 13 (New York: Harper and Bros., 1837), 307.

custom,"[42] they frequently describe the association of ideas as an experience that God directs and guides. It is this model of experience and learning that I am calling "providential empiricism."[43]

Eighteenth-century thinkers and theologians classify providence into two categories: the general and the particular. According to Jacob Viner, general providence is "God operating through secondary causes, or through the 'laws of nature,'" and particular providence is "God operating directly, either in a special manipulation of the laws of nature, or without reference to the laws of nature, or in direct suppression of them."[44] In this article, I discuss particular providence—God's intervention in the lives of individuals. Importantly, as Viner points out in his survey of providence, during the eighteenth century, both of these forms had been considered beneficial to humanity. He argues further that "it was for many men psychologically impossible to believe that God did not constantly have man in his providential care, and that the physical order of the cosmos was not one of the tools he had designed to serve that purpose. The period in fact abounded, as never before, and perhaps never since, in attempts to demonstrate the manner in which the cosmos served man."[45]

However, I want to position the writers I am discussing against the theological utilitarianism that Viner identifies as crucial to eighteenth-century thought on providence. As he explains it, the theological utilitarians argue that humans do not possess an innate moral sense and that humans are prompted to act as a result of pain or pleasure. Thus "rewards often go to the undeserving, and the virtuous are often in

---

42. Locke, *Essay*, 335.

43. George Berkeley makes a similar argument, for all sense impressions. Jonathan Bennett summarizes Berkeley's argument thus: "(a) My ideas of sense come into my mind without being caused to do so by any act of my will; (b) The occurrence of any idea must be caused by an act of the will of some being in whose mind the idea occurs; therefore (c) My ideas of sense occur in the mind of, and are caused by acts of the will of, some being other than myself"; *Locke, Berkeley, Hume: Central Themes* (Oxford: Clarendon Press, 1971), 165. Locke's argument would be more pervasive and more influential for writers of children's literature, however, and it is his argument they would adapt.

44. Jacob Viner, *The Role of Providence in the Social Order: An Essay in Intellectual History* (Philadelphia: American Philosophical Society, 1972), 4–5.

45. Ibid., 19.

misery."[46] In this system, humanity is not naturally good, earthly goodness ensures no reward, and morality has no rational basis; an unjust world can only be endured because everything would be sorted out in a future life. However, in children's literature, pain and pleasure come from God and thus trouble the categories of "innate" and "deserving." If God sends suffering, pain is thus part of a divine plan and the person's resulting virtue or vice is not irrational.

Providential empiricism thus posits an epistemology structured around the belief that God directs one's actions and suggests that ethics are divinely inspired and thus potentially universal. For example, eighteenth-century British children's writers often attribute the suffering of characters to God's direct intervention. Such suffering is a demonstration of God's concern for the child's spiritual well-being because it encourages the child to develop not only sympathy but also faith, as numerous references to Job, Lamentations, and Hebrews illustrate.[47] Locke's empiricism, on the other hand, leads to moral relativism because, in that theory, each person builds his or her own notions of ethical responsibility from a distinct set of experiences that have no foundation in either innate morality or a divine plan.

Barbauld's writings best capture the nuances of the providential empiricism found in eighteenth-century British children's literature. Barbauld is now perhaps best known for her political poems, but she is also a revolutionary children's writer. Her earliest children's books, *Lessons for Children* (1778–79) and *Hymns in Prose for Children* (1781), are books that, for the first time, consider the needs of the child reader, being printed with large type and wide margins. Even more important, she developed a style of "informal dialogue between parent and child" that was widely imitated.[48] Her books were read, recited, and

---

46. Ibid., 70–71.

47. For example, "And ye have forgotten the exhortation which speaketh unto you as unto children . . . despise not thou the chastening of the Lord, nor faint when thou art rebuked of him: For whom the Lord loveth he chasteneth, and scourgeth every son whom he receiveth. . . . Now no chastening for the present seemeth to be joyous, but grievous: nevertheless afterward it yieldeth the peaceable fruit of righteousness unto them which are exercised thereby" (Hebrews 12:5–11, Authorized (King James) Version [AV]).

48. William McCarthy, "Mother of all Discourses: Anna Barbauld's *Lessons for Children*," in *Culturing the Child, 1690–1914: Essays in Memory of Mitzi Myers*, ed.

memorized for over one hundred years.[49] Like most eighteenth-century educators, Barbauld is, in many ways, a firm believer in the Lockean self. In the "Preface" to her *Hymns in Prose*, an updating and recasting of Watts's *Divine Songs*, she describes the goals of her text in phrases evoking empiricism and associationism:

> The peculiar design of this publication is, to impress devotional feelings as early as possible on the infant mind; fully convinced as the author is, that they cannot be impressed too soon, and that a child, to feel the full force of the idea of God, ought never to remember the time when he had no such idea—to impress them by connecting religion with a variety of sensible objects; with all that he sees, all he hears . . . and thus by deep, strong, and permanent associations, to lay the best foundation for practical devotion in future life.[50]

Barbauld repeats the word *impress* three times in a single sentence, conjuring up Locke's image of the mind as malleable wax. Moreover, she adopts the modern language of "mind" over the older one of "soul:" it is not the child's soul, but rather his or her mind, that must learn to recognize God. Finally, Locke's association of ideas theory is the basis of Barbauld's argument for "connecting" religious ideas with "sensible objects" in the child's mind.

But while it may appear in this preface that Barbauld is a thoroughgoing Lockean, the hymns themselves complicate this interpretation as the reader discovers what the "full force of God" really is.[51] In "Hymn VIII," Barbauld writes, recalling Watts, "he [God] knoweth every one of them [God's family], as a shepherd knoweth his flock . . . none are so great, that he cannot punish them; none are so mean, that he will not protect them."[52] Barbauld paints a picture of a powerful and involved God. Her God is interested in each individual. And, as Barbauld

Donelle Ruwe (Lanham, MD: Scarecrow Press, 2005), 85–111.

49. Sarah Robbins, "Re-making Barbauld's Primers: A Case Study in the Americanization of British Literary Pedagogy," *Children's Literature Association Quarterly* 21, no. 4 (1996): 158–69; and McCarthy, "Mother of All Discourses," 85–111.

50. Barbauld, *Hymns in Prose for Children*, v–vi.

51. Ibid., vi.

52. Ibid., 59–60.

repeatedly states throughout the hymns, "his anger is terrible; he could make us die in a moment, and no one could save us out of his hand."[53] God wills events, so Barbauld describes his providence as something to fear. Yet she writes in a more comforting tone in her essay "What is Education?"[54] Originally published in 1798 in *The Monthly Magazine*, she tells parents that they can rest assured that God will guide their child: "Providence continues his education upon a larger scale, and by a process which includes means far more efficacious. Has your son entered the world at eighteen, opinionated, haughty, rash, inclined to dissipation? Do not despair, he may yet be cured of these faults, if it pleases heaven."[55] God can effect extraordinary changes in the self, but only "if it pleases" him.

It is debatable to what extent one can control the development of one's own or another's identity under the Lockean system. Locke himself does not seem to have been optimistic on this point. Not only does he fear irrational associations and the deleterious effects of having servants, but he also repeatedly frets over the problems of "custom." For Locke, "custom settles habits of thinking in the understanding, as well as of determining in the will, and of motions in the body . . . which once set a going, continue in the same steps they have been used to, which by often treading, are worn into a smooth path, and the motion in it becomes easy, and as it were natural."[56] Such "ease" and comfort in one's ideas worry Locke, who argues that feelings of "uneasiness" are essential to human progress.[57] Although Locke, like the writers I am looking at in this article, invokes the "all-wise Maker" at this juncture in his argument and claims that said Maker "has put into man the *uneasiness* of hunger and thirst, and other natural desires" in order to prompt human "industry" and "action," writers for children see a more direct divine influence on each individual.[58] Rather than claiming God endows all

---

53. Ibid., 22.
54. Anna Laetitia Barbauld, "What Is Education?" in *Anna Letitia Barbauld: Selected Poetry and Prose*, ed. William McCarthy and Elizabeth Kraft (Peterborough, Ontario, Canada: Broadview Press, 2002).
55. Ibid., 331–32.
56. Locke, *Essay*, 355.
57. Ibid., 234.
58. Ibid.; emphasis in the original.

humans with general "uneasinesses" that are part of human nature, these writers argue that God chooses specific experiences for each person. Once one introduces direct divine intervention, as Barbauld does, the bulk of human agency vanishes. Barbauld, in her most explicit articulation of providential empiricism—"What Is Education?"—describes the process this way:

> Providence takes your child, where you leave him. . . . There are remedies which you could not persuade yourself to use, if they were in your power ... Faded beauty, humbled self-consequence, disappointed ambition, loss of fortune, this is the rough physic provided by Providence, to meliorate the temper, to correct the offensive petulancies of youth, and bring out all the energies of the finished character.[59]

Although Barbauld leaves some room for human agency in the formation of the self—providence steps in only after the parents have tried their best (and presumably failed, as all will do since humanity lives in a fallen world)—in the end, it is unquestionably God who "bring[s] out all the energies of the *finished* character."[60] Moreover, suffering is one potent way in which God shapes personal identity—it is painful experiences that mold the self.

As a way to explain painful life experiences and articulate the maturation process, Barbauld, Wollstonecraft, and Sherwood offer child readers the discourse of Christian sensibility; feeling, sympathy, and compassion dominate these writers' understanding of what it means to be a human, particularly one with a relationship to God. Importantly, however, all three agree that, as Sherwood puts it in *The Governess* (1820), "children naturally want [lack] feeling."[61] The role of the educator thus becomes to nurture and to direct the child's passions. God may deliberately expose children to suffering, but it is the parent's or instructor's responsibility to teach them how to interpret those afflictions. Such

59. Barbauld, "What is Education?," 331–32.
60. See also "An Address to the Deity" for an expression of Barbauld's providential empiricism, in *Anna Letitia Barbauld*, 41; emphasis added.
61. Mary Martha Sherwood, *The Governess; or, the Little Female Academy* (Wellington, UK: F. Houlston and Son, 1820), 138.

training must begin early, for how and what one learns as a child greatly impacts the mature self (here, the three authors are in agreement with Locke). Once children have learned how to properly channel their suffering and how to empathize with others, they have reached adulthood.

For Wollstonecraft, the self is a construction of perceptions that providence carefully chooses. In Wollstonecraft's *Original Stories from Real Life*, first published anonymously in 1788, Mrs. Mason, a maternal teacher, educates two young charges—Mary, aged fourteen, and Caroline, aged twelve—through example, story, and precept.[62] Slowly, over the course of the episodic text, the girls correct some of their faults and exhibit more virtuous, although not perfect, characters. In the beginning, Wollstonecraft adopts the Lockean language of the wax-like tabula rasa:

> This employment [caring for children] humanized my [Mrs. Mason's] heart, while, like wax, it took every impression; and Providence has since made me an instrument of good—I have been useful to my fellow-creatures.[63]

Once again, we see the fusion of the empirical and the providential. Mrs. Mason has a malleable heart that has received "impressions" (the same word Barbauld uses). She has learned charity. And God is active in her life, making her "useful." Importantly, Wollstonecraft locates the essence of the self in the "heart," the organ of sympathy. It is Mrs. Mason's heart, rather than her mind or consciousness (as Locke would argue), that receives "impressions"; and it is these "impressions" (i.e., providence's guidance) that enable her to become benevolent.

---

62. Wollstonecraft, *Original Stories from Real Life; With Conversations, Calculated to Regulate the Affections, and Form the Mind to Truth and Goodness* (London: J. Johnson, 1788). Wollstonecraft seems to have drawn on her own life in creating these characters. Mrs. Mason appears to have been inspired by Miss Mason, "a good girl" whom she employs in her school at Newington Green, and Mary and Caroline had been inspired by two of Lady Kingsborough's daughters; Mary Wollstonecraft to George Blood–Newington Green, July 20, 1785, in *The Collected Letters of Mary Wollstonecraft*, ed. Janet Todd (New York: Columbia University Press, 2004), 56. Interestingly, Lady Kingsborough's third daughter, Margaret, the one on whom Wollstonecraft had perhaps the greatest impact, after an unhappy marriage, "abandoned her husband and called herself Mrs. Mason"; Todd, *Collected Letters*, 124n286.

63. Wollstonecraft, *Original Stories*, 17.

Although Wollstonecraft's writings show that, for her, benevolence and sympathy are deeply bound up with Christianity, Wollstonecraft scholars have not been eager to address her faith or her religious discourse until fairly recently. Perhaps, for many, her spirituality undermines her place as an early feminist or positions her too closely to conservative figures, such as Hannah More. Those who have attempted to analyze Wollstonecraft's relationship to the religious, such as Mary Poovey, often comment positively on Wollstonecraft's "progress" away from orthodox Anglicanism. Poovey traces the evolution of Wollstonecraft's religious thought from the *Vindication of the Rights of Men* (1790) through *Letters Written during a Short Residence in Sweden, Norway, and Denmark* (1796).[64] After doing so, Poovey concludes that Wollstonecraft has a "new willingness to explore the face of death, to accept the fact of human limitations without automatic recourse to religious consolation"; this, Poovey writes, is "an index of [her] maturity."[65] We see in Poovey a modern, liberal desire to devalue Wollstonecraft's faith—Wollstonecraft's "maturity" in Poovey's narrative is marked by Wollstonecraft's adopting more unorthodox religious opinions. But this explanation of Wollstonecraft's "progress" does not help us understand eighteenth-century valuations of the ties between, for example, sensibility and religion; in fact, as Poovey admits in a footnote, "even though many liked the *Letters*, Wollstonecraft's contemporaries reacted strongly—and generally negatively—to the less orthodox theology this work contained."[66]

As Barbara Taylor explains, it is precisely through a proper understanding of Wollstonecraft's religious thought that we can understand her "ambiguous attitude toward sensibility" because it is "part of her

---

64. Mary Wollstonecraft, *Vindication of the Rights of Men, in a Letter to the Right Honourable Edmund Burke; Occasioned by His Reflections on the Revolution in France* (London: J. Johnson, 1790); and Mary Wollstonecraft, *Letters Written During a Short Residence in Sweden, Norway, and Denmark* (London: J. Johnson, 1796).

65. Mary Poovey, *The Proper Lady and the Woman Writer: Ideology as Style in the Works of Mary Wollstonecraft, Mary Shelley, and Jane Austen* (Chicago: University of Chicago Press, 1984), 87.

66. Ibid., 256n8.

wider endeavor to define an authentic religious subjectivity."[67] Wollstonecraft's central project is to understand her relationship to God and to create a moral selfhood that best expresses the foundation of that relationship—a moral selfhood that she articulates through the, at times, confusing and contradictory language of sensibility. For example, in her *Thoughts on the Education of Daughters* (1787), Wollstonecraft writes,

> While we are looking into another's mind, and forming their temper, we are insensibly correcting our own; and every act of benevolence which we exert to our fellow creatures, does ourselves the most essential services. Active virtue fits us for the society of more exalted beings. Our philanthropy is a proof, we are told, that we are capable of loving our Creator. Indeed this divine love, or charity, appears to me the principal trait that remains of the illustrious image of the Deity, which was originally stampt on the soul, and which is to be renewed.[68]

She invokes the language of Locke, writing that "charity . . . was originally stampt on the soul," while simultaneously resisting his core ideas, emphasizing the Christian notions of charity and the soul, which Locke downplayed in favor of reason and the mind. Furthermore, she contends that it is sympathy and love, conveyed through religious feeling, that will eventually unite society and bring it closer to God.

As Wollstonecraft clarifies later in *Thoughts*, it is not only teachers who help individuals "form" the self but also God: he, "who is training us up for immortal bliss, know[s] best what trials will contribute to make us so [i.e., virtuous]; and our resignation and improvement will render us respectable to ourselves, and to that Being, whose approbation is of more value than life itself."[69] Like Barbauld, Wollstonecraft argues that the experiences, particularly the "trials," that each person undergoes are providential. Experiences are not random—God intends them to shape each and every person. In *Original Stories*, Wollstonecraft

---

67. Barbara Taylor, *Mary Wollstonecraft and the Feminist Imagination* (Cambridge: Cambridge University Press, 2003), 97.

68. Mary Wollstonecraft, *Thoughts on the Education of Daughters: With Reflections on Female Conduct, in the More Important Duties of Life* (London: J. Johnson, 1787), 66–67.

69. Ibid., 78.

dramatizes these trials. Mrs. Mason guides Mary and Caroline through much God-given pain and suffering before they can reach the ideal for which they are striving. In chapter 21, which focuses on "fortitude," for example, Caroline is stung by a bee, and Mrs. Mason elaborates on the blessings of God's torments:

> The Almighty, who never afflicts but to produce some good, first sends diseases to children to teach them patience and forti- tude; and when by degrees they have learned to bear them, they have acquired some virtue. In the same manner, cold or hunger, when accidentally encountered, are not evils; they make *us feel what wretches feel*, and teach us to be tender-hearted. Many of your fellow-creatures daily bear what you cannot for a moment endure without complaint. . . . I should not value the affection of a person who would not bear pain and hunger to serve me; nor is that benevolence warm, which shrinks from encounter- ing difficulties, when it is necessary, in order to be useful to any fellow creature.[70]

Wollstonecraft explains to her readers the virtues of disease, stressing God's role—one might even say that it is through the blessing of disease that they first learn to sympathize. This passage, which describes God as the one who "sends diseases" so that readers can acquire "patience and fortitude," also illustrates the role of providential empiricism in the cre- ation of the self. Furthermore, to Wollstonecraft, "cold [and] hunger" are not "accidentally encountered" but are rather further "afflictions" sent from God to assist one in learning to be "tender-hearted."

Barbauld, Wollstonecraft, and Sherwood all highlight the role of providential empiricism, but it is Sherwood who most strongly empha- sizes the benefits of God-given suffering. Sherwood, one of the most prolific writers of children's literature at the beginning of the nine- teenth century, would write more than four hundred works covering every major genre.[71] She is most famous for her Evangelical children's

70. Wollstonecraft, *Original Stories*, 156–160; emphasis in original.
71. M. Nancy Cutt, *Mrs. Sherwood and her Books for Children* (London: Oxford Uni- versity Press, 1974), ix.

literature, such as *The History of the Fairchild Family* (1818, 1842, 1847).[72] Although Sherwood is not usually compared to eighteenth-century writers, most of her books retain a style strongly indebted to the Puritan and Dissenting works of the period. She would even revise and repackage popular eighteenth-century children's works such as Sarah Fielding's *The Governess* (1749) and John Bunyan's *The Pilgrim's Progress* (1678).[73] Also, Sherwood herself had been educated in a quintessentially eighteenth-century environment. Like both Barbauld and Wollstonecraft, as a female, she was lucky to have been exposed to stimulating intellectual conversations at a formative time in her life. As a child and as a young woman growing up in Lichfield, she had been in the company of Erasmus Darwin, Anna Seward, the Edgeworth family, Thomas Day, and occasionally Samuel Johnson and David Garrick.[74]

Despite the religious differences between Sherwood's works and those of Barbauld and Wollstonecraft, Sherwood's still display a similar providential empiricism. For example, in 1820, Sherwood revised Sarah Fielding's *The Governess; or, Little Female Academy* (1749), a novel in which the girls at Mrs. Teachum's school tell each other stories in order to reconcile their differences. As the tale begins, the reader learns why Mrs. Teachum had established the school. Sherwood begins her version like so: "It pleased God, during one period of [Mrs. Teachum's] life, to exercise this excellent person with many severe trials, no doubt in order to bring her the nearer to himself."[75] Fielding, in contrast, highlights the "Christian fortitude" of Mrs. Teachum, who expertly runs the school despite the loss of her husband, children, and fortune.[76] Fielding chooses to emphasize Mrs. Teachum's capable recovery from intense sorrow and near bankruptcy while Sherwood chooses to emphasize

---

72. Mary Martha Sherwood, *The History of the Fairchild Family* (New York: Garland Publishing, 1977).

73. Sarah Fielding, *The Governess; or the Little Female Academy* (London: A. Millar, 1749); and John Bunyan, *Pilgrim's Progress: From This World to That which Is to Come* (London: Nath. Ponder, 1678).

74. F. J. Harvey Darton, ed. *The Life and Times of Mrs. Sherwood from the Diaries of Captain and Mrs. Sherwood* (London: Wells Gardner, Darton & Co., 1910).

75. Sherwood, *Governess*, 1.

76. Sarah Fielding, *The Governess; or, the Little Female Academy*, ed. Candace Ward (Peterborough, Ontario, Canada: Broadview Press, 2005), 49–50.

God's role in Mr. Teachum's death and in Mrs. Teachum's suffering and progress toward a stronger faith. For Fielding, it is "accident" and "misfortune"[77] that force Mrs. Teachum into her present situation, whereas, for Sherwood, it is God's providence.

Sherwood's firm faith in the power of suffering to instruct and redeem and her fervent belief in predestination often seem to deny her characters agency. Even when characters appear to have contributed to their own destinies, Sherwood quickly reminds us to whom the real credit is owed: God. For example, after Jenny Peace, the eldest of the girls at Mrs. Teachum's school, restores harmony among the quarreling students, Fielding's Mrs. Teachum compliments the girls approvingly on the quick reestablishment of their friendships. Sherwood's Mrs. Teachum, on the other hand, reminds her scholars to whom the true thanks are due: "Let us thank God for this blessed change which has taken place among you, and give the glory to him who maketh men to be of one mind in a house."[78] Although Jenny is still the peacemaker in Sherwood's version, she is God's agent rather than an independent one. Sherwood's narrators and authority figures consistently remind readers to give their hearts to God so that they can be guided by his will. In fact, throughout Sherwood's works, most of her characters are reduced to praying for God's intercession in their hearts as it is the only thing that can truly affect any change. Despite Sherwood's strong evangelical bent, as evident in these examples, one should not overlook the ultimate—and surprising—similarities between her works and Wollstonecraft's and Barbauld's. All emphasize the crucial role of divine affliction in the formation of the self.

Although Barbauld, Wollstonecraft, and Sherwood all argue that God plays a pivotal role in forming the child's self, they also leave room for human influence, particularly via authority figures such as teachers and parents. As Sherwood's Mr. Fairchild intones to his son Henry, "I stand in the place of God to you, whilst you are a child."[79] These writers had to believe that their works would impact children's development, thus their texts reflect a tension between their desire to acknowledge

---

77. Ibid.
78. Ibid., 43.
79. Sherwood, *Fairchild Family*, 269.

God's guidance and their desire to acknowledge their own agency as authors. This tension is perhaps most evident in their inset tales of suffering, which are manifestations of what Barbauld refers to as God's "rough physic." As authors, they take on the role of God; that is, they "authorize" and narrate stories of suffering that will shape their readers' selves in the same way that they see God inflicting suffering in order to mold human beings—they are enacting a godly pedagogy, as it were.

Wollstonecraft's Mrs. Mason represents this figure of the godly pedagogue, educating her charges through stories meant to cause sympathy and appreciation for suffering. For example, in *Original Stories*, she relates "The History of Jane Fretful," a miniature spiritual biography inspired by Puritan children's literature. Wollstonecraft employs the language and topoi of what was then seen as an uplifting and inspiring genre to play on the reader's fears:

> This [death of Jane Fretful's mother] though, and [Jane's] peevish temper, preyed on her impaired constitution. She had not, by doing good, prepared her soul for another state, or cherished any hopes that could disarm death of its terrors, or render that last sleep sweet—its approach was dreadful!—and she hastened her end, scolding the physician for not curing her. Her lifeless countenance displayed the marks of convulsive anger; and she left an ample fortune behind her to those who did not regret her loss. They followed her to the grave, on which no one shed a tear. She was soon forgotten; and I only remember her, to warn you to shun her errors.[80]

The reader experiences the horror of Jane's death through Wollstonecraft's vivid deathbed scene, complete with the exclamatory, "[Death's] approach was dreadful!"[81] Readers are meant to live through this terrifying scene with Jane in their imaginations in order to avoid living it out in reality; presumably, they will learn what sorts of actions to avoid because they have already "experienced" the horror of consequences from such wicked actions. Moreover, she indicates that authority figures

---

80. Wollstonecraft, *Original Stories*, 36.
81. Ibid.

should learn to model this method of telling stories that shape the self through suffering.

Just such a story constitutes one of the most memorable episodes in Barbauld's *Lessons for Children of Three Years Old, Part I* (1779), in which the mother tells Charles an extended narrative set in winter:

> There was a naughty boy; I do not know what his name was, but it was not Charles, nor George, nor Arthur, for those are all very pretty names: but there was a robin came in at his window one very cold morning—shiver—shiver, and its poor little heart was almost frozen to death. And he would not give it the least little crumb of bread in the world, but pulled it about by the tail, and hurt it sadly, and it died. Now a little while after the naughty boy's papa and mamma went away and left him; and then he could get no victuals at all, for you know he could not take care of himself. So he went about to every body—Pray give me something to eat, I am very hungry. And every body said, No, we shall give you none, for we do not love cruel naughty boys. So he went about from one place to another, till at last he got into a thick wood of trees, for he did not know how to find his way any where; and then it grew dark, quite dark night. So he sat down and cried sadly; and he could not get out of the wood; and I believe the bears came and eat him up in the wood, for I never heard any thing about him afterwards.[82]

At the beginning of the passage, Barbauld places the mother-narrator in the role of the godly pedagogue and the reader in the position of the unnamed child. Barbauld thus cedes authority here to any oral narrator; once someone begins reading this story aloud to another, Barbauld also inhabits the godly pedagogue role. Barbauld begins her assault on the reader by describing the physical suffering of the bird; words such as *shiver* help the reader imagine the cold body of the bird. Turning from the merely literal depictions of its near-death state, she invokes the language of sensibility by focusing on the animal's heart in a literal and a figurative

---

82. Anna Laetitia Barbauld, *Lessons for Children, of Three Years Old. Part I* (Dublin: R. Jackson, 1779), 73–77.

sense: "its poor little heart was almost frozen to death." In a simple yet elegant demonstration of poetic justice, the boy's situation at the end of the tale resembles that of the bird he had tortured—like the robin, he is now forlorn and starving. This becomes a common trope of eighteenth-century British literature for children: children who torture an animal are made to undergo the very same torture themselves.[83]

In the companion book *Hymns in Prose*, Barbauld overtly connects the mother who tells these stories to God:

> There is an eye that never sleepeth; there is an eye that seeth in dark night, as well as in the bright sun-shine . . . that eye seeth every where, in all places, and watcheth continually over all the families of the earth. The eye that sleepeth not is God's; his hand is always stretched out over us.... As the mother moveth about the house with her finger on her lips, and stilleth every little noise, that her infant be not disturbed; as she draweth the curtains around its bed, and shutteth out the light from its tender eyes; so God draweth the curtains of darkness around us; so he maketh all things to be hushed and still, that his large family may sleep in peace.[84]

Barbauld draws on the same images with which I began this essay—God's eye and hand—to remind readers that God is physically present, that we feel him in our lives every day. Significantly, however, she connects that feeling to the mother figure. The empirical experience of being a child reader here is one of being touched by God and mother together.

These writers yearn to affect their readers with the Godly power that they see in providential empiricism, and they wrote this power into their stories. They not only depict a God who is involved in the daily lives of their child readers by shaping those readers through suffering, but they also model their own literary personas on that divine figure.

83. See chapter 4 in Adrianne Wadewitz, *"Spare the Sympathy, Spoil the Child": Sensibility, Selfhood, and the Maturing Reading, 1775–1815* (PhD diss., Indiana University, 2011).

84. Barbauld, *Hymns in Prose for Children*, 30–34.

Sacred Alliance? The Critical Assessment of Revelation in Fichte and Kant

Tom Spencer
Brigham Young University

Religion encountered a host of problems in the eighteenth century: the decline of Biblical authority, the rise of scientific skepticism, and an emerging spirit of human autonomy.[1] Each of these developments diminished the function of religious institutions in public life, but this is not to say that religion lost its importance. Western modernity has not been able to ignore or replace Christianity—even if modernity generally cannot incorporate it. As Jonathan Sheehan observes, "secularization always is and always must be incomplete. Even as religion seems to vanish from politics and public culture, it never ceases to define the project of modernity."[2]

But for eighteenth-century thinkers, religion was not merely an unavoidable, *negative* reference point in the story of progress. On the one hand, it remained invaluable for morality, such that even Voltaire displays a deep reluctance to abandon belief in divine justice, which he

---

1. On the decline of biblical authority in the eighteenth century, see Hans Frei, *The Eclipse of Biblical Narrative* (New Haven, CT: Yale University Press, 1974). For a discussion on the modern society of "mutual benefit" in which prevails a feeling of human self-sufficiency vis-à-vis God and the spiritual realm, see Charles Taylor, *A Secular Age* (Cambridge, MA: Harvard University Press, 2007).

2. Jonathan Sheehan, *The Enlightenment Bible* (Princeton, NJ: Princeton University Press, 2005), ix.

feels is necessary for social stability.[3] Immanuel Kant, who holds that moral rectitude does *not* require religion, nevertheless feels that a belief in God's justice meets a "natural need, *which would otherwise be a hindrance to moral resolve*, to think for all our doings and nondoings taken as a whole some sort of final end which reason can justify."[4] On the other hand, religion provided a counterbalance to the cognitive epistemology of the Enlightenment. Martin Jay comments that "the reduction of experience [after Hume and Kant] to a question of cognition . . . left a gnawing sense that something important in human life had been sacrificed," and this feeling gave rise to the modern experiential theory of religion.[5] Although their challenges to religion were often serious and fundamental, very few intellectuals of the eighteenth century sought its demise. On the contrary, there was a widespread attempt to re-legitimate religion, or some version of it, within the critical-scientific idiom of the day.

In this article, I investigate one very specific instance of this religious accommodation: Johann Gottlieb Fichte's and Immanuel Kant's assessment of revelation in the early 1790s. Like many of their contemporaries, these thinkers were committed to disentangling religion from "superstition" and to reorienting it toward morality. Critical philosophy provided a rich, a priori account of the constitution and limits of knowledge as well as a powerful practical philosophy—and this would seem to leave little room for a philosophical discourse on divine intervention. But like many of their contemporaries, they also felt the need to consider the rights of revelation. In this respect, they can be included in a specifically German

---

3. See, for instance, the entries "Athée, Athéisme," "Fraude," "Préjugés," and "Théiste" in Voltaire, *Dictionnaire Philosophique* (Geneva: Gabriel Grasset, 1764).

4. Immanuel Kant, *Religion innerhalb der Grenzen der bloßen Vernunft*, vol. 6, *Werke (Akademie Ausgabe)* (Berlin: de Gruyter, 1968), 5; emphasis added. All citations from Kant provide the volume and page number from the *Akademie* edition (e.g., *Religion*, 6.5). Unless noted otherwise, all translations are taken from the *Cambridge Edition of the Works of Immanuel Kant*, ed. Paul Guyer and Allen W. Wood (Cambridge: Cambridge University Press, 1998).

5. Martin Jay, *Songs of Experience: Modern American and European Variations on a Universal Theme* (Berkeley: University of California Press, 2006), 78. Jay presents Friedrich Schleiermacher, William James, Rudolf Otto, and Martin Buber as the key theologians on religious experience. See chapter 3, "The Appeal of Religious Experience," in *Songs of Experience*.

tradition of rational-religious conciliation beginning with Gottfried Wilhelm von Leibniz. According to religious historian Johannes Wallmann, Leibniz demonstrates the "theoretical possibility (*Denkmöglichkeit*) and reasonableness" of miracles and ecclesiastical dogma, and this opens a German "alliance . . . between philosophy and theology, which is based on the idea of a harmony between revelation and reason."[6] Classic examples of this alliance are Johann Joachim Spalding's extremely popular *The Vocation of Man* (1748), which merges the Enlightenment ideal of progressive perfection into the Christian vision of the afterlife, and Gotthold Ephraim Lessing's profoundly influential view of the Old and New Testaments as "primers" (*Elementarbücher*) assisting humanity along its path to moral autonomy.[7] Fichte's *Attempt at a Critique of All Revelation*

6. Johannes Wallmann, *Kirchengeschichte Deutschlands seit der Reformation*, 6th ed. (Tübingen, Germany: Mohr Siebeck, 2006), 152. I acknowledge, however, that not all of the German enlightened are of a piece. Thomas Saine and Jonathan Israel have identified an early "radical" Enlightenment in Germany that offers no olive branch to religious orthodoxy. See Thomas Saine, *The Problem of Being Modern, or, The German Pursuit of Enlightenment from Leibniz to the French Revolution* (Detroit, MI: Wayne State University Press, 1997); and Jonathan Israel, *Radical Enlightenment: Philosophy and the Making of Modernity, 1650–1750* (Oxford: Oxford University Press, 2001), 628–63. Saine in particular bemoans the gradual dissolution of this rigorously secular Enlightenment as German intellectuals struggled to keep "as much as possible of the old while embracing the new" (16). The secularist view has been recently challenged by David Sorkin, who believes that "the Enlightenment could be reverent as well as irreverent, and that such reverence was at its very core"; *The Religious Enlightenment: Protestants, Jews and Catholics from London to Vienna* (Princeton, NJ: Princeton University Press, 2008), xiv. Of course, the secular/religious question is a perennial one for any general characterization of the Enlightenment.

7. A similar spirit of "alliance" between reason and revelation can, I believe, be found in the combination of philological brilliance and verbal literalism in the Biblical scholarship of Johann Albrecht Bengel, the most prominent of the Württemberg Pietists, or in the combination of historical biblical criticism and religious establishmentarianism in Johann Salamo Semler and the German "neologists." See Johannes Wallmann, *Der Pietismus* (Göttingen, Germany: Vandenhoeck & Ruprecht, 2005), 213–25; Wallmann, *Kirchengeschichte*, 56–160; Frei, *Eclipse of Biblical Narrative*, 175–79; and B. A. Gerrish, "Natural and Revealed Religion," in *The Cambridge History of Eighteenth-Century Philosophy*, ed. Knud Haakonssen (Cambridge: Cambridge University Press, 2006), 659. Lessing is admittedly a double-edged sword in this context, because his publication of Reimarus's infamous Biblical criticism (which unleashed the so-called *Fragmentenstreit*) and his own posthumously exposed Spinozism were major affronts to orthodox piety. Hermann Timm even views Lessing as a counter to Leibniz: "Leibniz hatte noch davon ausgehen können, daß die christliche Tradition sich selbst trägt . . . Die Beweislast liegt auf Seiten des Gegners . . . Durch den Fragmentenstreit ist die Beweislast auf die Gegenseite

(1792) fits into this story of a German philosophical-theological alliance insofar as it attempts to reconcile revelation and the new Kantian philosophy, and Kant, in his own cautious way, continues Fichte's initiative in *Religion within the Boundaries of Reason Alone* (1793).

My investigation begins with Fichte's view, as evidenced in *Attempt*, that some historical peoples might lose their sensitivity to the moral law and might require God's empirical intervention if they are to overcome evil and embrace their moral destiny. This is similar to Lessing's position, but Fichte's position is novel insofar as he presents it as a consequence of purely Kantian or "critical" principles, which in turn forces Kant to decide whether Fichte's argument is indeed critically viable.[8] Kant expressed mild public praise for Fichte's work in 1792,[9] yet Kant's real verdict—and the main focus of my argument—comes one year later in *Religion*. If we read this work with Fichte in mind, we can see Kant agreeing that evil is a central problem for the philosophy of religion but strongly resisting Fichte's idea that an individual's moral or "practical" reason might lack self-sufficiency and *require* divine intervention. I show that, although Kant clearly champions the self-sufficiency of practical reason, the necessity of a nonempirical divine intervention as an antidote to radical evil nonetheless remains a serious possibility in *Religion*, if only for the power of reflective judgment.

I should say that the point of my reading of *Religion* is not to expose its various weaknesses as a philosophical text because these have been well noted and thus require no repetition.[10] Rather, by

---

verlegt worden. Das vorgängige Vertrauen in die Überlieferung erlischt" (26). Perhaps John H. Smith says it best when he argues that the German attempts to reconcile faith and reason often turns out to be historically self-defeating. See John H. Smith, *Dialogues Between Faith and Reason: The Death and Return of God in Modern German Thought* (Ithaca, NY: Cornell University Press, 2011).

8. Fichte meant the work to be purely Kantian, since he wished to ingratiate himself with Kant and thereby open the door to an academic career beyond that of a private tutor. In this regard, it proved very successful, becoming the principle cause for his appointment to a professorship at the University of Jena in 1794.

9. Erich Fuchs, *J. G. Fichte im Gespräch: Berichte der Zeitgenossen. Band 1: 1762–1798* (Stuttgart, Germany: Fromann-Holzboog, 1978), 34, 38–39.

10. Kant scholars' accusations against the coherence of *Religion* are summarized at length in Chris L. Firestone and Nathan Jacobs, *In Defense of Kant's Religion* (Bloomington: Indiana University Press, 2008), 13–19, 28–36, 48–57, 83–100.

reading Fichte and Kant side by side, I wish to show that Kant's *Religion* responds to the challenge to the Kantian system posed by Fichte's *Attempt*. More specifically, when I demonstrate that the necessity of divine intervention remains a serious possibility in Kant's work, I am saying that Kant did not entirely succeed in deflecting Fichte's challenge to the self-sufficiency of practical reason. The nature of my own argument is thus ultimately historical, although my method is largely analytical.

As a preliminary matter, I must point out that I use terms such as *revelation, miracle,* and *divine intervention* interchangeably in this essay. Unless evident otherwise, the notion behind these terms is a supernatural interference in the natural order, whether through the empirical transmission of scripture, the inward gift of grace, or some more obscure manipulation of history itself. On this view, genuine revelation cannot be the imaginative grasp of rational truth, as it is for Spinoza, nor can it be a pronounced moment of self-discovery in the dialectic of Spirit, as Hegel would have it. Spinoza and Hegel immanentize the divine in a way that leaves little or no room for transcendence, whereas the God-talk of Fichte and Kant often implies a Beyond from which God operates (or could, in principle, operate). In other words, Fichte and Kant retain the central Christian notion that revelation, like all miracles, is a "free manifestation by God of that which lies beyond the normal reach of human inquiry."[11]

Fichte and the Conditional Necessity of Revelation

Johann Gottlieb Fichte is the founder of what became German Idealism, a philosophical movement characterized in part by an abandonment of the transcendent as the ground of being. Reality, in Fichte's view, is the production of the self-positing self (i.e., the "I") as it passes through an endless series of negations (i.e., encounters with the "not-I"), which are overcome in two ways: through a *reflective* reconstruction of the original unity of consciousness as "I," and through a *practical* subjection of nature to the rationality of the "I."

11. Avery Dulles, *Models of Revelation* (Garden City, NY: Doubleday, 1983), 9.

Because Idealism is not my focus here, I do not unpack or critique this position; it is enough to observe that, in this worldview, any notion of religion based on supernatural revelation does not fare terribly well. Fichte implies, long before Ludwig Feuerbach overtly argues, that God is the externalization of human spirit.[12]

This being the case, it is ironic that *Attempt at a Critique of All Revelation*, the work announcing Fichte's appearance on the intellectual scene, revolves entirely around a religious question: "Is the concept of revelation possible *a priori*, or does it have a merely empirical origin?"[13] To answer this question, *Attempt* begins with a general "deduction of religion" (chap. 2), followed by a treatise on the distinction between natural and revealed religion (chap. 3), then a "deduction" of revelation and its rational possibility (chap. 4–7), and finally a discussion of the "criteria" for judging revelations (chap. 8–12). In chapter 2, Fichte reaffirms the Kantian postulate of a divine, moral Lawgiver, albeit through a somewhat different line of reasoning than Kant's. The chapter's opening sentence announces the a priori imperative of reason to achieve the highest good, which consists of moral perfection united with perfect happiness. Because our happiness depends on our well-being as sensual creatures, however, we are unable to bring about the highest good, for natural laws are, from the human perspective, completely insensitive to moral commands. Therefore, in order to avoid a contradiction within reason—namely, to avoid reason making a practical demand that it knows theoretically is impossible to fulfill, thus compromising the authority of the moral law within the economy of reason as a whole— we must assume, "as assuredly as we must assume that the promotion of the end goal of the moral law within us is possible," that there is a God

---

12. See Johann Gottlieb Fichte, *Versuch einer Kritik aller Offenbarung (1792)*, ed. Hansjürgen Verweyen (Hamburg, Germany: Felix Meiner, 1983), 24. Also see Allen Wood, introduction to *Attempt at a Critique of all Revelation*, by Johann Gottlieb Fichte, trans. Garrett Green (Cambridge: Cambridge University Press, 2010), xxiv–xxv; and George die Giovanni, *Freedom and Religion in Kant and His Immediate Successors* (Cambridge: Cambridge University Press, 2005), 212.

13. Fichte, *Versuch*, 33. Translations throughout are based on Green's translation, but I have modified them in many instances. Because the chronological priority of Fichte's text over Kant's is important here, I cite from the first edition in 1792 as published by the Meiner Verlag rather than the more frequently cited second edition of 1793 as published in the fifth volume of the de Gruyter edition.

who rules over the domains of both freedom and nature.[14] This conclusion is particularly important for our "lower faculty of desire" (*unteres Begehrungsvermögen*), which looks after our material happiness. Our "upper" faculty is content with the disinterested pleasure (*Lust*) of achieving an aesthetic conformity between our actions and the moral law.[15] We can successfully subordinate our "lower" faculty of desire to our "upper" one partly out of fear or admiration for the divine Lawgiver's power and partly because the Lawgiver promises an ultimate satisfaction to our "lower" faculty should it conform to virtue.[16] We can, futhermore, trust God's promise because reason requires us to attribute moral goals not only to the divine mind but also to the omnipotent *will* of the Creator.[17]

The indirect consequences of the concept of the divine will are, however, what really drive the argument of *Attempt*. Should it be possible for our respect for the moral law as such to grow weak, then representing morality as the will of God—a representation that revelation actuates—might serve as a secondary moral incentive to lead us back to moral health. Fichte is quite explicit about this:

> We can imagine individual cases of the application of the [moral] law, in which reason alone would not have enough strength to determine the will; rather, to reinforce its efficacy, it

---

14. Fichte, *Versuch*, 8–10, cf. 17. Fichte is adopting here Kant's philosophical motives for including the ideas of freedom (agency), God, and immortality within the project of moral philosophy. Without these, practical reason would, on reflection, find itself irreconcilably at odds with nature. Despite the novelties he introduces into Kant's argument, Fichte perceives himself to be proceeding in a rigorously Kantian fashion.

15. Ibid., 13.

16. Ibid., 12, 19–20.

17. Ibid., 20. There are two main differences from Kant's argument. First, Fichte does not follow the order in which Kant's practical concepts unfold. Skipping the postulate of immortality, Fichte begins with the highest good and then jumps to God as the Guarantor of the highest good. (None of this is developed as carefully as we might wish.) Hansjürgen Verweyen notes that the order of these concepts may reflect the influence of Pezold, introduction to *Versuch einer Kritik aller Offenbarung (1792)*, by Johann Gottlieb Fichte, ed. Hansjürgen Verweyen (Hamburg, Germany: Felix Meiner, 1983), x. Second, Fichte presents the God of revelation, in Allen Wood's terms, as "intimately connected to moral motivation and the authority of the moral law, which requires that we be able to think of morality as legislated both by our own will and by the will of God which is external to us" (introduction to *Attempt*, xv).

additionally requires the representation that a certain action be commanded by God.[18]

We might well doubt whether an incentive other than the moral law itself can be considered "moral," but Fichte's text provides two interrelated ways of defending this proposition. First, although the representation of a moral Lawgiver outside of ourselves cannot "in the strict sense strengthen our respect for the moral law at all," it can "increase our respect for the decisions of the moral law in specific cases, where a strong counterweight of inclination is present."[19] In other words, revelation, because it directly evokes the representation of God, can promote moral sensitivity and thereby empower the moral will. As Hansjürgen Verweyen puts it, "[w]hen people are brought to at least temporarily listen to God, their moral feeling can develop."[20] In providing this service, revelation belongs to the category of moral "helps and hindrances" that recent scholarship has identified and defended in the context of Kantian anthropology.[21] Second, revealed commandments can be moral incentives in the sense that they invoke our relationship to a being "in regard to whom it is not up to us whether we respect [*achten*] him or deny him due respect . . . a being the mere thought of whom must impress the deepest reverence upon us, and whom it would be the greatest absurdity not to honor."[22] Revelations are thus not only a moral "help" in fostering moral sensitivity but also directly invoke the moral law via their practical-dialectical unity with the idea of God.[23]

---

18. Fichte, *Versuch*, 23.

19. Ibid., 24.

20. Verweyen, introduction to *Versuch*, xxxi.

21. See, for instance, Patrick Frierson, *Freedom and Anthropology in Kant's Moral Philosophy* (Cambridge: Cambridge University Press, 2003), 48–67. It would be good to see Kant scholars eventually acknowledge Fichte as a representative of this "Kantian" moral anthropology.

22. Fichte, *Versuch*, 24.

23. It should be noted that the practical-dialectical unity of God and revelation could not be spelled out in Kantian terms in 1792 because Kant had not yet provided such terms. Fichte therefore provides his own: "The only purely moral stimulus is the inward holiness of right," he says, and "by a postulate of pure practical reason this is in God *in concreto* (and consequently available to sensibility)"; *Versuch*, 40. Although an elaboration of this dense argument would be helpful, it is clear that, for Fichte, we must think of God's inward holiness as "available to sensibility," which means that the mere experience of

Whichever way we explain the possibility of a secondary moral incentive, the bottom line is that the senses, usually seen as a source of temptation, can, in fact, facilitate morality by receiving revelation:

> Should beings . . . become entirely incapable of morality, their sensuous nature must itself be determined by sensuous stimuli to allow itself to be determined by the moral law. . . . This can only be taken to mean that purely moral stimuli are to be brought to these beings via the path of the senses.[24]

"Purely moral stimuli" can be none other than the commands of moral reason, and to present them "via the path of the senses" can only be to receive them from the mouth of God. To be sure, we have no general duty to regard the moral law as sensuously revealed, because that would be an a priori challenge to the autonomy of reason. Fichte merely speculates that, in some cases, it might be crucial for the law to be represented as coming immediately from God, who "personally would have to announce himself and his will as lawful for [finite moral beings] in the sensuous world."[25] In any case, this sensuous reinforcement marks, for Fichte, the divide between sterile "theology" and living "religion."[26]

But could the weakening of the moral law, on which all this is predicated, actually occur? Despite protestations of doubt in chapter 2, Fichte defends this possibility. "It can certainly be conceived a priori," he argues, that a primitive or indigent society might "come into a situation . . . such

---

(perceived) revelation already has a priori resonance with the moral law. Kant, by contrast, will never say that we must assume God's holiness is "available to sensibility" because he is afraid it could lead to non-moral forms of religion, or "counterfeit service" (*Afterdienst*); *Religion*, 6.151.

24. Fichte, *Versuch*, 40.

25. Ibid., 41.

26. Scholars typically classify this distinction between "theology" and "religion" as Fichte's innovation on Kant's philosophy of religion, although Fichte may have acquired the idea, as Marco Olivetti points out, from the conclusion of Kant's third *Critique*; "Zum Religions- und Offenbarungsverständnis beim jungen Fichte und bei Kant," *Fichte-Studien* 23 (2003): 193–94. "Theology" concerns merely those ideas that arise from reflection on the moral law, while "religion" concerns the total relation, including the sensuous relation, between the subject and the divine. See Xavier Léon, *Fichte et son temps*, vol. 1 (Paris: Armand Colin, 1954), 104–5; for the complex development of Fichte's *Religionsbegriff*, see Verweyen, introduction to *Versuch*, xxiv–xxviii.

that it was compelled . . . to hear no other law than that of need," in which case God would have to intervene to awaken their beleaguered moral sense.[27] Or, if primitive humans should, as is likely, gradually emerge from the thoughtlessness of indigence by making practical rules for themselves based on their experience, it is likely that these rules would "contradict possible moral rules," and such rules passed down as tradition could conceivably "destroy the possibility of morality" altogether.[28] Finally, certain individuals can exhibit deficiencies to "a degree of intensity at which the moral law loses its causal force on their sensuous nature entirely, either permanently or only in certain cases."[29] In any of these cases, humans remain moral beings, but the sensuous obstacles preventing them from properly harkening to the moral law are too great. Assuming Fichte has correctly described the human predicament, the argument for a secondary moral incentive in the form of revelation becomes urgent.

Fichte sums up his argument as follows:

> Mankind can fall so deep into moral corruption [through indigence, culture, or personal defect] that it can be brought back to morality in no other way than by religion, and to religion in no other way than by the senses. A religion that is to affect such men can be based on nothing but direct divine authority. Since God cannot will that any moral being should fabricate such an authority, he must himself be the one who confers it on such a religion.[30]

In short, the moral Lawgiver must intervene to alleviate such moral incapacitation. Additionally, we must be able to represent this intervention to ourselves as fully real. It is not symbolic or metaphorical. If it is to convince the lower faculty of desire, and thereby rehabilitate the higher faculty, revelation must quite literally be an "appearance in the world of sense and must be *given* (cannot be *constructed*)."[31] Can we expect such an extraordinary thing? On a priori grounds, Fichte says yes, because

---

27. Fichte, *Versuch*, 74.
28. Ibid.
29. Ibid., 40.
30. Ibid., 79–80.
31. Ibid., 132.

the a priori logic of the moral law dictates that God must "promote the greatest possible morality in all rational beings by all moral means."[32] We can therefore anticipate that if moral incapacitation "really should exist, [God] will use [sensuous] means" to recover us for the good.[33]

Such, in brief, is Fichte's a priori argument for what Verweyen calls the "conditional necessity of revelation" (*bedingte Notwendigkeit der Offenbarung*).[34] Even if we grant its Kantian premises, Fichte's theory is not without its problems. For instance, by arguing from a priori principles for the conditional necessity of historical revelation, Fichte makes what appears to be an "ontological" argument. If he can antecedently deduce that (a) reason must believe in a God guaranteeing the moral law and the highest good and (b) moral incapacitation, as previously discussed, is possible, then reason must also believe that God, in cases of such incapacitation, *will cross over into the empirical domain* to promote his own moral ends. By insisting on this as a real possibility, we must also assume that God is, or could at any time become, real.

Of course, this argument differs from classic ontological argumentation in a couple ways. First, the logical necessity for the idea of revelation is not "original" to practical reason in the way that the necessity for God and immortality are; no "*datum* of pure reason" requires us to embrace the concept of revelation, as, for instance, the a priori principle of causation requires us to posit the existence of a First Cause and an "absolute world-whole."[35] Rather, the idea of revelation becomes necessary only after reflecting on experience. But does this diminish the force or legitimacy of the argument? It does not, because experience may create new practical needs, and from these needs, new practical ideas (such as conditionally necessary revelation) may flow and potentially receive a priori justification.[36] Such ideas do not arise on their own, but their possibility, their "lawful origin *in abstracto*," can be demonstrated once the matter has been raised.[37]

---

32. Ibid., 41.
33. Ibid.
34. Verweyen, introduction to *Versuch*, xxix.
35. Fichte, *Versuch*, 35–36.
36. Ibid., 35.
37. Ibid., 36.

Second, Fichte's argument differs from classic ontological reasoning because it rests on *practical* a priori principles, which means its conclusions do not have theoretical status. But, again, this does not diminish the argument for revelation, because the ideas of practical reason must be given theoretical import in order to do their job. A rational belief is rational precisely inasmuch as we have no good reason to doubt it. In the words of Kant's third *Critique* (published two years before Fichte's own text), rational faith is "not like an opinion, without sufficient ground," but rather is "adequately grounded in reason," albeit "only in regard to its practical use."[38] The Kantian qualification of "only in regard to its practical use" is not meant to diminish the authority of rational faith, only to clarify its source. Fichte takes this source seriously enough—and I find this *very* serious—to warrant anticipation of "something outside [the idea of revelation] that corresponds to itself" when "an empirical need should arise."[39] He plainly states that

> theoretical propositions can be derived from a practical commandment which is absolutely a priori and which is not based on any theoretical propositions as its premises, because to practical reason, a power certainly is to be ascribed over the theoretical, though suitable to its own laws.[40]

Here, Fichte is merely a disciple of Kant, who never felt that rational self-coherence required, at some level, the subjugation of practical to theoretical reason, as scientific-materialists might. Rather, the ideas of practical reason—immortality, God, the highest good—derive immense authority from the factual status of moral law itself. Thinking along these lines, Frederick Beiser observes that Kant's account of the highest good *must* be taken as serious metaphysics. As the dialectic of practical reason unfolds, says Beiser,

> the underlying problem . . . and the postulate [Kant] proposes to solve it, are metaphysical. If we were to purge metaphysics from the argument of the "Antinomy [of Pure Practical Reason],"

---

38. Kant, *CPJ*, 5.472.
39. Fichte, *Versuch*, 132.
40. Ibid., 18.

Kant would have no basis to connect the realms of freedom and nature . . . In the end, then, to read the metaphysics out of Kant's concept of the highest good is only to beg the question of its possibility.[41]

If the practical argument for Kant's highest good is to have any meaning, it must be telling us something authoritative about divine reality. The same insight holds for Fichte's argument for revelation. If it has any force at all, then we really should expect discrete, empirical divine intervention, given certain historical contingencies, because the God of a priori reason is just this kind of interventionist being. To be sure, identifying specific moments (if any) in actual human history that satisfy these criteria for revelation is probably impossible and may always involve an act of faith.[42] For his part, Fichte offers only a single, tentative historical example, and that in a footnote.[43] This epistemological difficulty in *verifying* an actual instance of divine intervention does not, however, invalidate the point made here, which is that a priori practical reason entitles us to expect that God will intervene empirically under certain plausible circumstances. This expectation distinguishes revelation from the practical ideas of God and immortality, which do not entail any empirical consequences (at least not in this life), and it is precisely this "impurity" in Fichte's a priori reasoning that Kant does not like, as we shall now see.

Kant's Radicalization of Fichtean Evil

We do not know what Kant thought of Fichte's conditional necessity argument for revelation (however much of it he read) after the younger

---

41. Frederick Beiser, "Moral Faith and the Highest Good," in *Kant and Modern Philosophy*, ed. Paul Guyer (Cambridge: Cambridge University Press, 2006), 602.

42. Wolfgang Ritzel remarks emphatically, "It can never be categorically declared that in this or that instance or in any instance whatsoever God has announced himself"; *Fichtes Religionsphilosophie* (Stuttgart, Germany: Kohlhammer, 1956), 45.

43. Fichte, *Versuch*, 75n. The example is ancient Israel's stubborn moral backwardness, which apparently elicited supernatural threats and admonitions.

man sent him a copy of the *Attempt* manuscript in August 1791.[44] But at the least, he must have had in mind a critical defense of revelation as he wrote the first section of *Religion*, which was submitted to the *Berlinische Monatsschrift* in February 1792, with the full text available to the public by the Easter book fair of 1793. Although he seems to have at least approved of Fichte's project, in the end, he resists the conditional necessity argument (how knowingly is hard to say) for two reasons.[45] The more obvious reason is that historical revelations of the type Fichte postulates can lead to scriptural idolatry and generally distract from the moral law, which alone has intrinsic authority.[46] A more fundamental reason, the one discussed here, is that an argument for the conditional necessity of revelation calls into question the self-sufficiency of the moral law, to which Kant is deeply committed. Nevertheless, I argue that Kant does not fully reject the necessity of revelation in *Religion*, despite his antipathy toward the idea, because the problem of evil ultimately calls into question, at the level of reflective judgment, the self-sufficiency of the moral law.

As a first step it is necessary to identify the obstacle to such a reading. In the preface for *Religion*'s first edition, Kant immediately makes the point that the moral law is to be regarded as self-sufficient. This is an up-front challenge to Fichte—and to any moral argument for the necessity of divine aid—in forceful and unambiguous terms:

> So far as morality is based on the conception of the human being as one who is free but who also, just because of that, binds himself through his reason to unconditional laws, it is in need neither of the idea of another being above him in order that he recognize his duty, nor, that he observe it, of an incentive other

---

44. Kant met with Fichte to discuss the manuscript on August 23, 1791, and in a letter to Ludwig Ernst Borowski dated September 16, 1791, Kant admits to having read only to "page eight." In a communication to Friedrich August Weißhuhn, Fichte calls it "about up to ch. 3." If this is true, Kant would not have encountered Fichte's specific argument for the conditional necessity of revelation. See Verweyen, introduction to *Versuch*, xv–xvii; and Fuchs, *Fichte*, 34.

45. Kant's general support of Fichte's work is most evident in his letter to Borowski recommending its publication; Fuchs, *Fichte*, 34.

46. A thorough treatment of the dangers of miracles and revelation for moral life is provided by the "Remarks" that Kant appends to each of the four parts of *Religion*.

than the law itself. At least it is the human being's own fault if such a need is found in him; but in this case too the need could not be relieved through anything else: for whatever does not originate from himself and his own freedom provides no remedy for a lack in his morality. Hence on its own behalf morality in no way needs religion (whether objectively, as regards willing, or subjectively, as regards capability) but is rather self-sufficient by virtue of pure practical reason.[47]

In describing morality based on the conception of freedom as both "objectively" and "subjectively" sufficient for a moral life, Kant seems to be responding to Fichte's distinction between theology and religion in chapter 2 of *Attempt* (a part that Kant likely read). Religion, for Fichte, is born from the influence (*Zurückwirkung*) of the theological ideas of pure practical reason on our lower faculty of desire. For example, when the moral law is represented sensuously as a command that God reveals—a religious idea—it may help the more sensual part of our will go along with it. In making this distinction, Fichte is opening a space, as we have seen, for the possibility that, without religious *Zurückwirkung* onto the lower faculty of desire, the "higher" desire of our rational will might be unable to determine our total will. This is also the scenario that Kant seems to reject by arguing that morality "in no way needs religion . . . but is rather self-sufficient." It is not, then, the idea of revelation that Kant rejects but the notion that revelation might actually be necessary.

At this point, Kant could fall in with the Deists, for whom revelation is at best a dispensable "republication of the religion of nature."[48] In this case, he would disagree with Fichte, and Fichte's *Attempt* would simply be a failed Kantian imitation. But Kant does take to heart a central tenet of Fichte's argument. Although Kant insists that practical reason must be regarded as self-sufficient, he recognizes from an empirical perspective that it can fail to determine moral choice. Even more serious, Kant believes it *always* and *universally* fails, a stunning insight that leads him to posit a "radical" or "innate" evil in humanity. Within the

47. Kant, *Religion*, 6.3.
48. Matthew Tindal, *Christianity as Old as the Creation: Or, The Gospel, a Republication of the Religion of Nature* (London, 1730). Lorenz Schmidt translated it into German in 1741.

Kantian system, this idea is a bit mysterious, since moral behavior is, by definition, that which adopts the primacy of rational incentives only to disobey them for no discernable reason. Why a moral subject—indeed *all* moral subjects—might behave this way is, as Kant repeatedly admits, impossible for him to explain, especially because he rejects the notion of a diabolical will, which actually desires to choose evil.[49]

Fichte might have been somewhat surprised at Kant's perplexing radicalization of his concept of moral incapacitation, even though Fichte, according to Verweyen, is the first to identify "a freedom [i.e., to choose evil] radically distinct from morality" as a central part of the critical philosophy of religion.[50] In any case, Kant cannot simply dispense with the necessity of revelation a priori because he is confronted with what appears to be a catastrophic, empirical failure of the very rational self-sufficiency he so rigidly defends. This is a philosophical problem that Kant obviously needs to address.

This problem can be further illuminated in two ways, which correspond to the two stories that Kant tells about the source of evil in *Religion*. In part I, he attributes radical evil to our original moral disposition (*Gesinnung*) as human beings, while in part III, he portrays it as a corrupting power springing directly from human sociality. One challenge of Kant scholarship is to decide whether or not these are two different evils or merely two faces of the same evil. But for the present, I treat them as coordinated yet separate problems.[51] In the following two

---

49. Note that Kant's "radical evil" does not necessarily correspond to the egregiously bad behavior that we might associate with this term. Rather, it denotes an unwillingness to act *purely* out of moral motives, and from an external perspective a radically evil person can accomplish a great deal of good. However, one can argue that horrendous evil is not *essentially* any different from outwardly harmless evil. On this "banality" of all evil within a Kantian framework, see Henry Allison, "Reflections on the Banality of (Radical) Evil: A Kantian Analysis," in *Rethinking Evil: Contemporary Perspectives*, ed. María Pía Lara (Berkeley: University of California Press, 2001), 86–100.

50. Verweyen, introduction to *Versuch*, xxxi. Marco Olivetti finds that Fichte's anticipation of Kant's use of "the subject of evil as a prerequisite for a religious-philosophical analysis" is "astounding" (198–99).

51. Allen Wood (following Sharon Anderson-Gold) seems to view the dispositional story of evil as a partial lens on the grander story of man's "unsocial sociability." More precisely, he sees the "nature and source" of evil as purely social, although "responsibility" still lies with the individual, since no collective subject can experience this responsibility; Allen Wood, *Kant's Ethical Thought* (Cambridge, England: Cambridge University

sections, I demonstrate how Kant's empirical assessment of human evil leads him, in both stories, to the threshold of divine intervention. I do not suggest that he actually argues for the necessity of revelation—he clearly does not—but I do suggest that he is unable or unwilling to foreclose such an argument. This detail turns out to be rather significant given Kant's dour assessment of humanity's moral condition.

The Private Story of Radical Evil: The Moral Disposition

One of the most important contributions in *Religion* to Kant's moral philosophy is his introduction of the moral disposition. This term designates our general attitude toward the moral law, that is, the inner command of reason to "act only in accordance with that maxim through which you can at the same time will that it become a universal law."[52] This disposition alone really determines whether or not we are moral beings, since it sets the standard for how all other maxims are to be made. Without a moral disposition, furthermore, it would be impossible to speak of moral responsibility, because no principle of continuity would underlie our various moral actions.[53]

The great dilemma of *Religion*—the insight that puts the whole text in motion—is Kant's assertion that every human being is born with an evil moral disposition, which means that, although they hear the voice and recognize the authority of the moral law, they choose not to incorporate it into their supreme moral maxim. Humanity, Kant posits, is

---

Press, 1999), 286–89. Chris Firestone and Nathan Jacobs, in contrast, approach the evil disposition as an independent problem with its own solution (i.e., "the prototype"), which can be undone by the entirely separate process of social corruption. They identify "a logical priority in Kant's work, which requires moral conversion to occur prior to building an ethical community" (*In Defense of Kant's Religion* 183). I think their approach better accommodates Kant's text. In any case, one of the general difficulties Kant faces as a philosopher—a difficulty that his Idealist successors seek to overcome—is navigating between ahistorical aspects of human nature (like the evil disposition and the prototype) and historical ones (like social corruption and ethical community building). On this last point, see Smith, *Dialogues Between Faith and Reason*, 87–90.

52. Kant, *Religion*, 4.421.

53. See Henry Allison, *Kant's Theory of Freedom* (Cambridge: Cambridge University Press, 1990), 136–37.

"radically evil" or "evil by nature" because, from the earliest glimmer of a moral conscience—"antecedent to every use of freedom given in experience (from earliest youth as far back as birth)"—*every* human exhibits a willingness to deviate from moral law.[54] For the purposes of this article, I do not evaluate the evidence for this dramatic claim; instead, I will simply accept, as most Kantian scholars do, that it is a certainty acquired at least partly through empirical means.[55]

What is most troubling about this claim is its universality. Kant clearly insists that pure practical reason must consider our original moral disposition to be the product of a free, albeit hidden choice. Yet, the fact that all people without exception choose the same moral disposition—and we can safely assume they will continue to do so—hardly rests easy with this assumption of an original freedom. One cannot appeal in this case to the physical constitution of the species as an explanation of our evil disposition, because (a) Kant believes that our natural predisposition (*Anlage*) is to moral goodness and (b) the presence of material incentives in whatever degree is ultimately irrelevant to our moral character.[56] Moral action is strictly a matter of how we prioritize moral and material incentives, and no material incentive can determine this, for then we would be dealing with natural causation and leaving the realm of freedom altogether. The universality of evil, therefore, does not flow from physical nature, yet reason cannot shake the sense that it flows from something other than sheer spontaneity or

---

54. Kant, *Religion*, 6.22.

55. This reading of radical evil as an empirical doctrine can be found, for instance, in Robert Louden, *Kant's Impure Ethics: From Rational Beings to Human Beings* (Oxford: Oxford University Press, 2002); Pablo Muchnik, "An Alternative Proof of the Universal Propensity to Evil," in *Kant's Anatomy of Evil*, ed. Sharon Anderson-Gold and Pablo Muchnik (Cambridge: Cambridge University Press, 2010); and Patrick Frierson, *Freedom and Anthropology in Kant's Moral Philosophy* (Cambridge: Cambridge University Press, 2003). Although Allen Wood has rejected his "own naïve conjecture long ago that the doctrine of radical evil is intended simply as an empirical generalization" (see *Kant's Ethical Thought*, 287) and Henry Allison has insisted on the importance to Kant of a "conceptual" understanding of radical evil, both of these major Kant scholars still concede that experience plays an indispensable role confirming the reality of this doctrine (see "Ethics, Evil, and Anthropology in Kant: Remarks on Allen Wood's *Kant's Ethical Thought*," *Ethics* 111, no.3 (2001): 605–10).

56. On the first point, see Kant, *Religion*, 6.26–28.

at least not from any *personal* spontaneity.[57] What is the likelihood that an effectively endless number of rational agents would, without exception, make the same choice of moral disposition, if they were not in some sense compelled to do so?

One answer could be that humans possess an overwhelming rational incentive for evil, which would explain our consistent rejection of the moral law without, however, necessitating it. Such a solution is merely verbal, however, because there is in fact no *im*moral law thundering in our consciousness alongside the moral law. Because the moral law is the only nonnatural incentive we know—and for Kant this is simply a fact of experience—morally worthy action is the only kind of true freedom we can conceive. Evil is thus a kind of freedom beyond freedom, or a freedom to pervert freedom, for which we cannot indentify any positive incentive. Once this freedom has been exercised, critical philosophy encounters one of its absolute limits. When it comes to evil, we can only make (a) the negative, conceptual point that it involves a knowing refusal to incorporate the moral law into our supreme moral maxim and (b) the positive, empirical point that it afflicts us universally as if it were a natural law.

More important for our purposes, the question, "Why evil?" prompts another question: "Why a return to moral goodness?" The seemingly obvious answer is that the moral law never stops commanding us with intrinsic authority. But is this really an answer? The law,

---

57. In a persuasive interpretation, Seiriol Morgan argues that radical evil is *precisely* to be identified with the spontaneity of will, albeit as a fetish. Evil results from the desire to exercise freedom, a "primal self-enticement to license" without realizing that any nonmoral use of freedom is ultimately self-defeating since it draws its incentives from natural self-interest; Seiriol Morgan, "The Missing Formal Proof of Humanity's Radical Evil in Kant's *Religion*," *The Philosophical Review* 114, no. 1 (January 2005): 94. We should note, however, that in order for this argument to work, Morgan must reject a rather major claim in *Religion*, namely, that "the propensity to evil amounts to the adoption of an evil disposition" (95). In other words, Morgan rejects the idea that evil flows from an evil meta-maxim, contrary to Kant's explicit claim to the contrary. I am not sure that the imputability of a maxim-less choice and a maxim-guided choice can have the same moral meaning, however, because they arise from different subjective moments or processes and are thus not "personal" in the same way. In any case, for the purposes of this historically oriented article, I simply accept Kant's text as it stands, which means that evil is to be seen, oddly, as the result of perverse maxim-making that is imputable to me, even though I am not conscious of ever having performed this maxim making.

without doubt, remains an incentive to morally worthy action, but radical evil is the categorical rejection of this incentive as our exclusive, supreme standard of action. The choice of an evil disposition may be too "knowing" to be corrected by the same moral law that it rejects. This seems to be an implication of moral "rigorism," which is Kant's doctrine that we are either entirely good or entirely bad, since we either do or do not embrace the absolute authority of the law. There is no third option.[58] An eventual deliverance from the "rigor" of our personal evil cannot be explained by a sudden adequacy of the same moral law that previously was inadequate.[59] (Or does Kant think that the moral law "wears down" our evil resistance to it? Would that not be a naturalistic reduction of freedom?)

A better answer, it would seem, is the appeal to our noumenally free power of choice (*Willkür*), which accompanies the rational will and freely incorporates or rejects rational incentives. To be sure, as an "explanation" of moral conversion, the appeal to the power of choice is very weak, because it is really, on the theoretical level, just an appeal to spontaneity. However, reason could never make sense of radical evil in the first place, so perhaps it is a wash. If that is so, then the "explanation" of conversion is best presented as a question: Given so many free, rational individuals with a naturalistically undetermined power of choice, what are the chances that *none* of them would undergo a reversal in their disposition?

This appeal to the spontaneous change of heart is not, however, an innocent hypothesis for the reason with which we are now familiar: radical evil bears the form of a necessary law. That being the case, one can counter the appeal to the power of choice with another question:

---

58. Kant, *Religion*, 6.22–25.

59. Philip Quinn has made essentially this same point: "There is no possible world in which (i) the thesis of rigorism is true, (ii) every human adopts a morally evil supreme maxim, and (iii) some human adopts a morally good supreme maxim"; "Original Sin, Radical Evil and Moral Identity," *Faith and Philosophy* 1, no. 2 (1984): 199. The upshot, for Quinn, is that we should not consider ourselves responsible for conversion. "We ought not to effect a moral revolution in our characters . . . because we cannot" (199). If this means becoming cynical about responsibility, then I think it would be a wrong way to read Kant (and I do not think Quinn wants to read him this way). But Quinn is right, I think, that we cannot imagine our own conversion flowing from our own strength.

Why should we think of moral conversion through the figure of spontaneity when we must think of corruption through the figure of necessity? It would make more rational sense to expect spontaneity in both cases, but the empirical data do not permit this. An asymmetry emerges that reason cannot ignore. At this point, the idea subjects itself to reflective judgment (i.e., the power to revise or complicate a priori judgments based on experience) that, in moral conversion, something must come to the assistance of freedom in order to counteract the law-like principle of evil in our original constitution—perhaps universally, perhaps only in certain cases. This counteractive force, completely indescribable in its particulars, is the basis of the reflective argument for revelation that I am proposing. Below, we will see that Kant does leave open the theoretical possibility of such aid, even if he is somewhat reluctant to develop this idea. Before discussing that, however, let us see how the struggle between a priori and empirical perspectives plays out in Kant's second story about evil.

The Social Story of Radical Evil: Mutual Corruption

Unlike the private story, in which the problem of evil (but not the solution to it) is very specific and clear, the social story struggles to identify the problem of evil in a consistent way. Indeed, it is this very absence of a consistent account of evil that suggests Kant's inability to rule out a possible need for divine aid. Such, at least, will be my argument in this section.

At the center of the social story is the rise of the ethical community, a society "solely designed for the preservation of morality by counteracting evil with united forces."[60] On the face of it, we should have no reason to deliberately construct such a community; because humanity's predisposition (*Anlage*) is to the good, a just society should naturally emerge over time through human interaction.[61] In fact, this is not the case. According to Kant, finite, rational beings have a natural tendency toward mutual corruption.

---

60. Kant, *Religion*, 6.94.
61. Ibid., 6.26–28.

Envy, addiction to power, avarice, and the malignant inclina-
tions associated with these, assail man's nature, which on its
own is undemanding, as soon as he is among human beings.
Nor is it necessary to assume that these are sunk into evil and
are examples to lead him astray: it suffices that they are there,
that they surround him, and that they are human beings, and
they will mutually corrupt each other's moral predisposition
[*moralische Anlage*] *and make one another evil* [*sich einander
böse machen*].[62]

Needless to say, this language is very strong, even to the point of paradox. How can you corrupt another person or "make" him evil when evil
is precisely an act of moral freedom? As disturbing as this claim is, Kant
does not immediately backtrack or qualify it. For him, it is an empirical
fact, however difficult it may be to make sense of this fact practically
or theoretically. Instead of dwelling on the a priori problems that arise
in attributing an absolutely corrupting power to human sociality, Kant
hurries to name the ethical community as the antidote to it:

The dominion of the good principle is not otherwise attain-
able . . . than through the setting up and the diffusion of a society
in accordance with, and for the sake of, the laws of virtue. . . .
For only in this way can we hope for a victory of the good principle over the evil one.[63]

The way Kant sets this up prompts an important question: Can the same
rational individuals who are inevitably corrupted by social life have the
moral strength, without some addition of grace, to produce the antidote
to this corruption? It is by no means obvious that they would, and it
indeed sounds hopeless in light of Kant's assurance that human beings

---

62. Ibid., 6.94; emphasis added. I have altered Allen Wood's translation here to read
"moral predisposition" instead of "moral disposition," because "predisposition" is Wood's
usual rendering of *Anlage*, with "disposition" being reserved for *Gesinnung*. Admittedly,
Gesinnung might be the more accurate term here in light of Kant's usage in part I of
Religion and elsewhere. But in part III, he seems to use *Anlage* as a blanket term for both
our moral capacity (the specific sense of *Anlage*) and the fundamental orientation of that
capacity (*Gesinnung*).

63. Kant, *Religion*, 6.94.

inevitably corrupt one another. Once social contact corrupts them, they are "rigorously" evil, and any rationally self-sufficient ethical community building becomes difficult to imagine.

Perhaps it is for this reason that Kant modifies his language in other passages, suggesting that, in the ethical state of nature (i.e., before any ethical community is attempted), we would not necessarily be morally doomed but only be in serious, constant danger: "However much the individual human being might do to escape from the dominion of this evil, he would still be held in *incessant danger of relapsing* into it."[64] Heroically, it might be possible, although unlikely, to stay morally afloat long enough to found the ethical community without divine aid; although, even then, we would have no guarantee that the community would maintain its integrity for long.

A few pages later, we see another description of the ethical state of nature, in which we again see Kant trying to allow just enough room for reason to save itself. He begins with the same language about radical social corruption but soon shifts to the milder language of moral endangerment.

> The ethical state of nature [is] one in which the good principle, which resides in each human being, is incessantly attacked by the evil which is found in him and every other as well. Human beings . . . mutually corrupt one another's moral predisposition [*sich einander wechselseitig ihre moralische Anlage verderben*] and, even with the good will [*guten Willen*] of each individual, because of the lack of a principle which unites them, they deviate through their dissensions from the common goal of goodness, as though they were instruments of evil, and expose one another to the danger of falling once again under its dominion.[65]

Here, my earlier objection—that rational agents necessarily corrupted by social interaction may not have the strength to be their own antidote—is not addressed, even though Kant is clearly suggesting that we might have this strength. It would seem that all we have to do is

---

64. Ibid.; emphasis added.
65. Ibid., 6.97.

hit on the appropriate uniting principle (i.e., the idea of the ethical community), and we are in the clear of both moral endangerment and direct moral corruption. Pursuing this hopeful line, Kant argues that

> there is . . . reason to assume that it is God's will that we should ourselves carry out the idea of [the ethical] community. And though human beings might have indeed tried out many a form of church with unhappy result, yet they ought not to cease striving after this end, if need be through renewed attempts which as much as possible avoid the mistakes of previous ones.[66]

Kant suggests that, through trial and error, we could, *in principle*, devise an adequate approximation to the ethical community, or "church", which would save us from endangerment or corruption and rescue our rational self-sufficiency.

The problem is this: a few paragraphs earlier, Kant established that people are, *in fact*, not good enough to pull this off, at least not directly. "Due to a peculiar weakness of human nature, pure faith can never be relied on as much as it deserves, [enough] to found a Church on it alone."[67] This means that "ecclesiastical faith," or a church based on a historical revelation, is ultimately required as a vehicle for the ethical community.[68] Such a concession seems like a victory of revelation over rational self-sufficiency. But, in yet another twist, we must remember that Kant does not accept every "revelation" at face value. Society generates plenty of "alleged revelations" (*angebliche Offenbarungen*), as Kant puts it, on which an ecclesiastical faith can be based, perhaps even to good effect.[69] Does this mean that we can defend the self-sufficiency of reason by demonstrating how a morally successful, historical faith can be grounded in a false revelation constructed by scheming or delusional people?

Understandably, Kant does not want to speak in such terms. However, his concession that "pure [rational] faith can never be relied on as much as it deserves" puts him in the precarious position of requiring ecclesiastical faith on the one hand and denying the need for revelation

---

66. Ibid., 6.105.
67. Ibid., 6.103.
68. Ibid., 6.102–7.
69. Ibid., 6.111.

on the other. When we think of how rare—or in Kant's European context, nonexistent—these non-revelation-based religions are, we see
what a difficult bind he has put himself in. He tries to minimize the
problem by speaking in conciliatory language about the general possibility (but not the necessity) of revelation-based religion:

> It would be . . . arrogant peremptorily to deny that the way a
> church is organized may perhaps also be a special divine dispen-
> sation, if, so far as we can see, the church is in perfect harmony
> with moral religion, and if, in addition, we cannot see how it
> could ever have made its appearance all at once without the req-
> uisite preparatory advances of the public in religious concepts.[70]

Kant admits that rapid advances in the religious development of a society may be too striking for any explanation but a supernatural one,
but this very claim implies that human societies generally may still be
capable, albeit slowly, of "advances . . . in religious concepts" *on their
own,* thus preserving the self-sufficiency of reason. This, however, once
again purchases rational self-sufficiency at the cost of a false revelation
promulgated by scheming or delusional people, unless we adopt a third
way in which ecclesiastical faith does not require even the appearance
of revelation. In favor of this latter possibility, Kant speaks, as we have
seen, of "trying out" churches and "avoiding the mistakes" of previous
ones, which sounds like a deliberately artificial endeavor. But ultimately,
Kant is not eager to adopt this way, because nothing is more valuable in
ecclesiastical faith (ironically) than a revelation, an "object of the highest respect" transmitted through a sacred text that can be continually
reinterpreted in the direction of pure, moral faith.[71] A man-made "tradition" is simply not a match for the "knockdown pronouncement, *Thus it
is written.*"[72] It seems, then, that Kant nearly forces himself into a choice
between a necessary revelation and a necessary deception.

In a final twist, we find the following statement on the need for
divine assistance—one that I believe best captures Kant's peculiar view
on the matter—in the introduction to part IV:

70. Ibid., 6.105–6.
71. Ibid., 6.107.
72. Ibid.

> To erect a church as a community under religious laws . . . seems
> to require more wisdom (of insight as well as of good disposi-
> tion) than human beings can be thought capable of; it seems
> that the moral goodness especially, which is aimed at through
> such an organization, must for this purpose be *presupposed* in
> them already. Nonsensical is in fact even the expression that
> *human beings* should *found* a Kingdom of God (as we might
> well say of them that they can establish the kingdom of a human
> monarch); God must himself be the author of his Kingdom.[73]

On the one hand, Kant tells us unambiguously that humans cannot
found an ethical community on their own. One can defend this proposition on the à priori level ("nonsensical is . . . even the expression")
as well as the empirical ("to erect a church . . . seems to require more
wisdom . . . than human beings can be thought capable of"). This
leaves little room to reduce "God" to a metonymy for "practical reason," especially when we consider that the function of God here is to
save practical reason by founding the ethical community, which God
could hardly do if he were no more than reason's self-projection or an
unreal postulate of reason. On the other hand, Kant seems to equate
God's authorship of the ethical community with the moral goodness
"presupposed" in humanity. To modern ears, this sounds very much
like an anthropological reduction of the divine; God is something that
has always already been part of us, just like our reason or our senses.
Can these two positions coexist?

I have quoted at length from Kant's own words concerning the
social narrative of evil in order to demonstrate the restlessness of Kant's
analysis. I do not conclude that Kant is forced to concede the necessity
of divine aid; rather, I argue that he seems genuinely unable to state
simply and unequivocally that ethical progress is possible without the
representation of divine aid. I do not deny the existence of passages in
Religion where Kant clearly asserts the self-sufficiency of reason, but I
do insist that, taken as a whole, the text does not permit us to embrace
the self-sufficiency postulate without ambivalence. The empirical data
do not permit it. The corrupting power of sociality and the challenge

---

73. Ibid., 6.152.

of the ethical community both seem to overtax human strength. Or, at least, Kant repeatedly speaks this way without adequately assuaging the doubts raised by such language.

Reflective Judgment and the Miracle of Grace

Having illuminated the problems in both the private and the social story of radical evil, I want to say more about the kinds of divine assistance that would be involved in the solution to evil in either story. If, after reading Kant's puzzling social story of evil, we (a) understand revelation to be a requirement of a successful ecclesiastical faith and (b) find it incompatible for the dignity of reason to rely on phony revelation, then a historical-empirical intervention of the type that Fichte suggests—a supernatural deliverance of scripture—is necessary. And yet, in both stories Kant is primarily interested in divine aid of a different sort. Breaking away from the law-like grip of the evil disposition or summoning the strength to resist societal corruption (with or without the help of a church) may require an inward dispensation of grace rather than, or in addition to, the deliverance of scripture.

To get a handle on this type of revelation, we can take as our starting point the moral law itself, which Kant finds so different from nature in that it "proclaims a divine origin."[74] One might read the word *origin* here in a deistic spirit, imagining that God built the moral law into our original human nature, after which it should perform its function perfectly and without mishap, like clockwork. We have seen, however, that the moral law fails despite its absolute, intrinsic authority and that humans have no easy way to remedy this without calling on divine aid. Fortunately, we can read the "divine origin" of the law in another way that is friendly to the possibility of such aid. Because freedom issues from the noumenal, where the categories of time and space do not apply, it is permissible to imagine (because we can only deal with metaphors here) that God continually dispenses the moral law in an "occasionalist" manner. It continually "originates." The disadvantage to thinking this way is that we can never represent the moral subject as fully self-responsible,

---

74. Ibid., 6.49–50.

since the law, in this view, cannot be defined as part of our autonomous rational nature; the advantage is that we can more easily imagine God "adjusting" his influence on our will to address contingencies like our fall into radical evil. This assistance will necessarily be of a kind that does not alter the immediate existence of free will, which is hardly possible, but will nonetheless assist reflective faith in making sense of humanity's total situation. A "hidden" miracle of this kind may be suggested in Kant's description of "the basis for the transition to the new order of things" lying in the "principle of the pure religion of reason, as a revelation (though not an empirical one) permanently taking place within all human beings."[75] On this account, something about the persistence of the law itself can be understood, on reflection, as a form of divine intervention, and, indeed, as part of the same intervention that gives us the moral law in the first place.

The notion of a nonempirical, inward miracle may be what underlies the supernaturalist language in Kant's account of the "prototype [*Urbild*] of the Son of God" in part II of *Religion*.[76] Kant speaks of this prototype as a rational ideal enabling us to believe in the possibility of moral progress. Because we cannot consider ourselves the authors of this idea or comprehend how it came to us (a religiously loaded premise similar to ones found in Plato, Augustine, Descartes, and Jacobi), reason finds it best to say that "the *prototype* has *come down* to us from heaven, that it has taken up humanity (for it is not just as possible to conceive how the *human being, evil* by nature, would renounce evil on his own and *raise* himself up to the ideal of holiness, as it is that the latter take up humanity—which is not evil in itself—by *descending* to it)."[77] In other words, it is more rational to actually think of the prototype as a divine gift than as a natural endowment that merely seems like a divine gift. In a compact phrase, Firestone and Jacobs call this prototype a "transcendentally chastened form of Platonic idealism"—"transcendental" because it resides in reason and "Platonic" because it is, in some sense, beyond what finite rationality could itself produce or expect.[78] In any

---

75. Ibid., 6.122.
76. Ibid., 6.60–62.
77. Ibid., 6.61.
78. Firestone and Jacobs, *In Defense*, 155.

case, one can make the case that the prototype represents an addition or supplement to our human nature.

Whether or not we associate revelation with the prototype, I suggest we label the elusive Kantian theology that has emerged here as "moral occasionalism." This would be the doctrine that God occasionally supplies, or at least supplements, the causal force of certain moral ideas (e.g., the prototype of the Son of God or the vision of the ethical community), which would otherwise be empty or inadequate incentives because of our preexisting "rigorous" evil and the overwhelming corrupting power of society. Such divine supplementation is truly miraculous, but since it is eternally active—and here is the crucial difference from Fichte—we can never *phenomenally* distinguish it from reason's natural drives. It thus fits Kant's requirement that "either miracles are to be admitted as daily [events] (though hidden under the appearance of natural occurrences), or never."[79]

Let me emphasize, however, that I do not argue for this inward miracle, be it moral occasionalism or some other form, as a necessary component of Kant's practical philosophy. It is quite clear that the authority of the moral law and its corollary doctrine of freedom are entirely sufficient, in Kant's view, for moral life. The need for divine intervention arises only negatively in the dialectic between a priori and empirical reason. Such intervention is not absurd in principle, and Kant concedes that a "certain moral strength perceivable to us" can rationally be considered evidence of "supernatural assistance," even when theoretical insight into this act of supplementation "totally escapes us."[80] His objections to such moral grace are only that (a) it is a "transcendent" concept of which no experience can make us certain and that (b) it is

---

79. Kant, *Religion*, 6.89n. My use of this passage is admittedly ironic, because Kant goes on to say that the idea of miracles as everyday realities "hidden under the appearance of natural occurrences . . . is in no way compatible with reason," and therefore "nothing remains but to accept the latter maxim [i.e., that miracles never occur]"; *Religion*, 6.89n. I would argue, however, that this conclusion only holds—and Kant would agree—from a purely rational perspective. For "reflective faith" (Kant, *Religion*, 6.52) and "moral discipline" (Kant, *Religion*, 6.51), Kant's idea of a "daily miracle hidden under the appearance of natural occurrences" is both possible and helpful, as the conclusion of my discussion of Kant demonstrates.

80. Kant, *Religion*, 6.191.

morally "very risky" and "hard to reconcile with [practical] reason."[81]
A response to both objections is, in fact, provided by reflective judgment, to which we must now turn our attention.

I have invoked the power of reflective judgment at a few key moments in my reading of Kant and have defined it as a power to revise or complicate a priori judgments on the basis of experience. I wish now to explain that a little more fully. Judgment in general is the power to "think the particular as contained under the universal."[82] If the universal is something already given a priori, judgment is "determinative"; if the universal is not given and instead must be found, then the judgment is "reflective."[83] In other words, reflective judgment is the process of finding concepts to cover contingent facts and, more specifically, to cover those facts exhibiting some kind of formal regularity or "purposiveness" that calls for interpretation. This distinction between determinative and reflective judgment is required because "there is such a manifold of forms in nature, as it were so many modifications of the universal transcendental concepts of nature that are left undetermined by those laws," that we must invent new concepts to cover the creative diversity of nature.[84] In short, science needs imagination as well as logic. It requires an aesthetic skill of anticipating or sensing how contingent things might fit together. Just as importantly, reflective judgment requires, for the sake of rational self-coherence, that the principles it uncovers "must be considered in terms of the sort of unity they would have if an understanding (even if not ours) had likewise given them for the sake of our faculty of cognition, in order to make possible a system of experience in accordance with particular laws of nature."[85] In other words, in trying to make sense of the contingent world, we must assume that laws can exist beyond the ones that *human* reason can deduce a priori, but laws that nonetheless fit into a rational system. These are the laws, also called "regulative" concepts, that reflective judgment can intuit. Most important, regulative concepts can

---

81. Ibid.
82. Kant, *CPJ*, 5.179.
83. Ibid., 5.179.
84. Ibid.
85. Ibid., 5.180.

depart from the types of narratives that the a priori categories of the understanding would lead us to expect. In other words, reason, in its fullest form, does not demand exclusive naturalism.

Let us apply this more fleshed-out notion of reflective judgment to Kant's two objections to inner grace mentioned earlier. His first objection is that experience can never make us certain of this grace. This, however, is only a problem for theoretical understanding, not for reason as a whole. Earlier, we saw that, for both Fichte and Kant, the moral law bears theoretical import, even if it produces no theoretical certainty. Something like this can apply to the representations of reflective judgment as well. For instance, in the third *Critique*, Kant uses the reflective notion of the "supersensible" to deal with the paradox of organic form (among other things) and to thereby help reason obtain its broader goal of self-coherence. Reflective judgment patches the holes, as it were, that experience places in our a priori picture of the world. For this reason, the productions of reflective judgment deserve rational respect, even though they do not produce certain knowledge. My argument here is that the same respect Kant gives to the supersensible is due, or could be due, to the postulate of inner grace, which deals reflectively with the equally paradoxical problem of radical evil. Although we cannot be certain of inner grace, we can hardly use this uncertainty as an argument against its rational value as a reflective judgment. Radical evil is, after all, just as serious a problem for reason as organic form.

This brings us to the response of reflective judgment to Kant's second objection about the "riskiness" and "irreconcilability" of inward grace. The point I would make here is that experience requires us to entertain notions that are, from some rational perspective, incomprehensible and unsettling. Therefore, "riskiness" and "irreconcilability" are decidedly not a problem if we have broader rational reasons for entertaining a notion. Quantum mechanics has made this truth very easy for us to perceive today. In Kant's work, we see it play out, once again, in his analysis of organic form. The a priori concept of nature only permits phenomena to have external causes, while organic form seems internally purposive. To address this logical impasse, reflective reason adopts the "risky" notion of a supersensible substrate that, in some incomprehensible way, "transitions" between freedom and nature at the site of organic form.[86] Reason justifies this theoretically suspect move inasmuch as the supersensible "brings reason into harmony with itself."[87] In the present case, I simply argue that the reflective notion of inner grace performs a similar kind of damage control or "transitioning" within the broader economy of reason, this time to address the paradox of radical evil. Labeling it "irreconcilable" and "risky" is thus a bit disingenuous on Kant's part, whose third *Critique* provides a strong defense for such regulative ideas.

Conclusion

I have shown that Fichte and, in a more limited and reluctant way, Kant, participate in the "alliance" between reason and revelation that characterizes the German Enlightenment. In this spirit, Fichte argues for the possible necessity of revelation based on the potential failure of the moral law under certain circumstances. More precisely, he argues that historical and other contingent factors could diminish the appeal of the moral law to the point that moral development is out of the question without divine intervention. Kant, in contrast, defends the self-sufficiency of the moral law against all contingencies, but he takes Fichte's notion of moral failure even more seriously than Fichte does. Specifically, he argues—using an "inner" dispositional story and an "outer" social story—that human beings are innately and universally evil, such that one need not look for historical causes of their moral failure. Kant tells us we must think of the innate evil as a free choice, but he neither adequately explains how, in this case, freedom and the strict universality of evil can coexist. He also does not tell us how deliverance from this quasi-deterministic scenario is possible. Therefore, I have argued that reflective judgment may require us to postulate divine intervention in some form if we are to avoid terminal moral

86. Kant specifically says that the supersensible makes "possible the transition from the manner of thinking in accordance with the principles of [nature] to that in accordance with the principles of [freedom]"; *CPJ*, 5.176.

87. Ibid., 5.341.

discouragement. In the broader framework of reason, this "risky" idea is not only permissible, but valuable.

Recovering the Rhetorical Tradition: George Campbell's Sympathy and its Augustinian Roots

Brian Fehler
Texas Woman's University

T he year 1776 saw the production of two important documents of the Enlightenment: the US Constitution and George Campbell's *The Philosophy of Rhetoric*. Both documents were products of Enlightenment thought, and both demonstrate the conflicting attitudes in the era toward the rhetorical use of emotional appeals. Recent scholarship by John Witte examines the religious roots of the anti-emotionalist rhetoric expressed by Federalist politicians in the Constitutional era and in particular the influence of the Calvinist clergy of New England, with their "Puritan covenantal theory of ordered liberty and orderly pluralism."[1] Like the Federalists who were in charge of the new US government, the Calvinists of New England not only celebrated the victory achieved in the Revolution but also worked to ensure that the new American republic did not descend into the kind of chaos that later consumed revolutionary France. The Federalist politicians and the Calvinist clergy shared a suspicion of mass rule, of mobs enflamed by emotion. Politicians such as John Adams and James Madison were careful to acknowledge that the US Constitution was not too easily subjected to the whims of the mob, what Adams famously called "the tyranny of the majority" and what

---

1. John Witte, *The Reformation of Rights: Law, Religion, and Human Rights in Early Modern Calvinism* (Cambridge: Cambridge University Press, 2008), 278.

Madison called the "violence of faction."[2] For their part, the members of the Calvinist clergy of New England, the heirs of the tradition of Jonathan Edwards, who were known as the New Divinity men or Consistent Calvinists, hoped to do their part to restrain the emotions of the mob by advocating for religious revivals that were sober in tone, revivals in which participants conducted themselves with the decorum expected of responsible, self-governing citizens of a new republic.

On the other side of the Atlantic, rhetorician and Scottish divine George Campbell presented a rhetoric that privileged the place of emotions in communication. Campbell was concerned less with continuing the rhetorical tradition than with modernizing it. As Lois Agnew points out, Campbell wished both "to synthesize classical precepts and incorporate the contemporary insights of science into a groundbreaking philosophical approach."[3] Campbell's primary concern was integrating the classical rhetorical tradition and the new sciences of his own era into a rhetorical system that would serve students studying for the ministry.

In so many ways, Campbell's *The Philosophy of Rhetoric* (published as a whole in 1776 but presented and written in various forms over the course of many years) brought the rhetorical tradition into the new era of philosophy and learning and has been "lauded as the most important Enlightenment theory of rhetoric produced in Great Britain."[4] Campbell's contribution to the rhetorical tradition is most often noted for its incorporation of faculty psychology. Campbell's theory is, in fact, "a theory of rhetoric based on mental operations."[5] These mental operations, or faculties, must be addressed in order for a subject or an audience to be persuaded. For Campbell, the faculties, reflecting John

---

2. John Adams, *The Political Writings of John Adams: Representative Selections*, ed. George A. Peek (Cambridge, MA: Hackett Publishing, 2003), 154; and James Madison, "Federalist No. 10," in *The Federalist Papers*, ed. Clinton Rossiter (New York: Penguin, 2003), 73.

3. Lois Agnew, "The 'Perplexity' of George Campbell's Rhetoric: The Epistemic Function of Common Sense," *Rhetorica* 18, no. 3 (2000): 80.

4. Arthur E. Walzer, "On Reading George Campbell's 'Resemblance' and 'Vivacity' in the *Philosophy of Rhetoric*," *Rhetorica* 18, no. 3 (2000): 321.

5. Arthur E. Walzer, *George Campbell: Rhetoric in the Age of Enlightenment* (Albany: State University of New York Press, 2003), 40.

Locke's categories, are understanding, imagination, passion, and will. "The path to persuasion in Campbell's theory," Patricia Bizzell and Bruce Herzberg write, "passes through each of the faculties in turn."[6] Accordingly, an audience's understanding must be engaged, by facts or information, which results in conviction that the problem being discussed is a serious or relevant one. Then, an audience's imagination must be pleased, usually by examples of beauty or experience. Following that, an audience must have its passion stirred by emotional examples of sympathy and pathos. Finally, an audience's will must be moved, which a speaker achieves through vigor of written or spoken expression. For the first time in a major rhetorical treatise, Campbell introduces faculty psychology to a rhetorical treatise in English, and in his formulation of it he validates the use of emotion in rhetoric.

Campbell cannot be entirely credited with developing a process of faculty psychology from scratch; his ideas reflect the earlier work of Locke. Campbell's contribution to rhetoric results from his presenting faculty psychology, as it relates to communication, in what would become a popular textbook as well as a theoretical treatise: *The Philosophy of Rhetoric.* Similarly, Campbell was not alone among Enlightenment thinkers in privileging a sense of sympathy and emotional connection in human relations. Throughout history, various sources on sympathy can be identified, although these sources echo what Francis Hutcheson calls, in this case, benevolence, that "determination of our nature to study the good of others; or some instinct, antecedent to all reason from interest, which influences us to the love of others."[7] Lloyd Bitzer recognizes the philosophy of David Hume as a special influence on Campbell in terms of sympathy and other matters as well. Bitzer writes, "Major elements of Hume's view—including the primacy of imagination and feeling . . . were taken over by Campbell without significant modification." Bitzer further maintains that Campbell's view of sympathy, "that means by which one person communicates emotion to another," is essentially

6. Patricia Bizzell and Bruce Herzberg, eds., *The Rhetorical Tradition: Readings from Classical Times to the Present* (Boston: Bedford, 2001), 898.
7. Francis Hutcheson, *An Inquiry into the Original of Our Ideas of Beauty and Virtue* (London: J. Darby, 1726), 155.

222

Humean.[8] More recently, Dennis Bormann has suggested that Bitzer overemphasized Hume's influence on Campbell. Bormann looks further afield for influences on Campbell's work, across the English Channel, in fact, to the eighteenth-century French treatises on style and belletrism, "those popular works in France with which Campbell was so well acquainted" with their "emphasis on the Longinian sublime in literature and rhetoric."[9] Norman Fiering takes an even more extensive view, considering classicism as sources for Enlightenment notions of sympathy. Using interchangeably the terms *sympathy, humanity,* and *irresistible compassion,* Fiering suggests that Enlightenment thinkers "inherited from the ancient world many of the ingredients of the doctrine of irresistible compassion." He cites as sources Juvenal on compassion (as translated by Dryden in his 1693 edition of the *Satires*) and Cicero on the preference of avoiding cruelty (as presented by John Cockman in his 1699 translation of *De Officiis*).[10]

To this long line of antecedents of eighteenth-century sympathy, particularly in the way Campbell recognized the concept as important for rhetoric, this study suggests one additional source be added: St. Augustine's *De doctrina Christiana* (*On Christian Doctrine*).[11] Gerald Press recognizes that *De doctrina Christiana* "has long been considered an important text in the history of rhetoric because Book 4 has been judged to be the first Christian homiletic"; Douglas Ehninger, many years ago, concluded that Campbell's *The Philosophy of Rhetoric* "stands without challenge as one of the great classics in the field of rhetorical theory."[12] In terms of sacred rhetoric, *De doctrina Christiana* and *The Philosophy of Rhetoric* probably stand as the two most important contributions to understandings of sacred rhetoric by major rhetorical

8. Lloyd Bitzer, "Hume's Philosophy in George Campbell's 'Philosophy of Rhetoric,'" *Philosophy and Rhetoric* 2, no. 3 (1969): 140, 156.

9. Dennis R. Bormann, "George Campbell's *Cura Prima* on Eloquence—1758," *Quarterly Journal of Speech* 74, no. 1 (1988): 46.

10. Norman S. Fiering, "Irresistible Compassion: An Aspect of Eighteenth-Century Sympathy and Humanitarianism," *Journal of the History of Ideas* 37, no. 2 (1976): 196–97.

11. I am referencing an English translation of Augustine's work but refer to it by its Latin name, a practice common in Campbell's time.

12. Gerald A. Press, "*Doctrina* in Augustine's *De doctrina Christiana,*" *Philosophy and Rhetoric* 17, no. 2 (1984): 98; and Douglas Ehninger, "George Campbell and the Revolution in Inventional Theory," *Southern Speech Journal* 15, no. 4 (1950): 270.

theorists. This study not only suggests that Augustine's work serves as an important antecedent to Campbell's eighteenth-century notions of sympathy but also draws the conclusion that sympathy, although it might sometimes be found absent in secular rhetoric (such as Aristotle's), should be recognized as an important factor in Western sacred rhetorics.

As Bitzer, Bormann, and Fiering suggest, sympathy as a philosophical concept was well recognized by the time Campbell produced *The Philosophy of Rhetoric*. For Campbell, sympathy was especially important, as his aim was to produce a theory of communication, a theory to which a sense of emotional connection and compassion for preachers, congregations, audiences, and interlocutors was vital. Campbell's support of the validity of emotional appeals countered the anti-emotional attitude of the earlier Enlightenment philosopher Locke but allowed Campbell to establish the possibility of a sacred rhetoric in the age of reason that was both intellectually respectable and spiritually satisfying. Augustine's notion of *caritas* (brotherly love) can be seen as an antecedent of Campbell's rhetoric of emotion and sympathy. The importance of *caritas* in Augustine's rhetoric has been largely overlooked by scholars of rhetoric; by viewing *caritas* as a precursor to Campbell's more widely recognized reliance on sympathy, one will also begin to recognize and trace the importance of compassion in Western conceptions of sacred rhetoric.

Whereas Campbell wished to revitalize the rhetorical tradition by informing his work with findings of science and overlooking the formulaic sermon guides of the Middle Ages, Augustine, for his part, had wished to recover a Platonic search for truth in rhetoric and to reject the Second Sophistic of his day. Charles Baldwin recognizes Augustine's innovative spirit and suggests that Augustine, in fact, "begins rhetoric anew" and that Augustine's rhetoric "ignores sophistic" and goes "back over centuries of lore of personal triumph to the ancient idea of moving men to truth."[13] Baldwin places Augustine's rhetoric in the context of sophistic rhetoric of the day, and thus, given the excesses and

---

13. Charles Baldwin, "St. Augustine on Preaching," in *Essays on the Rhetoric of the Western World*, ed. Edward P. J. Corbett, James L. Golden, and Goodwin F. Berquist (Dubuque, IA: Kendall Hunt Publishing, 1990), 195.

flourishes of the Second Sophistic, Augustine's emphasis on truth and clarity seems especially distinctive. In the days of the Roman Republic, classical rhetoric had reached a zenith, as politicians and orators such as Cicero debated the issues of importance in people's lives. As the Roman Republic gave way to the Roman Empire, however, rhetoric's agonistic and useful role slipped into the background. Public debate was replaced by imperial decree. The practice of rhetoric did not altogether disappear in the Roman Empire, of course. The teachings of the Second Sophistic still maintained a role of entertainment and even social mobility, and the educational rhetoric of Quintilian proved valuable in private spheres. However, vigorous public debate declined.

The new rhetoric that Augustine proposed in his principal rhetorical work *De doctrina Christiana*, as Thomas Conley suggests, "continued to be read and copied . . . even during the darkest of the Dark Ages, because it made any other such treatise unnecessary, if not impossible to supersede."[14] In book 1, Augustine begins to establish his theory of *caritas*. Augustine makes the rather remarkable claim that no interpretation of scripture that advocates a spirit of goodwill and brotherly love is incorrect or deceptive, although it may be faulty. If a reader of scripture, Augustine writes, "draws a meaning from [scripture] that may be used for the building up of love, even though he does not happen upon the precise meaning . . . his error is not pernicious, and he is wholly clear from the charge of deception."[15] According to Augustine, no reading that advances a theory of brotherly love can be discounted, and the person who proposes such a "misreading" is likened to a traveler who takes a different road but reaches the "same place to which the [correct] road leads."[16] Later, Augustine clearly defines his use of the central terms of *caritas* and *cupiditas*. He writes:

> I mean by *caritas* that affection of the mind which aims at the enjoyment of God for His own sake, and the enjoyment of one's self and one's neighbor in subordination to God; by *cupiditas* I

---

14. Thomas Conley, *Rhetoric in the European Tradition* (Chicago: University of Chicago Press, 1994), 78.

15. Augustine, *On Christian Doctrine*, trans. J. F. Shaw (Boston: Benton, 1952), 635.

16. Ibid.

mean that affection of the mind which aims at enjoying one's self and one's neighbor, and other corporeal things, without reference to God.[17]

Augustine clearly distinguishes between *caritas* (brotherly love but also charity) and *cupiditas* (lust, cupidity). Gerald Schlabach suggests that the straightforwardness of Augustine's distinction between these two kinds of love actually masks an ambiguity between their definitions. Schlabach writes that "Augustine's very definition of Christian charity in *On Christian Doctrine* hints that love for God itself might not be quite so straightforward," and in order to define love of God, "Augustine had to do so in relation to other loves, including the false loves it was not."[18] For Schlabach, there is a certain uneasiness regarding Augustine's definition by negative—defining *caritas* by defining what it is not. At this point, Schlabach probably overlooks the fact that Augustine was trained as a rhetorician, that to define his terms was a necessary act, and that to define by negatives is really the only way he could define anything. In any case, philosophical uneasiness aside, Augustine sets up his terms, *caritas* and *cupiditas*, in a way that is important for his rhetoric and that foreshadows Campbell's work centuries later.

Hannah Arendt, whose doctoral dissertation *Love and Saint Augustine*, published in 1996, provides a discussion that is relevant to an understanding of Augustine's rhetoric on "love understood as craving" and on "the neighbor's relevance" to this love.[19] Considering *caritas* and *cupiditas*, Arendt makes the important observation that "they are distinguished by their objects, but they are not different kinds of emotion" (LSA 18). *Caritas* and *cupiditas*, in other words, are both "craving," the one for God, the other for the world. However, given that human beings must actually live in the world among other human beings, "would it not be better," Arendt asks, "to love the world in *cupiditas* and be at home? Why should we make a desert out of this world?" (LSA 19). Arendt hints at the answer: "The justification . . . can only lie in a deep dissatisfaction with what

---

17. Ibid., 662.

18. Gerald W. Schlabach, *For the Joy Set Before Us: Augustine and Self-Denying Love* (Notre Dame, IN: Notre Dame University Press, 2001), 30–31.

19. Hannah Arendt, *Love and St. Augustine*, ed. Joanna Scott and Judith Stark (Chicago: University of Chicago Press, 1996), 7 (hereafter cited in text as LSA).

the world can give its lovers" (LSA 19). Craving, in short, is not a "sinful" desire, and Augustine's reason that craving for God (*caritas*) is superior to craving for the world (*cupiditas*) is a pragmatic one: in craving for God, humanity finds the fulfillment, not the repression, of its desires, while in craving for the world, humanity finds only frustration. Arendt writes, "The reason that self-love, which starts with forsaking God, is wrong and never attains its goal is that such love" will always be outside of the person seeking love (LSA 20). In Augustine's thought, *caritas* is the only way to achieve the goal of happiness, and Augustine wanted humanity to achieve that goal.

Though the goal in Augustine's work is love of God, love of neighbor plays an integral role in a person's attainment of the love of God. Humanity's love of neighbor is perhaps the least understood concept in Augustine's *De doctrina Christiana*, and Arendt does a good job of clarifying love of neighbor as an attribute of *caritas*. Arendt writes that "love of neighbor is man's attitude toward his neighbor, which springs from *caritas*. It goes back to two basic relations: first, a person is to love his neighbor as God does; and second, he is to love his neighbor as he loves himself" (LSA 93). The topic of love of neighbor is important in understanding Augustine's rhetoric, for, although Arendt herself does not pursue this rhetorical line of inquiry, loving a neighbor must include attention to how to understand a neighbor, encounter a neighbor, and communicate with a neighbor. Ideally, as Arendt suggests, "for the lover who loves as God loves, the neighbor ceases to be anything but a creation of God" (LSA 94). This concept of all humanity as a creation of God existed in Christianity before Augustine, yet Augustine provides a new emphasis—a new communicative emphasis—on loving one's neighbor. When one loves a neighbor as a creation of God, *caritas* enables an ideal level of communication.

Augustine's notion of neighbor-love is seen by some critics as problematic. The problem is simply this: if Augustine commands Christians only to love—to use—neighbors in order to gain one's own salvation, the role of the neighbor is reduced to a usable "thing" (*res*). This problem is one recognized primarily by twentieth-century scholars. Helmut Baer, in "The Fruit of Charity," surveys and then rejects this line of criticism. Baer writes that, apparently, "when Augustine speaks of 'using' the neighbor, he offends our basic moral sensibilities by recommending what appears to be an instrumental treatment of the neighbor."[20] The controversy arises primarily from Augustine's use of the words *uti* (use) and *frui* (enjoy). Augustine advocates that people "use" their neighbors and "enjoy" God; neighbors can teach people much about love, yet even so, neighbors are only to be "used" for this knowledge, not "enjoyed."

Baer offers that scholars who suggest that Augustine intends "using someone" to mean something like it does in current, popular idiom do not understand the context of Augustine's discussion. Importantly, Baer points out, Augustine also suggests humans "use" Christ. Elsewhere in *De doctrina Christiana*, Baer writes, "*uti* is the key term for understanding the relationship between God and humanity. Human persons 'use' Christ to find their blessedness in God, or to speak more properly, God makes himself 'useful' to humanity through Christ."[21] In short, then, a comprehensive reading of the many passages in *De doctrina Christiana* that mention "*uti*" suggests that, "for Augustine, to 'use' another is to relate to that person in charity."[22]

In fact, the critics who suggest Augustine, in the *uti* passages, means something like our modern sense of the term "use" ignore one of the major themes of *De doctrina Christiana*: that love of neighbor is necessary for salvation and for present happiness. Moreover, Augustine would hardly contradict the Christian scriptures on so vital a matter, and, as Carol Harrison points out, although Augustine wrote a good deal about brotherly love, the idea is present throughout the New Testament. Harrison writes, "Christianity's distinctive emphasis upon the practice and rhetoric of love in its Scriptures and preaching allowed it to create a linguistic community in which the central message of faith could be communicated and understood in such a way that it was then practiced and lived."[23] In a way, friendships among Christian believers were strengthened because they believed those friendships

20. Helmut David Baer, "The Fruit of Charity: Using the Neighbor in *De doctrina Christiana,*" *Journal of Religious Ethics* 24, no. 1 (1996): 48.

21. Ibid., 53.

22. Ibid., 63.

23. Carol Harrison, *Augustine: Christian Truth and Fractured Humanity* (Oxford: Oxford University Press, 2000), 67.

enabled them to experience a love that reflected an even greater, more perfect love.

The interpretations that suggest Augustine meant something pernicious, simply overlook a long history of scholarship regarding Augustinian friendship. In order to counter the negative *uti* interpretations, Donald Burt looks at Augustine's letters to his own friends as well as references to passages in the *Confessions* where Augustine discusses friendship. Burt cites Augustine's letter to a friend, in which Augustine wrote that friends "spread no small comfort about them even in this life. . . . If such people are with us, then in large measure, our bitter trials become less bitter, the heavy burdens become lighter."[24] Undoubtedly, Augustine well understood the benefits of earthly friendships.

In addition to his rhetorical advice on preaching, a spirit of *caritas* can also be identified in Augustine's exegetical work. Augustine has been credited, since medieval times, with helping to establish rules of interpretation that allow allegorical readings of scripture. Discussions of Augustine's enormous influence in contributing to an allegorical understanding of the Bible do not often address Augustine's rhetorical and sympathetic preoccupations, however. Although it is true that Augustine's training as a rhetorician allowed him to recognize tropes and figures in the Bible, a recognition that some critics have felt seems sometimes strained, Augustine's influence as a rhetorician was not limited to tropological issues. Indeed, in Augustine's establishment of an allegorical hermeneutics, he hearkens back to Aristotle's rhetoric, which sought to identify the importance of arguing by probabilities as well as reasoning by certainties. It hearkens back, too, to the perhaps "purer" sophistry of the early generations of sophists, such as Isocrates and Gorgias, who sought to teach people how to live practically in the world—how to adapt to a changing society. While Augustine, the scathing critic of the Second Sophistic, would probably not wish to be associated with any form of sophistry, his efforts to establish an allegorical tradition of scriptural hermeneutics demonstrate his concern not only with the unchanging truth he believed was found in the Bible

---

24. Donald Burt, *Friendship and Society: An Introduction to Augustine's Practical Philosophy* (Grand Rapids, MI: Eerdmans, 1999), 59.

but also with ways in which biblical truth could be applied in a variety of ages and situations. In short, Augustine absolutely believed that the Bible contained God's truth; however, he would remain suspicious of humans who claimed to fully know that truth. Human nature, he felt, was simply too fraught with sinfulness. Rules could be set down, generalities proposed, and communities established that could do their best to ascertain the truth, but, in the end, the human agent would always be prone to error (and this is one reason why *caritas* was so important: it served as a safeguard against those who adopted a harmfully dogmatic hermeneutics).

Augustine's allegorical hermeneutics may be more revolutionary than scholars have long supposed, for while "ancient Christian allegorical readings of the Bible have often been regarded as the means by which interpreters translated the unique images and stories of the Bible into the abstractions of classical metaphysics and ethics," David Dawson writes, "Augustine's recommendations concerning how to interpret Scripture suggest that nonliteral translation ought to move in the opposite direction." That is, instead of "dissolving scriptural language into nonscriptural categories, allegorical reading should enable the Bible to refashion personal experience and cultural ideals by reformulating them in a distinctively Biblical idiom."[25] Dawson's claim presents an intriguing scenario, one that is important for an understanding of *caritas*.

In order that we do not miss the significance of Dawson's claim, it is important to draw out its implications, for these implications are also applicable to the work of Campbell. Although Augustine has been long credited for refashioning classical rhetoric—as Baldwin, among others, has noted—it is important to emphasize that Augustine's rhetoric was not *only* a refashioning. Instead, it is useful to consider that Augustine intended to create a wholly new rhetoric, and, being a rhetorician, Augustine understood that classical rhetoric could help him accomplish his aim. Augustine's reputation as a sacred rhetorician, then, should spring not only from his attempt to "save" some elements

---

25. David Dawson, "Sign Theory, Allegorical Reading, and the Motions of the Soul in *De doctrina Christiana*," in *De doctrina Christiana: A Classic of Western Culture*, ed. Duane Arnold and Pamela Bright (Notre Dame, IN: Notre Dame University Press, 1995), 123.

of classical rhetoric but also from his recognition of the rhetorical
situation in which he found himself. Dawson suggests that Augustine's
allegorical hermeneutics represent more than an attempt to make
scripture acceptable according to a classical standard. Indeed, we should
probably extend this notion to Augustine's entire rhetorical project,
for Augustine, in his writings, starts with the human condition (the
rhetorical situation) and then applies whatever intellectual traditions
are at his disposal to explain and clarify humanity's journey out of
an earthly rhetorical situation toward what Arendt calls "not-time," a
nonsituation—salvation. For this reason, long lists of oratorical and
interpretive rules should be learned only by students who are gifted in
this way. Augustine writes that "the rules and precepts" of oratory and
interpretation must be acquired "by those who can do so quickly."[26] For
Augustine, the ultimate expression of sympathy for fellow humans, and
of his rhetoric of *caritas*, was to bring listeners to Christian salvation—
no other act, for him, showed love so clearly.

In this way, perhaps, Augustine's rhetoric is pragmatic as well
as sympathetic; he wants his allegorical hermeneutics to illuminate
specific conditions of specific people's lives, not necessarily to confirm
eternal truths. Similarly, his advice to preachers in book 4 of *De
doctrina Christiana* displays this pragmatic bent; Augustine's rules
are there for guidance, but the preacher should remember that the
specific situation of a church or a person might cause certain rules to
be altered, amended, or discarded. David Tracy recognizes Augustine's
willingness to accept arguments that are not only eternal but also
adaptable. Tracy considers Augustine to be "the first great rhetorical
theologian" and *De doctrina Christiana* the first great statement of
rhetorical theology, for in *De doctrina Christiana* "one may find both
a classical reformulation of 'theology and culture' as well as a rhetoric
of both discovery and communication."[27]

John Schaeffer suggests a valuable reason for Augustine's acceptance
of the adaptability of interpretive rules. Augustine was, in short, "bending

---

26. Augustine, *On Christian Doctrine*, 453.
27. David Tracy, "Charity, Obscurity, Clarity: Augustine's Search for a True Rhetoric,"
in *Morphologies of Faith*, ed. Mary Gerhart and Anthony Yu (Atlanta, GA: Scholars Press,
1990), 124.

the rules" himself in many ways: by adapting classical rhetoric, by giving a new direction to allegorical hermeneutics, and by emphasizing a law of love based on *caritas*. Augustine's many efforts to "refashion" rhetoric for Christianity resulted from, in no small part, the transition from orality to literacy that occurred during Augustine's lifetime. Schaeffer suggests that book 4 of *De doctrina Christiana* is probably laying out advice for preachers to deliver sermons extemporaneously. In disavowing the Second Sophistic, then, Augustine is "returning to the orally based rhetoric of republican Rome," Schaeffer writes, "which he is adapting to a textually based religion attended by an emerging sense of interiority."[28] In this interpretation, Augustine's system of rhetoric must necessarily be highly adaptable, and this adaptability eschews rigid codification. "The paradox of Christianity in late antiquity," Schaeffer writes, "is that people were taught to believe in a written teaching that most could not read but only heard."[29] Although Schaeffer does not make this point—a point that would become more important in the Reformation, when attention was given to individual interpretation of scripture—Augustine's *caritas* was important in an age when few people were literate. *Caritas*, which demands self-humility, is something any interpreter of scriptures must practice, for in claiming a rigid dogmatic interpretation, a preacher could easily lead his (illiterate) flock into error. But above all, extemporaneous performances demand adaptability in order to ensure an audience's understanding. Schaeffer correctly recognizes that "an orator must sense the audience's thoughts and feelings and adjust to them."[30]

What prevents Augustine's orator, dedicated though he may be, from straying too far in his extemporaneous performances? What keeps the orator grounded in scriptural truth? The answer is that an orator must possess *caritas*. Here the importance of *caritas* becomes apparent. In an orally taught culture, the orator must be careful to avoid pride and error. This task would perhaps intimidate many orators, but Augustine provides assurance. Training in interpretation under respected teachers,

---

28. John Schaeffer, "The Dialectic of Orality and Literacy: The Case of Book 4 of Augustine's *De doctrina Christiana*," *PMLA* 111, no. 5 (1996): 1134.

29. Ibid., 1136.

30. Ibid., 1140.

coupled with a true spirit of *caritas*, will enable an orator to behave rightly, and even, after an orator has done his best, should he fail, if he acted in a spirit of love, God would forgive the failure. Thus *caritas* is not simply a virtue an orator must teach; it is a safeguard against preaching error.

Like Augustine, George Campbell was an adapter and an innovator of the rhetorical tradition. As Augustine proved innovative in his allegorical and rhetorical hermeneutics, Campbell would prove innovative in his studies of faculty psychology and motive. The times in which Campbell lived required him to be both an adapter and an innovator. By the time Campbell was born in Scotland, Enlightenment notions of truth and meaning had already begun to thrive both in the old world and the new. Campbell could not assume, as medieval and even Renaissance rhetoricians could, that his audience would understand the finer points of the Christian tradition. The age of reason had dawned, and adherents of religious dogma found themselves increasingly on the defensive. This age of reason saw the birth of many capable defenders of Christian theology, not the least of whom were Jonathan Edwards in America and Campbell in Scotland. Campbell and Edwards shared some similar characteristics. Both were well educated, impassioned ministers in the provinces of the British Empire. Both were influenced by Enlightenment philosophers, such as Locke, yet they rejected the primacy of the scientific method, believing that truth could be found through other sources, particularly through religious feeling and sensation. Campbell was driven to develop as complete a system of persuasion and motivation as he was capable of doing, "a tolerable sketch of the human mind," as he famously states in the introduction to his *The Philosophy of Rhetoric*.[31] In any event, Campbell was clearly more a theorist of the rhetorical tradition than Edwards or other ministers who practiced oratory with skill but never looked specifically to the history of rhetoric for information on effective preaching. Campbell remains a unique blend of rhetorician: a student of rhetoric and a rhetor—an oratorical practitioner. As both a practitioner

31. George Campbell, *The Philosophy of Rhetoric* (1841; repr., Delmar, NY: Scholars Facsimiles and Reprints, 1992): 2.

and theoretician, Campbell advocated an emotional connection and the spirit of sympathy as a foundation for rhetoric.

Campbell's *The Philosophy of Rhetoric*, a collection of lectures that were presented at Marischal College (where Campbell served as principal) and before the Aberdeen Philosophical Society (of which Campbell was a founding member) finally appeared in print in 1776, although the lectures were already well known. It should not be forgotten (as Corbett and Golden point out, and as Arthur Walzer does in *George Campbell: Rhetoric in the Age of Enlightenment*) that Campbell was a churchman—a reverend of the Church of Scotland. Campbell's interest in the sciences of human nature resulted from his curiosity to better understand the workings of what he believed to be one of God's great creations, the human mind. In addition, much of Campbell's advice on oratory was presented to support successful pulpit oratory, as evidenced by one of Campbell's other works, *Lectures on Pulpit Eloquence.*

Campbell's goal of creating a new sacred rhetoric for his times, however, did not permit him to accept all characteristics of faculty psychology as previously described by Locke. Campbell differed from Locke in an important area: Campbell, like Hutcheson in his philosophical treatises, maintained throughout his work the importance of sympathy as a motive. In doing so, Campbell demonstrated that on this topic he had more in common with St. Augustine than with his own near-contemporary Locke. Connecting the motive of sympathy to the broader category of emotional appeals, Beth Innocenti Manolescu writes, "For Augustine emotional appeals cure disorder; for Locke they cause it."[32] Whereas Augustine celebrated emotion and its connection to religious experience, Locke displayed, according to Gerald Cragg, an "almost pathological fear of religious emotion."[33] As a rhetorician concerned with religious propagation, Campbell recognized the importance of religious feeling, and, like Augustine, the central feeling for Campbell's rhetoric was also compassion.

---

32. Beth Innocenti Manolescu, "Religious Reasons for Campbell's View of Emotional Appeals in *Philosophy of Rhetoric*," *Rhetoric Society Quarterly* 37, no. 2 (2007): 160.

33. Gerald R. Cragg, *Reason and Authority in the Eighteenth Century* (Cambridge: Cambridge University Press, 1964), 10.

Campbell writes that sympathy "is not a passion but that quality of the soul which renders it susceptible of almost any passion, by communication from the bosom of another."[34] Unsurprisingly, because sympathy is a social quality moved by others, it is affected by the company it keeps. Campbell writes, "Sympathy may be greatly strengthened or weakened by the influence of connected passions. Thus love associates to it benevolence, and both give double force to sympathy. Hatred, on the contrary, associates to it malice, and destroys sympathy."[35] It is this view on the importance of sympathy, and of religious emotion generally, that allows Campbell to fall on the side of Augustine and revise an ancient rhetorical attitude toward pity. As far back as Aristotle, philosophers, including Cicero and Hobbes, recognized pity as, really, a self-reflection. For Aristotle, for example, pity is a "feeling of pain caused by the sight of some evil . . . which we might expect to befall ourselves."[36] For Campbell, however, pity is "a full participation by sympathy in the woes of others."[37] In this definition, sympathy provides the background quality of the soul on which the proper passion of pity plays out.

A genuine concern for the needs of others rather than for one's self, the importance of reaching out in sympathy, is a hallmark of Campbell's rhetoric. Thus Campbell accepts the Enlightenment notion of the importance of sympathy, and he brings that concern to rhetoric and communication. While he defines sympathy in his instructional lectures that compose *The Philosophy of Rhetoric*, Campbell also practiced what he preached in his public disputations. The most well-known of these in his day was Campbell's *A Dissertation on Miracles*, which was written in response to Hume's "On Miracles," a chapter in his *An Enquiry Concerning Human Understanding*. Hume had suggested that since miracles could not be subject to scientific validation, he himself could not believe in the biblical miracles. As mentioned previously, Bitzer draws many parallels between the work of Hume and Campbell and suggests that Hume was an important source for Campbell's work. In "Some 'Common Sense' about Campbell, Hume, and Reid," Dennis

---

34. Campbell, *Philosophy*, 131.

35. Ibid.

36. Aristotle, *Rhetoric*, trans. Rhys Roberts (Mineola, NY: Dover Publications, 2004), 77.

37. Campbell, *Philosophy*, 131.

Bormann takes further exception with Bitzer's claims.[38] Bormann suggests that Campbell and his contemporaries saw Campbell's work in frequent opposition to Hume's work and more in line with the philosophy of Thomas Reid.[39] Campbell, in any case, took up the debate with his fellow Scotsman Hume. In doing so, Campbell demonstrated what he had declared in *The Philosophy of Rhetoric*—that reasonable debate was best practiced when interlocutors engaged in a feeling of sympathy for one another.

In *Dissertation*, Campbell writes that the sheer weight of evidence— moral evidence—supported the biblical accounts of miracles. In defending miracles, Campbell drew on the importance of testimony. It would be likely, he admitted, that miracles would be doubtful if only a few people testified to their occurrence, but the numbers of people in the Bible who witnessed miracles were too substantial to overlook. In reasoning from analogy, Campbell suggested miracles, like all religious revelation, were similar to accounts of any historical record. For example, one did not have to scientifically demonstrate that the Norman Conquest occurred. Written records, in such cases, are valuable and often proof enough.

Campbell certainly begins *Dissertation* in a spirit of charity and sympathy. He writes, in the very first sentence of what he calls his "advertisement," that "it is not the only, nor even the chief design of these sheets, to refute the reasoning and objections of Mr. Hume with regard to miracles: the chief design of them is to set the principal argument for Christianity in its proper light."[40] The whole of what would be called the Campbell–Hume debate on miracles was conducted in a respectful, genteel fashion. To be sure, Campbell disagreed with Hume's argument that miracles could not be verified because they could not be reproduced. Campbell felt Hume's empiricism too rigorous and narrow, but Campbell nonetheless counted himself among the many admirers of Hume's thought. This debate, then,

---

38. Dennis R. Bormann, "Some 'Common Sense' about Campbell, Hume, and Reid: The Extrinsic Evidence," *Quarterly Journal of Speech* 71, no. 4 (1985): 395–421.

39. Ibid.

40. George Campbell, *A Dissertation on Miracles* (London: Thomas Tegg, 1824), iii (hereafter cited in text as DM).

carried out in the name of the skeptic and the divine, was a debate inspired by the writings of the two men, although Campbell and Hume did not really participate in the debate after their respective works were published. Hume, in fact, did not even feel it necessary to respond to Campbell in later editions of *An Enquiry Concerning Human Understanding*, although he revised the work in other ways. Campbell did include letters exchanged among himself, Hume, and belletristic rhetorician Hugh Blair on the subject of miracles in later editions of *A Dissertation*. To the end, Campbell remained an enthusiastic supporter of Hume's overall body of work, and Hume remained complimentary, in a general way, toward Campbell's objections, although Hume never discussed them specifically.

Interestingly, Campbell's *Dissertation* is much longer than the essay it responds to; the *Dissertation* runs to more than 123 pages, whereas Hume's essay, which made up part 10 of his *An Enquiry Concerning Human Understanding*, filled fewer than 40 pages. Campbell's primary contention against Hume—that human knowledge consists of more than the empirical scientific method—anticipated twentieth-century notions of knowing, such as new rhetorical and metaphorical ideas. In fact, much of Campbell's *Dissertation* consists of examples and extensions of this claim: "The whole [of Hume's argument] is built upon a false hypothesis. . . . Testimony has a natural and original influence on belief. . . . Accordingly youth, which is inexperienced, is credulous; age, on the contrary, is distrustful. Exactly the reverse would be the case, were this author's [Hume's] doctrines just" (DM 38). Hume, in his essay, had hoped to show that doubt is the primary act of the mind, the Cartesian principle that only that which could not be doubted should be believed. Campbell held that assent, rather than doubt, was prior in the human mind, an idea Cardinal Newman would later develop. In Campbell's *Dissertation*, testimony replaces Hume's empiricism as the primary way in which humans are convinced, the surest way in which we come to know.

Walzer suggests that Campbell's *Dissertation* was the most highly regarded of the refutations to Hume's "Of Miracles" because Campbell "raised the issue to a general philosophical issue—the epistemological question of the validity of testimony."[41] Campbell did not produce an invective in response to "Of Miracles," a work considered in many quarters at the time to be an attack on Christianity. Instead, Campbell responded reasonably, suggesting that Hume's definition of human knowledge was not sufficiently capacious. Campbell's work, especially *The Philosophy of Rhetoric* and *A Dissertation on Miracles*, provides examples of a rational Christian thinker attempting to demonstrate the reasonability of religious faith in an era of increasing Enlightenment skepticism. Perhaps for this reason, of all his published works, Campbell instructed that only *Dissertation* be mentioned in his eulogy.

In addition to *Philosophy* and *Dissertation*, Campbell penned two other major works, both also reflecting the influence of the *caritas*–sympathy tradition. The first of these two works is Campbell's two-volume translation of the Gospels. In the preface to this work, Campbell, always eager to provide insight into his motives for publication, defends his decision to produce a gospel translation when many other versions were already available. In Campbell's estimation, simply, many English translations did not seem quite right. "As far back as 1750," Campbell writes in his original preface to the 1788 translation, he began to take "notice of such proposed alterations on the manner of translating the words of the original [Greek New Testament], as appeared not only defensible in themselves, but to yield a better meaning, or at least to express the term with more perspicuity and energy."[42] Campbell the rhetorician, even in his early days as a parish pastor, recognized certain deficiencies of language, deficiencies he set out to improve (and one should not be surprised that one of Campbell's primary aims was increased *perspicuity*, a term he discusses at length in *The Philosophy of Rhetoric*). Although Campbell seemed to anticipate that some people would find his rendering superfluous, he hoped that his work would be given a fair reading. For, he writes it had been one of the goals of his life to "give a patient hearing and impartial examination to reason and argument, from what corner soever it appears," and Campbell wished for his readers to return this favor (FG 2). His motivation for producing

41. Walzer, *George Campbell*, 10.

42. George Campbell, *The Four Gospels* (Boston: Wells and Wait, 1811), ii (hereafter cited in text as FG).

this work, and other works, is simple, Campbell insisted: always to seek the "love of Truth" (FG iv). Campbell expected that the reader would realize that his translation was an effort to clarify the truth of the Gospels.

Campbell astutely realized that an unoriginal work such as a translation (unoriginal in the sense that a translation is a rendering of some work that already exists) nonetheless comprises an argument. Living in an age of proofs and warrants, Campbell understood that even the seemingly objective, value-free acts of literal translation and of philological study were rhetorical enterprises. Campbell concedes that the "essential quality of philology" lies in the ability to "trace such changes [in language use] with accuracy" (FG xv). To trace with accuracy involves judgment calls and choices of value, the limits of which are determined by audience, for "when a change is made from what people have long been accustomed to, it is justly expected that the reason, unless it is obvious, should be assigned" (FG xv). This attention to a reader's response, even in the matter of translation, demonstrates Campbell's concern with building sympathy. "Sympathy," for Campbell, writes Silvia Xavier, "identifies speaker with auditor."[43] Any communication, be it an original sermon or a translation of an ancient text, Campbell believed, required a writer or speaker to make rhetorical choices with attention to building sympathy.

Another of Campbell's works, *Lectures on Pulpit Eloquence*, deals directly with the topic of sacred rhetoric and demonstrates how sympathy can be applied to teaching. This work, as its title suggests, consists of lectures Campbell produced for his students at Marischal College. Campbell understood that not all of his students wished to engage in a close study of rhetorical theory, quibbling with Aristotle, for example, as Campbell himself did, over the usefulness of the enthymeme. For these students, preparing for parish work, their teacher wished to lecture on the practical nature of rhetoric. (One recalls Augustine's insistence, in Book 4 of *De doctrina Christiana*, that a student, should he be unable to grasp the theoretical implications of rhetoric, must move on to practical matters,

---

43. Silvia Xavier, "Engaging George Campbell's 'Sympathy' in the Rhetoric of Charlotte Forten and Ann Plato, African-American Women of the Antebellum North," *Rhetoric Review* 24, no. 4 (2005): 440.

for a preacher's cause is sacred, but his time is scarce.) Walzer recognizes Campbell's attempts to reach out to students in plain, practical language and suggests that of all Campbell's works, *Lectures on Pulpit Eloquence* "is written in a readable, collegial style—creating a professional stance in which the assumed difference between the professor and student is a matter of experience only."[44] Campbell was sensitive enough regarding audience to know that the essays on rhetoric that he presented before the Aberdeen Philosophical Society (published as *The Philosophy of Rhetoric*) were too theoretical in nature to suit the practical needs of the students at Marischal. Campbell, who had reached out in sympathy to his intellectual peer David Hume in *A Dissertation on Miracles*, approached his students in a simpler, but just as sympathetic, manner.

This is not to say that Campbell lowered his intellectual standards in his lectures to his students. To do so would have represented a merely shallow view of sympathy. Instead, one must conclude that, in fact, Campbell's divinity students received a solid rhetorical education. In the twelve lectures that appear in *Lectures on Pulpit Eloquence*, Campbell touches upon many valuable topics. In the introductory lecture, he provides a brief history of the discipline, claiming, as he does in *The Philosophy of Rhetoric*, that his contemporary rhetoriticians have made little improvements on the classical rhetoric of Aristotle, Cicero, and Quintilian. In this lecture, too, Campbell insists, as does Augustine, that "knowing the truth of the gospels" is insufficient if one cannot also effectively proclaim that truth.[45] In lecture 6, which deals with the composition rather than the delivery of sermons, Campbell reveals his fondness for a vivid image, insisting that a powerful demonstrative sermon must be "almost equal in vivacity and vigour with the perceptions of sense."[46] Campbell's concern for vivacity is apparent throughout the lectures. Vivacity and vigor are important in Campbell's lectures for a practical reason: the preacher must gain and maintain an audience's attention. In lecture 7, Campbell suggests that a "good choice [illustration] may contribute previously to rouse attention, and even

44. Walzer, *George Campbell*, 118.

45. George Campbell, *Lectures on Pulpit Eloquence* (London: John Bumpus Company, 1824), 152.

46. Ibid., 238.

to put the hearers in a proper frame for the subject to be discoursed on as well as to keep their minds in the time of preaching from wandering from the subject."[47] In this way, effective rhetorical choice and illustration are ways of reaching out in sympathy to an audience or congregation. In taking a look at these lectures, a reader familiar with *The Philosophy of Rhetoric* will recognize typical Campbellian topics, such as the distinction of will and of passion and of other allusions to faculty psychology, while gaining a fuller understanding of the practical, sympathetic aims of Campbell's rhetorical endeavors.

Of the various sources recognized as ingredients of eighteenth-century sympathy, Augustine's notion of *caritas* should be recognized as one, particularly when considering the rhetorical work of Campbell. Neither Augustine nor Campbell, with their wide-ranging interests, was a rhetorician only, of course. Jeffrey Suderman, for one, laments that Campbell's original works (with the exception of *The Philosophy of Rhetoric*) are studied too little today by scholars other than historians of rhetoric because most of the current scholarship on Campbell is produced by rhetoricians.[48] Although both men wrote on a variety of subjects—theology, education, and ethics for Augustine and criticism and the New Testament for Campbell—their interests certainly centered on finding the best way to communicate the Christian beliefs they both held. Undoubtedly, it is because Augustine and Campbell were interested in so many things that the rhetorics they produced have been recognized and studied for so long; Campbell and Augustine's rhetorical treatises, in other words, were not merely formulaic textbooks, as were many of the homiletics texts of the nineteenth century. Of course, because of the variety of topics Augustine and Campbell addressed, their treatises have been read by many people other than preachers-in-training. Their audiences have been Christian and non-Christian alike, resulting in a richer field of scholarly response from both.

Still, we must recognize that Augustine's *De doctrina Christiana* and Campbell's *The Philosophy of Rhetoric* are special kinds of rhetorical treatises; they are sacred rhetorics and probably the most important

---

47. Ibid., 268.

48. Jeffrey M. Suderman, *Orthodoxy and Enlightenment: George Campbell in the Eighteenth Century* (Montreal: McGill Queen's University Press, 2001), xiii.

contributions of their kind to the larger rhetorical tradition. Although Augustine's and Campbell's works are separated by centuries, the status of *De doctrina Christiana* and *The Philosophy of Rhetoric* as significant sacred rhetorics helps us to make some generic comments regarding the concerns of Western sacred rhetorics through the centuries. In recent years, scholarly attention to sacred rhetorics has increased, evidenced by Laurent Pernot's plenary address at the International Society for the History of Rhetoric. In his address, Pernot claimed that "we are today witnessing the return of religion. As the French writer and statesman André Malraux predicted, the twenty-first century would be religious. This is why it is important—and perhaps why it is the duty of academics and intellectuals—to find new ways of thinking about religion in a world where unthinking and depraved uses of religion can be dangerous."[49] In a similar way, Luigi Spina, echoing Pernot, claims, "We are today witnessing the return of religion . . . and we are today witnessing also the return of rhetoric."[50] Other recent works look more specifically at generic concerns of specific works of sacred rhetoric, such as Paddy Bullard's commentary on Jonathan Swift's pulpit advice. Though Swift is not often considered in the realm of sacred rhetoric, Bullard demonstrates the value of Swift's pulpit commentary and emphasizes that the "most consistent feature of Swift's sermons and of his writings about sacred eloquence is this emphasis on conciliation and mutual attentiveness."[51] Old as the tradition of sacred rhetoric is, scholarly attention to the field, as a subset of the larger rhetorical tradition, has grown especially lively in recent decades, as Bullard's work shows, as texts from the past are reconsidered in light of their contributions to sacred rhetoric.

This study's examination of Augustine and Campbell demonstrates that more can be learned about the interests and limits of sacred rhetoric by looking at figures squarely in the sacred rhetoric tradition. In both Augustine's *De doctrina Christiana* and Campbell's *The Philosophy of Rhetoric*, we have been able to identify the *caritas*–sympathy tradition

---

49. Laurent Pernot, "The Rhetoric of Religion," *Rhetorica* 24, no. 3 (2006): 236.

50. Luigi Spina, "Fall and Rise of Rhetoric and Religion," *Rhetorica* 26, no. 3 (2008): 214.

51. Paddy Bullard, "Pride, Pulpit Eloquence, and the Rhetoric of Jonathan Swift," *Rhetorica* 30, no. 3 (2012): 276.

as an important element of these two treatises, and in so doing, we have been able to recognize *caritas*–sympathy as not only an important element of Christian theology but of Christian sacred rhetoric as well.

American Unitarians and the George B. English Controversy

Bradley Kime
Utah State University

*You seem not to have heard of the book which engages all the attention
here at present;—Mr. English's apology for leaving his profession. You will
have heard of it, however, before you receive this,—for it will pass like
wildfire through the country; and like that too it will flash, and crackle,
and sparkle, and dazzle, and amaze for a moment, and then go out, or
be put out.*

—*Henry Ware Sr.*[1]

In late September 1813, a Harvard graduate named George Bethune
English published an attack on the historical evidences of Christianity titled *The Grounds of Christianity Examined, by Comparing
the New Testament with the Old.*[2] English denied the relevance of miracles and argued that Jesus's claims to divine authority hinged solely on
his fulfillment of Messianic prophecies. Only by twisting such prophecies beyond their obvious meanings, English argued, could Christians

---

1. Henry Ware Sr. to Henry Ware Jr., 20 October 1813, in *Memoir of the Life of Henry
Ware, Jr.*, ed. John Ware, vol. 1 (Boston: James Munroe, 1846), 63.
2. George Bethune English, *The Grounds of Christianity Examined, by Comparing the
New Testament with the Old* (Boston: privately printed, 1813).

RAE, vol. 5, 2015
Copyright © 2015 AMS Press, Inc

conceivably claim that Jesus fulfilled them. In their own day, the apostles and Evangelists did just that—misapplying the prophecies to Jesus either out of ignorance or dishonesty. In either case, English concluded, the New Testament was not inspired, Jesus was not the prophesied Messiah, and the traditional historical evidences—miracles and prophecy—could not support the claims of Christianity.

The controversy English ignited has long since been forgotten, true to the senior Ware's prediction, but during an important moment in American Unitarian history it held Boston's collective attention and engaged some of the city's most talented preachers and scholars. The reverends William Ellery Channing and Samuel Cary published the first hasty rebuttals, but these only fanned the flames. In English's heated responses to both ministers, his confidence appeared unshaken. The *General Repository and Review* added its own critique and alluded eagerly to a forthcoming work that would finally "put out" the fire. In August 1814, the young Edward Everett's five-hundred-page monument, *A Defence of Christianity*, decisively ended the debate.[3]

Although several broader works include brief synopses of the George B. English controversy, the full story has never been explored.[4] Historians have, unfortunately, often dismissed the importance of the controversy, seeing it as merely a parochial rehashing of

---

3. Edward Everett, *A Defence of Christianity, Against the Work of George B. English, A. M., entitled The Grounds of Christianity Examined, by Comparing the New Testament with the Old* (Boston: Cumming and Hilliard, 1814).

4. The most well-known account, although not the most informative, is Paul Revere Frothingham, *Edward Everett: Orator and Statesman* (Boston: Houghton Mifflin, 1925), 28–30. The most insightful account is included in Jerry Wayne Brown, *The Rise of Biblical Criticism in America, 1800–1870* (Middletown, CT: Wesleyan University Press, 1969), 36–38. The most inclusive is Albert Post, *Popular Freethought in America: 1825–1850* (New York: Columbia University Press, 1943), 29–31. Others include Stuart Horn, "Edward Everett and American Nationalism" (PhD diss., The City University of New York, 1972), 41–44; Richard H. Popkin, *Disputing Christianity: The 400-Year-Old Debate over Rabbi Isaac Ben Abraham of Troki's Classic Argument* (Amherst, NY: Humanity Books, 2007), 29–31; and Irving H. Bartlett, "Edward Everett Reconsidered," *The New England Quarterly* 69, no. 3 (1996): 431. The preceding Henry Ware Sr. epigraph illustrates the paucity of primary research on the controversy. Frothingham was the first to use the quote but mistakenly attributed it to Henry Ware *Jr.* rather than *Sr.*, his father. Subsequent accounts of the controversy have copied the quote and its mistaken attribution from Frothingham. See, for example, Popkin, *Disputing Christianity*, 29.

eighteenth-century contests. And, to some extent, it was. A century before English's publication, Deist and Christian scholars in Britain had debated the historical evidences of the Bible in scores of volumes.[5] The Boston controversialists drew from this Enlightenment tradition extensively (and in English's case, unscrupulously). Thus, one historian has written that the lengthy efforts of Everett and others to refute English "finally seemed a bit ludicrous, since [English] had simply lifted large portions" from other Deist works.[6] But neither English nor his opponents claimed that his central arguments were new, and yet, Everett and others saw purpose in writing lengthy rebuttals of English's work.

The significance of the controversy lay not in new arguments but in a new context. In 1813, Boston Congregationalists were dividing over major tenets of the establishment's Calvinist (Reformed) orthodoxy.[7] Liberal Christians had come to reject these tenets, particularly the Trinity and substitutionary Atonement, in favor of a Unitarian God and an essentially Arian Jesus.[8] They had also made the earliest efforts

---

5. Diego Lucci, *Scripture and Deism: The Biblical Criticism of the Eighteenth-Century British Deists* (New York: Peter Lang, 2008).

6. Cynthia Stokes Brown, "The American Discovery of the German University: Four Students at Göttingen, 1815–1822" (PhD diss., Johns Hopkins University, 1964), 38. For another similar assessment, see Eugene Robert Chable, "A Study of the Interpretation of the New Testament in New England Unitarianism" (PhD diss., Columbia University, 1955), 104.

7. For useful accounts of the American Unitarian controversy, see Conrad Wright, "The Election of Henry Ware: Two Contemporary Accounts, Edited with Commentary," *Harvard Library Bulletin* 17 (1969): 245–78; Conrad Wright, "The Controversial Career of Jedidiah Morse," *Harvard Library Bulletin* 31 (1983): 64–87; Charles C. Forman, "Elected Now by Time," in *A Stream of Light: A Sesquicentennial History of American Unitarianism*, ed. Conrad Wright (Boston: Unitarian Universality Association, 1975), 3–32; and Sydney E. Ahlstrom and Jonathan S. Carey, eds., introduction to *American Reformation: A Documentary History of Unitarian Christianity* (Middletown, CT: Wesleyan University Press, 1985), 3–42. For the controversy's eighteenth-century roots, see Conrad Wright, *The Beginnings of Unitarianism in America* (Boston: Starr King Press, 1955). For a revisionist account emphasizing the impact of Joseph Priestley and English Unitarianism, see J. D. Bowers, *Joseph Priestley and English Unitarianism in America* (University Park: The Pennsylvania State University Press, 2007), 151–204.

8. On this, David Robinson echoes Daniel Walker Howe's *The Unitarian Conscience: Harvard Moral Philosophy 1805–1861* (Cambridge, MA: Harvard University Press, 1970). Robinson has noted that "the name 'Unitarian' has long suggested that the dominant idea among the liberal Congregationalists was a rejection of Trinitarian doctrine, when in fact the stress on moral culture and the corresponding rejection of innate depravity were

to understand and appropriate higher biblical criticism from Germany, which they used to ground their theology in what they saw as defensible New Testament history.[9] English's public opponents were all prominent liberal Christians and, given the growing rift in Congregationalism, they were eager to prove that a historically grounded Unitarian faith was more defensible than a Christianity burdened with the theological accretions of Calvinism. Boston's homegrown heretic gave liberals the opportunity to demonstrate that they could defeat infidelity and defend Christianity in ways the conservatives could not.

Participants on both sides of the George B. English controversy drew from the previous century's Deist debates, but they used the works produced during those debates to engage in the emerging Unitarian conflict. In doing so, they highlighted an important transition in American religious discourse—from general defenses of Christianity to debates about which forms of Christianity (liberal or conservative) were most defensible in the face of long-standing rationalist critiques. English and his opponents also participated in laying the groundwork for another later transition toward the transcendentalist thought of figures like Emerson and Theodore Parker. Unitarians' preoccupation with historical evidences, exemplified by Everett and his colleagues, fed transcendentalists' disillusionment with traditional Christianity and their subsequent radical insistence on immediate revelatory experience,

---

the defining impulses of that tradition"; *The Unitarians and the Universalists* (Westport: Greenwood Press, 1985), 29. Nevertheless, "to the orthodox, the rejection of the Trinity seemed to be the most heinous of the liberal crimes"; Robinson, *Unitarians*, 29. Thus, in the context of controversy, like the George B. English debate, defensiveness toward orthodox criticism rhetorically elevated Trinitarianism above other disputed doctrines. See also Sydney E. Ahlstrom and Jonathan S. Carey, eds., *An American Reformation: A Documentary History of Unitarian Christianity* (Middletown, CT: Wesleyan University Press, 1985), 35.

9. For historical evidences and biblical criticism in the context of early New England Unitarianism, see Michael J. Lee, *The Erosion of Biblical Certainty: Battles Over Authority and Interpretation in America* (New York: Palgrave Macmillan, 2013); Brown, *Biblical Criticism*; Howe, *Unitarian Conscience*, 45–92; Chable, "Interpretation of the New Testament"; Elizabeth Hurth, *In His Name: Comparative Studies in the Quest for the Historical Jesus* (Frankfurt: Peter Lang, 1989); Theodore Dwight Bozeman, *Protestants in an Age of Science: The Baconian Ideal and Antebellum American Religious Thought* (Chapel Hill: The University of North Carolina Press, 1977); and E. Brooks Holifield, *Theology in America: Christian Thought from the Age of the Puritans to the Civil War* (New Haven, CT: Yale University Press, 2003), 159–96.

fostering a new transatlantic conversation; Unitarians, drawing from and debating English Deism and German higher criticism, so prominently displayed in the George B. English controversy, would help give rise to American transcendentalist engagement with English romanticism and German idealism—an important nineteenth-century reverberation of Enlightenment religious discourse in America.[10]

Although debates similar to the English controversy had engrossed those on both sides of the Atlantic in the previous century, a new context meant that English's book was "indeed a new thing," as Cary put it.[11] English's attacks on Christianity were, as another reviewer wrote, "entitled to the bad distinction of being the first original works of this character, ever published in New England."[12] Exploring the controversy within its New England context and in relation to broader movements in religious thought will illuminate how the supposedly superfluous responses to this forgotten figure were a timely demonstration of Unitarian strength.

George English and *The Grounds of Christianity Examined*

George Bethune English graduated from Harvard in 1807. He was an exceptional student—much like his future foe, Edward Everett.[13] He was

10. For information on the role of Everett and others in Unitarian historicism and the subsequent transcendentalist discontent, see Elizabeth Hurth, "Sowing the Seeds of 'Subversion': Harvard's Early Göttingen Students," in *Studies in the American Renaissance,* ed. Joel Myerson (Charlottesville: University of Virginia Press, 1992), 91–106. For a discussion regarding transcendentalist engagement with romanticism and idealism as an outgrowth of Unitarian engagement with Enlightenment scholarship and higher criticism, see Philip F. Gura, *American Transcendentalism: A History* (New York: Hill & Wang, 2007). For an exploration of Emerson's engagement with European thought, see Patrick J. Keane, *Emerson, Romanticism, and Intuitive Reason* (Columbia: University of Missouri Press, 2005).

11. Samuel Cary, *Review of a Book Entitled: "The Grounds of Christianity Examined, by Comparing the New Testament with the Old, by George Bethune English, A. M."* (Boston: Isaiah Thomas, 1813), 32.

12. "Article 9," *General Repository and Review* 4 (October 1813): 299–300. Note: The October issue was not actually published until November.

13. English and Everett were the top two Boylston Prize winners in 1812 for their respective dissertations. See "Intelligence: Harvard College," *The General Repository and Review* 2 (October 1812): 392.

also noted for his eccentricities by nearly all who mentioned him.[14] He studied law after graduating and gained admittance to the bar of Suffolk but never practiced. A fellow law student who lived with English during his school years later wrote a brief newspaper article about him, recalling that his religious opinions had been deeply unsettled. English had consequently studied the historical evidences of Christianity extensively and told his roommate, "If my understanding were once convinced, nothing would defer me from devoting my life to the cause. I would study divinity to-morrow."[15]

Eventually, English's understanding was convinced. Immediately after being admitted to the bar, English returned to Harvard to study divinity for three years. According to his description in the introduction to *Grounds of Christianity*, he became a believer in the religion of the New Testament for a time, after "a sufficient examination of its evidence for a divine origin."[16] On completing his divinity studies, he received his license to preach from the Boston Association of Ministers; but his preaching was, by most accounts, not popular. At some point, in the basement of the Harvard library, English discovered what he believed were some lesser-known arguments against the Christian evidences. After a thorough examination, he felt "finally, very reluctantly," as he put it, "compelled to feel persuaded, by proofs he could neither refute nor evade," that the New Testament contradicted the Old Testament, the foundation on which it claimed to build, and, therefore, Christianity could not be true.[17]

English's emphasis on his "understanding" being "convinced" and his mind being "compelled . . . by proofs" reflected the epistemological assumptions underlying the debate. E. Brooks Holifield had noted that, in relation to conversion and faith, it was "commonplace" for "[earlier] Protestant thought to distinguish intellectual assent from a heartfelt consent made possible by the spirit."[18] But, as James Turner has written,

---

14. See, for example, "Ploughboy Summary," *The Plough Boy, and Journal of the Board of Agriculture* (December 10, 1822): 218.

15. "George B. English," *Christian Philanthropist* (July 30, 1822): 48.

16. English, *Grounds of Christianity*, xii.

17. Ibid.

18. Holifield, *Theology in America*, 110.

after over a century of defending the reasonableness of Christianity from Deist arguments, "'belief' gravitated toward the connotation it had for Deists: intellectual assent to a definable proposition."[19] The English debate presupposed this equation of faith with intellectual assent to logical propositions.[20] With a convinced mind and an Englishtenment insistence on intellectual honesty, English believed he was obligated not only to renounce Christianity and leave the ministry but also to publish his reasons for doing so.

However, the timing of English's discovery in the Harvard library fostered skepticism about his motives. Paul Revere Frothingham, in his brief 1925 account, suggested that English left the pulpit because he was not succeeding in the ministry and then, "partly perhaps in pique," published his "attack upon the Christian claims."[21] In contrast, English claimed that his honest discovery came first and his departure from the ministry second. English actually went to several ministers, including Cary and Channing, before publishing *Grounds of Christianity*. While still uncertain and still a minister, English presented them with his concerns and a manuscript of his book, but he received no satisfactory answers or counsel. Instead, he heard false rumors circulating that he was an atheist. English claimed that only then did he publish his book. Neither Cary nor Channing ever refuted that claim. But regardless of whether his stated motives were sincere, substantial plagiarisms his opponents later uncovered in his book ensured that questions about his personal motives would always plague his public arguments.

English's central argument was that Jesus could only be the Christ—the Messiah—if he had fulfilled Messianic prophecies. The New Testament's authors themselves, English argued, always proved the truth of Christianity from Old Testament prophecies, not from miracles, and not from other evidences. Even Jesus himself, English noted, told his disciples after his resurrection, "All things must be fulfilled which were written in the law of Moses, and in the Psalms, and

---

19. James Turner, *Without God, Without Creed: The Origins of Unbelief in America* (Baltimore: The Johns Hopkins University Press, 1985), 103.

20. Ibid.

21. Frothingham, *Everett*, 28.

in the Prophets concerning him."[22] Fulfillment of Messianic prophecy, then, was the only valid evidence of Jesus's authority, miracles notwithstanding, "for miracles can never render a foundation valid, which is in itself invalid; [and] can never make a false inference true."[23]

After narrowing the evidential grounds of Christianity to prophecy, English traced the characteristics of the Messiah as prophesied in the Old Testament. First, Christ was to be a "mighty monarch"[24] who would conquer Israel's enemies and establish a universal reign of peace and happiness; Israel was to be established as the seat of Christ's government. Second, Christ was to be a descendant of David and was to rule from Jerusalem. Third, English emphasized, the restoration of Israel would be contemporaneous with Christ's mortal manifestation. In contrast, English argued, the historical Jesus's kingdom was "not of this world."[25] The Jews, far from being gathered, were scattered and oppressed for eighteen centuries after Jesus's death. Jesus was not called by the name of David and he never reigned in Jerusalem. "Indeed," English wrote, "nothing seems to be more dissimilar than the character of the Messiah as given by the Hebrew prophets, and that of Jesus of Nazareth."[26]

With such obvious disparities between the two figures, English asked why New Testament writers tried to prove Jesus's authority by quoting inapplicable Old Testament passages. The standard defense was what English referred to as "the principle of accommodation."[27] Christian scholars argued that the apostles and Evangelists justifiably "accommodated" Old Testament passages to New Testament events even though

---

22. English, *Grounds of Christianity*, 1–5.

23. Ibid., 7.

24. Ibid., 13.

25. Ibid., 21.

26. English, *Grounds of Christianity*, 22. The Andover archconservative Moses Stuart was unimpressed by English's interpretation of Messianic prophecies. In an 1813 letter to Edward Everett, Stuart wrote, "It is indeed the most absurd scheme of argument I have ever seen . . . 'It is the coincidence of the character of Jesus with the descriptions of the Old Testament which alone can support his claims.'—But who is to determine what these descriptions mean? Why Mr. E. to be sure—But have not thousands misinterpreted these passages?"; Moses Stuart to Edward Everett, 14 October 1813, in Edward Everett Papers, Massachusetts Historical Society, Reel 1; hereafter cited as Everett Papers.

27. English, *Grounds of Christianity*, 32.

such passages were likely not actually intended as prophecy.[28] According to this argument, accommodated quotations were often simply illustrations applied to the present, meant to appeal to Jewish audiences. This practice was supposedly justifiable because it was "of established authority among the Jews" at the time.[29] Throughout the debate, each of English's opponents would touch on this argument—admitting that some New Testament quotations of Old Testament passages were questionable, and suggesting that such quotations were perhaps "merely arguments ad hominem, to convince the Jews of the truth of Christianity, who *allowed* such a method of arguing to be valid."[30]

To English, this was a fatal admission. If this was the interpretive method used in every case, then "the whole affair of Jesus being *foretold* as the *Messiah* is reduced to *an accommodation of phrases!*"[31] But if Old Testament passages quoted in the New Testament were, in some cases, actually prophecies fulfilled yet, in other cases, merely phrases accommodated, then by "what rule," English asked, could one judge which was which?[32] The apostles themselves were no help in differentiating between the two because they introduced all Old Testament quotations in the same way. English concluded that if accommodation was an accepted Jewish practice adopted by the apostles, then any actual prophecies were indecipherable from accommodated phrases. And if the apostles did not adopt the accommodation principle from their contemporaries, then they simply misapplied prophecies out of ignorance or dishonesty. As Jesus's claims rested solely on his supposed fulfillment of Old Testament prophecy, "each horn of the Dilemma," English wrote, "must prove as fatal as the other."[33]

---

28. Ibid.
29. Ibid., 29.
30. Ibid., 30; emphasis added.
31. Ibid., 32.
32. Ibid.
33. Ibid., 33. English's critique of the accommodation principle was thought-provoking to his contemporaries. Henry Ware Sr. wrote to his son, "I shall be anxious to hear how the book strikes you"; Henry Ware Sr. to Henry Ware Jr., 20 October 1813, in *Life of Henry Ware, Jr.*, vol. 1, 64. The junior Ware's response, still in the first month after English's publication, was perplexity: "I don't know what to think of the subject of the typical [as in types and shadows] application of the Old Testament. Ought we to say that the tabernacle was built in order to prefigure the church, or is it only referred to as an apt

As English advertised, he had discovered his central arguments in some "lesser-known" texts in the Harvard library basement. Yet, as Everett would later expose, English's articulation of these arguments often included an unattributed amalgam of the works of British Deists, principally Anthony Collins.[34] English's more original work was not his largely plagiarized central argument but his rhetorical hedging of that argument. English used comparisons to Mahometanism (i.e., Islam) to try to keep the debate centered on Messianic prophecy. Each of his opponents would predictably attempt to maintain other evidences for Christianity—most prominently, miracles, moral truths, and missionary successes—but English asserted that the same evidences existed for Mahometanism. Such common evidences, English argued, could not prove any exclusively Christian truth claims. (Later developments in English's personal religious journey would make his rhetorical stance toward Islam intriguing.)

In the century of American religious history preceding the English debate, the most important historical evidences for Christianity alongside the fulfillment of Old Testament prophecies were the New Testament miracles, but English denied their uniqueness. "Innumerable volumes" were written to record and revere the miracles of Mahomet (i.e., Muhammad) too: "Christian reader, thou seest how much can be said, and how many respectable witnesses and authorities can be adduced to prove that Mahomet wrought miracles. Canst thou adduce more, or better, authorities in behalf of the miracles of the New Testament?"[35] As English anticipated, his opponents would also point to supposedly distinctive moral truths in the New Testament as an evidence of Christianity. "That the New Testament inculcates an excellent morality,

---

comparison? Was Jonah three days and nights in the whale's belly *because* the Messiah was to be so long in the earth, or did Christ, finding the fact to be so, only allude to it by way of similitude? And so of other instances."; Henry Ware Jr. to Henry Ware Sr., 26 October 1813, in *Life of Henry Ware, Jr.*, vol. 1, 64.

34. English drew his central argument regarding the incompatibility of Old Testament prophecy and its supposed fulfillment in the New Testament from Anthony Collins, *Discourse of the Grounds and Reasons of the Christian Religion* (London: privately printed, 1724). In contrast to most of the Boston controversialists, Collins was known for his unflappable courteousness in Christian controversies.

35. English, *Grounds of Christianity*, 120–21.

cannot be denied," English admitted.[36] Otherwise, he asked, why would anyone have believed Jesus and the apostles? But Mahomet and the Koran also promoted excellent moral truths. And "surely that will not prove Islamism to be from God, nor that Mahomet was his prophet!"[37] Finally, English argued that the "rapid propagation"[38] of Christianity was not a unique evidence of Christ's divinity. "Islamism," English asserted, "made more progress in one hundred years, than Christianity did in a thousand . . . [although] Mahomet was a poor camel-driver."[39] The then-standard Christian response was that Mahomet spread his message with the sword. But English argued that, in fact, more people voluntarily embraced Islam than Christianity. He reminded his readers of Constantine, Charlemagne, the Teutonic Knights, and the soldiers who had forcefully established Christianity in Europe. The spread of Mahometanism, he concluded, was no more violent and no less legitimate or rapid than that of Christianity.

Thomas Kidd has written that, by the middle decades of the eighteenth century, "citing the similarities between an opponent's views and the 'beliefs' of Islam as a means to discredit one's adversaries" had become "a staple of religious polemics" in America.[40] Identifying one's opponents with Islam was effective because all parties involved in a given debate normally agreed on the degenerate nature of Islamic culture and religion. While English drew from this well-established Western tradition, he also departed from it in some innovative ways. True to form, he cited similarities between Christianity and Islam to discredit his opponents, yet English used shared *virtues*, rather than shared vices, to deflate Christian evidences. Islamic characteristics functioned not as a foil for English's position but as a contradiction of Christian claims to uniqueness. The negative image of Islam in the American cultural imagination made this a biting comparison and a considerable deconstruction of Christian evidential exclusivity. The irony is that English

---

36. Ibid., 75.

37. Ibid., 75–76.

38. Ibid., 121.

39. Ibid.

40. Thomas Kidd, "'Is It Worse to Follow Mahomet than the Devil?' Early American Uses of Islam," *Church History* 72, no. 4 (2003): 773.

tapped into those assumptions without actually sharing them. English did not consider Islam self-evidently false or evil; he recognized that his opponents did and took full advantage.[41]

Although English's book had provided Boston liberals with a timely opportunity, English's rhetorical strategy did not make it easy for them to assert Unitarianism as *the* definitive and defensible Christianity. It forced them to maintain multiple boundaries—not only between liberal and orthodox positions but around Christianity generally. English's opponents would have to simultaneously defend Christianity from Deism, differentiate Christianity from Mahometanism, and define Christianity as Unitarianism. English understood what he had required of his opponents and concluded his book with confidence: "If any person should feel inclined to attempt to refute this book, let him do it like a man; without evading the question, or equivocating, or caviling about little things. Let him consider the principal question."[42]

English's opponents took up that challenge during a lacuna in liberal leadership created by the death of Joseph Stevens Buckminster Jr. in 1812. Nine years before English's publication, in 1804, Buckminster entered the New England ministry and rose quickly. "Every other Boston divine" soon "moved in his shadow."[43] During his eight years at the Brattle Street pulpit, Buckminster introduced German higher criticism to America, with the expectation that it would support liberals in New England's theological battles. As Robinson has explained, "[i]nsofar as the higher criticism called certain parts of the canon into question, Buckminster thought that it undermined the foundations of Trinitarian

---

41. English's approach to Islam foreshadowed those of great minds such as Thomas Carlyle. In his *On Heroes, Hero-Worship, and the Heroic in History* (London: Chapman and Hall, 1840), Carlyle described Mahomet as a prophet-hero and questioned the uniqueness of Christian evidences—its spread, its moral truths, and its martyrs—as he compared these to the same virtues within Islam. See Paul E. Kerry, "The Outsider at the Gates of Victorian Society: Thomas Carlyle's *On Heroes, Hero-Worship, and the Heroic in History*," in *The Image of the Outsider in Literature, Media, and Society*, ed. Will Wright and Steven Kaplan (Pueblo: University of Southern Colorado, The Society for the Interdisciplinary Study of Social Imagery, 2002), 369–73. In particular, see Carlyle, *On Heroes*, 56–57, 67, 70.

42. English, *Grounds of Christianity*, 175.

43. Jack Mendelsohn, *Channing: The Reluctant Radical* (Boston: Little, Brown and Company, 1971), 94.

doctrine and helped to establish more securely the form of purified Christianity [i.e., Unitarianism] that he believed he and his colleagues preached."[44] Because Buckminster was not only a renowned minister and scholar but New England's most promising opponent of orthodoxy, his sudden death the year before the English controversy left behind the mantle of leadership and an "unprecedented lament."[45]

William Ellery Channing would assume that mantle during the 1815 controversy, but in 1813, Buckminster's successor was yet to be determined. When English published his book, Channing was popular at his Federal Street pulpit but still relatively unknown outside of Boston and relatively averse to participating in religious controversy, let alone leading what would be perceived as a dissenting faction.[46] Samuel Cary, though virtually unknown now, was recognized then as the heir apparent of Stone Chapel's James Freeman, the first self-declared Unitarian minister in America.[47] But Freeman's Unitarianism was that of the British radicals, not the New England liberals, so Cary's association with Freeman had excluded him from the possibility of liberal leadership. In contrast, nothing hindered Edward Everett from filling Buckminster's role, and many rightly looked to him for the definitive answer to English's work; he would inherit Buckminster's Brattle Street pulpit four months into the controversy and in the process of refuting English he would surpass

44. Robinson, *Unitarians and Universalists*, 28. See also Gura, *American Transcendentalism*, 21–45. For Buckminster's impact on New England Unitarianism, see Lawrence Buell, "Joseph Stevens Buckminster: The Making of a New England Saint," *Canadian Review of American Studies* 10 (1979): 1–29. For Buckminster's introduction of higher criticism to America, see Brown, *Biblical Criticism*, 1–21.

45. Robinson, *Unitarians and Universalists*, 30.

46. See Arthur W. Brown, *William Ellery Channing* (New Haven, CT: Twayne Publishers, 1961), 35; and David P. Edgell, *William Ellery Channing: An Intellectual Portrait* (Boston: Beacon Press, 1955), 32.

47. In 1815, a Unitarian periodical in England dedicated several pages of praise to Cary both before and after his unexpected death. The magazine considered Freeman "the father of Unitarianism in the Eastern States" and described Freeman and Cary together as being "as avowed Unitarians, as the late Mr. Lindsey"; "Foreign Intelligence: Unitarians in America," *The Monthly Repository of Theology and General Literature* 10 (1815): 657. At the time of the controversy, Cary had recently expressed his strong anti-Trinitarian views in print. See his 1808 letter discussed and reprinted as "Mr. Cary's Letter on the Trinity," *Christian Examiner and Religious Miscellany* 44, no. 1 (January 1848): 34–47.

Buckminster's biblical scholarship.[48] But those outcomes were still uncertain when English deposited his manuscript at the district clerk's office for publication on September 24, 1813, and the "wildfire" that Ware predicted began.

Channing's *Sermons* and Cary's *Review*

Channing countered English within weeks in his *Two Sermons on Infidelity* (1813).[49] It was actually only one sermon, delivered on October 24, 1813, at Channing's Federal Street Church and published soon after with an extended introduction. Channing was unique in his avoidance of personal attacks—refraining from even using English's name.[50] He focused his sermon on the interpretation of Messianic prophecies. Such prophecies, he noted, were communicated in "the language of the boldest metaphors," which could easily be misinterpreted.[51] Was it any wonder, Channing asked, "that *Jews* beheld in these predictions their own nation raised to universal empire, and enjoying ease and plenty under their victorious leader?"[52] In contrast, interpretations of the Messiah as a "teacher, a light to the Gentiles . . . who should introduce universal peace . . . by instruction . . . [were] more generous and

---

48. For Everett's biblical scholarship, see Brown, *Biblical Criticism*, 36–39. The best Everett biography looks to be Matthew Mason, *From Knapsack to Gettysburg: Edward Everett, Slavery, the Sacred American Union, and the Coming of the Civil War* (Chapel Hill: University of North Carolina Press, forthcoming). Roland F. Reid's *Edward Everett: Unionist Orator* (Westport, CT: Greenwood Press, 1990) contains a nearly exhaustive bibliography of primary and secondary sources and a bibliographic essay.

49. William Ellery Channing, *Two Sermons on Infidelity* (Boston: Cummings and Hilliard, 1813).

50. Six years later, Channing would be heavily involved in another theological debate with arch-conservative Trinitarian Moses Stuart. At that time, Channing wrote that "the controversy should have as little to do with individuals as possible. It is one of the chief wiles of party to mix up extraneous considerations with subjects of debate, to turn the publick mind from the true point of discussion"; William Ellery Channing to Andrews Norton, 2 May 1819, quoted in Brown, *Biblical Criticism*, 69. Channing's distaste for debate was consistent over these years of involvement in New England religious controversies. His response in 1813 was a striking contrast to the otherwise deeply personal polemics that other opponents directed at English.

51. Channing, *Two Sermons*, 17.

52. Ibid., emphasis in the original.

sublime, more worthy of God, and more desirable to mankind, than that to which the Jews adhered."[53]

Channing admitted, however, that applications of Old Testament passages in the New Testament were often questionable. "We are told," wrote Channing, "that [the apostles] have quoted and applied incorrectly passages from the Old Testament."[54] This objection "is . . . perhaps the most plausible with which Christianity has been assailed."[55] Channing mentioned the accommodation principle as a possible explanation, but was more inclined to simply acknowledge the humanity of the apostles and rely on non-prophetic evidences. "Suppose . . . that the apostles have erred in some quotations," Channing wrote. "The apostles, indeed, will in this case appear to have been men, whose memories and reasoning powers sometimes failed them; but does this destroy their credibility?"[56] The apostles, Channing argued, were still reliable witnesses to the miracles and resurrection of Jesus. Even without prophecy, these and the other non-prophetic evidences could bear the burden of proof.

Yet English had already countered non-prophetic evidences. For example, Channing wrote that the truth of Christianity was evidenced by "the wonderful rapidity" with which it spread.[57] "I know the answer which is made to this," he admitted, "Mahometanism, we are told, triumphed as rapidly as Christianity."[58] But Channing argued that Mahometans brandished a sword in one hand and a Koran in the other while Christianity flourished peacefully, English's contrary evidence notwithstanding. Channing maintained that "[a]ll history presents nothing parallel with the diffusion of Christianity."[59] Channing acknowledged and rejected English's Mahometan parallels without actually countering English's arguments. The miracles, morals, and providential propagation of Christianity were, to Channing, unique evidences that Jesus was the Messiah.

---

53. Ibid.
54. Ibid., 21.
55. Ibid.
56. Ibid., 24.
57. Ibid., 26.
58. Ibid.
59. Ibid., 27.

Channing concluded with a theme that all of English's opponents would repeat. The ravings of infidels were unoriginal but ultimately beneficial for Christianity because they revealed its strength. Channing reasoned that, "had [Christianity's] truth never been questioned before, we might fear for the result of inquiry. . . . But this uncertainty is removed. Christianity has passed the trial. . . . We may now dismiss our fears for our religion."[60] What Christianity meant to William Ellery Channing in 1813 and what *type* of Christianity was strengthened by the attacks of infidels would become clearer as English's liberal opponents continued their efforts to refute him.

Less than four weeks later, the young but noted liberal minister, Samuel Cary, began where Channing left off: "The Christian religion . . . rests upon a rock of adamant and cannot be subverted by man. For this . . . it is principally indebted to *infidelity*—to the severe scrutiny which it has been compelled to receive, and to an open and thorough discussion of its pretensions."[61] Deist attacks on historical evidences were thus a welcome refiner's fire to Cary. Opponents such as English consumed systematic theology that could not withstand the heat of Biblical criticism, leaving only the solid core of rational, primitive, Unitarian Christianity. Like English's other opponents, Cary saw English's *Grounds of Christianity* as a benefit to Christianity because, to him, Christianity was Unitarianism.

Cary spent his next forty pages attacking English personally for his questionable methods and motives—a fact Cary's eulogizer, Henry Colman, would regret publicly at Cary's death while recounting the English controversy.[62] When Cary came to English's arguments, he critiqued English's dismissal of miracles as interpretively presumptuous. English had argued that miracles were invalid evidences because they could only prove a contradiction—that a man who did not fit the prophetic pattern was nevertheless the Messiah. Cary responded that miracles did

---

60. Ibid., 32.

61. Cary, *Review of a Book,* 5.

62. Of Cary's *Review of a Book,* Colman wrote, "we must always regret, that anything personal should be mingled in our discussions of a subject of such immense importance and dignity as the truth of our religion"; "Character of the Rev. Samuel Cary," *Christian Disciple,* August 4, 1816, 241.

not prove *directly* that Jesus was the Messiah. Rather, miracles proved that Jesus was a teacher from God. Therefore, Cary asserted, Jesus had divine authority to interpret the Messianic prophecies as being fulfilled in him. Because Jesus was a teacher from God, his interpretations of scripture were infinitely more reliable than English's. Did English and his sources, Cary asked, have "the vanity to believe that . . . the prophecies themselves are in their hands, and that they are as competent judges of their relevancy to Christ as he himself could be?"[63] Given the transmission history of Jesus's words, it was a difficult argument to make, but Cary believed the argument solved the interpretive problem surrounding Jesus's fulfillment of Old Testament prophecies.

Most notable to the controversy's significance in 1813 Boston, Cary argued that orthodox Christianity was, in contrast to Unitarian Christianity, deeply vulnerable to English's attacks. One of English's central recurring arguments was that Jesus encouraged idolatry by commanding that he himself be worshiped. By doing so, "he taught the worship of other Beings besides Jehovah" and contradicted numerous Messianic prophecies.[64] Cary was quick to respond that English's attack assumed the orthodox reading of scripture. What English had claimed was an idolatrous "doctrine of Christianity,"[65] Cary argued was actually creedal theology that Trinitarians had erroneously read into the original text. For them, this was a vulnerability, but not for Cary: "How they [i.e., Trinitarians] who believe that Jesus . . . can be entitled to the same kind of adoration with the Deity himself will vindicate themselves from this charge of Mr. E. is an affair with which I have no sort of concern."[66] For Unitarians, English's argument posed no such problem. Cary argued that "Jesus taught in the most explicit manner . . . the unity and unrivalled excellence of God."[67] When Jesus said, "I and my Father are one," he meant "nothing more than that the will of his Father and his will, that

63. Cary, *Review of a Book*, 48.
64. English, *Grounds of Christianity*, 131. Bostonians took particular notice of this argument. As Everett commented, it was "in the mouth of everyone who knew Mr. English"; *A Defence*, 417.
65. Cary, *Review of a Book*, 87.
66. Ibid.
67. Ibid., 88.

they were one in design, intention, object."[68] In contrast to a Trinitarian Jesus who claimed his own divinity, Cary concluded, the Unitarian Jesus taught the worship of the one true God, in fulfillment of Messianic prophecies.

Besides demonstrating the defensibility of Unitarian Christianity, Cary used the opportunity to assert that Unitarianism *was* Christianity: "The errors of Calvinists are not to be confounded with Christianity."[69] Such presuppositions of Unitarianism *as* Christianity illuminate the recurring theme of infidelity's benefits to Christianity. In short, to Cary and his colleagues, the Christianity benefitting from English was the only Christianity that could withstand Deist attacks—Unitarianism. Understandably, then, those who made the effort to publicly respond to English were all liberals; more than one religious battle occupied Bostonians at the time, and liberal Christianity had the most to gain by engaging with English's attack on the historical evidences of the Bible.

English's Letters to Channing and Cary

Before the end of 1813, English responded to Channing and Cary in print. His confidence was unshaken and his rhetorical strategies were unrevised. Channing's sermon had argued that the Messiah foretold in the Old Testament, spiritually understood, would be a divine teacher, a light to the Gentiles—which described the Jesus actually recorded in the New Testament. According to Channing, "[t]he extension of the knowledge of the true God among the heathen nations" that Jesus accomplished had fulfilled prophecy and distinguished him from every other human teacher of religion.[70] At the same time, Channing had tried to shift the burden of proof from the apostles' questionable interpretations of prophecy to what he considered to be their unquestionable witnesses of Jesus's miracles. He argued that their humanness influenced their hermeneutics without invalidating their testimonies.

---

68. Ibid., 89.
69. Ibid., 131.
70. Channing, *Two Sermons*, 18.

Turning once again to Mahometanism, English asked how Jesus's teaching could prove any kind of unique authority. He scoffed at Channing's belief that Jesus's "teaching and enlightening of the Gentiles" was "sufficient to prove him the Messiah"; such a characteristic would "prove Mahomet the Messiah sooner than Jesus; since Mahomet in person converted more Gentiles to the worship of one God during his life time, than Christianity did in one hundred years."[71] And although apostles could have misread the Old Testament without mistaking Jesus's miracles, English stated that the textual history of the Gospels excluded the possibility of eyewitness testimonies. Matthew and John were the only apostles supposed to have seen Jesus's miracles, and, as English outlined at length, scholars were unsure if Matthew and John themselves wrote their eponymous Gospels.

English responded well to the impersonal nature of Channing's sermon. He argued with Channing "respectfully"—a titular adverb conspicuously missing from the Cary letter. But he was dismissive of Channing's logic. He attributed Channing's influence instead to his eloquent appeals to sentiment. English believed that one of the crudest such appeals in Channing's *Two Sermons* was the idea that if Christians gave up Christianity, they would have no religion left. On the contrary, English argued, devout Gentiles could easily give up the New Testament, worship the one true God, and keep the moral law contained in the Old Testament—mere "Theism garnished," as he described it.[72] He closed by affirming, in the face of false rumors, his belief in God and his support of public worship, sans Christianity.

In contrast to the Channing letter, English's response to Cary's bitter criticism was perhaps the most heated moment in the controversy. Why, English asked, had Cary suppressed English's investigation with such vitriol if it were beneficial to Christianity?[73] The question was rhetorical; already understanding how his infidelity was beneficial to

71. George Bethune English, *A Letter Respectfully Addressed to the Reverend Mr. Channing, Relative to His Two Sermons on Infidelity* (Boston: privately printed, 1813), 11.
72. Ibid., 26.
73. George Bethune English, *A Letter to the Reverend Mr. Cary, Containing Remarks upon His Review of The Grounds of Christianity Examined by Comparing the New Testament with the Old* (Boston: privately printed, 1813), 22.

liberals in Boston, English considered Cary's assertions of Unitarian theology evasions of Christianity's vulnerabilities. Cary had argued that English made Christianity accountable for Trinitarian doctrines, but English critiqued that argument as an identification of Christianity with Unitarianism. "Now sir, when a man argues about the Christian System, as I do," English wrote, "[one] suppose[s] that he means the System established and agreed on by Christians in general"; did not that system in Christian churches inevitably "begin with the doctrines of the Trinity and Incarnation?"[74] Of course they did, English answered, "and my opinions, nor your opinions cannot invalidate this fact."[75] English recognized that a Trinitarian Jesus was less compatible with Messianic prophecy than a Unitarian Jesus and therefore worked to refute Cary's assertion of the latter.

In another instance, Cary had mishandled the careful boundary maintenance of Unitarianism and Trinitarianism while defending Christianity from English's Deism. English had argued in *Grounds* that the crucial, contested prophecy in Isaiah 53 described the suffering people of Israel, not a suffering Messiah. The "righteous servant" in Isaiah was to be wounded for our iniquities and bear our sins as an "intercession for the transgressors."[76] So Cary had mocked English's interpretation by asking whose sins and iniquities the Jews had borne. But Cary's rhetoric implied acceptance of the traditional Christian interpretation of Isaiah 53, which presupposed a substitutionary Atonement. "Did the Unitarian, Antisatisfactionist, Mr. Cary, mean to intimate, by his manner of arguing upon these passages, a hint in favour of such a shocking Doctrine?" English asked. "God forbid!"[77] Well aware of his opponent's layered loyalties, English was quick to mock any transgressions of the Unitarian–Trinitarian boundary.

While such oversights highlight the complex negotiation of religious boundaries involved in the controversy, Cary's *Review* had other issues as well. Hastily composing the work in just four weeks, Cary had failed to trace some quotations to their primary sources, resulting

---

74. English, *Reverend Mr. Cary*, 33.
75. Ibid., 33–34.
76. Isaiah 53:11, 12 (Authorized [King James] Version).
77. English, *Reverend Mr. Cary*, 80.

Religion in the Age of Enlightenment

in several citation errors. English took full advantage of these errors, although they were not as serious as his own. Cary's petty, personal tone had weakened his tract, too, and ultimately English emerged from the first round of counterattacks embittered and emboldened.

The *General Repository and Review*

Soon after Cary's response, the *General Repository and Review* assessed the current state of the controversy and added its own indictment of English. The *Repository* had been founded in January 1812 as a voice for New England Unitarianism, and in 1813 its editors were eager to point out the controversy's potential benefits.[78] They wrote that liberal Christians were indebted to men like English "for the clearing away of all which human folly . . . has connected with Christianity."[79] "The efforts of the enemies of Christianity," they continued, have aided "the destruction of what its most sincere and intelligent friends are laboring to remove."[80] Henry Ware Sr. had predicted that English's book would "pass like wildfire" through New England; the *Repository* articulated the benefits of that blaze: "The foundation, which no man has laid, cannot be removed by man; but the wood, and the hay, and the stubble, which have been built upon it, have very often blazed in the contest with the assailants. We expect some advantages of this kind from the publications of Mr. English."[81] As Calvinistic superstructures burned to the ground, they

78. The *General Repository and Review* was the creation of Andrews Norton, who would go on to become one of the most strident defenders of New England Unitarianism, earning himself the title of "Unitarian Pope." In its first year, under Norton as editor, the *Repository* was confrontational in its critique of orthodox Christianity and its promotion of liberal Christianity. By 1813, Norton's approach had lost some favor, and in April, he accepted the Dexter Lectureship at Harvard, resigning as editor of the *Repository*. But in the issue covering the George English controversy, the *Repository*'s editors reiterated their liberal loyalties: "The members of the society . . . all claim to be liberal Christians"; they "feel no other interest in the work than as liberal Christians"; "The Editors to the Public," *General Repository and Review* (October 1813), 403, 405. For the history and significance of the *Repository*, see Lillian Handlin, *"Babylon est delenda*—the Young Andrews Norton," in *American Unitarianism: 1805–1865*, ed. Conrad Erick Wright (Boston: The Massachusetts Historical Society and Northeastern University Press, 1989), 53–86.

79. "Article 9," 301.

80. Ibid.

81. Ibid.

argued, a Unitarian foundation would be revealed. Mr. English was the most recent in a long line of infidels, the editors asserted. And the broader tensions in New England Congregationalism made his attacks a particularly timely invitation to demonstrate liberal strength.

The *Repository* article included personal and scholarly critiques. The editors traced English's life history to illustrate his intellectual vacillations. How seriously could one take the man's religious opinions, they asked, considering how temporary they might be? In their scholarly critique, the editors analyzed some of English's methodological errors, which foreshadowed Everett's approach. The *Repository* concluded with an eloquent and emotional evocation of Christian miracles, moral truths, and remarkable growth. The editors did not fail to acknowledge English's Mahometan critiques of these evidences. Nor did they fail to see the sympathy for Mahometanism that lay behind English's rhetoric and the potential implications of his restless religiosity. Their comment on the subject would prove prophetic: "With his sort of mind, if he were to happen to get engaged in the history of Mahomet, we should be not at all surprised, if he were to suffer a new change, as extraordinary as any that have preceded."[82]

Edward Everett's *Defence of Christianity*

On February 9, 1814, Edward Everett was ordained at the Brattle Street church. He had been working on his *Defence of Christianity* for about four months, and his parishioners knew about his work. The *Religious Remembrancer*'s article on his ordination ceremony expressed supreme confidence in Everett and perhaps a continuing awareness of the still unresolved controversy: "While our churches are instructed and defended by such enlightened and pious Teachers . . . the friends of Christianity need not be alarmed by . . . the cavils of infidelity."[83]

Earlier, on October 14, 1813, English's book had reached Moses Stuart in Andover, Massachusetts. In a letter to Everett, Stuart dismissed

---

82. Ibid., 307–8.
83. "Article 3," *Religious Remembrancer* (February 26, 1814): 104.

Grounds of Christianity and advised Everett on the response he had already begun writing:

> Will you permit me to suggest one thing? Do not undertake to answer all that Mr. E. has said, for it will make your volume too large. Seize the fundamental points—expose their weakness, & (though tenderly) their wickedness—give specimens of his misstatements, perversions, etc.—& leave it. The answer, to be read, should be brief—& a brief one will be all that is necessary.[84]

Whatever Everett's initial intentions, his five-hundred-page book was not brief, and by the time he wrote the book, it had become clear that a brief response was not all that would be necessary. Stuart's overly optimistic prediction corresponds with Frothingham's 1925 assessment of Everett's *Defence*. While it was well done, wrote Frothingham, "whether the book was necessary or not, is another question. Probably it was not."[85] But Stuart made his prediction before Channing and Cary failed to silence English, and Frothingham's judgment was based solely on Everett's self-effacing preface. Until Everett published his book, Bostonians felt that English was yet to be refuted; those who were not outright critical of Cary's response were, at the least, unsatisfied with it. The *Repository* linked its lingering dissatisfaction with Cary to its anticipation of Everett's book. "There are some oversights" in Cary's work, the editors opined, but "we expect a more complete answer to English's book than has yet appeared, from a gentleman, whom we are gratified to speak of as one of our number."[86] As another Bostonian remembered the story, *Grounds of Christianity* "unsettled the faith of many, and, if left unanswered, seemed destined to do this for many more," even after "several older men . . . attempted without success" to answer English.[87] Later historians have questioned the need for Everett's lengthy work, but Everett's liberal contemporaries believed his book was necessary

---

84. Stuart to Everett, 14 October 1813, Everett Papers, Reel 1.
85. Frothingham, *Everett*, 30.
86. "Article 9," 313.
87. Samuel Lothrop, "Tribute to Edward Everett. Special Meeting," *Proceedings of the Massachusetts Historical Society* 8 (1864–65): 119.

and anticipated it being a triumphant answer to English. Their lofty expectations were not disappointed.

Everett has been most remembered for exhaustively exposing English's unattributed source materials. As George Ticknor told the story, the previous responses to English "from the pulpit and the press" were unsatisfactory because "their authors had not frequented the strange by-paths of learning in which Mr. English had . . . been wandering."[88] But Everett "followed him everywhere with a careful scholarship . . . unknown to his presumptuous adversary."[89] Everett began with a table listing the pages English had plagiarized (in total, seventy-four pages out of two hundred) and the sources from which he had taken them. He filled every chapter thereafter with meticulously traced examples of English's sloppy or dishonest scholarship. In the memory of his contemporaries, Everett "so destroyed [English's] credit as a scholar and as an honest controversialist, that he sent the pamphlet down to oblivion."[90]

But Everett also engaged English's own (i.e., non-plagiarized) arguments. He presented rival interpretations of the Messianic prophecies that English had examined, arguing that the major ones, like Isaiah 53, were indeed fulfilled in Jesus of Nazareth. He displayed a mastery of European scholarship, particularly German higher criticism, far beyond English's.[91] His logic was as meticulous as his research and, in many places, revealed contradictions and inconsistencies in English's reasoning that Channing and Cary had missed. He also tersely dismissed English's equation of Christian and Muslim evidences. Like Christianity, Mahometanism had its "alleged miracles," Everett acknowledged, but "it is as easy to discern between true and false miracles, as between true and false prophecy."[92]

---

88. George Ticknor, "Tribute to Edward Everett. Special Meeting," *Proceedings of the Massachusetts Historical Society* 8 (1864–65): 136.

89. Ibid., 136–37.

90. Richard Henry Dana, *An Address upon the Life and Services of Edward Everett: Delivered before the Municipal Authorities and Citizens of Cambridge, February 22, 1865* (Cambridge, MA: Sever and Francis, 1865), 14.

91. Everett had access to Eichhorn and other German works through Moses Stuart. Stuart obtained the German works in 1812 at the auction of Buckminster's famous library by narrowly outbidding the young Everett. See Gura, *American Transcendentalism*, 22–23.

92. Everett, *Defence of Christianity*, 16–17.

Everett's lasting legacy in his own mind was his revision of the standard accommodation theory. As all of English's opponents had done, Everett acknowledged that many Old Testament passages quoted as prophecies in the New Testament were not actually intended as prophecies. But Everett argued that the apostles accommodated these passages out of their original context because they, as Jews, quoted the Old Testament in the same way rabbis did in the Mishna, not simply because their audiences were Jewish.[93] In 1855, Everett noted this insight in his personal account of the controversy. Of his own book, he wrote, "there are many parts of it which would not stand the test of modern criticism. There are some parts of it however which if I may be permitted to say so threw new light upon . . . the quotations of the Old Testament by the New Testament writers."[94] Jerry Wayne Brown has likewise described Everett's explanation of Old Testament quotations in the New Testament as an original contribution: "Everett's innovation turned the light of historical criticism on the Gospels, a giant stride forward in biblical studies and a significant American development."[95] Later, commentators would legitimately criticize *Defence*'s short shelf life, but Everett's contemporaries found this particular insight relevant beyond the controversy itself. In 1832, for example, a Boston periodical called the *Scriptural Interpreter*, exploring how the Old Testament was quoted in the New Testament, praised and reprinted Everett's entire treatment of the subject from his book.[96]

To his liberal contemporaries, there was another reason why Everett's book was not superfluous. The Christianity whose strength Everett demonstrated was thoroughly Unitarian; *Defence* was Boston Unitarianism's own contribution to the long evidentialist dialogue that had strengthened liberal Christianity. The review of *Defence* in the *Christian Disciple*, which Everett still remembered and quoted with pleasure in 1855, stated that the evidences of Christianity had received a "full examination . . . during the last century," having "been assailed and

---

93. Brown, *Biblical Criticism*, 37.

94. Autobiography, Everett Papers, Reel 41a.

95. Brown, *Biblical Criticism*, 37–38.

96. "On the Quotation of the Old Testament in the New: From Everett's *Defence of Christianity,*" *Scriptural Interpreter* (February 1, 1832): 75–81.

defended by men on both sides."[97] Christianity had been found "vulnerable only in some points, which made no part of it as it came from the hands of its Author." But a century of scrutiny spurred by evidential debates had brought "the real . . . doctrines of the Gospel . . . back nearly to their primitive simplicity . . . as they are understood by men of liberal and enlightened minds."[98] The *Disciple* linked Everett's *Defence* to this tradition and lauded its unique contribution to the liberal cause in Boston.

Most responses to Everett's book were as positive as the *Disciple's*, and for Bostonians, the controversy was over. After reading *Defence*, Boston judge F. A. Van de Kemp wrote to Everett with a representative assessment in appropriately Biblical language: "You have discovered the nakedness of Mr. English . . . exploded his objections—shown the futility of his mean and scurrilous calumnies—and with all this treated him with a gentleman like regard."[99] Everett's work was, as he would put it in his autobiography, "overwhelming."[100] Later commentators would often remark that *Defence* disappeared as quickly as *Grounds of Christianity* because the debate was so decisively settled. Everett himself also disappeared quickly. His masterful engagement with German higher criticism in *Grounds of Christianity* foreshadowed his departure to Germany just months later. While abroad, Everett received two years of Harvard-funded education that included training from the great Johann Gottfried Eichhorn, founder of modern Old Testament criticism.

The year after the publication of Everett's book, Jedidiah Morse sparked the first of several pamphlet wars by conflating New England liberals with their more radical English Unitarian counterparts, forcing a public self-definition and initiating the culminating stages of the American Unitarian controversy. As that controversy engrossed Boston Congregationalists, the George B. English controversy was largely, but not completely, forgotten. In some ways, the evolving public tensions

---

97. "Review: *A Defence of Christianity*," *Christian Disciple* (December 2, 1814): 369.
98. Ibid.
99. F. A. Van de Kemp to Edward Everett, 3 April 1815, Everett Papers, Reel 1.
100. Autobiography, Everett Papers, Reel 41a.

between Unitarians and Trinitarians would actually perpetuate and revise the English controversy's significance.

Conclusion

Although scholars have described Channing as "bound" to assume Buckminster's mantle of liberal leadership, that mantle seemed at least equally accessible to Everett after his preeminent role in the English controversy.[101] Ironically, Everett's role in the controversy contributed to his disillusionment with the liberal cause during his study of higher criticism in Germany. In January 1816, Everett looked back "with disapprobation" on many parts of his book, loathing "to think how near [he] had come to giving credit to that poorest of all systematizing, systematic Theology" and longing to "separate the public worship of God and the public teaching of duty, from all connection with arbitrary facts, supposed to have happened in distant nations and ages."[102] Devoting himself to classicism instead, Everett decided to leave "the world to fight out the cause of Religion, as piously as they have fought it out hitherto."[103] Although he was at the forefront of American biblical criticism and nascent New England Unitarianism in 1814, Everett is known today for his oratory and political career. Cary became ill, traveled to England to try to recover, and died in October 1815. Channing alone stayed involved in the liberal cause and became the defining voice of American Unitarianism.

English's religious path continued to be eccentric. He had shown some healthy self-awareness when he proclaimed his intellectual impartiality to Cary: "I have given too many proofs already that I am not one apt to be influenced by the pride of consistency to stand to opinions because they were mine."[104] In the years following the controversy, English traveled to Turkey and Egypt, where, according to reports in the *London Jewish Expositor*, he converted to Islam. Under

---

101. Mendelsohn, *Channing*, 94.
102. Everett to Alexander Everett, 5 January 1816, Everett Papers, Reel 1.
103. Ibid.
104. English, *Reverend Mr. Cary*, 123.

the name Mohamed Effendi, he published an exposition of the Koran before returning to the United States in 1822.[105] Two years later, English published *Five Pebbles from the Brook*, a response to Everett's *Defence*, but it went unnoticed (according to Everett, English wrote it while living in Robert Owen's New Harmony, Indiana, community and printed it at the community's expense).[106] English died in 1827, having journeyed through skepticism, Unitarianism, Judaism, Deism, Islam, and possibly Utopian Socialism—a path surely traveled by few nineteenth-century Americans.

The works English and his opponents produced during the debate did not disappear from the American religious scene.[107] An episode in 1821 illustrated their continuing significance in the context of Trinitarian-Unitarian tensions. That year, the General Assembly of the Presbyterian Church publicly accused Jared Sparks and his Baltimore, Maryland Unitarian congregation (significant for being the first outside of New England) of propagating a modified form of infidelity under the guise of Christianity. With their Christian credentials at stake, Sparks held up Unitarianism's history of defending the historical evidences of the Bible, particularly in the George B. English controversy. "We are charged with infidelity. But . . . with what justice?" Sparks asked.[108] "Let us," he continued, "pursue this subject in relation to facts. Does it appear that Unitarians have rejected, or even slighted the evidences of Christianity? . . . Have we done nothing for the truth of the Christian religion?"[109]

---

105. "Mr. Wolff, and Mr. English—From the London Jewish Expositor," *Boston Recorder* (June 8, 1822): 89; "George B. English," *Reformer* (August 1, 1822): 191; and "Article VI—Joseph Wolff," *Christian Examiner* (November 1861): 422.

106. Autobiography, Everett Papers, Reel 41a.

107. Books from the debate made their way into the libraries of John Adams, Thomas Jefferson, and Ralph Waldo Emerson, among others. Adams wrote on the final page of his copy of *Defence*: "Read through November 16, 1814, having before read English, Cary and Channing: i.e. all the previous controversy." Jefferson received copies of *The Grounds*, Cary's *Review*, and English's letter to Cary from a Jewish acquaintance named Israel Baer-Kursheedt. See J. Jefferson Looney, ed., *The Papers of Thomas Jefferson: Retirement Series* (Princeton, NJ: Princeton University Press, 2010), 7:435–36. Emerson recorded having read Everett's *Defence* in his journal in 1829.

108. Jared Sparks, "Infidelity Modified," *Unitarian Miscellany and Christian Monitor* (July 1, 1821): 309.

109. Ibid., 310–11.

Noting that, "[i]n the present case, it is our duty to vindicate ourselves at home," Sparks turned to the Boston controversialists and recounted the "singular and labored attack . . . made on the Christian religion . . . by Mr. English [in 1813]."[110] He reminded his readers of the powerful defenses that Channing, Cary, and especially Everett had produced. With these as some of his primary examples, Sparks argued that Unitarians had done more to defend the cause of Christianity and to earn the Christian name than any other denomination.

In comparison, he asserted, Unitarians' accusers had contributed little to the defense of Christianity. As Sparks pointed out, "[t]he Trinitarian clergy often complain of the alarming progress of infidelity. But what have they done to oppose it?"[111] Beyond negligence, Trinitarians had, in one case, even claimed Unitarian efforts as their own. The *Evangelical Magazine* had recently reported that English's book was still being read with "mischievous effect" in parts of Virginia.[112] To oppose it, the magazine had reprinted an excerpt of Everett's *Defence* without actually crediting the Unitarian author. The magazine, Sparks wrote, was suspiciously "sparing of names" that might attribute merit or draw attention to "the works of unitarians."[113] The Evangelicals' dubious move was an implicit acknowledgment that the English controversy demonstrated Unitarian strength.

This episode signaled the completion of an important rhetorical realignment. With the American Unitarian controversy then in full bloom, the significance of the English debate as a blow to Deism was fully subsumed by its meaning for Unitarians and Trinitarians. It was no longer important that Christianity had been defended; what mattered was who had more ably defended it and which Christianity had been more defensible. In 1813–14, amid multiple cross-currents of religious controversy, Boston liberals demonstrated that their historically grounded Unitarianism could put out the wildfire that George Bethune English had ignited.

---

110. Ibid., 311.
111. Ibid., 312.
112. Ibid., 311.
113. Ibid.

The Potential Convergence of Religious and Secular Interests in Voltaire's *Traité sur la tolérance*

John C. O'Neal
Hamilton College

W hen the Toulouse parliament condemned Jean Calas to death on March 9, 1762, and had him executed on the following day, Voltaire took up his pen to denounce what he saw as a brutal act of intolerance against a Protestant. Although Henry IV had signed the Edict of Nantes in 1598, guaranteeing freedom of conscience for all religions, Louis XIV revoked this edict in 1685 and claimed Catholicism as the one official religion of France. Already well known for his anticlericalism, Voltaire questioned a number of religious practices. But in his *Traité sur la tolérance* he does not reject religion so much as he presents an idealized form of it that converges with the secular notion of justice he is trying to protect. The question, as he poses it in the *Traité sur la tolérance*, is to "examiner si la religion doit être charitable ou barbare" (examine whether the true religious spirit is more consistent with charity or with cruelty).[1] Voltaire's answer to this question reveals his own form of religion. By examining both tendencies

---

1. Voltaire, *Traité sur la tolérance*, ed. René Pomeau (Paris: GF Flammarion, 1989), 40 (hereafter cited as *Traité*). The English translation by Brian Masters used here follows Voltaire's later 1765 text, which is reproduced in René Pomeau's widely available edition. See *Treatise on Tolerance*, trans. Brian Masters (Cambridge: Cambridge University Press, 2000) (hereafter cited as *Treatise*). The English translations of the French will always be given in parentheses, as here (*Treatise*, 11).

RAE, vol. 5, 2015

inherent in religion, Voltaire presents a choice between justice and injustice, humanity and inhumanity that, through his ironic treatment of the subject, is largely determined in advance.

Voltaire believed that religion could tend toward barbarity by excessive passions, beliefs, and actions. Passions, hatred, and fanaticism combined in a particularly pernicious way in the *affaire Calas*, as it came to be known. Voltaire criticizes the brotherhood of white penitents for being behind much of the irrational public fervor, as he does all religious brotherhoods when they give themselves over to their worst passions:

> Elles semblent instituées par le zèle qui anime en Languedoc les catholiques contre ceux que nous nommons huguenots. On dirait qu'on a fait voeu de haïr ses frères, car nous avons assez de religion pour haïr et persécuter, et nous n'en avons pas assez pour aimer et pour secourir.

> (Their very foundations appear to be built upon that extremism, which in Languedoc, so manifestly excites Catholics against those whom we call Huguenots. You would think they had made a vow to hate their fellow man, for though we have in our country sufficient religious feeling to revile and persecute, it is not yet strong enough to love and to cherish.)[2]

The frenzy of hatred spreads quickly from the religious orders and the people to the judges of Toulouse, who

> entraînés par le fanatisme de la populace, ont fait rouer un père de famille innocent.

> (led astray by the fanaticism of the populace, have caused an innocent man to perish on the wheel.)[3]

Fanaticism can have disastrous results not only for others but also for one's own group. In Roman times, Christians themselves could endanger the lives of their fellow believers through their excessive zeal, which

---

2. *Traité*, 41 (*Treatise*, 12).
3. *Traité*, 40 (*Treatise*, 11).

Voltaire sees as the probable source of all their persecutions.[4] People's errors should be punished as crimes only when they inspire fanaticism.[5]

As with excessive passions, superstitious and dogmatic beliefs can also dehumanize religion. Voltaire views the worst kind of superstition as a form of hatred:

> Mais de toutes les superstitions, la plus dangereuse, n'est-ce pas celle de haïr son frère pour ses opinions?
>
> (Yet of all superstitions is not the most dangerous that which demands we hate our neighbour on account of his opinion?)[6]

Like his *confrères* the philosophes, Voltaire fostered diversity of opinion in all matters, secular and religious. Conformity of views, he feared, could lead not just to intellectual stagnation but actual persecution of others. He was all too aware of

> cette sombre superstition qui porte les âmes faibles à imputer des crimes à quiconque ne pense pas comme elles.
>
> (that grim superstition which persuades the weak-minded to impute a criminal character to whoever does not think as they do.)[7]

Voltaire devotes all of chapter XX to the question of superstition: "S'il est utile d'entretenir le peuple dans la superstition" (Whether it is useful to hold the people in superstition).[8] He seems to acquiesce to some superstition in the early stages of a society but believed it becomes useless as the society evolves. Ironically, Voltaire adopts a kind of relativism about superstitions; some are much more harmful than others:

> Et n'est-il pas évident qu'il serait encore plus raisonnable d'adorer le saint nombril, le saint prépuce, le lait et la robe de la vierge Marie, que de détester et de persécuter son frère?

4. *Traité*, 70 (*Treatise*, 37).
5. *Traité*, 121 (*Treatise*, 78).
6. *Traité*, 132 (*Treatise*, 86).
7. *Traité*, 157 (*Treatise*, 105).
8. *Traité*, 129 (*Treatise*, 83).

(Is it not evident that it would be far more in accordance with reason to worship the holy navel, the holy foreskin, the milk and the robe of the Virgin Mary, than to detest and to persecute one's fellow man?)[9]

Not surprisingly for a treatise on tolerance, what determines the unacceptability of a given superstition depends on the degree of intolerance or actual harm involved.

Voltaire links a dogmatic frame of mind in religion to dangerous passions that have ravaged Europe. He writes:

> La fureur qu'inspirent l'esprit dogmatique, et l'abus de la religion chrétienne mal entendue a répandu autant de sang, a produit autant de désastres, en Allemagne, en Angleterre, et même en Hollande, qu'en France.

> (The fury unleashed by both the dogmatic spirit and the misuse of a poorly understood Christianity has spilt as much blood and caused as many disasters in Germany, in England, and even in Holland, as in France.)[10]

Yet he suggests at the same time that certain dogmas do not necessarily belong in true Christianity. He cites the belief in purgatory and the adoration of relics that heretics did not subscribe to and who, consequently, were cruelly tortured to death.[11] The ambiguity surrounding some dogmas arises from the lack of unequivocal explanations in Jesus's own teachings and universal approval in the church:

> On sait que tous nos dogmes n'ont pas toujours été clairement expliqués et universellement reçus dans notre Église. Jésus-Christ ne nous ayant point dit comment procédait le Saint-Esprit, l'Église latine crut longtemps avec la grecque qu'il ne procédait que du Père: enfin elle ajouta au symbole qu'il procédait aussi du Fils. . . . Il n'y a pas longtemps que l'immaculée conception est établie: les dominicains n'y croient pas encore.

---

9. *Traité*, 132 (*Treatise*, 86).
10. *Traité*, 48 (*Treatise*, 19).
11. *Traité*, 44 (*Treatise*, 15).

(It is well known that our dogmas have not always been properly explained, nor universally received in our church. As Jesus Christ did not inform us in what manner the Holy Ghost operated, for a long time the Latin Church believed, along with the Greek, that it operated only through God the Father; later, they added that it could also work through God the Son. . . . It is not so long ago that the dogma of the Immaculate Conception was established; the Dominicans still refuse to believe it.)[12]

Voltaire cannot help concluding toward the end of the *Traité*:

moins de dogmes, moins de disputes; et moins de disputes, moins de malheurs: si cela n'est pas vrai, j'ai tort.

(The fewer dogmas one has to deal with, the fewer the disputes over them; and the fewer the disputes, the less the risk of calamity. If this is not true, then I am much mistaken.)[13]

Dogmatic thinking leads to disputes, which in turn lead to human misery.

When Voltaire considers the misery arising from religious intolerance, he thinks not only in terms of the emotional suffering it causes but also in terms of the physical suffering or the actions by which people are persecuted. These actions vary in their degree of intensity from the unjust to the absurd to the violent. Like numerous other acts of intolerance, the *affaire Calas* follows to some extent this progression. Sieur David, the municipal magistrate of Toulouse in charge of the case had the whole Calas family imprisoned in chains without adhering to the standard operating procedures in such cases, thereby flouting the rules of justice, law, and order. At best, the system of justice in eighteenth-century France lacked a number of protections and rights for the accused, who could not argue their cases in public. The system safeguarded the secrecy of court proceedings and, in many cases, the arbitrariness of the court's decisions, as Jean-François Perrin has pointed out.[14] Jean Calas's

---

12. *Traité*, 85 (*Treatise*, 51).

13. *Traité*, 133 (*Treatise*, 87).

14. Jean-François Perrin, *Politique du renonçant : le dernier Rousseau : des Dialogues aux Rêveries* (Paris: Éditions Kimé, 2011). Rousseau, Perrin claims, was acutely aware of

son Marc-Antoine had probably committed suicide, but the father is wrongly accused of having hanged his own son, supposedly to keep him from converting to Catholicism. Jean Calas's wife and his other son, Pierre, are also implicated as accomplices, as are a friend of the family named Lavaisse and a woman servant. The subsequent series of events takes on absurd theatrical qualities that Voltaire is quick to point out:

> Jamais aucune Église ne célébra la fête d'un martyr véritable avec plus de pompe; mais cette pompe fut terrible. On avait élevé au-dessus d'un magnifique catafalque un squelette qu'on faisait mouvoir, et qui représentait Marc-Antoine Calas, tenant d'une main une palme et de l'autre la plume dont il devait signer l'abjuration de l'hérésie, et qui écrivait en effet l'arrêt de mort de son père.

> (Never had any church celebrated the feast of a martyr with greater display. Yet there was something dreadful about this ceremony. Above a magnificent catafalque they placed a skeleton, which they contrived to move and jerk. It bore in one hand a palm, and in the other a quill. The skeleton represented Marc-Antoine Calas, the quill the instrument of his supposed recantation; except that it signed instead the death warrant of his father.)[15]

The events draw to a grisly end with the violent and awful death of Jean Calas on the wheel. Despite the painful blows to his limbs that his executioners presumably break one by one, as was the custom with this type of punishment, Jean Calas continues to profess his innocence before he dies.

Although merely one event, Jean Calas's painful death typifies for Voltaire the long history of religious intolerance. The city of Toulouse itself still celebrates a feast day for having "égorgé, il y a deux cents ans, quatre mille des ses concitoyens" (massacred, two hundred years ago, four thousand of the city's inhabitants), marking the victory of Catholics

---

the injustices of the legal system and structured the arguments in his *Dialogues* accordingly to counter these deficiencies.

15. *Traité*, 34 (*Treatise*, 6).

over Protestants during the religious wars of the Renaissance.[16] Some religious practices, when not merely absurd, can be horribly violent. Voltaire does not have to look far in France's history to find examples of religious bloodletting. The Reformation furnishes ample proof, as Voltaire enumerates the cases in chapter III: the annihilation of six thousand Vaudois (or Waldenses), nine civil wars, the assassinations of Henri III and IV by the Catholic League, and, of course, the infamous Saint Bartholomew's Day massacre. Ironically, by the late 1750s, shortly before the Calas case, the Protestant problem was beginning to find sympathetic supporters "among liberal Catholic theologians and lawyers."[17] But serious problems clearly remained.

Given the excesses to which religions can go in their barbarity, one wonders with Voltaire whether there remains any hope of a charitable form of religion. In his *Traité*, Voltaire presents, however, not just the barbaric side of religion but also a human side that takes on secular characteristics. When properly practiced, religion shares political, social, intellectual, and emotional or behavioral goals with the secular order that Voltaire was promoting. In the political realm, freedom constitutes just as important an objective for religious leaders as it does for secular ones. Voltaire cites a number of sources as authorities for the connection he makes between religion and freedom:

C'est une impiété d'ôter, en matière de religion, la liberté aux hommes, d'empêcher qu'ils ne fassent choix d'une divinité: aucun homme, aucun dieu, ne voudrait d'un service forcé.

(In matters of religion, it is impious to rob men of their liberty, to prevent them from choosing their deity. No man, and no god, would wish for an enforced adherence.)[18]

Si on usait de violence pour la défense de la foi, les évêques s'y opposeraient. (Saint HILAIRE, liv. Ier)

---

16. *Traité*, 79–80 (*Treatise*, 46).

17. See the pertinent section of John Renwick's introduction to his critical edition of Voltaire's *Traité sur la tolérance in Les Oeuvres complètes de Voltaire*, vol. 56c (Oxford, UK: Voltaire Foundation, 2000), 11–27, esp. 18.

18. *Treatise*, 70: *Apologeticum*, chap. 24.

(If violence were employed to defend the faith, the bishops would oppose it.)[19]

La religion forcée n'est plus religion: il faut persuader, et non contraindre. La religion ne se commande point. (LACTANCE, liv. III)

(Enforced religion is no religion at all; the essence is to persuade, not compel. Religion cannot be adopted on command.)[20]

Voltaire reasserts the freedom of conscience that allows men and women to choose the religion they desire to practice without fear of persecution. Partisans of tolerance at the time advocated freedom of conscience to seek truth in matters of religion and spirituality, whereas those on the side of intolerance used their self-proclaimed duty of protecting a more absolute, dogmatic notion of truth to justify the persecution of others.[21] The depiction of human beings as free agents here foreshadows what will come at the end of the century in the *Déclaration des droits de l'homme et du citoyen (Declaration of the Rights of Man and of the Citizen)*. The right to choose freely in all matters, including religion, should be a universal right. Intolerance, Voltaire suggests, infringes on that right by the use of force, violence, or both.

The social goals of progress, civilization, law, and fraternity also apply to religious and secular worlds. Voltaire believed society had made great strides and France had shown the way to a better world. He writes of the enormous progress achieved under Louis XIV in his *Essai sur les moeurs* and *Le Siècle de Louis XIV*.[22] He was also aware that he himself was living in times of tremendous change and in his *Traité* calls attention to it:

19. *Treatise*, 70: St. Hilarius, book I.
20. *Traité*, 109. Although Voltaire presents all the quotations in chapter XV as "Témoignages contre l'intolérance" (or "Authorities against persecution"), they also clearly point to the innate freedom in humans. *Treatise*, 70: Lactantius, book III.
21. Sébastien Charles, "De Pascal à Locke: sources et enjeux philosophiques du concept de tolérance chez Voltaire" in *Voltaire: La Tolérance et la justice*, ed. John Renwick (Leuven, Belgium: Peeters, 2011), 158.
22. See John C. O'Neal, "Perceptual Dimensions of French Culture in Voltaire's Historical Writings," in *Changing Minds: The Shifting Perception of Culture in Eighteenth-Century France* (Newark: University of Delaware Press, 2002), 46–69.

et ne nous apercevons-nous pas que presque toute l'Europe a changé de face depuis environ cinquante années?

(and have we not noticed that practically the whole face of Europe has changed over the last fifty years or so?)[23]

Using the interrogative form for his observation, Voltaire realizes, however, that much still remains to be done. But his question does not eclipse the fact that

la douceur de la société [a] pénétré chez ceux qui conduisent l'esprit de ces peuples.

(gentle manners [have] reached to the men who instruct the minds of these people.)[24]

In writing his *Traité*, Voltaire looks both to the immediate future for a positive outcome for the Calas family's case and to posterity for a wholly transformed society:

Je sème un grain qui pourra un jour produire une moisson. Attendons tout du temps.

(I have tried to sow a seed from which one day there might be gathered a harvest. For the rest, we depend upon the fullness of time.)[25]

Voltaire frequently associates progress with "civilized manners" (my translation) or, as he puts it in the *Traité*, "la douceur des moeurs." Yet he cannot help pointing out the cruel irony of the Toulouse bicentennial celebration of the 1562 massacre of Protestants with its overheated speeches at the same time as "cent académies écrivent pour inspirer la douceur des moeurs!" (a hundred academies have devoted their energies to the promotion of decency and gentleness in public affairs!).[26] However much religion can stoke humans' passions, it has also in the middle of a war "adoucissait quelquefois leurs fureurs" (acted . . . occasionally

---

23. *Traité*, 47–48 (*Treatise*, 18).
24. *Traité*, 47 (*Treatise*, 18).
25. *Traité*, 151 (*Treatise*, 100).
26. *Traité*, 35 (*Treatise*, 6).

[as] a mollifying stay upon their ferocity).[27] Religion can contribute to what Norbert Elias has called "the civilizing process," or what the period itself called *politesse*.[28] Voltaire's own religion, as professed in the *Traité*, consists in "l'unique dessein de rendre les hommes plus compatissants et plus doux" (the sole desire of making mankind more compassionate and charitable [read "gentle," which corresponds more to the tenor of Voltaire's writings here]).[29] In making humans more compassionate and gentle, Voltaire recognizes the appropriate connection between religion and humanity. In fact, he points out the hypocrisy of the abbé Malvaux's title *Accord de la religion et de l'humanité*, which should read "*l'inhumanité*" (*Inhumanity*), Voltaire says, and he presents it as diametrically opposed to his own goal.[30]

A substantial section of the *Traité*, chapters XII–XIII, studies the correlation between divine law and tolerance. Voltaire examines first Judaism, then Christianity to determine if these religions condone or even command intolerance. No great admirer of the Jewish religion and at times bordering on the anti-Semitic, even Voltaire must conclude that Judaism cannot be accused of intolerance:

> En un mot, si l'on veut examiner de près le judaïsme, on sera étonné de trouver la plus grande tolérance au milieu des horreurs les plus barbares. C'est une contradiction, il est vrai; presque tous les peuples se sont gouvernés par des contradictions. Heureuse celle qui amène des moeurs douces quand on a des lois de sang!

> (In a word, if one is prepared to examine Judaism closely, one will be surprised to find, in the midst of barbaric horrors, the most extraordinary spirit of tolerance. Yes, it is a paradox, but then nearly all people have been governed by some measure of

---

27. *Traité*, 61 (*Treatise*, 29).

28. Norbert Elias, *The Civilizing Process: The History of Manners and State Formation and Civilization*, trans. Edmund Jephcott (1939, 1968; Oxford, UK: Blackwell, 1994). See also Peter France, *Politeness and its Discontents: Problems in French Classical Culture* (Cambridge: Cambridge University Press, 1992).

29. *Traité*, 143 (*Treatise*, 94).

30. Ibid.

contradiction; happy are those whose society is gentle though their laws be bloody!)[31]

As for Christianity, Voltaire finds few passages in the Gospels that might legitimize intolerance.[32] For the most part he considers Christianity a tolerant religion and places Jesus Christ on the side of the persecuted rather than on that of the persecutors:

> Je demande à présent si c'est la tolerance ou l'intolérance qui est de droit divin? Si vous voulez ressembler à Jesus-Christ, soyez martyrs, et non pas bourreaux.

> (I will now enquire whether it is tolerance which is divinely ordained, or intolerance. If you want to be like Jesus Christ, better be a martyr than a hangman.)[33]

Although hardly going so far as to advocate religious laws for the secular state he ultimately desires, Voltaire more or less favorably compares divine laws from the two major Western religions with the shambles of civil laws he sees around him. Whereas divine laws usually, if not always, reinforce tolerance, the laws meting out justice in Voltaire's day are at best insufficient, arbitrary, or confusing.[34] At worst, they bring about gross injustices, as in the *affaire Calas*. Lacking justification either in divine law or human law, intolerance has no "base rationnelle," as Stéphane Pujol has observed.[35]

In addition to the social goals of progress, civilization, and law, Voltaire also envisions a possible shared sense of social solidarity or fraternity between religion and the state. In his prayer to God, the subject of chapter XXIII, Voltaire prays for a great many things, but he ends his prayer with a powerful plea for fraternity: "Puissent tous les hommes se souvenir qu'ils sont frères!" (May all men remember that they are

---

31. *Traité*, 99 (*Treatise*, 63).

32. *Traité*, 101 (*Treatise*, 64).

33. *Traité*, 107 (*Treatise*, 69).

34. *Traité*, 36, 152 (*Treatise*, 7, 100).

35. Stéphane Pujol, "Tolérer l'intolérance: de la pétition de principe aux actualisations littéraires" in *Voltaire: La Tolérance et la justice*, ed. John Renwick (Leuven, Belgium: Peeters, 2011), 119. Intolerance has no "rational basis."

brothers!).[36] The religious notion of fraternity has particular resonance in the *Traité* because it rejoins the related notion of humanity that Voltaire emphasizes throughout this work and which he largely associates with tolerance.[37] Voltaire suggests in his prayer that, in our intolerance and the persecution of our fellow human beings that it inevitably entails, we can lose sight of any sense of our sameness and equality in the eyes of God, for whom differences in clothing, language, customs, laws, opinions, and social classes mean nothing.[38] Rather than use our hearts and our hands to hate or hurt others, we should, Voltaire prays,

> nous nous aidions mutuellement à supporter le fardeau d'une vie pénible et passagère.
>
> (help one another to bear the burden of a difficult and transient life.)[39]

The church and state have common ground not just in political and social values but also in intellectual ones, such as truth, reason, and philosophy. But the church would have to be one much more closely aligned with its original form that, according to David Diop, derived from natural religion.[40] Or, as Sébastien Charles suggests, the best solution would be one in which civil religion, which could help reinforce social order—always a priority for Voltaire—is not allowed to degenerate into theological religion and its fanaticism.[41] It may seem odd that Voltaire, whose quick

---

36. *Traité*, 142 (*Treatise*, 92).

37. See, for example, the passage on the banishment of the Jesuits from Japan, which Voltaire considers "un exemple de tolérance et d'humanité" (*Traité*, 51), translated "a supreme example of tolerance and humanity" (*Treatise*, 22).

38. *Traité*, 141 (*Treatise*, 92).

39. *Traité*, 141 (*Treatise*, 92).

40. In referring to chapter XXV, Diop states, "Voltaire lays out his concept of natural religion [here] by playing on the etymology of the word church, which not only designates the assembly of the first Christians but also the edifice where they assembled. A clever way to suggest that Christian religion was built on the ruins of natural religion" (my translation). David Diop, "La rhétorique de la crédulité dans le *Traité sur la tolérance*: de la lecture à l'écriture de l'allégorie"; *Revue de Littératures Françaises et Comparées* 13 (1999): 119.

41. Charles, "De Pascal à Locke," 171. On Voltaire's desire for social order, see also Gerhardt Stenger, "L'intolérance catholique, 1750–1770," in *Voltaire: La Tolérance et la justice*, ed. John Renwick (Leuven, Belgium: Peeters, 2011), 99–118; and John Renwick's introduction to his critical edition of Voltaire's *Traité sur la tolérance*, 29–40.

eye was often drawn to outrageous errors—the fables of history or the superstitions of religion—could find any truth in religion. Like many philosophes, he saw it as his duty to root out error.[42] But in the *Traité*, he aims not only to expose error but to untangle truth from the web of lies fabricated by historians of secular and religious history:

> Le mensonge en a trop longtemps imposé aux hommes, il est temps qu'on connaisse le peu de vérités qu'on peut démêler à travers ces nuages de fables qui couvrent l'histoire romaine depuis Tacite et Suétone, et qui ont presque toujours enveloppé les annales des autres nations anciennes.

> (Falsehood has for too long held sway over the minds of men. It is time we sought to discover the few truths which we may discern through the vast clouds of fable which cover Roman history from the time of Tacitus and Suetonius, and which have nearly always smothered the annals of other nations in the ancient world.)[43]

The same rigor he uses for ancient history he applies to religion. Voltaire in fact distinguishes between true and false religion, a pure form from God and one to which humans have added numerous unnecessary, and sometimes corrupt, accretions. Many people, weary of the "fraudes pieuses et de toutes les superstitions" (pious fraud and superstition),[44] may even turn away from true religion:

> Tous ces faux miracles par lesquels vous ébranlez la foi qu'on doit aux véritables, toutes ces légendes absurdes que vous ajoutez aux vérités de l'Évangile, éteignent la religion dans les coeurs.

> (All these false miracles by which you unsettle the confidence due to true ones, and all these absurd legends with which you clutter the truth of the Gospels, stifle religion in the hearts of men.)[45]

42. For this Enlightenment project, see David William Bates, *Enlightenment Aberrations: Error and Revolution in France* (Ithaca, NY: Cornell University Press, 2002).

43. *Traité*, 77 (*Treatise*, 44).

44. *Traité*, 81; "pious fraud and superstition" (*Treatise*, 48).

45. *Traité*, 81 (*Treatise*, 48).

Paradoxically for religion more so than for secular history, Voltaire's method for uncovering errors consists in the judicious use of reason and of philosophy, which informs it. Voltaire reunites the two traditions of philosophy and religion that are, on his account, too often opposed. They can indeed work together to accomplish much good for both religious and secular worlds:

> La philosophie, la seule philosophie, cette soeur de la religion, a désarmé des mains que la superstition avait si longtemps ensanglantées; et l'esprit humain, au réveil de son ivresse, s'est étonné des excès où l'avait emporté le fanatisme.

> (Philosophy, that is the only true philosophy, the sister of Religion, has now disarmed hands so long bloodied by superstition, and the human spirit, as it recovers from its toxic madness, stands astonished at the excesses to which bigotry once brought it.)[46]

Like reason, philosophy is making progress in Voltaire's times and is necessary for continued progress.[47] Moreover, the march of reason, advanced considerably by the enlightened thinking of Pascal, Descartes, Bayle, and Fontenelle, among others, cannot be stopped:

> Chaque jour la raison pénètre en France, dans les boutiques des marchands comme dans les hôtels des seigneurs. Il faut donc cultiver les fruits de cette raison, d'autant plus qu'il est impossible de les empêcher d'éclore.

> (With each day that passes, the power of reason is seeping as much into the houses of tradesmen as into the grand mansions of the nobility. We must needs harvest the fruits of this reason, particularly since it is impossible to prevent their blossoming.)[48]

The link between reason and religion becomes especially clear in Voltaire's analysis of the emotional or behavioral goals of religion and society. Some of these, such as love (and, to some extent, charity) and

---

46. *Traité*, 49 (*Treatise*, 20).
47. *Traité*, 35, 47 (*Treatise*, 6, 18).
48. *Traité*, 131; (*Treatise*, 85).

gentleness, echo the social calls for fraternity and civilization, whereas others, such as forgiveness and pity, complement the general purpose of cultivating all of these emotions, namely, tolerance. Revealingly, Voltaire does not speak much of love or charity in the *Traité*.[49] More often and more conservatively, as the following passage and passages quoted in the first part of this study underline, he enjoins human beings not to hate or detest one another:

> ne nous haïssons pas, ne nous déchirons pas les uns les autres dans le sein de la paix.

> (let us at least not hate one another or tear each other apart in the midst of peace.)[50]

Voltaire avoids the stronger expression of love because, faced with the carnage of intolerance, he keeps minimal expectations. If humans can merely tolerate one another—love being practically too much to ask—they will have made enormous progress. In one of the rare references to the Christian human emotion of love, Voltaire reminds the followers of a merciful God of the words from the Gospel of Luke: "Aimez Dieu et votre prochain" (Love thy God and thy neighbour), as they have "surchargé cette loi pure et sainte de sophismes et de disputes incompréhensibles" (smothered that pure and holy doctrine with sophistries and unfathomable controversies).[51] All too often humans separate the objects of love in this divine commandment by loving God but not their fellow human beings.[52] Again, Voltaire underscores the purity of the original religious message that humans have corrupted.

Likewise, charity proves somewhat problematic for Voltaire. He does indeed ask the fundamental question in the *Traité* about religion's barbaric or charitable tendencies. In its adjectival form, the word

---

49. The only two occurrences of the word *amour* are in a secular context: "l'amour de l'équité" or "love of equity," referring to the judges' sense of this in the appeal (*Traité*, 149; *Treatise*, 98) and "l'amour de la nation" or "love of the nation" (*Traité*, 156; *Treatise*, 105).

50. *Traité*, 142; (*Treatise*, 93).

51. *Traité*, 139; (*Treatise*, 91).

52. The other occurrences of the verb *aimer* (to love)—loving more unequivocally with God than with humans as the object—bear out such a distinction. See *Traité*, 41 (*Treatise*, 12, also in note 2); *Traité*, 141 (*Treatise*, 92); and *Traité*, 143 (*Treatise*, 94).

charitable appears to maintain its positive connotation.[53] When describing the general emotions and the tears shed over Madame Calas and her daughters, who have joined her in prison at the time, the appeal seems finally to be moving in her favor, however, Voltaire carefully avoids using the word *charité*:

> L'humanité, la générosité, leur prodiguaient des secours. Ce qu'on appelle la *charité* ne leur en donnait aucun. La charité, qui d'ailleurs est si souvent mesquine et insultante, est le partage des dévots, et les dévots tenaient encore contre les Calas.
>
> (Humanity and nobility of heart lavished assistance upon the women; 'charity' gave them none. Charity, which is besides often mean and insulting, belonged to those of a religious disposition, and they were still very much against the Calas family.)[54]

Voltaire discerns a certain hypocrisy in the so-called charity of those who supposedly practice their religion devoutly.

Instead of speaking in terms of love and charity, Voltaire prefers to characterize the desired emotions or behaviors that promote tolerance as gentleness, forgiveness ("indulgence" in French according to Masters's translation), and pity. The goals of religion reinforce those of the ideal society Voltaire has in mind in the *Traité*. In the Gospel's parables, "Jésus-Christ prêche la douceur, la patience, l'indulgence" (Christ exhorts patience, gentleness and forgiveness).[55] Voltaire's own goal in the *Traité*, as mentioned previously, consists in making humans more compassionate and gentle.[56] Voltaire reflects in part here the seventeenth-century moralists' view of the passions, which one should moderate as much as possible. A passion such as hate, for instance, could be regulated by the positive quality of generosity, as Descartes suggests in his *Passions de l'âme*.[57] In the case of Voltaire, gentleness, forgiveness, and pity would all presumably serve to attenuate the passion

---

53. See *Traité*, 40 (*Treatise*, 11); *Traité*, 69 (*Treatise*, 36); and *Traité*, 104 (*Treatise*, 66).

54. *Traité*, 155 (*Treatise*, 104).

55. *Traité*, 104 (*Treatise*, 66).

56. *Traité*, 143 (*Treatise*, 94).

57. René Descartes, *Les Passions de l'âme*, in *Oeuvres de Descartes*, ed. Charles Adam and Paul Tannery, vol. 11 (Paris: Vrin, 1996), III: clvi, clviii, 447–48.

of hatred, which poses one of the greatest threats to true tolerance. For Voltaire, forgiveness represents a "devoir sacré" (sacred duty), by which he valorizes not only the importance of forgiveness for a just and tolerant society, but also for a religious one.[58] Moreover, forgiveness comes to play an integral part in our happiness, which religion guides for this world and the next:

> La religion est instituée pour nous rendre heureux dans cette vie et dans l'autre. Que faut-il pour être heureux dans la vie à venir? être juste. Pour être heureux dans celle-ci, autant que le permet la misère de notre nature, que faut-il? être indulgent.
>
> (Religion is instituted in order to make us happy in this life and in the next. What is necessary to be happy in the life to come? That we be just. And to be happy in this life, in so far as our perverse nature will allow, what is necessary? That we be tolerant and merciful.)[59]

By being forgiving, we not only follow Jesus' preaching and gain in our spirituality according to Christianity but also accomplish the secular goals of improving our lot and the lot of others on this earth. Finally, pity or commiseration, as Voltaire sometimes refers to it, can also lead to tolerance. Voltaire seems to concur with Rousseau in his view of pity as a sign of our humanity.[60] Voltaire speaks of commiseration in the same breath as tolerance and forgiveness, and, as would Rousseau, calls it "l'apanage de la nature" (the natural prerogative of Humanity).[61] According to Voltaire, Paris and all of Europe are moved to pity by the *affaire Calas*.[62] Voltaire implies that one would have to be devoid of any humanity—a beast or a barbarian—not to pity the Calas family.

---

58. *Traité*, 111 (*Treatise*, 71).

59. *Traité*, 133 (*Treatise*, 87).

60. Rousseau saw in pity one of the last vestiges of natural man. See Jean-Jacques Rousseau, *Discours sur l'origine et les fondements de l'inégalité parmi les hommes*, in *Oeuvres complètes*, ed. Bernard Gagnebin and Marcel Raymond, vol. 3 (Paris: Gallimard, 1964), 126, 154–55.

61. *Traité*, 39–40 (*Treatise*, 11).

62. *Traité*, 39 (*Treatise*, 10).

The political, social, intellectual, and emotional or behavioral goals that Voltaire illustrates as potentially shared ideals for religion and the state may lead one to question Voltaire's own secularism. But Voltaire endeavors to reorient the status quo in the eighteenth century that had the state serving a corrupt form of religion. In the new world he imagines in the *Traité*, Voltaire believes either that a purified religion would actually serve the purposes of the state or that the two would work hand in hand. It is not clear from the *Traité* which of these two scenarios prevails. Voltaire begins to conclude the *Traité* on a pious, religious note with a prayer to God in chapter XXIII. But the last two chapters of the 1763 edition focus less on God or religion than on humanity.[63] In chapter XXIV, he implies that he does a better job than the abbé Malvaux of showing the connection between religion and humanity, and is therefore the best spokesman for humanity. The final chapter includes Voltaire's revealing response to a letter he received from someone in the Languedoc region. In his reply, which Voltaire practically reproduces in full and which represents his final word in the 1763 *Traité*, Voltaire has nature, not God, speak. More remarkable, Voltaire personifies nature, which speaks at some length in the first person: "La nature dit à tous les hommes: Je vous ai tous fait naître faibles et ignorants" (Nature tells us all, 'You have been born weak and ignorant').[64] Nature goes on to give men commandments: "Secourez-vous . . . éclairez-vous et supportez-vous" (You must look after one another . . . you must educate each other).[65] It is also nature, in Voltaire's response to his Languedoc correspondent, that has given us a "germe" (seed) of reason that we are commanded not to snuff out or corrupt, as it is "divin" (divine).[66] With the word *divin* Voltaire seems to pay respect to God or a Supreme Being. But a series of "moi seule" ("I alone"), all referring to nature, reestablish the authority of this secular voice:

---

63. The 1765 edition adds yet another chapter that recapitulates the final and favorable verdict in the appeal of the Calas case. It is in this additional chapter that Voltaire bitterly calls attention to the lack of charity among supposedly devout people.

64. *Traité*, 151 (*Treatise*, 100).

65. Ibid.

66. *Traité*, 151–52; "seed" and "divine" (*Treatise*, 100).

C'est moi seule qui vous unis encore malgré vous par vos besoins mutuels. . . . C'est moi seule qui, dans une nation, arrête les suites funestes de la division interminable. . . . Moi seule je conserve l'équité dans les tribunaux. . . . Seule je peux inspirer la justice.

(I alone bind you still further to one another, despite yourselves, by your mutual needs. . . . I alone can put a stop to the disastrous consequences of those interminable divisions. . . . I alone preserve fairness in the law-courts. . . . I alone can inspire true justice.)[67]

This shift to a secular tone at the very end of the *Traité* makes of Voltaire ultimately not so much a defender of the faith as a defender of humanity. So, too, does it illustrate the occasionally troubled relation between Christianity and enlightenment for the period.[68] In any event, Voltaire's form of religion remains problematic in the *Traité* and in his *oeuvre* as a whole.[69] Religion does not have to be barbaric; Voltaire knows enough about its original, essential qualities to see how it can fill for the state a truly charitable function, which for him consists in putting people back in touch with their humanity. At the end of the Calas appeal, Voltaire

67. *Traité*, 152; (*Treatise*, 100).

68. For René Pomeau, the sincerity of Voltaire's prayer in chapter XXIII is obvious. See the introduction to his edition of the *Traité*, 25. Current eighteenth-century research is exploring the nexus between Christianity and enlightenment, and is proposing new terms such as *humanisme chrétien* or "Christian humanism" (my translation), which might possibly apply—I would suggest—to certain passages of Voltaire's *Traité*. See Sylviane Albertan-Coppola, "Présentation et état des recherches," in "Christianisme et Lumières," ed. Sylviane Albertan-Coppola and Antony McKenna, *Dix-Huitième Siècle* 34 (2002): 8.

69. According to René Pomeau, Voltaire, obsessed as he was both with the idea of a fearsome God and of cruel priests, was greatly influenced by English philosophy's notion of a lenient God, and he adhered ultimately and most consistently in his life to deism as a religion. See his *La Religion de Voltaire* (Paris: Nizet, 1969), 463–64. Related, of course, to deism is natural religion—devoid of any identification with existing religions—which is what Raymond Trousson finds in the *Traité*. Raymond Trousson, "Voltaire et la liberté de pensée: le *Traité sur la tolérance*," *Revue de Littératures Françaises et Comparées* 13 (1999): 150–51. Both Pomeau and Trousson, however, point out Voltaire's strong aversion to atheism, which might allow the powerful to "justify their crimes" (my translation). See Raymond Trousson, "Tolérance et fanatisme selon Voltaire et Rousseau," in *Rousseau and l'Infâme: Religion, Toleration, and Fanaticism in the Age of Enlightenment*, ed. Ourida Mostefai and John T. Scott (Amsterdam and New York: Rodopi, 2009), 39.

celebrates the renewed reign of "l'humanité et de la justice chez les hommes" (justice and humanity . . . in the breasts of men!).[70] Tolerance prevails, Voltaire believed, when men and women recognize they are human, and Voltaire strove admirably throughout his life to remind us of our fundamental humanity.

---

70. *Traité*, 149; (*Treatise*, 100).

Sacred or Profane Pleasures? Erotic Ceremonies in Eighteenth-Century French Libertine Fiction

Marine Ganofsky
University of St. Andrews

I n France, the Age of Enlightenment was also an age of literary lev-
ity that saw a proliferation of erotic and pornographic narratives in
which philosophy often fused with sexual gratification. The famous
Choderlos de Laclos with his *Liaisons dangereuses* (1782) and the infamous Marquis de Sade, along with authors such as Crébillon and Vivant
Denon, epitomize this moment in French literary history, when erotic
freedom paired with intellectual liberty. This "libertine" literature, as
it is known, is characterized by its focus on fleshly desires and pleasures. The subject matter of libertine novels, short stories, poems, and
paintings is the rendezvous that brings together the characters for an
initiation into, or a celebration of, erotic delights. Indeed, lovemaking
is often described as a religious ceremony. Why is this so? Why should
lust be narrated with a religious lexicon? Why should lovers express
rapture through imagery that is normally associated with the church?
Why should fornication be orchestrated as a ritual?

First, by blending together religious images and eroticism, libertine
authors highlight that libertinism stems from intellectual emancipation: parodying religious ceremonies and associating worship with lust
requires a certain audacity and independence with respect to what is
traditionally and institutionally held as sacred. Second, the comparison

of certain erotic scenes to religious ceremonies appears to be connected to the desire not only to profane religion but also to sacralize pleasures and paint them with the reverence they are deemed to deserve.

The objective of this article is to argue that the libertines' intellectual independence does not necessarily entail their rejection of religious concepts such as God, the sacred, and worship. Rather, their emancipation means that they feel free to redefine these concepts. The parody of ceremonies in libertine fiction stems less from a *rejection* than from a *redefinition* of what is sacred or divine. What libertines worship does not have to be the God of the Christian Church. Their deity can instead be Nature, Reason, Pleasure, or Liberty. And because they are free to rethink the concept of God as they please, libertines can develop a much more intimate relationship with this concept, hence its intrusion into bedrooms and boudoirs. In this article, therefore, I argue that the erotic ceremonies featured in libertine fiction permit the authors to underline their protagonists' intellectual emancipation but not necessarily their lack of a spiritual dimension.

The present analysis of the libertine stance toward religious matters touches upon the wider reality of the Age of Enlightenment. It raises the question of what follows in civilization when God is dead. Could there exist an ontological need for the concept of the Divine, whether the divinity in question be equated to the biblical God or to an abstract notion like reason or *jouissance*? Indeed, if Diderot's skepticism finally led him to atheism, Voltaire's enlightenment made him a deist, not an atheist. Later, during the French Revolution, the Committee of Public Safety abolished the Christian "cult" but replaced it with a worship of the Supreme Being, a paradox that Sade denounced: "Était-il besoin de briser les autels de la superstition et du fanatisme pour en arriver à reconstruire à l'envers ce culte grossier?"[1] (Was it necessary to break down the altars of superstition and fanaticism to come to rebuild upside down this vulgar cult?)[2] We must then wonder about the purpose of the erotic ceremonies that thrive in libertine fiction: Do authors want to suggest Man's

---

1. Donatien Alphonse François de Sade, "Sade contre l'Être suprême," in *"Sade contre l'Être suprême," précédé de "Sade dans le temps,"* ed. Philippe Sollers (Paris: Gallimard, 1996), 61.

2. Unless otherwise noted, all translations are my own.

all-too-human need for a divine dimension? Or do they want to ridicule this idea by creating such witty parodies of worship?

The question of the possible ontological need for a religion preoccupies many branches of the human sciences. While the psychology of religion tries to understand why men, whatever their epoch or culture, have felt the need to believe in a supernatural power, the evolutionary psychology of religion argues that answers are to be sought on the societal, rather than the individual, level. Academic battles are fierce between those who defend the theory that men and women neither need deities nor faith and that evolution will triumph in the twilight of the idols[3] and those who claim that religions are the backbone of human consciousness[4] as well as of societies. David Hume had already put forth such a justification for faith as early as 1757:

> No wonder, then, that mankind, being placed in such an absolute ignorance of causes, and being at the same time so anxious concerning their future fortune, should immediately acknowledge a dependence on invisible powers.[5]

The present article does not aim to answer these questions.[6] Neither does it aim to apply these modern theories nor to offer an anthropological perspective from which to understand libertine fiction. Rather, I explore a literary representation—perhaps a fantasy—of one of the

---

3. Echoed by Sam Harris in *The End of Faith: Religion, Terror, and the Future of Reason* (New York: W.W. Norton, 2004) and Christopher Hitchens in *God Is Not Great: How Religion Poisons Everything* (New York: Warner Twelve, 2007). Richard Dawkins, for instance, defines religion as a mass delusion and atheism as the healthy reaction to that disease or weakness of the mind. See *The God Delusion* (New York: Bantam, 2006).

4. A school of anthropology of religion regards positively what they call an ontological instinct to believe in the supernatural, akin to the survival instinct. See Pascal Boyer's *Religion Explained: The Evolutionary Origins of Religious Thought* (New York: Basic Books, 2001); and Justin L. Barrett's *Why Would Anyone Believe in God?* (Washington: Rowman & Littlefield, 2004).

5. David Hume, *The Natural History of Religion* (1757), quoted in Frank E. Manuel, *The Eighteenth Century Confronts the Gods* (Cambridge, MA: Harvard University Press, 1959), 127.

6. A synthesis of the impact of the laicization of the post-eighteenth-century Western world can, however, be found in the fine and comprehensive work edited by Marcel Gauchet, *The Disenchantment of the World: A Political History of Religion* (Princeton, NJ: Princeton University Press, 1999).

various contemporary reactions to the "disenchantment of the world" that arose as a consequence of the Enlightenment.

Through the representations of erotic ceremonies in eighteenth-century French literature, I show that libertinism, one of the responses to the (relative) dechristianization of Europe, was characterized neither by a pure despair nor by a pure joy at the idea of a metaphysical void. Libertines enjoyed the freedom that came with the gradual vanishing of the Christian God and the weakening supremacy of Christian traditions—but often because it meant that they could toy more freely with the concept of religion. New idols replaced the old ones in the metaphysics of eighteenth-century libertinism. The libertines' universe is indeed dechristianized; their private lives are likewise freed from the dominion of the church, but these hedonists refuse to have their world altogether "disenchanted." The persistence of religious structures and images allows libertine pleasures to truly thrive, either through the delights of an ultimate, blasphemous transgression of old principles or through the experience of sex as the ultimate form of bliss, a mystical *jouissance* reaching both the flesh and the mind at once. To understand the libertine literary representations of sex as sacred, and their attachment to religious concepts despite their intellectual emancipation, we must refer to Sigmund Freud. In his later days, he came to regard the need for idols as the sign of a desire to open up the mind to possibilities set beyond the empirical world.[7] Therefore, from a libertine perspective, transforming lovemaking into a ceremony can reveal a conceptualization of erotic bliss as an emotion beyond the everyday experience of the common people.

At the core of the present reflection on the literary representations of libertine ceremonies is the idea of blasphemy and what it might signify. This article progresses by addressing successively the two main aspects of blasphemy: first, blasphemy blatantly arises from the desire to show scant respect for a thing held divine. Indeed, these libertine ceremonies

---

7. Freud developed this idea in his last book, *Der Mann Moses und die monotheistische Religion* (1939; Ditzingen: Reclam, 2010). Previously, he had regarded faith as a childish rampart against the dread of death and the desire for the existence of God as akin to a child's crying need for a father. See *Die Zukunft einer Illusion* (1927; Bremen: Europäischer Literaturverlag,).

first and foremost belong to a libertine manifesto affirming their participants' intellectual insubordination. The tone is light, irreverent, droll, and provocative; it is part and parcel of the libertine's reaction to any institution that seeks to impede the fulfillment of their desires. In the first part of this article, I therefore analyze why libertine lessons are narrated as ceremonies of initiation and explain how this relates to the blasphemous stance that characterizes libertinism. In particular, I argue that the ceremonial overtone of erotic lessons is driven by the fact that such educations aim to debunk the church's notion of what is sacred, revealing instead to pupils where sacredness really lies for a libertine: not in institutions and usual hierarchies but in the abandonment to Nature's impulses. Born anew after their first lessons, novices are now able to let go of, and even ridicule, former restrictions and definitions.

Second, however, blasphemy remains a gesture through which the sacred and the profane are united. Could we see, beyond the libertine bravado of parodying ceremony and demystifying the Christian ritual, a hint of a longing to bridge the gap between the two dimensions and perhaps even to touch the sacred? In the second part of my article, I consider libertine ceremonies as genuine celebrations of Pleasure—a new deity deserving worship.

Libertine Education as Initiatory Ceremonies

In libertine fiction, the ceremonious nature of certain rendezvous is often the spontaneous outcome of the education it represents for one of the participants. The lessons that libertine masters share with their pupils go beyond the scope of usual tutoring. They represent less an education than an initiation, more a rite of passage than a lesson. Whereas education just reforms one's way of thinking, an initiation radically transforms one's being.

The term *initiation* in the most general sense denotes a body of rites and oral teachings whose purpose is to produce a decisive alteration in the religious and social status of the person to be initiated. In philosophical terms, initiation is equivalent to a basic change in existential condition; the novice emerges from his or her ordeal endowed as a totally different being from that which he or she was before his or her initiation; the novice has become *another*.[8]

So frequent are scenes akin to an initiation ritual present in libertine fiction that initiatory ceremonies can be considered as a topos of the genre. This should not be a surprise in a literature that, although ranging from the sentimental to the pornographic across the span of the century, finds a unifying principle in the educational motive. Whatever their stance toward pleasure, whether they condemn or condone one's abandonment to temptations, all libertine authors describe the enlightenment of a character with regard to sexuality, a new facet of which is revealed to him or her in the course of the story.

The crux of a libertine education is erotic. Yet, an entire new perspective on the world is revealed through sexuality. Patrick Wald Lasowski, perusing the depths of libertine frivolity and resorting to the imagery of liberation ("s'est délivré" [freed himself]), comments on the existential dimension of the countless erotic discoveries that punctuate the history of libertine literature:

> Il y a, à travers la diversité des formes, une structure romanesque dominante. Le roman libertin est . . . roman de formation. Il fait le récit d'une initiation, d'une découverte, d'une exploration du monde, au terme de laquelle le héros s'est délivré des doutes, des hésitations, des terreurs qui l'habitaient.[9]

> (There is, despite the diversity of forms, a governing novelistic structure. The libertine novel is . . . a novel of education. It tells the story of an initiation, a discovery, an exploration of the world, at the end of which the hero has freed himself from the doubts, hesitations, and terrors that haunted him.)

Characters learn from their encounters with one another. Should one be younger or obviously less experienced than his or her partner, the erotic narrative borrows heavily from the didactic lexicon. A mistress remains

---

8. Mircea Eliade, *Rites and Symbols of Initiations: The Mysteries of Birth and Rebirth* (1958), trans. Willard R. Trask (Woodstock, NY: Spring, 1995), x.

9. Patrick Wald Lasowski, foreword to *Romanciers libertins du dix-huitième siècle*, ed. Patrick Wald Lasowski, 2 vols. (Paris: Gallimard "Pléiade," 2005), 1:xlvii.

a mistress, but a lover becomes another's pupil or master, and an intercourse becomes a lesson taught by "immoral teachers" (as in Sade's *La Philosophie dans le boudoir, ou les instituteurs immoraux* [1795]). The one-night affair described in *Point de lendemain* (1777) has been called "une leçon de nuit"[10] (a night lesson) whereas, through the libertine perspective of Andréa de Nerciat (1739–1800), the surprising discovery of sodomy becomes an "impromptu doctorate" (*Le Doctorat impromptu* [1788]). This collusion of eroticism with education serves as a reminder that historically, libertinism has its roots in intellectual emancipation rather than in debauchery.

When the term *libertine* first appeared in the early modern period, it was to describe and denounce a sect of Anabaptists. It was then synonymous with "atheist," "skeptic," "deist," and any kind of religious dissident. What defined a libertine was his or her intellectual independence from dogma, as if echoing the word's ancient meaning—a *libertinus* was a freed slave in ancient Rome. By the seventeenth century, this independence often walked hand in hand with a disregard of certain socioreligious values, such as monogamy and temperance. It was also punishable by fire: many a free spirit died on the stake in the first decades of the Grand Siècle[11] for having refused to conform to the sanctioned definition of God and finding divinity, instead, in their appetites: "Ils n'ont d'autre Dieu que leur ventre"[12] (They have no other God than their stomach). As the century progressed, under Louis XIV's ever tighter moral codes, prudery increased, which relegated sexual freedom to secrecy and relative silence. At the same time, the progress of Reason was digging a channel for emancipated spirits to express themselves. Fontenelle's, Bayle's, and Saint-Évremond's intellectual independence no longer made libertines of them but, already, men of the Enlightenment. The eighteenth century's free spirits—Montesquieu, Voltaire, Diderot—are labeled as *philosophes*. A century earlier, they would have

---

10. Philippe Sollers, *Le Cavalier du Louvre : Vivant Denon, 1747–1825* (Paris: Plon, 1995), 79.

11. Such was the fate of Jules César Vanini in 1619. Théophile de Viau was condemned to the same sentence but was eventually burned only in effigy.

12. Le Père Garasse, *La Doctrine curieuse des beaux esprits de ce temps* (Paris: Charpillet, 1622), 37.

been "libertines," but by the beginning of Philippe d'Orléans regency (1715–23), the term is reserved for rakes and fornicators, prostitutes and fallen ladies. Until recently, French history tended to consecrate the idea of a shift from one type of libertinism—intellectual or *érudit*[13] in the seventeenth century—to another—merely physical in the eighteenth.

However, libertine literature, as has been widely recognized, blurs traditional boundaries by multiplying examples of texts that partake at once of the pornographic novel and of the philosophical essay.[14] In an age when adultery and fornication are still officially condemned by society and the church, sexual freedom demands a certain form of intellectual emancipation. Therefore, any erotic story somehow narrates the independence (acquired or being acquired) of a protagonist with regard to institutions and the Christian religion. Religious dissidence, while tacit in some novels,[15] can be central in other libertine writings. Blasphemy then takes center stage.

Such novels often advertise their anti-ecclesiastical stance in their very titles, as can be seen in the famous examples of *Histoire de Dom Bougre ou le portier des chartreux* (1740), *Histoire galante de la tourière des carmélites* (1743), and *Les Lauriers ecclésiastiques* (1748).[16] These novels continue a tradition of philosophical and theological dialogues infused with pornography that Aretino (often regarded as the father of Western pornographic literature) consecrated with his *Ragionamenti: La Vita delle Monache, La Vita della Maritate, La Vita delle Puttane* (1534–36), in which the lives of married women and of prostitutes come second only to the beguiling lives of nuns. The late seventeenth century had given libertine authors from the Age of Enlightenment new models reviving this

13. The expression *libertins érudits* was coined by René Pintard in his thesis. See *Le Libertinage érudit dans la première moitié du dix-huitième siècle* (Paris: Boivin, 1943).

14. To such an extent that in his effort to categorize eighteenth-century literature, Henri Coulet has labeled pornographic texts *romans philosophiques*. See *Le Roman jusquà la Révolution*, 2 vols. (Paris: Colin, 1967).

15. The tales of Crébillon, Duclos, and Dorat, for instance, do not emphasize the necessary "enlightenment" of their protagonists.

16. Respectively written by Gervaise de Latouche, Meusnier de Querlon, and La Morlière. One can also think of the anonymous *Le Triomphe des religieuses ou les Nonnes babillardes* (1748), *Lettres galantes et philosophiques de deux nonnes* (1777), and *Les Exercices de dévotion de M. Henri Roch* (1786).

tradition, such as *Vénus dans le cloître ou la Religieuse en chemise* (1683). The authors and the implicit readers of such texts seem to have relished the collision of two mutually exclusive discourses and images: the pornographic and the religious.

These texts' anti-ecclesiastical stance manifests itself in the most vivid manner as nuns, monks, priests, and devout women are revealed as the most lustful creatures of the libertine universe. Yet, they also show that transgression is pleasure's best accomplice. The more transgressive, the better—hence the bliss of the nuns and monks who pervert the Christian ritual they live by. Most famously, the monks who capture, rape, torture, and kill their victims in dark orgies in Sade's *Justine, ou les infortunes de la vertu* (1791), as well as the monks and nuns from two neighboring institutions who meet in nocturnal debauchery in *Dom Bougre,* illustrate the pleasure of perverting the most sacred symbols of an institution. When these rakes meet, they do not free themselves from the order of the ritual. Quite the contrary: they reproduce the structure of a mass and repeat the words of the religious service. Sexual excitation is enhanced by the libertines' self-consciousness about breaking the rules as well as by their pride at managing to wittily pervert the would-be pure meaning of religious ceremonies.

One text, the highly anti-ecclesiastical *Thérèse philosophe* (1748), best illustrates the pleasure—both sensual and intellectual—to be gained from perversion. It opens with the fantasized details of an actual and well-known scandal in the eighteenth century: the seduction of a young nun by her priest. From a closet, the narrator and protagonist, Thérèse, is watching it all happen. Père Dirrag makes his penitent kneel and pray, promising that her obedience and devotion will make her feel the presence of the "cordon de Saint François" (Saint François's knot), which he administers from behind: "Par ce moyen il s'assure qu'elle ne tournera pas la tête, qu'elle ne verra rien de son impudicité"[17] (He can thus make sure that she will not turn her head, that she will see nothing of his impudicity). The extreme innocence of Eradice makes the scene comic, albeit acid: "Elle croit tomber dans une extase divine, purement

17. Jean-Baptiste de Boyer d'Argens, *Thérèse philosophe, ou Mémoires pour servir à l'histoire du P. Dirrag et de Mlle Éradice* (1748), in *Romanciers libertins du dix-huitième siècle*, 1:892.

spirituelle, lorsqu'elle jouit des plaisirs de la chair les plus voluptueux"[18] (She thinks she is falling in a divine ecstasy when she is in fact enjoying the most voluptuous pleasures of the flesh). The religious discourse is used on two parallel levels for many pages in *Thérèse philosophe*, as if to signify that this language is in itself pregnant with vice.

Such texts are obviously highly blasphemous. Their authors, not content to simply mock the church, also mock religious feelings when they conflate physical ecstasy with religious emotion. This contributes greatly to the humor and satire of these texts. A devout woman succumbs, to the delight of her libertine lover, with ejaculatory prayers:

> Quelle jouissance qu'une dévote! Que de charmants riens! Comme cela vous retourne! Quel moelleux! Quels soupirs! . . . Ah! ma bonne Sainte Vierge! . . . Ah! mon doux Jésus![19]

> (What an ecstasy a devout woman can be! So many charming little things! How it can upset you! What a softness! What sighs! . . . Ah! Holy Virgin Mother! . . . Ah! Sweet Jesus!)

Another devout woman confuses her apprentice's cries of pleasure for an ecstatic prayer; she just fails to notice the young man hidden under the apprentice's skirts:

> La voilà qui se persuade que Cécile récitait ses prières. "Continuez, mon enfant, continuez. . . . Vous êtes dans la voie du salut." . . . C'étaient les titillations de cette langue agile qui avaient causé dans les sens de Cécile ce désordre que Geneviève avait pris pour un élan de dévotion.[20]

> (Here she is, convinced that Cécile was repeating her prayers. "Keep going, my child, keep going. . . . You are on the way to salvation." . . . It was the tease of that dexterous tongue that had

---

18. Ibid., 1:891.

19. Honoré-Gabriel de Riquetti, Comte de Mirabeau, *Ma Conversion, ou Le Libertin de qualité* (1783), in *Romanciers libertins du dix-huitième siècle*, 2:982.

20. Charles Pigault-Lebrun, *L'Enfant du bordel* (1800), in *Romanciers libertins du dix-huitième siècle*, 2:1239.

caused in Cécile's senses that disorder that Geneviève had mistaken for an impulse of devotion.)

Similar examples abound, and all serve the same purpose of profaning the religious discourse and underlying its vacuity. Such passages aim to reveal that the believers' virtue is but an illusion (at best, it is fragile and ready to crumble at the first temptation) and that religion can only be an absurdity because its language makes no sense to the point of lending itself to the emotion it condemns: erotic bliss. Through blasphemy, libertine authors aim to reveal the legitimacy and even the supremacy of pleasures of the flesh over religious or social prejudices.

Beyond the lack of respect, blasphemy is a demonstration of independence and of defiance toward God and his word as proclaimed by the Ten Commandments: "You shall not make wrongful use of the name of the Lord your God."[21] Through blasphemy or blasphemous behaviors, libertines claim that they have no fear of God's punishment, an act of bravado that Don Juan and most of his fictional avatars, from Molière's Dom Juan (1660) to Mozart's Don Giovanni (1687), have epitomized in their challenge to the statue of the commander, as if to say that if there exists a metaphysical power in the universe, it should manifest itself to punish their insults. Jean Starobinski has detected in such provocations the possibility of a tacit, desperate cry for a God:

Ils préfèrent blasphémer la figure traditionnelle du Père. Ils se replient dans le rêve du défi et de la faute, pour susciter en fin de compte une punition où ils trouveront la preuve d'une Présence dont ils ne peuvent se passer.[22]

(They prefer to blaspheme the traditional figure of the Father. They lock themselves in the dream of a challenge and a fault, to eventually trigger a punishment in which they will find the proof of a Presence without which they cannot live.)

Still, beyond this doubt, this possibility, there is one certitude: the libertine thus advertises himself or herself as free from the bondage of fear

---

21. Exodus 20:7 (New Revised Standard Version [NRSV]).
22. Jean Starobinski, *L'Invention de la liberté: 1700–1789* (Geneva: Skira, 1987), 74.

and submission to a higher power. The only power to which a libertine might concede is that of his or her appetites and drives. The fear of damnation, just like the belief in virtue, belongs, according to them, to inferior beings. In a fine study of three supreme examples of eighteenth-century libertinism—Versac from Crébillon's *Les Egarements du cœur et de l'esprit* (1735–1738), Valmont from *Les Liaisons dangereuses*, Sade through his heroes—Pierre Saint-Amand has portrayed libertines as "immortals,"[23] promethean figures set above the rest of common men, satanic seducers rivalling God, should God exist. They rival, if not with God, at least with the concept, through a battle they lead in the minds of the devout women they seduce.[24] Valmont reveals his project to his accomplice the Marquise de Merteuil in terms that lift his enterprise of corruption to the metaphysical sphere: "J'aurai cette femme ; . . . j'oserai la ravir au Dieu même qu'elle adore. . . . Je serai vraiment le Dieu qu'elle aura préféré"[25] (I shall have this woman; . . . I shall dare stealing her from the very God she adores. . . . I shall truly be the God she will have preferred). Seduction, worldly as it is, can take cosmic proportions. Through sin and blasphemy, libertines affirm their belonging to a chosen few who have refused to let the church and its Christian God limit their impulses.

Yet, these chosen few sometimes decide that a novice is worthy of being initiated to their wisdom and is invited to join their superior sphere from which God has been dethroned. Thus what they provide is no longer a simple education but an initiation, and the enlightenment they offer is considered to be of such a magnitude that it is worthy of a ceremony. Of course, the fact that the demystification of the church and its dogma should be staged as a ceremony is in itself a blasphemy; it is yet another challenge to the concept of an Almighty God and to the idea that the church alone has the right to declare what to worship. The libertine ceremonial, which sublimates depravation into an initiation,

---

23. Pierre Saint-Amand, "The Immortals," trans. Jennifer Curtis Gage, in *Libertinage and Modernity*, ed. Peter Cryle and Catherine Cusset, Yale French Studies 94 (New Haven: Yale University Press, 1998), 116–29.

24. Betty Becker-Theye also saw a satanical grandeur in these seducers' enterprises. See *The Seducer as Mythic Figure in Richardson, Laclos and Kierkegaard* (New York: Garland, 1988).

25. Pierre Ambroise François Choderlos de Laclos, *Les Liaisons dangereuses*, in Laclos, *Œuvres complètes*, ed. Laurent Versini (Paris, 1979), p.1–386 (p.22).

constitutes in itself a first step toward intellectual independence: what used to be the sole property of the church in eighteenth-century France is now owned by libertines. Libertines have redefined what is sacred and what is profane. Erotic desire, they explain, is only profane for the "profanes," for the nonenlightened souls who "détournent les éjaculations naturelles de leur cœur pour en diriger les élans vers des êtres fantastiques. L'amour est un dieu profane qui ne mérite pas leur encens. . . . C'est pour nous un blasphème que d'exprimer l'amour."[26] (Deviate the natural ejaculations of their hearts and address such impulses to fantastical beings. Love is a profane god that does not deserve their incense. . . . It is for us a blasphemy to express love). This erotic love is what is presented as worthy of reverence and secrecy, of being wrapped in a silence that confers it its sacred dimension, as we shall see in the second part of this article. The novices' acceptance of this reversal of values is a first step toward their libertine enlightenment, toward the revelation of what libertines hold as sacred.

The blasphemous nature of these initiatory ceremonies is symbolically reinforced by their setting: they take place at night. The surrounding darkness acts as a metaphor for the intellectual journey that the novice is about to undertake and that will set him or her free from the rule of Christ, the Light of the World.[27] Libertine narrators enjoy the polysemy of their descriptions when it comes to darkness. Indeed, the tenebrous setting envelops the scene in a depth of religious resonances. It is sometimes said in passing, casually, but this feigned airiness only highlights the novice's momentous move from light to darkness, virtue to vice, as in *Thémidore* (1744), in which the young narrator follows a courtesan into the dark recesses of her alcove: "Nous passâmes vers le côté obscur"[28] (We moved to the dark side). The transition is both literal and metaphorical for this young man who surrenders to depravity. Libertine authors are here playing with the codes of the Johannic Manicheism

---

26. Anon. [Mirabeau?], *Le Rideau levé, ou L'Éducation de Laure* (n.p., 1786, n.p.: Au Palais sous les robes, 1882), 1.

27. "I am the light of the world. Whoever follows me will never walk in darkness, but will have the light of life" (NRSV, John 8: 12).

28. Claude Godard d'Aucour, *Thémidore* (1744), in *Romanciers libertins du dix-huitième siècle*, 1:523.

used by the church: if light is the domain of Christianity and virtue ("God is light, and in Him is no darkness at all" [NRSV, John 1:5]), night will be theirs, lending them and their pupils a perfect setting for educations that will be in fact countereducations, teaching the reverse of what is taught in daylight.

Libertine literature displays a taste for ironic contrasts as sharp as the day-night dichotomy: harp classes in the afternoon for Cécile de Volanges but "catéchisme de débauche"[29] (catechism of debauchery) at night with Valmont in *Les Liaisons dangereuses*,[30] a father-and-daughter relationship in the daytime for Laure and her stepfather in *Le Rideau levé* but lessons of voluptuousness together and with her governess in hours of darkness, prayers and religious instruction from dawn to dusk in convents but sapphic initiations from dusk to dawn for the countless nuns of anti-ecclesiastical fiction who admit to "[se] branl[er] du soir au matin"[31] (masturbating from evening to morning). This duality also serves to proudly advertise the successful hypocrisy of these masters of libertinism who manage to live two antithetic lives. Even before the advent of libertine fiction, it was commonly acknowledged that nocturnal lessons could only be deviant: emblematically, the medieval scholar Pierre Abelard recalled how his theological tutoring of Héloïse would metamorphose itself at night: "Mes nuits éta[ie]nt données à l'amour, mes journées au travail"[32] (My nights were given to love, my days to work). If sunlit hours must be lived in accordance with public laws and religious prejudices, nocturnal educations can teach disciples to dedicate themselves to the ideals of individual happiness, truth, and nature. The lesson, from Rousseau's *Emile* to the pornographic *Mémoires de Suzon* (1778), is invariably the same: society and the church have wronged humankind in setting up laws that are in perfect contradiction to Man's nature:

29. Choderlos de Laclos, *Les Liaisons dangereuses*, Letter CX, 354.

30. On the educative motive in Laclos's novel, see Susan Dunn, "Education and Seduction in *Les Liaisons dangereuses*," *Symposium* 34 (1980): 125–37.

31. Anon., *Mémoires de Suzon, sœur de D.B. . . ., portier des Chartreux, écrits par elle-même* (1778), in *Romanciers libertins du dix-huitième siècle*, 2:900.

32. Pierre Abelard and Héloïse, *Correspondance* (1120s), ed. Edouard Bouyé and trans. Octave Gréard (Paris: Gallimard, 2000), 68.

L'homme même a forgé de ses propres mains son malheur, et aiguisé les traits qui doivent lui percer le cœur. Ne serait-il pas à désirer qu'il n'eût jamais suivi que l'instinct de la nature, plutôt que de s'être soumis à des lois et à des coutumes qui n'ont été inventées que pour le malheur de l'humanité?[33]

(Man himself has crafted his misery with his own hands and sharpened the darts that shall pierce his heart. Should not one wish that he had only ever followed nature's instinct rather than submitting himself to laws and customs that have been invented only for humanity's misery?)

This is the introductory lecture of all libertine educations, hence Sade's opening his *Philosophie dans le boudoir* with an introductory warning to his readers:

Ces passions, dont de froids et plats moralistes vous effraient, ne sont que les moyens que la nature emploie pour faire parvenir l'homme aux vues qu'elles a sur lui; n'écoutez que ces passions délicieuses.... Détruisez, foulez aux pieds ... tous les préceptes ridicules inculqués par d'imbéciles parents.[34]

(These passions, with which cold and pointless moralists scare you, are but the means that Nature uses to lead Man to the ambitions it has for him; listen only to these delicious passions.... Crush, trample over all the ridiculous precepts taught by imbecile parents.)

Thus the "immoral teachers" of libertine literature are shown encouraging their disciples to listen to the call of the wild and to escape from what in their view is an arbitrary and absurd social order.

This emancipation constitutes the core material of the anonymous novel *Le Rideau levé, ou l'éducation de Laure* (1786), in which a man and a governess teach his stepdaughter to become an independent spirit and

---

33. Anon., *Mémoires de Suzon*, 898.
34. Sade, *La Philosophie dans le boudoir* (1795), in *Œuvres*, ed. Michel Delon, 3 vols. (Paris: Gallimard "Pléiade," 1990), 3:1.

therefore a happy woman. From an early age onward, Laure has been taught the virtues of skepticism; philosophy must replace her prejudices: "Apprends de bonne heure à réfléchir et à former ton jugement, en le dégageant des entraves du préjugé"[35] (Learn rapidly to think and to form your judgment by freeing it from the shackles of prejudice). She must rethink the boundaries that the church and society have set between Good and Evil. The Christian God, in this libertine catechism, as in Sade's, is replaced by Nature, which willfully made men as creatures of cravings:

> Consultons la nature : quels ont été son but et ses desseins? La reproduction des êtres, et elle n'a imprimé tant de plaisirs dans l'union des sexes que pour y parvenir d'une manière agréable et par conséquent plus sûre.[36]

> (Let's consult Nature: what were its goals and objectives? The reproduction of beings, and it has only put so many pleasures in the union of the sexes in order to fulfill its objective through agreeable—and therefore safer—means.)

The enlightenment described in this novel is given a metaphysical air from the title page onward. The lifted curtain of the title, the one thanks to which Laure will discover the physical bliss of her two tutors, is a direct reference to the etymology of "apocalypsis": the lifting or tearing of the curtain hiding the truth. Through the allusion to a revelation, Laure's very factual education (sexual and philosophical) becomes a parable for an initiation to a new definition of the sacred. As Mircea Eliade explains, initiation not only signifies the end of childhood and ignorance, it also implies the end of one's profane condition.[37] Thus, the hierophany featured in Le Rideau levé can be understood as revealing to the novice Laure that the truly sacred is in fact the laws of Nature prompting man to seek jouissance.

To further highlight the sacred nature of the revelation made to Laure, when she is finally about to be initiated into the mysteries of sexuality,

---

35. Anon. [Mirabeau?], Le Rideau levé, ou L'Éducation de Laure, 18–19.
36. Ibid., 155.
37. Eliade, Rites and Symbols of Initiations, x.

her tutors are careful to re-create all the attributes of an initiatory ceremony. In a boudoir, a mystical night is reproduced through dimmed blue lights ("la lumière du jour en était absolument bannie. . . . Les foyers de quatre réverbères . . . adoucis par des gazes bleues" [daylight was absolutely banned from the room. . . . The fire of four torches . . . softened by blue veils]), and the bed is transformed into a sacrificial altar ("Je me jetai de moi-même sur l'autel" [I threw myself on the altar]).[38] The use of the semantic field of ritual sacrifices can be justified by its aesthetic function within the text. These references are rhetorical allusions to the ancient world, and their role is to ornate the text just as statues of Greek gods ornate interiors and gardens in the early modern period. Yet, these mentions of sacrifices and altars, of crowns and worships, also serve to startle the reader and convey the intensity of the impact that the sexual discovery has on the existence of the initiated character.

This moment, the culmination of Laure's initiation, must result in her transformation into a new being; Laure's old self is therefore ritually sacrificed. Her blood must be spilled—"mets-moi toute en sang" (make me bleed)—to make room for the new, enlightened woman that her defloration will have turned her into. The masters of this initiation ceremony tie her waist, hair, and arms with "rubans couleur de feu" (ribbons the color of fire) and place the neophyte on a sacrificial cushion of the same color—"un petit coussin de satin couleur de feu, mis au milieu, qui formait la pierre sur laquelle devait se consommer le sacrifice" (a small pillow the color of fire, put in the center, which stood for the stone on which the sacrifice was to be consummated)—that shall evoke the purification through fire followed by the phoenix-like rebirth of her whole being. Ritually, on this altar, Laure dies—"J'étouffais, je mourais ; mes bras, mes jambes, ma tête tombèrent de toutes parts ; je n'étais plus à force d'être" (I could not breathe, I was dying; my arms, my legs, my head fell altogether; by being, I stopped being)—and starts her life on a new first day: "Le premier où j'ai connu les délices de la volupté" (The first when I knew the delights of voluptuousness). Although erotic ecstasies have often been described as little deaths far beyond the scope of libertine writings, libertine authors are careful to emphasize the rebirth

---

38. All quotes on this page come from Anon. [Mirabeau?], *Le Rideau levé*, 60.

that follows certain of these blackouts. Once reborn a libertine, one can finally worship the new sacred that has been revealed throughout this initiation: pleasure.

Ceremonies as Celebrations of Pleasure

When libertine authors paint sexual gratification with poses and colors that are normally the prerogatives of the religious sphere, they are not necessarily positioning themselves against all religious notions.[39] Their characters' blasphemy, their defiance, and their insults are directed against the Christian Church and its polarization of the erotic and the divine alongside the dichotomy of evil and good, profane and sacred. Refusing the dogmatic premises on which the devaluation of sexuality in the Western world has been based, libertines and libertine authors return to an original and actual definition of the sacred when they associate it with the pleasures of the flesh. They show an understanding of the fact that the sacred and the divine are two different things, despite the Christian tradition of assimilating them.

Anthropologists such as Émile Durkheim, Rudolf Otto, and Mircea Eliade[40] have remapped the two domains of sacred and divine. They stress the fact that the sacred can exist independently from the church. Whereas the divine is necessarily sacred or sacralized by religious institutions, the sacred is not necessarily divine: it does not have to relate to a god. The sacred, they explain, is characterized by its remoteness from the normal order of things—from the profane, the everyday—hence Man's instincts to erect temples in remote places, to perform ceremonies at night while others sleep (from Bacchanalia to Aphrodisies to Easter or Christmas wakes), and to provide heavy doors to churches

---

39. Alexis de Tocqueville, at the end of the century, had already remarked that the hatred for the church was greatly due to the clergy's disproportionate riches, not exclusively to the symbols it used. On this subject, see Starobinski, *L'Invention de la liberté*, 116.

40. Émile Durkheim, *Les Formes élémentaires de la vie religieuse : Le Système totémique en Australie* (1912; Paris: Presses Universitaires de France, 2013); Rudolf Otto, *The Idea of the Holy [Das Heilige]* (1917; Oxford: Oxford University Pres, 1968); and Mircea Eliade, *The Sacred and the Profane: The Nature of Religion*, trans. Willard R. Trask (New York: Harper Torchbooks, 1961).

behind which believers are separated from the buzz of the modern world. In all these situations, what is experienced is something new and different from the normality of the everyday. The *ganz andere*, the "absolutely other," and the *mysterium tremendum*, the "overwhelming mystery," that accompanies its contemplation, define the sacred, according to Otto and his followers.[41] Only the divine is associated with gods. The sacred, by contrast, can be found anywhere, even in something as worldly and earthly as physical pleasures. The sacred is a way of seeing and existing in the world by being aware of the *majestas*[42] characterizing this other dimension.

To understand what prompted libertines to associate sexuality with a form of sacredness, we must remember that since the early seventeenth century, sexuality belonged to a dimension severed from daily life, relegated to the nocturnal and to the bedroom or closet.[43] As Michel Foucault has seminally explained in his *Histoire de la sexualité* (1976–1984), sex and the discourses of pleasure have not only been *demonized* but also—paradoxically—*sacralized* by centuries of repression.[44] The libertine novel, as one of these discourses about eroticism, is therefore endowed with the sacredness that used to be the privilege of religious predication:

> C'est le sexe aujourd'hui qui sert de support à cette vieille forme, si familière et si importante en Occident, de la prédication. . . . Demandons nous comment il a pu se faire que le lyrisme, que la religiosité . . . se soient . . . reportées, pour une bonne part au moins, sur le sexe.[45]

---

41. Otto introduced the terms *ganz andere*, *mysterium trememdum*, and *mysterium fascinans* in *Das Heilige*. His theories and definitions are summed up by Mircea Eliade in the introduction to *The Sacred and the Profane: The Nature of Religion*, trans. Willard R. Trask (New York: Harper Torchbooks, 1961).

42. Eliade, *The Sacred and the Profane*, 17.

43. Philippe Ariès and Georges Duby have commented on this exacerbation of the notions of privacy and intimacy with regard to the body (and consequently to sexuality) in *Histoire de la vie privée*, vol. 3, *De la Renaissance aux Lumières* (Paris: Seuil, 1985).

44. Michel Foucault, *Histoire de la sexualité*, vol. 1, *La Volonté de savoir* (Paris: Gallimard, 1976), 14.

45. Ibid., 15.

(It is sex nowadays that serves as a support to this old form of predication that is so familiar and so important in the Western world. . . . Let's ask ourselves how it can have happened that lyricism, religiosity . . . could have been transferred, if only partially, onto sex.)

Foucault does not mention any blasphemous stance in this collusion of the former sacred with the new. Confined to secrecy, it was natural that libertine texts and pleasures gained an almost numinous aura that libertine narrators only magnify, and with which they ironically play, when they turn orgies into ceremonies or see sacred ecstasies where there is but a physical orgasm. In fact, the man who can perceive the presence of the sacred in the world, whether in the spectacle of the nocturnal sky or in erotic bliss, is not necessarily a blasphemer but truly a "religious man."[46]

Thus the provocation addressed against the Church's sacred (when libertines become nuns or when they use altars and calices for their sexual pleasures) is not necessarily a blasphemy of that wider definition of sacredness and of that religious feeling. Rather, libertines' blasphemous ceremonies become a celebration of this exceptional, otherworldly dimension that has been revealed to them in the awe-inspiring intensity of erotic bliss.

Besides, even their actual blasphemy of a certain form of (mostly Christian) sacredness can perhaps be interpreted as meaning more than disrespect, even if only on a subconscious level. It is indeed one of the attributes of blasphemy to bridge the gap between sacred and profane, or divine and worldly, as Alain Cabantous has remarked in his study of blasphemy in the Western world:

Avec le blasphème, il s'agit de prendre la mesure de la relation entre le divin et l'humain, de saisir la limite entre deux mondes co-existants et pourtant de plus en plus distincts dans l'approche spirituelle de l'Europe moderne.[47]

---

46. This is how Mircea Eliade defines the "religious man" throughout *The Sacred and the Profane.*.

47. Alain Cabantous, *Histoire du blasphème en Occident: XVIe–XIXe siècles* (Paris: Michel, 1998), 10–11.

(With blasphemy, what is at stake is the evaluation of the relation between the divine and the human, the capture of the limit between worlds which co-exist although they are getting more and more distinct in the spiritual approach of modern Europe.)

This would explain why libertines and libertine authors were not willing to get rid of the symbols and religious cults that punctuate their narratives, such as altars, temples, and ceremonies. By redefining the sacred as independent from any instituted religion, they could have forsaken all these signs and traditions. Yet, the choice to keep these symbols reinforces the impression that pleasure is truly sacred. Besides, jouissance is enhanced by being experienced as something fabulous, beyond the everyday:

Au lieu de promouvoir une réalité neuve, l'on prend pour modèle un théâtre d'ombres : ainsi, faisant irruption dans le monde moderne, la liberté commence par ajuster sa figure sur de grands précédents fabuleux.[48]

(Instead of promoting a new reality, they take a theater of shadows as their model: thus, breaking in the modern world, freedom starts by shaping its form on grand and fabulous precedents.)

Pleasure is thus celebrated in a manner normally reserved for deities.

Of course, the ceremonial staging of libertine orgies must be deemed blasphemous. The intention to parody is undeniably present. However, the religious discourse and its imagery represent the best—if not the only—way to express intense emotions. This corroborates Cabantous's suggestion that what motivates blasphemy is not always solely a blasphemous intention. Referring to pleasure by resorting to the imagery of religious bliss is a natural, almost instinctive attempt to cope with the ineffable. Ejaculatory prayers such as "ah mon Dieu" come out instinctively. Beyond the comical effect produced by the proximity of sin and faith, these prayers that punctuate many a love scene in libertine fiction efficiently underline the characters' automatic recourse to religion to describe unearthly feelings rather than to provoke the Church or God.

---

48. Starobinski, *L'Invention de la liberté*, (Villeneuve d'Ascq: Presses Universitaires du Septentrion, 2003), 117.

Félicia, narrating her hedonist youth, often faces the impossibility of translating her emotions in order to share them with her readers. Nevertheless, ellipses and prayers can equally well suggest the boundless nature of her bliss: "Dieux! . . . Quelle nuit! . . . Quel homme! . . . Quel amour!"[49] (Gods! . . . What a night! . . .What a man! . . . What a love!) The sacred discourse of the church and the erotic narrative share the deep consciousness of their unavoidable failure to express the unfathomable nature of the emotions they are concerned with. As Florence Deschamps remarks in her analysis of the meaning of blasphemy in libertine texts:

> Au-delà d'une simple perversion du lexique religieux effec-
> tuée dans une intention parodique, le recours au sacré pour
> dépeindre une jouissance amoureuse s'inscrit en fait dans la
> tradition des grands textes chrétiens. Pensons au *Cantique des
> Cantiques.*[50]

> (Beyond the simple perversion of the religious lexicon per-
> formed with a satirical intention, resorting to the sacred in order
> to represent an amorous bliss inscribes itself in fact in the tradi-
> tion of great Christian texts. One can think of the *Song of Songs.*)

Staging lovemaking as a ceremony, or expressing pleasure with words borrowed from the religious lexicon, is thus a form of reverence, a way to acknowledge the awe-inspiring and unfathomable nature of the pleasure one seeks. For libertines, it is a sign of a refusal to reduce sex to a simple fact and instead to magnify the impact it has on their lives. It is part and parcel of the libertines' efforts toward refinement that so often characterize their eroticism. Michel Delon calls this "le passage de la pulsion sexuelle au raffinement érotique"[51] (the shift from sexual pulsion to erotic refinement). Although they admit to being driven by

---

49. André-Robert Andréa de Nerciat, *Félicia, ou Mes Fredaines* (1775), in *Romanciers libertins du dix-huitième siècle*, 2:861.

50. Florence Deschamps, "'Au commencement était le verbe . . .': Parole sacrée et blasphème au sein des écrits érotiques du XVIIIe siècle," in *Libertin, mon ami*, ed. Patrick Wald Lasowski, Revue des Sciences Humaines 271 (Lille: Villeneuve d'Ascq: Presses de l'Univ. Charles-de-Gaulle, 2003), 83–84.

51. Michel Delon, "L'espace de la séduction dans le roman français du dix-huitième siècle," in *Littérature et séduction*, ed. Roger Marchal (Paris: Klincksieck, 1997), 382.

their appetites, most libertines do not welcome the prospect of copulating like animals. Their pleasures thus demand a mise-en-scène, hence, sometimes, their games of seduction, repetitions, accessories, and ceremonies too. Anything susceptible to giving emotions and sensations a special, possibly stupefying, resonance is priceless in a century when Man discovers he exists only through these sensations. As Georges Poulet has shown in his *Études sur le temps humain*, the Age of Enlightenment corresponds to a period in Western history when only the here and now mattered once the certitude of an afterlife had been shattered by the Enlightenment. Beyond the here and now is a void of apathy from which only sensations can lift Man: "A la place de Dieu, il y a des sentiments, des sensations, tout ce qui cause ces sensations."[52] (Instead of God, there are feelings, sensations, everything that causes these sensations), hence the libertines' cry for extreme emotions that can touch not only their bodies but also their minds. Ceremonies therefore appear as an efficient way to condition the mind for great pleasures and to build up expectations and desires by postponing their satisfaction.

The longing, not to say the need, to compare lovemaking to a ceremony is best exemplified in the short story *Point de lendemain* (1777). With this text, Vivant Denon wrote an apotheosis of libertine literature, before the dark libertinism featured in *Les Liaisons dangereuses* and the Marquis de Sade's fiction took over. *Point de lendemain* tells the story of one night between two lovers. Mme de T*** has abducted the young Damon from the opera and takes him for a night with "no tomorrow" to her husband's castle outside Paris. From the onset of the tale, this night has a peculiar resonance: "Le flambeau mystérieux de la nuit éclairait un ciel pur d'un demi-jour très voluptueux"[53] (The mysterious torch of night was lighting a pure sky with a very voluptuous *chiaroscuro*). The plot is simple and could be regarded as a dull, banal one-night stand between two strangers. Yet, the way in which it is narrated and the way in which it is actually experienced by the two protagonists forbids us from seeing a commonplace episode of fornication in this short story. Throughout the tale, we witness the couple's efforts to raise their

52. Georges Poulet, *Études sur le temps humain*, 4 vols. (Paris: Plon, 1949–68), 1:25.
53. Dominique de Vivant Denon, *Point de lendemain* (1777; Paris: Liseux, 1876), 9.

pleasures to the level of a sacred communion. This desire leads them
to perceive the presence of an otherworldly enchantment in the world:
"Notre imagination faisait d'une île qui était devant notre pavillon un
lieu enchanté"[54] (Our imagination transformed an island that was in
front of our pavilion into an enchanted place). From then on, a garden
pavilion can become a sanctuary (*sanctuaire*);[55] a boudoir, a temple; and
lovemaking a ceremony of worship to the god of erotic love.

What characterizes a ceremony is its careful and meaningful
orchestration. The lovers, conscious of this, decide to enjoy this night
by following a (worldly) ritual of seduction and by devising a buildup
toward the climax of their celebration:

> Tout ceci avait été un peu brusqué. Nous sentîmes notre faute.
> Nous reprîmes avec plus de détail ce qui nous était échappé.
> Trop ardent, on est moins délicat. On court à la jouissance en
> confondant toutes les délices qui la précèdent.[56]

> (All this had been a bit rushed. We felt our mistake. We started
> again, in more detail, what we had missed. Too eager, one is less
> delicate. By running to jouissance, one confuses all the delights
> that precede it.)

Their preliminary homage culminates with the perfect imitation of a
ceremony that starts as an initiation: "Tout cela avait l'air d'une initiation. . . . Mon cœur palpitait comme celui des grands prosélytes que l'on
éprouve avant la célébration des grands mystères"[57] (All this looked like
an initiation. . . . My heart was beating like that of a proselyte about to
be tried before the celebration of great mysteries). A temple has been
re-created within a boudoir where a statue of the god of love presides:
"Devant cette statue était un autel, sur lequel brillait une flamme; au bas
de cet autel étaient une coupe, des couronnes et des guirlandes"[58] (In
front of this statue was an altar, on which a flame was shining; at the

---

54. Ibid., 30.
55. Ibid., 53.
56. Ibid., 28.
57. Ibid., 43.
58. Ibid., 43.

base of this altar was a cup, wreaths, and garlands)—all the parapher-
nalia of religious worship instead of erotic accessories. Later, when their
celebration is complete, the lover is crowned: "La déesse prit une cou-
ronne qu'elle posa sur ma tête"[59] (The goddess took a wreath, which she
put on my head).

Vivant Denon is here reproducing a common trope of libertine art[60]
whereby lovemaking becomes a ceremony by blending together various
traditions, from Masonic meetings[61] to ancient rituals. Allusions to the
Masonic ritual are numerous: in *Point de lendemain*, such references
range from the blindfolding of the novice to his circumambulation in
a labyrinthine castle to a transit through the Room of Reflections (the
boudoir being full of mirrors) to his admission into the Temple to his
final fall and symbolic death. Still, despite these many details that often
fill the descriptions of libertine love scenes, the overall comparison
refers to ancient nocturnal ceremonies such as Priapées,[62] Aphrodisies, and Bacchanalia. Emblematically, in *La Nuit merveilleuse* (ca.
1790), the anonymous pornographic rewriting of *Point de lendemain*,
the Masonic atmosphere with its gospel of unselfish love gives way to
the worship of Priapus: "La scène avait changé : au lieu du temple et de
la statue de l'Amour, c'était celle du dieu des jardins"[63] (The scene had
changed: instead of the temple and statue of Love, it was that of the
god of gardens). Yet it is Bacchanalia, rather than Priapées, that provide libertine authors with the aptest comparison for the love scenes

59. Ibid., 46.

60. One can think of the paintings of Boucher and Fragonard, notably the latter's
allegories of love.

61. Mirabeau, Caylus, Nerciat, Duclos, Laclos, and Vivant Denon, to name but a few,
were all Freemasons.

62. This was indeed the time when "the arrogant connoisseur" Richard Payne Knight,
A Discourse on the Worship of Priapus (1786; London: Forgotten Books, 2008), and the
Londonian dilettanti, like libertine authors, were discovering the Priapic celebrations of
the ancient world. Vivant Denon himself was fascinated by Priapus, as witnessed by his
travelogues *Voyage en Sicile* (1788), ed. by Patrick Mauriès(Paris: Le Promeneur, 1993) and
Voyage dans la Basse et la Haute égypte pendant les campagnes du général Bonaparte (1802;
Paris: Gallimard, 1998). See also Hélène Lafont-Couturier, *Priapées et sujets divers gravés
par Dominique-Vivant Denon* (Paris: Réunion des Musées Nationaux, 2000).

63. Anon. [Vivant Denon?], *La Nuit merveilleuse, ou Le Nec plus ultra du plaisir* (ca.
1790), in *"Point de lendemain" suivi de "La Nuit merveilleuse,"* ed. Paul Emmanuel Auguste
Poulet-Malassis and Jean-Jacques Pauvert (Paris: Les Belles Lettres, 1993), 45.

they narrate. Euripides's *The Bacchae* (405 BC) offers an example of the extreme furore and forgetting of the self as of limits that characterize trance. We already noted the violence of the images used in *Le Rideau levé*, in which the girl's sacrifice requires the actual spilling of her blood. Likewise, in *Point de lendemain* the lovers' passion is described as a Dionysiac sacrifice: "On arrache un nœud, on déchire une gaze: partout la volupté marque sa trace, et bientôt l'idole ressemble à la victime"[64] (One tears down a bow, one tears a veil, everywhere voluptuous prints its mark, and soon the idol resembles the victim).

However, when libertine authors resort to the model of the Bacchanalia, it is not only to refer to the furore of the trance. They also aim to highlight the communion of souls that can take place in physical ecstasy. In *The Birth of Tragedy* (1872), Friedrich Nietzsche famously remarks that what defines the Dionysiac is this spiritual communion:

> Now, with the gospel of world harmony, each man feels himself not only united, reconciled, and at one with his neighbour, but one with him, as if the veil of Maya had been rent and now hung in rags before the mysterious primal oneness.[65]

Libertine authors seem to have had a strong intuition of what Nietzsche would later argue. Erotic bliss can be a communion beyond the limits of the material world. It is described as the utmost form of pleasure toward which lovemaking should tend, as La Mettrie remarks in his essay on the art of bliss: "Ce n'est point la jouissance des corps, c'est celle des âmes qu'il me faut"[66] (It is not the jouissance of the bodies but of the souls that I need). Even a cynical libertine like Valmont discovers the superiority of this jouissance—"ce charme inconnu que j'ai ressenti" (this unknown delight that I experienced)—when he finally makes love with the devout Mme de Tourvel. To describe it, he is forced to use the image of a Dionysiac trance: "L'ivresse fût complète et réciproque"[67] (The

---

64. Vivant Denon, *Point de lendemain*, 9.

65. Friedrich Nietzsche, *The Birth of Tragedy from the Spirit of Music* (1872), trans. Shaun Whiteside, ed. Michael Tanner (London: Penguin, 1993), 15.

66. Julien Offroy de La Mettrie, *L'Art de jouir* in *"L'Homme machine" suivi de" 'L'Art de jouir"* (1748 and 1753; Paris: Bossard, 1921), 148.

67. Choderlos de Laclos, *Les Liaisons dangereuses*, Letter CXXV, 295.

intoxication was complete and reciprocal). For once, his soul, too, has been convened to this erotic intoxication. This conception of lovemaking as a religious communion is where libertine writing merges with sentimental prose, and the pornographic description of a sacrifice-like intercourse is told with the same terms as Saint-Preux's in Rousseau's *Julie* (1761): bliss is a "tight union of the souls" (Rends moi cette étroite union des âmes).[68] There is a sublime dimension in such a bliss. Through the assimilation with a Dionysiac trance, jouissance is represented as a vertigo in which one can contemplate infinity, and in the eighteenth century, according to its "esthétique de l'infini" (aesthetics of infinity), what one perceives by contemplating infinity is God himself: "Dans l'infinité du monde, l'infinité de Dieu nous est rendue sensible"[69] (In the infinity of the world, the infinity of God is made sensible to us). From a libertine perspective, jouissance may thus have an organic justification for being experienced and represented as a religious ceremony.

Behind the libertine representation of lovemaking as a religious ceremony is the unifying principle of the characters' desire to transcend all limits. Through their blasphemy, they place themselves beyond society's laws, beyond the word of God, and beyond the limits normally prescribed to mortals. Their jouissance is described as an experience of infinity. On the one hand, one could argue that this effort to replace a form of worship (the Christian) with another is but a sign of their eagerness to fill in the void left by the "disenchantment of the world," as if the secularization of the Enlightenment had left behind it an existential despair and a longing for new deities to worship, whether these be Reason, Nature, or Pleasure. On the other hand, one could argue that through their blasphemous parodies of ceremonies, these libertine writers have seconded the Enlightenment's enterprise of debunking the vacuity of religious discourses and practices. As ever with libertine literature and libertinism, the answer must be sought between these two interpretations, in the libertines' carelessness, or, as Catherine Cusset

---

68. Jean-Jacques Rousseau, *Julie, ou La Nouvelle Héloïse* (1761), in *Œuvres complètes*, 2:148.

69. Starobinski, *L'Invention de la liberté*, 166.

would phrase it, in "la conscience ironique de ce rien"[70] (the ironical consciousness of this nothingness). If there is no God, then metaphysics is a blank page ready to be filled, just for pleasure's sake, with an abundance of fabulous references ranging from Masonry to the parodied Christianity to Bacchanalia. For libertines, God may be dead, but the enchantment of the religious is not.

---

70. Catherine Cusset, "Cythère et l'Élysée: jardin et plaisir de Watteau à Rousseau," in *Jardins et châteaux*, ed. Roland G. Bonnel, Dalhousie French Studies 29 (Halifax, Canada: Dalhousie Press, 1994), 83.

Pentecost 1794: Robespierre's Religious Vision and the Fulfillment of Time

Muriel Schmid
University of Utah

Après les flots de sang, vous savez quoi? Je vous le donne en cent, en mille, en cent mille: l'Être Suprême! Ne riez pas, c'est le nom regonflé de la Chimère, on nous a changé la marionnette d'habits . . . Ah, Lumières, Lumières, n'étiez-vous donc que la préparation des Ténèbres?

—Philippe Sollers[1]

Publications on the religious history of the French Revolution were in vogue during the second half of the nineteenth century.[2] Several important essays published then are still regarded as landmarks for this topic, including those by Edgar Quinet (*Le christianisme et la Révolution française*, 1845), François-Alphonse Aulard (*Le Culte de la Raison et le Culte de l'Être Suprême*, 1892), and Albert Mathiez (*Les origines des cultes révolutionnaires*, 1904). After this initial wave of interest, the religious paradigm of the French Revolution disappeared from scholarly discussions for more than half a century.

---

1. *Sade contre l'Être Suprême* (Paris: Gallimard, 1996), 62, 69.
2. In his introduction to *Conscience religieuse en Révolution* (Paris: Éditions Picard, 1969), Bernard Plongeron presents the major developments of this research and notices new trends as of 1955.

Not until the 1970s do we see a revival of interest in the topic, with the production of a significant amount of studies in a short period. In 1990, just after the two hundredth anniversary of the French Revolution, Claude Langlois reviewed ninety French titles dedicated to the relationship between religion and the French Revolution that had been published during the late 1980s.[3]

This recent scholarship is traditionally divided into two groups: essays written by secular historians and essays written by historians who belong to the Catholic Church. The latter often express an antirevolutionary view, focusing on the violence perpetrated during the French Revolution against the church, its members, and its representatives; they are generally not interested in presenting a constructive critique of the revolutionary religious paradigm. In response, since the 1990s, as Langlois notes, the so-called secular approach has grown in popularity among historians and has slowly superseded the voice of confessional historians, claiming to formulate a more scientific understanding of the French Revolution and its religious tenets.

A discussion of the mere opposition between these two approaches, however, does not seem entirely productive. The present article seeks to reconcile both discourses and suggests points of encounter between historical and theological perspectives that can illuminate the complex relationship between religion and the French Revolution. Due to limited space, I have chosen to focus my analysis on one of the most significant moments of the French Revolution and its religious paradigm: the Festival of the Supreme Being orchestrated by Robespierre in June 1794. The Festival of the Supreme Being plays a decisive yet paradoxical role in the development of the revolutionary religious paradigm; often seen as its apogee, it marks, at the same time, the last manifestation of this new religion.[4]

When read in the larger context of the Revolution and its ideology, scholars agree on the festival's symbolic power for the entire Revolution, delivering a strong message of cohesion and renewal. Aulard links it to Robespierre's deep mysticism; Mathiez reads it as the perfect synthesis

---

3. Claude Langlois, "Religion et Révolution: bibliographie critique," *Archives des sciences sociales des religions* 71, no. 1 (1990): 189–204.

4. Robespierre was executed on July 28, 1794.

between the god of the philosophers and the god of the church. Frank Tallett, in his 1999 study on Robespierre's religion,[5] sees in it Robespierre's unique opportunity to teach the value of the republican virtues; Christopher Dawson develops similar views in *The Gods of the Revolution*.[6] Mona Ozouf, in her 1976 study of the revolutionary festivals,[7] reads it as the perfect ritual of regeneration and renewal. Finally, Marie-Hélène Huet, in her article on the representation of the sublime during the French Revolution, analyzes the Festival of the Supreme Being as the palimpsest of all the other revolutionary festivals, particularly the Festival of Reason celebrated in November 1793, and situates it as the culmination of all revolutionary festivals.[8]

Among all those interpretations, however, no one addresses the fact that the Festival of the Supreme Being was celebrated on the official date of the Christian Feast of Pentecost, June 8, 1794. The surprising overlap between one of the most important revolutionary festivals and the Christian liturgical calendar offers the opportunity to investigate the relationship between the Revolution and its religious claims in new ways. Expanding on Huet's reading of the Festival of the Supreme Being as the palimpsest of the Festival of Reason, I suggest that the Festival of the Supreme Being cannot be fully understood without uncovering another palimpsest: the Christian Feast of Pentecost. This overlap not only renews our understanding of the Festival of the Supreme Being and its ideological function but sheds a new light, as I argue, on the overall religious revolutionary paradigm.

Scholars who study the religious history of the revolutionary period generally recognize two distinct phases of dechristianization in France

---

5. Frank Tallett, "Robespierre and Religion," in *Robespierre*, ed. Colin Haydon and William Doyle (Cambridge: Cambridge University Press, 1999), 92–108.

6. Christopher Dawson, *The Gods of the Revolution* (New York: New York University Press, 1972).

7. Mona Ozouf, *La fête révolutionnaire, 1789–1799* (Paris: Gallimard/NRF, 1976).

8. Marie-Hélène Huet, "Le Sacre du Printemps: Essai sur le sublime et la Terreur," *MLN* 103, no. 4 (September 1988): 783. A few years after the publication of the original French version, Huet published an English version of her essay: "The Revolutionary Sublime," *Eighteenth-Century Studies* 28, no. 1 (Autumn 1994): 51–64. Ruth Scurr, in her biography of Robespierre, *Fatal Purity: Robespierre and the French Revolution* (New York: Metropolitan Books, 2006), reads the entire history of the French Revolution as "an extraordinary palimpsest" (273).

during the eighteenth century. Nigel Aston provides a helpful definition of these two phases:

> At risk of over-simplification, it may be said that there are basically two ways in which the term "dechristianisation" can be deployed. The first is its use to describe the deliberate attempt by the First Republic from 1792 to 1794 to use the resources of the state to extirpate Christianity and replace it as the dominant cultural mode of French society with a new frame of references springing directly from the Revolution itself. The second meaning of the word characterises the longer-term trends that suggest the gradual detachment during the eighteenth century of a growing number of the French population from (Catholic) Christianity. Scholars who have taken up this second, more diffuse definition tend to argue that the official dismantling of Christian culture in 1792–4 was facilitated at grass-roots level by men and women who already stood at a remove to the historic faith.[9]

Even if this twofold understanding of dechristianization[10] does not entirely account for the complexity of the religious history of eighteenth-century France, it helps us situate the Festival of the Supreme Being in a continuum that slowly and profoundly transforms the religious references in France during that period from a Christian cultural paradigm to a new revolutionary understanding of time, culture, and history. As a palimpsest of the Christian Feast of Pentecost, the Festival of the Supreme Being is to be read as the marker of a radical change of times: it inaugurates a new era in which the old Christian understanding of history and salvation is fulfilled and consecrated by the Revolution.

My argument is divided into three parts: first a brief presentation of the festival itself that enumerates its main elements; second, a

---

9. Nigel Aston, *Religion and Revolution in France, 1780–1804* (Washington, DC: The Catholic University of America Press, 2000), 259. Similar views can be found in Michel Vovelle, *La Révolution contre l'Église: de la raison à l'Être Suprême* (Paris: Éditions Complexe, 2001), 14–17; and Noah Shusterman, *Religion and the Politics of Time* (Washington, DC: The Catholic University of America Press, 2010), 116–22.

10. As Bernard Plongeron reminds us, the neologism "dechristianization" initially provoked many negative reactions; see Plongeron, *Conscience religieuse*, 1200.

theological and biblical analysis of the festival explaining the Christian references that shaped it; and, third, a presentation of Gérard Genette's definition of "palimpsest" that helps articulate more specifically the use of Christian references in the revolutionary religious paradigm.

Description of the Festival of the Supreme Being

We possess descriptions of the Festival of the Supreme Being from a few archival documents (available in French) that contain the details of the festival. On May 7, 1794, in front of the Comité de Salut publique, Robespierre promulgated the dates of the various revolutionary festivals. The Festival of the Supreme Being was scheduled for June 8, 1794, and two hundred thousand pamphlets were immediately printed and sent throughout France to announce the date.

The painter Jacques-Louis David (1748–1825), official stage director of the revolutionary festivals, was given one month to plan the Festival of the Supreme Being. He worked closely with three other artists: Théodore Desorgues (1763–1808) wrote the lyrics of the hymns, and François-Joseph Gossec (1734–1829) and Étienne-Nicolas Méhul (1763–1817) composed the music. The day before the actual celebration, David presented a detailed program of the festivities to the National Assembly. This historical document indicates that a general call will be heard in Paris at dawn and a procession will form to go to the National Garden (known today as the Jardin des Tuileries) for the first half of the celebration. The following description then is provided:

> Lorsque toutes les sections seront arrivées au Jardin National, une députation ira annoncer à la Convention que tout est préparé pour célébrer la fête de la Divinité.
>
> La Convention Nationale descendra par le balcon du pavillon de l'Unité, sur l'amphithéâtre adossé audit pavillon.
>
> Le Président, placé à la tribune, fera sentir au peuple les motifs qui ont déterminé cette fête solennelle [sic] et l'invitera à honorer l'auteur de la nature.

Après ce discours, on exécutera une symphonie ; pendant ce temps, le Président s'approchera d'un monument élevé sur le bassin circulaire et représentant le monstre de l'Athéisme.

Du milieu de ce monument, incendié par le Président, apparaîtra la Sagesse.

Après cette cérémonie, le Président remontera à la tribune et parlera de nouveau au peuple, qui lui répondra par des chants et des cris d'allégresse.

(When each group has arrived at the National Garden, a delegation will tell the members of the Convention that everything is ready for the celebration of the Divine Being.

The members of the Convention will then come to the balcony of the Pavilion of Unity. . . .

The President, at the tribune, will impress upon the people the meaning of this solemn festival [*sic*] and will invite the audience to honor the maker of nature.

After this speech, the orchestra will play a symphony while the President reaches a monument sets on the central fountain representing the monster of Atheism.

From the middle of this monument, set on fire by the President, will appear Wisdom.

After this ceremony, the President will go back to the tribune and speak again while the people will cheer him with songs and joyful cries.)

The Festival of the Supreme Being was organized into two distinct parts. The first took place in the National Garden, whereas the second, which was longer and more elaborate, was held on the Field of the Reunion (known today as Champ de Mars), where an artificial mountain had been built:

La Représentation Nationale occupera la partie la plus élevée de la montagne et les musiciens se placeront sur le milieu. . . .

Aussitôt que tout sera rangé . . ., le corps de musique exécutera un hymne à la Divinité.

Après cet hymne, on exécutera une grande symphonie.

Cette symphonie finie, les vieillards et les enfants, qui seront sur la montagne, chanteront une première strophe sur l'air des Marseillais, et jureront ensemble de ne poser les armes qu'après avoir anéanti les ennemis de la République.

Tous les hommes répandus dans le Champ de la Réunion répèteront en chœur le refrain.

Les mères de famille et les jeunes filles placées sur la montagne chanteront une seconde strophe ; celles-ci promettront de n'épouser que les

Citoyens qui auront servi la patrie et les mères remercieront l'Être Suprême de leur fécondité.

Toutes les femmes répandues dans le Champ de la Réunion répèteront ensemble le refrain.

La troisième et dernière strophe sera chantée par tout ce qui sera sur la montagne. . . .

Le Peuple entier répètera en chœur le dernier refrain. . . .

Après la dernière strophe, une décharge générale d'artillerie, interprète de la vengeance nationale, se fera entendre ; et tous les Français, confondant leurs sentiments dans un embrasement fraternel, termineront la fête en faisant retentir les airs du cri général : "Vive la République!"[11]

(The National Representatives will stand on the highest point of the mountain and the musicians will stay in the middle of the slope. . . .

As soon as everything is in place . . ., the orchestra will play a hymn to the Divine Being.

After this hymn, a grandiose symphony will be played.

When the symphony is performed, old and young, who will be standing on the mountain as well, will sing the first stanza of the Marseillaise, and swear together not to give up arms before defeating the enemies of the Republic.

Every man standing down in the Field of the Reunion will repeat the refrain.

---

11. The entire document is reproduced by Marie-Louise Biver, *Fêtes révolutionnaires* (Paris: PUF, 1979), 192–98.

Mother and young daughters, standing on the mountain will sing a second stanza; the latter will promise to marry only the Citizens who have served their country while the former will give thanks to the Supreme Being for their fertility.

Every woman in the Field of the Reunion will repeat the refrain.

The third and last stanza will be sung by the entire group standing on the mountain. . . .

The People, all united, will repeat the last refrain. . . .

After the last stanza, a general firing will be heard, sound of the national revenge; and every French person, sharing his/her feelings of fraternity, will end the festival cheering and screaming, "Long live the Republic!")

These two phases indicate an important ideological choice: the first act was devoted to the destruction of the representation of Atheism in order to unveil in its place the figure of Wisdom; the second act celebrated the Supreme Being and the glory of the French Republic protected and chosen by divinity.

In 1831, nearly forty years after the festival, Charles Nodier (1780–1844) wrote what has become one of the most famous descriptions of it:

Jamais un jour d'été ne s'était levé plus pur sur notre horizon. Je n'ai trouvé que longtemps après, au midi et au levant de l'Europe, cette transparence de firmament à travers laquelle le regard semblait pénétrer d'autres cieux. Le peuple y voyait du miracle, et s'imaginait qu'il y avait, dans cette magnificence inaccoutumée du ciel et du soleil, un gage certain de la réconciliation de Dieu avec la France.[12]

(Never did we see a purer summer day on our horizon. I saw only years later, in the South and East of Europe, similar transparency in the sky inviting my gaze to penetrate other dimensions. The people believed then in a miracle, and thought that there was, in this unusual beauty of the sky and the sun, the ultimate proof that God was reconciled with France.)

---

12. See Huet, "Le Sacre du Printemps", 783.

The historian Jules Michelet (1798–1874) spoke of the hope the festival represented for the people, as the guillotine had been dismantled for the occasion:

> Nulle fête n'excita jamais une si douce attente, nulle ne fut jamais célébrée avec tant de joie. La guillotine disparut, le 19 prairial au soir. On crut que c'était pour toujours.[13]

> (No other festival had been so exciting, no other celebrated with so much joy. The guillotine had been removed in the evening of the 19th of Prairial. Everybody believed it was forever.)

This hope was betrayed, as history tells us, and the Festival of the Supreme Being was but a brief reprieve in the terror instilled by Robespierre. The festival, however, was quickly regarded as a unique episode in the Revolution and the most remarkable of its public ceremonies. Grasping the specificity of this episode requires a close reading of its context and Christian undertone as will be discussed in the following paragraphs.

Robespierre's Pentecost

As stated earlier, June 8, 1794, coincided with the Christian Feast of Pentecost. If historians occasionally mention it,[14] they fail to incorporate this detail into a broader analysis of the festival and often dismiss it as mere coincidence.[15] To my knowledge, only Aulard comments on the date and the Feast of Pentecost, stating:

> On ne sait si Robespierre avait prémédité cette coïncidence, mais elle fut très remarquée. Si certains catholiques en furent

---

13. Jules Michelet, *Histoire de la Révolution Française*, Tome 9 (Paris: Alphonse Demerre, 1888), 204.

14. For instance, see Marie-Louise Biver, *Fêtes révolutionnaires*, 93; or Nigel Aston, *Christianity and Revolutionary Europe c.1750–1830* (Cambridge: Cambridge University Press, 2002), 214.

15. For instance, see Scurr, *Fatal Purity*, 326; and Aston, *Religion and Revolution in France*, 271.

contristés comme d'un sacrilège, d'autres y virent un hommage rendu à l'ancienne religion.[16]

(We don't know whether or not Robespierre had premeditated this coincidence, but it was certainly widely noticed. If some Catholics were offended by this sacrilege, others took it as a way of honoring the old religion.)

If this coincidence might have been widely noticed at the time, it is today ignored by most scholars and authors writing on the Festival of the Supreme Being. It seems, however, quite unlikely that the overlap between the Gregorian and Republican calendars had been missed by Robespierre, considering his attention to detail in the preparation of the festival. Moreover, theologically and biblically this choice illuminates the liturgical power of the festival. In order to fully appreciate the importance of this overlap, it is essential to reread the biblical narrative of Pentecost in Acts 2:1–41.

Luke, the author of Acts, begins his account of the life of the early church by telling the story of the Holy Spirit descending on the apostles. Following Jesus's command, the apostles are gathered in Jerusalem after Easter. Before departing, Jesus promises them the coming of the Holy Spirit and asks them to wait for it in Jerusalem. Luke describes this event with imagery of thunder and fire: a loud noise is heard, and tongues of fire descend from the sky and touch each apostle. Filled with the Spirit, the apostles preach in other languages; each person in the crowd can hear the apostles' words in his or her own language. When the crowd expresses wonder and skepticism, Peter responds with a long discourse, the first in the Book of Acts. The biblical narrative makes two important theological points that I wish to briefly explore: (1) the Christian Pentecost is built on the meaning of the Jewish Pentecost and (2) the experience of the apostles that day structures a fundamental shift in history.[17]

---

16. François-Alphonse Aulard, *Le culte de la Raison et le culte de l'Être Suprême* (Paris: Félix Alcan, 1892), 340.

17. For detailed commentaries on the book of Acts, see Robert C. Tannhill, *The Narrative Unity of Luke–Acts. A Literary Interpretation* (Minneapolis: Fortress Press, 1994); and Ulrich Wilckens, "Interpreting Luke–Acts in a Period of Existentialist Theology," in *Studies in Luke–Acts*, ed. by Leander E. Keck (Minneapolis: Fortress Press, 1980), 60–83.

In the Jewish tradition, the Feast of Pentecost commemorates the gift of the Law on Mount Sinai and the establishment of the covenant between God and his/her people. As such, Pentecost is at the heart of the election of Israel as the chosen people. Luke immediately announces the reference to the Jewish Feast of Pentecost in Acts 2:1 ("when the day of Pentecost had come . . .")[18] and thus aligns his narrative in the history of the covenant. In the actual description of the Holy Spirit's descent, Luke uses a terminology inspired by both the appearance of God on Mount Sinai (Exodus 19:16–19) and Jesus's baptism (Luke 3:21–22), blending the two episodes. The theology of this narrative is then very deliberate: a new covenant is about to be established between God and his/her people, while the apostles, who are about to announce it to the world, are invested of an authority similar to the authority granted to Jesus at the beginning of his ministry. Representatives of every known nation are present in Jerusalem that day to witness the events; their presence opens the proclamation of the new covenant to the entire world (Acts 1:8). By extension, the text suggests that the new covenant is not restricted to Israel only but includes all nations on earth. The new covenant is resolutely universal.

After the coming of the Spirit, Peter speaks to the crowd and explains the meaning and importance of this moment. His discourse is loaded with a vocabulary that evokes the biblical theme of fulfillment. Peter borrows from the prophet Joel, emphasizing the eschatological tone of his words: "In the last days it will be, God declares, that I will pour out my Spirit upon all flesh" (Acts 2:17–21). This very moment, Peter reminds his audience, is the beginning of a new era in which salvation is offered to all. After reminding the people of God's miraculous power (against those who wanted to kill him) manifested in Jesus's resurrection, Peter calls everyone to repent and receive the Spirit: "Repent, and be baptized every one of you in the name of Jesus Christ so that your sins may be forgiven; and you will receive the gift of the Holy Spirit" (Acts 2:38). Peter's speech not only signals the beginning of the new era but invites those who are present to enter it and take part in the new covenant.

---

18. All biblical quotes are taken from the New Revised Standard Version.

Keeping in mind that the Festival of the Supreme Being was celebrated on the very day of the Christian Feast of Pentecost in 1794, the
themes identified in the biblical narrative of Pentecost resonate deeply
with some elements of the festival, particularly Robespierre's rhetoric.
In the first phase of the festival, Robespierre speaks to the crowd twice,
before and after the destruction of the monument representing Atheism. The tone of his sermon is deeply inspired by eschatological imagery.
Robespierre opens his harangue by acknowledging this unique occasion in which the French people at last celebrate the Supreme Being ("Il
est enfin arrivé, le jour à jamais fortuné que le peuple français consacre
à l'Être Suprême"). The rest of his discourse is centered on the notion
of fulfillment: God's divine plan has led the world from the beginnings
of time to this very moment when the republican virtues are to be
manifested eternally for all nations ("pour tous les siècles et pour tous
les peuples"). France becomes, in this divine plan, the chosen people,
elected by the Supreme Being, and she is now invested with the responsibility to combat false leaders and tyrants who oppose the Revolution.
Those who sought to block this divine plan and annihilate the Supreme
Being (such as those who tried to kill Jesus, according to Acts 2) have
failed. Wisdom, in Robespierre's vision, receives a role identical to the
one of the Spirit: she is the protector of the people and the Republic,
granting them prosperity and success.

In short, Robespierre introduces in his sermon themes and imagery that closely echo Luke's narrative, especially Peter's discourse: the
renewal of the covenant (here, between the Supreme Being and the
French people), the end of those who opposed the coming of a new era,
the protection of the Spirit/Wisdom, and the universality of salvation:[19]

> Français républicains, c'est à vous de purifier la terre qu'ils ont
> souillée, et d'y rappeler la justice qu'ils en ont bannie. La liberté
> et la vertu sont sorties ensemble du sein de la divinité, l'une ne
> peut séjourner sans l'autre parmi les hommes. Peuple généreux,
> veux-tu triompher de tous tes ennemis? Pratique la justice et

---

19. Both of those speeches are reprinted at the end of the article by Jean Deprun titled
"Les 'noms divins' dans deux discours de Robespierre," *Annales Historiques de la Révolution Française* 44, no. 208 (April–June 1972), 161–80.

rends à la divinité le seul culte digne d'elle. Peuple, livrons-
nous aujourd'hui, sous ses auspices, aux transports d'une pure
allégresse.

Homme qui que tu sois, tu peux concevoir encore de hautes
pensées de toi-même; tu peux lier ta vie passagère à Dieu même
et à l'immortalité. Que la nature reprenne donc tout son éclat,
et la Sagesse tout son empire; l'Être suprême n'est point anéanti.

(French Republicans, you are the ones to purify the earth soiled
by them and to call back justice. Freedom and virtue are born
of the Divinity, one cannot dwell among human beings without
the other. Generous people, do you want to triumph over your
enemies? Practice justice and respectfully worship the Divinity.
Today, people, let's put ourselves under its protection and celebrate the Divinity with joy.

Man, whoever you are, you can conceive high regards for
yourself; you can attach your passing life to God and immortality. May nature finds its brilliance and Wisdom its reign; the
Supreme Being is not destroyed.)

Frank Tallett, in his essay on Robespierre's religious views, analyzes documents written by Robespierre between 1789 and 1794; his
reading allows him to identify Robespierre's creed[20] around three
elements: the divine election of the French people, an apocalyptical
vision of history, and the essential role of the Revolution in renew-
ing divine moral values. Robespierre's tone during the Festival of the
Supreme Being is therefore entirely consistent with his longstand-
ing beliefs. However, the implicit reference to the Christian Feast of
Pentecost situates Robespierre's vision in a broader frame in which
France adopts the role of the first Christian church and, by extension,
Robespierre adopts Peter's role. In so doing, Robespierre defines the
revolutionary religious paradigm as the renewal of the old Christian
paradigm in several ways.[21]

20. Tallett, "Robespierre and Religion," 93.
21. It might be possible to add a third element, but the constraint of space does not
allow me to expand on this possibility. Between November 1789 and October 1791,
strong antirevolutionary rhetoric was published in the journal *Les Actes des Apôtres*

By indirectly taking Peter's role, Robespierre draws a parallel between his authority and Peter's authority (Peter is traditionally regarded as the church's cornerstone and the first bishop of Rome). In that sense, Robespierre inserts himself in the apostolic succession, with the Festival of the Supreme Being celebrating his enthronement. In her discussion of the festival, Ozouf wonders if Robespierre at that moment was deliberately strategic or genuinely religious.[22] Reading the festival through the lens of the Feast of Pentecost suggests that Ozouf's question ultimately offers a false dichotomy—both perspectives are not mutually exclusive. On the contrary, planning the Festival of the Supreme Being on the very date of the Feast of Pentecost reveals Robespierre's mastery of religious representations and a clear strategy to articulate his new religious paradigm on the old one, thus rooting it in common cultural references. At the same time, Robespierre takes on a pontifical role, presenting himself as the head of the revolutionary church; such a function reinforces for the believer the continuity between the old and the new paradigms. In short, Robespierre indicates a clear interest in building his new religious paradigm on the old one, forcing his audience to interpret it in light of Christian cultural references. In this context, the second stage of dechristianization, often read as purely destructive, can be seen as a reinterpretation of the old paradigm rather than a pure destruction of it.[23]

The Festival as Palimpsest

In her essay, Huet mentions that on July 1, 1794, less than a month after the Festival of the Supreme Being, a decree was promulgated prohibiting any theatrical representation of the festival.[24] This decree is unique in the history of the revolutionary festivals and, according to

---

(*Acts of the Apostles*), directed by Jean-Gabriel Peltier (1760–1825); Robespierre strongly condemned the journal and its political views. Robespierre's takeover of Pentecost and his allusion to the biblical narrative may fit in this controversy as well.

22. Ozouf, *La fête révolutionnaire*, 126.

23. Jean Deprun and Frank Tallett independently recognize the essential role Christian terminology plays in Robespierre's speeches.

24. Huet, "Le Sacre du Printemps," 784.

Huet, signals the particularity of the festival as a religious event. Huet lists two characteristics that set it aside: first, unlike theater performances, the festival does not tolerate viewers but requires participants; second, unlike the other revolutionary festivals, this festival does not tolerate any visual representation of the Supreme Being (only Atheism and Wisdom are represented). Based on these two characteristics, Huet reads the Festival of the Supreme Being as the achievement of the revolutionary religious paradigm. This religious paradigm is built, Huet insists, in stages and overlays, with one new concept added to an old one. However, in this analysis of the various layers of the Festival of the Supreme Being, Huet does not discuss the possibility and interest of identifying Judeo-Christian elements in this process. As suggested by the previous paragraphs, the rewriting process does not start with the first revolutionary festival, as Huet tends to suggest, but takes root in a strong Christian cultural environment that marks French history. The Festival of the Supreme Being may be the palimpsest of the Festival of Reason, as Huet describes it, but more profoundly it needs to be read as the palimpsest of the Christian Feast of Pentecost (itself a palimpsest of the Jewish Feast of Pentecost). If such is the case, the revolutionary religion cannot be fully understood outside of its Christian references. This conclusion sheds a new light on the concept of dechristianization.

In his famous study *Palimpsestes*,[25] Gérard Genette presents and analyzes diverse forms of hypertextuality. This category, created by Genette, defines the relationship between a text A (hypotext) and a text B (hypertext) that is grafted on A. In the relationship from B to A, Genette distinguishes two relational modes, transformation and imitation, and three registers, playful, satirical, and serious. The result is a series of six different possibilities of rewriting or recomposing text A through text B (see figure 1). The following is a reproduction of Genette's table adapted from the French original:[26]

---

25. Gérard Genette, *Palimpsestes* (Paris: Éditions du Seuil/Points, 1992).
26. Ibid., 43.

Register Relation	Playful	Satirical	Serious
Transformation	Parody	Travesty	Transposition
Imitation	Pastiche	Caricature	Plagiarism

Figure 1. Genette's table

The category of hypertextuality broadens the concept of palimpsest and, in our case, allows for a deeper understanding of the relationship between the Festival of the Supreme Being and the Christian Feast of Pentecost. At first glance, one may be tempted to classify the Festival of the Supreme Being under "satirical," but the intrinsic link between the festival and Pentecost forces us to place it under "serious" instead. Furthermore, the festival does not actually imitate Pentecost and so must be read as a transposition, the second possibility, according to Genette's classification, in this column. For Genette, transposition is the most important "pratiques hypertexuelles";[27] it possesses the largest array of devices and manifests itself under multiple forms (not just literary or textual forms). In a transposition, Genette adds, the hypertext establishes a unique relationship with its hypotext, using it as a real source of artistic inspiration, thus often making it essential to uncover the hypotext in order to interpret the hypertext.

Applied to the Festival of the Supreme Being, this interpretative key suggests that the biblical narrative of Pentecost plays a crucial role in the construction of the festival. Robespierre's final religious festival cannot be isolated from its broader religious cultural context, nor can it be univocally associated with the destructive second phase of dechristianization. In this light, Robespierre seems much more concerned by a full and intelligent appropriation of the Christian paradigm and the affirmation of the revolutionary model as the actual fulfillment of Christian promises.

A recent study by Noah Shusterman, *Religion and Politics of Time*, interprets the major events of the French Revolution through the lens of time and the imposition of the revolutionary calendar. Shusterman

27. Ibid., 291.

demonstrates how the implementation of a revolutionary calendar contributes to the effective transfer of power from the Catholic Church to the revolutionary government. Based on his observations, the overlap between the Festival of the Supreme Being and the Christian Feast of Pentecost, one of the most striking examples of the revolutionary calendar replacing the Gregorian calendar, fully participates in this shift and ultimately realizes it. The festival inaugurates a new era in which the French Revolution becomes the depository of divine salvation in perfect continuity with biblical times. The overlap of dates and calendars marks the convergence between the old and the new eras, symbolically indicating the actual turning point of time: June 8, 1794, is irrevocably transformed into 20 Prairial An II.

Religious Historiography

As of the 1970s, when interest in the revolutionary religious paradigm reappeared in the work of historians, historical research on religious mentalities in eighteenth-century France focused on archival documents and pamphlet literature in order to reveal an image of the religious landscape of the time that was less polarized (see in particular the work of Michel Vovelle). Among others, Susan Desan has greatly contributed to this shift in the history of religion during the French Revolution. In an article on the relationship between Catholics and the revolutionaries, Desan challenges "the prevalent assumption [established at the turn of the eighteenth and nineteenth centuries] that Catholics, almost inevitably adopted counterrevolutionary attitudes."[28] Analyzing petitions for the reinstitution of the Catholic mass written by French Catholic villagers after the fall of Robespierre, Desan notes that the rhetoric of those petitions is deeply informed by revolutionary ideology:

> Paradoxically, the Revolution opened up surprising and unexpected possibilities for the laity in prerevolutionary regions of

---

28. Susan Desan, "Redefining Revolutionary Liberty: The Rhetoric of Religious Revival during the French Revolution," *The Journal of Modern History* 60, no. 1 (March 1988): 2.

France to find within the Revolution itself political techniques and ideology to aid their reestablishment of Catholicism.[29]

Whereas revolutionaries sought to separate religious and political realms, postrevolutionary attitudes toward Catholicism show a more complex picture in which, as Desan's findings suggest, "religion and revolution might mix in unusual ways."[30] The overlap between the Festival of the Supreme Being and the Feast of Pentecost furthers Desan's conclusion and illustrates that the unusual mix between religion and revolution might have been inherent to the revolutionary ideology itself and Robespierre's vision in particular.

Desan's study challenges the assumption that Catholics unilaterally manifested antirevolutionary sentiment, yet it does not challenge the traditional understanding of revolutionary ideology as being strongly and unanimously anti-Christian. As Desan reminds us, "the revolutionary leadership had created a whole cultural system of revolutionary rituals, symbols, and language that aimed at replacing Christianity . . . the frame and underpinning of the monarchy," but it did not necessarily develop "a rhetoric of opposition"[31] as she wants us to think. If, on one hand, Desan's study demonstrates that the postrevolutionary Catholic revival was to some extent inspired and motivated by revolutionary rhetoric, on the other hand, a reading of the Festival of the Supreme Being through the lens of Pentecost shows Robespierre's attempt at equating the revolutionary religious rhetoric and ideology with the fulfillment of Christian promises.

The historical focus on popular religious mentalities has tremendously modified our understanding of the religious landscape of pre- and postrevolutionary France; in return there might still be new elements to uncover in the revolutionary religious paradigm itself that would challenge our presuppositions regarding the interpretation of the dechristianization movement.

---

29. Ibid., 26.
30. Ibid., 27.
31. Ibid., 4.

Songs without Music: The *Hymnes* of Le Franc de Pompignan

Theodore E. D. Braun, emeritus professor
University of Delaware

I n the first edition of his *Poésies sacrées* (1751), Jean-Jacques Le Franc de Pompignan (1709–1784) published 40 poems in four books, each containing ten poems.[1] These *Poésies sacrées*, or *Sacred Poems*, were to be printed three times in his *Oeuvres choisies* or *Selected Works* of 1753, 1754, and 1754–55. This modest collection was to be enlarged to 85 poems divided into five books of unequal length in its definitive form in the *de luxe quarto* edition of 1763 and finally as the first volume of his *Oeuvres* in 1784, which is the text I am using in this article.[2] Although at least one critic, the Canadian poet Robert Finch, maintained that we should consider as sacred songs the *Odes* (translations of certain psalms), the *Cantiques* (drawn from texts chosen from several Old Testament books), and even the selections from the *Prophéties* as well as the *Hymnes*,[3] these observations are limited here to the hymns.

The ten hymns published in the first cycle of four editions are paraphrases of texts found in the New Testament and were intended

---

1. Jean-Jacques Le Franc de Pompignan, *Poésies Sacrées de Monsieur L* F*****, *divisées en Quatre Livres, Et ornées de Figures en taille douce* (Paris: Chaubert, 1751).

2. Jean-Jacques Le Franc de Pompignan, *Oeuvres* (Paris: Nyon l'aîné, 1784), I:261–314. Unless otherwise indicated, all quotations from Le Franc's poems come from this edition.

3. Robert Finch, *The Sixth Sense: Individualism in French Poetry, 1686–1760* (Toronto: University of Toronto Press, 1966).

RAE, vol. 5, 2015

to be sung during the high mass on certain Sundays and important holy days during the liturgical year. Of the six hymns added in 1763, four celebrate saints (St. John the Baptist and three saints of national importance, Saint Genevieve, Saint Clotilde, and Saint Louis) and would be sung on their feast days, while the other two are a translation of Psalm CXII (*In exitu Israel de Aegypto*) in the Vulgate (Psalm CXIII in the other editions of the Bible) and a hymn of thanksgiving based on the *Te Deum*, and could be sung at other appropriate occasions. I have examined elsewhere different aspects of the first three books of the *Poésies sacrées*,[4] but the hymns have been neglected, even in the three monographs devoted to the poet in the twentieth century.[5] I propose to address the *Hymnes* in the present article. Very little work has been done on the hymns, and nothing has been published on them as songs.

Poetry, for Le Franc, consists of many elements, not the least of which is inspiration. In the present case, that is sacred verse, divine inspiration is needed, and Le Franc does not hide his belief that the poetry of the Bible is the oldest, the most venerable, and the closest to God's conception. Indeed, he addresses this question directly:

> God himself inspired men to write poetry. To celebrate his grandeur, his power, his mercy, his goodness, to express his anger and his indignation, he wanted men to use a language that is at once full of images, bold, melodious, subject to sonorous and cadenced measures, so as to distinguish it from the ordinary and common way of speaking.[6]

---

4. Theodore E. D. Braun, "Antiphilosophie dans les *Poésies sacrées* de Le Franc de Pompignan," *Revue de l'Université d'Ottawa* 54 (July–September 1984): 9–15; "La Bible dans les *Poésies sacrées* de Le Franc de Pompignan," in *Le Siècle des Lumières et la Bible*, ed. Yvon Belaval and Dominique Bourel (Paris: Beauchesne, 1986), 355–56; and "Truth, Beauty, Harmony, Order, and Muscularity in Le Franc de Pompignan's *Poésies Sacrées*," in *1650–1850: Ideas, Aesthetics, and Inquiries in the Early Modern Era*, ed. Kevin L. Cope, Laura Morrow, and Anna Battigelli (Brooklyn: AMS Press, Inc., 1997), 219–38.

5. Abbé François-Albert Duffo, *Jean-Jacques Lefranc, Marquis de Pompignan, Poète et Magistrat (1709–1784): Étude sur sa vie et sur ses œuvres* (Paris Picard, 1913); Theodore E. D. Braun, *Un Ennemi de Voltaire. Le Franc de Pompignan: sa vie, ses oeuvres, ses rapports avec Voltaire* (Paris: Lettres Modernes Minard, 1972); and Guillaume Robichez, *J.-J. Lefranc de Pompignan: Un Humaniste chrétien au siècle des lumières* (Paris: Sedes, 1987).

6. Le Franc de Pompignan, *Oeuvres*, xv–xvi. "Dieu a lui-même inspiré la poésie aux hommes. Il a voulu que pour célébrer ses grandeurs, sa puissance, ses miséricordes, sa

If poetry, and especially biblical poetry, is almost as close to the language of God as human beings can get, a step closer yet is poetry put to music, "melodious, subject to sonorous and cadenced measures." One of the many ways poetry can be made musical is by the use of harmony.

Harmony is the subject of one of Le Franc's very first known poems, the text of a kind of salon opera titled *Le Triomphe de l'Harmonie* written when he was just twenty years old.[7] He later used a slightly revised version of this text as the prelude to his very successful full-scale opera, produced seven years later in 1737 and bearing the same title.[8] The goddess Harmony, in part with her song and her verse, in part with her reason and her grace, conquers the forces of War, Discord, and Disputes of all sorts.

Harmony triumphs in his sacred verse in other ways, too—ways more appropriate to the subject of this article. *Harmonie* serves as an antonym and as a resolution not only of *désaccord* (discord in the sense of disagreement) but also of *discordance* (discord in the sense of dissonance); that is, it has in French, as in English, a musical value, too, along with its social and political meanings. It is the musical sense of the word that is of interest to us here.

Harmony is not just musicality, however; it is also the unity between a thought or an image and its expression, or what we might call Proportionality. It follows that if an idea or a person is "pleasing, tender, and brilliant," the language used to express this idea must reflect or incorporate these qualities; and if an idea or event is "majestic" or

---

bonté, que pour exprimer sa colère et son indignation, on se servît d'un langage figuré, hardi, mélodieux, assujetti à des mesures sonores et cadencées qui le distinguassent de la marche unie du discours ordinaire et commun." It is perhaps worth noting here that the book is not divided into chapters. The *Poésies sacrées* consists of a fairly long introduction, the *Discours préliminaire*, followed by five *Livres*, or books, of which the *Hymnes* is the fourth (the others are the *Odes*, the *Cantiques* or Canticles, the *Prophéties*, and the *Discours philosophiques* or Philosophical discourses). All five books are contained in vol. I: thus, *Oeuvres*, I, xv–xvi means vol. I, pp. xv–xvi of the 1784 edition. This is the case throughout the article.

7. Jean-Jacques Le Franc de Pompignan, *Le Triomphe de l'Harmonie*, score, 1730, Collection de Solleine, Bibliothèque Nationale, Manuscrits fonds français 9293, 47–51. Dated and signed, the manuscript consists of two scenes in one act.

8. *Le Triomphe de l'Harmonie, ballet héroïque*, musique de Grenet, *Oeuvres* (Paris: Nyon l'aîné, 1784), III:1–56. This opera-ballet was performed in Paris in 1737 and 1738.

"sublime," "lugubrious but consoling," or "terrifying . . . triumphant, full of love and happiness,"[9] the language used to express it must possess these qualities. In some cases, particularly in the *Prophéties* and the *Odes*, the subject matter and the Hebrew text (although not necessarily the Latin text of the Vulgate) require the powerful imagery that I have analyzed elsewhere as Muscularity (see note 4). The nature of the hymns does not lend itself to this aspect of Le Franc's poetic register.

Le Franc states clearly that the canticles were poems intended to be sung. It goes without saying that the hymns were also intended to be sung. Speaking specifically of his hymns written in French (instead of Latin), the poet builds into his aesthetic ideal uniting poetry and music the concepts of harmony and proportionality. On this matter, he says,

> My hope is for this genre to succeed enough so that our finest poets will cultivate it and our best musicians will compose songs in it. The motets of Lalande, Campra, Mondonville are enjoyed even by people who don't know Latin. They would hear this delightfully exciting music with even greater pleasure if it were supported by French words. Using as models the psalms and canticles, all the component parts of poetry would have to be brought to these French poems. I would like to see them *pleasing, tender and brilliant* for the feasts of the Virgin, for Christmas; *majestic and sublime* for the Resurrection, Pentecost, the Ascension; *lugubrious but consoling* for the All Souls Day; *terrifying* for the Last Judgment; *triumphant, full of love and happiness* for All Saints Day. Music appropriate to odes fashioned in this taste would surely produce an astonishing effect. My hymns will be thought of, perhaps, as only rough drafts of these great paintings; but the sketch is good, and others can fill in the details and the colors.[10]

---

9. Le Franc de Pompignan, "Discours préliminaire of the Poésies sacrées," in *Oeuvres* (Paris: Nyon l'aîné, 1784), I:lix–lx

10. Ibid.; emphasis added. "Je souhaiterais que ce genre réussît assez parmi nous pour engager nos bons poètes à le cultiver, et nos habiles musiciens à y consacrer leurs chants. Les motets de Lalande, de Campra, de Mondonville charment les personnes même qui ne savent pas le latin. Elles entendraient avec bien plus de plaisir cette musique ravissante, si elle était sur des paroles françaises. Il faudrait qu'en se proposant pour modèles

True to his words, he sought to put his hymns to music: hymn II, a Christmas hymn simply titled "Pour le Jour de la Nativité du Seigneur," had been performed in Bordeaux in 1742, as we have discovered in an imprint.[11] Unfortunately, the text does not contain the music. And we know that, even when the words of a song can stand on their own as true poetry (think of simply reading Georges Brassens, a laureate of the Académie Française in 1967, instead of hearing him sing),[12] or perhaps more to the point for eighteenth-century music, Handel's "Hallelujah Chorus" or a Bach cantata gives them a life they would otherwise not have. We consider, similarly, the renowned fourteenth-century French poet and composer, Guillaume Machaut (1300–77), whose music has been lost. We can only imagine what his song-poems would have sounded like. Likewise, without hearing what must have been echoing in Le Franc's ears as Le Franc composed his hymns, we must consider them in an imperfect form—that is, as songs without music.[13] Even so, they are effective verbally and lyrically and often possess a musicality

les Psaumes et les Cantiques, on rassemblât dans ces petits poèmes français tous les caractères de la poésie. Je les voudrais agréables, tendres et brillants pour les fêtes de la Vierge, pour la Nativité; majestueux et sublimes pour la Résurrection, la descente du Saint-Esprit, l'Ascension; lugubres, mais consolants, pour le jour des Morts; terribles pour le jugement dernier; triomphants, remplis d'amour et d'allégresse pour la fête de tous les saints. Une musique assortie à des odes travaillées dans ce goût ferait vraisemblablement une sensation étonnante. Mes Hymnes ne seront, si l'on veut, que des esquisses de ces grands tableaux; mais le dessein en est bon; d'autres y mettront le coloris."

11. According to MS 1696 (16) pièce 46 of the *Bibliothèque Municipale de Bordeaux* (4 pp. in-folio), this hymn had been set to music and performed in 1742. Below the title on the imprint, we see the words "Mis en musique par M. LEVENS, Maître de musique de l'Eglise Métropolitaine St. André de Bordeaux, l'Année 1742."

12. "Thèmes: Les differents themes abordés par Brassens dans ses textes [Themes: The different themes used by Brassens in his texts]," Eric M. Free, accessed January 8, 2014, http://eric.m.free.fr/. At the Brassens site constructed by Eric M. Free, the following poets (from the fifteenth century to the twentieth century) are among those listed: Paul Fort, 8 poems; Pierre Corneille, 1 poem; Antoine Pol, 1 poem; Gustave Nadaud , 2 poems; Alfred de Musset, 2 poems; Jean Richepin, 2 poems; Alphonse de Lamartine, 1 poem; Théodore de Banville, 2 poems; Victor Hugo, 2 poems; Paul Verlaine, 1 poem; Francis James, 1 poem; François Villon, 1 poem; Louis Aragon, 1 poem. Thanks to the music, and to Brassens's singing, each of these poems has taken on a new and more complete life.

13. Modern critics have not overlooked this important point. I cite but one example: "Like most songs, this work [Katherine Philips's 1664 poem "Mutual affection between Orinda and Lucatia"] is misrepresented if considered only as a text stripped of its musical setting." Dianne Dugaw and Amanda Powell, "Sapphic Self-Fashioning in the Baroque

that clearly comes from the eighteenth century. I look at the nature of that musicality to set the stage for brief analysis, emphasizing here harmony and proportionality.

Metrical feet, such as the iamb or the spondee, do not exist in French; instead, we count syllables.[14] The most common syllabic forms are the Alexandrine, a dodecasyllabic line with a caesura after the sixth syllable, used in meditative or philosophical verse, in comedies, in tragedies, and in sonnets; the octosyllabic line, originally used in narrative romances, which gives a more rapid, fleeting impression, and tends to be used in light verse forms; and the hexameter, or demi-Alexandrine, which breaks the predictable regularity of the Alexandrine and helps make the stanza lighter and airier. The decasyllabic line, popular in the Middle Ages and the Renaissance, is more rarely used; the tetrameter even more so.

One of the ways to express musicality in French verse, to get some of the lilt that is more easily produced in English, is to vary the meter, using lines of different lengths, and particularly to use lines of an odd number of syllables. The great symbolist poet Paul Verlaine, known for the musicality of his poems, wrote explicitly late in the nineteenth century in L'Art poétique,

> De la musique avant toute chose,
> Et pour cela préfère l'Impair . . .

> (Music first of all,
> And for that, prefer lines of odd-numbered syllables . . .)

Already in 1742, in the hymn mentioned above, for Christmas, Le Franc had incorporated this idea in his hymn. He opens the poem with a six-line stanza of hexasyllables; a second stanza with four lines of twelve, eight, twelve, and twelve syllables; a third four-line stanza with alternating lines of eight and six syllables, then two four-line stanzas of octosyllabic lines. Three stanzas of five-syllable lines follow:

Era: Women's Petrarchan Parody in English and Spanish," *Studies in Eighteenth-Century Culture* 35 (2006): 135–36.

14. For a full description of the evolution of French verse forms, see Frédéric Deloffre, *Les Vers français* (Paris: Sedes, 1973); the present question is addressed in chapter 6, "Naissance d'un art poétique: élaboration et spécialisation des différents types de vers," 59–67.

Suspends tes ravages,
Hiver rigoureux;
Aquilons fougueux,
Fuyez ces rivages.

Oiseaux qu'en nos bois
Leur souffle intimide,
Sur la branche humide
Ranimez vos voix.

Hâtez-vous d'éclore,
Fleurs, parez nos champs;
Ces heureux instants
Valent bien l'aurore
Du plus beau printemps.

(Suspend your harshness,
Rigorous winter;
Stormy winds,
Blow far from these shores.

Birds that in our woods
Are frightened by their gusts,
On your humid branches
Let your voices ring.

Hasten to bloom,
Flowers, decorate our fields;
These happy moments
Are every bit as lovely as dawn
In the most beautiful of springtimes.)

Nor is this the only example of the use of "musical" lines in the *Poésies sacrées*: Le Franc has lines of five and seven syllables scattered throughout the first four books of this volume.

The carol continues for some time in this vein, pleasing and tender; perhaps he heard the brilliant tones of flutes and trumpets when he wrote lines such as these that begin and end the hymn:

Quelle clarté perçante
Se répand dans les airs!
La flamme des eclairs
Est moins éblouissante. . . .

Chantons, mêlons nos voix aux célestes concerts.
Nuit à jamais célèbre! éclatante victoire!
La mort et le péché sont rentrés dans leurs fers.

Honneur, triomphe, gloire,
Au Dieu de l'univers.

(What a clear and piercing tune
Can be heard in the air!
The flame of lightning
Is less blinding.
What a clear and piercing tune
Can be heard in the air! . . .

Let's sing, let's lend our voices to the heavenly concert.
O Night forever famous! O brilliant victory!
Death and sin have retreated to their prison.

Honor, triumph, glory
To the God of the universe.)

The "pleasing and tender" qualities of this Christmas carol can also be seen in hymn IV, celebrating the presentation of the infant at the temple and the ritual purification of his mother. The musicality of this hymn is expressed by such elements as douceur (sweetness or softness) and sentiment, a word which Le Franc uses frequently in his prefatory remarks, and which he often succeeds in expressing. But the sweetness and the sentiment he refers to have nothing to do with human (and especially sexual) love. With few exceptions, the Bible—and particularly those passages Le Franc chose to translate or to paraphrase—is not lyrically effusive. Love of God, indignation, despair, terror, adoration, serenity—emotions such as these are the stuff of his verse. We will see some of these elements in a moment, but first, let us take a look at two short passages of this hymn ("Pour le jour de la Purification," 273–75), which Le Franc specifically calls a cantata (and just imagine what Bach could do with these texts!):

Accourez dans le saint lieu,
Volez, nations fidèles:
Couvrez des fleurs les plus belles
Le berceau de votre Dieu.

L'Enfant qu'ici je contemple,
De grands rois l'ont imploré.
Hélas ! encore ignoré,
Il est offert dans le temple
Où lui-même est adoré.

Volez, nations fidèles,
Accourez dans le saint lieu;
Couvrez des fleurs les plus belles
Le berceau de votre Dieu.

(Hasten to the sacred place,
Fly, faithful nations,
Cover with the most beautiful flowers
The crib of your God.

The child that I behold here,
Great kings have implored him;
Alas! Still unknown,
He is offered in the temple
Where he himself is adored.

Fly, faithful nations,
Hasten to the sacred place,
Cover with the most beautiful flowers
The crib of your God.)

Speaking of Bach, I cannot resist pointing out the baroque image of the second stanza of this piece. However classical or neoclassical he might have been, Le Franc had a penchant for baroque imagery, often

sublime, often fearsome, often violent; but here, all is harmonious, all is
sweetness and sentiment, all is pleasing and tender.

The closing passage of the hymn, a prayer in itself, consists almost
entirely of these elements:

> Gloire, triomphe au divin Père,
> Honneur au Fils, Dieu comme lui.
> Le tribut d'une foi sincère
> Obtient leur immortel appui.
>
> Esprit-Saint, recevez l'hommage
> Des coeurs qu'illuminent vos feux;
> Par vous seul nous faisons usage
> Des seuls biens dignes de nos voeux.
>
> Gloire, triomphe au divin Père,
> Honneur au Fils, Dieu comme lui.
> Le tribut d'une foi sincère
> Obtient leur immortel appui.
>
> (Glory, triumph to the divine Father,
> Honor to the Son, God like him.
> The tribute of a sincere faith
> Earns their immortal support.
>
> Holy Spirit, receive the homage
> Of hearts lit up by your flames;
> Through you alone we make use
> Of the only worship worthy of you.
>
> Glory, triumph to the divine Father,
> Honor to the Son, God like him.
> The tribute of a sincere faith
> Earns their immortal support.)

Variety of tone and form are also important to rendering in French
the musicality of the Hebrew original, according to our poet:

Mais si l'on avoue que [les psaumes] ont été faits pour être mis en musique et chantés, on ne saurait disconvenir qu'il n'ait fallu pour les plier avec plus de grâce aux différentes modulations du chant, un mélange de brèves et de longues arrangées avec plus d'art et de symmétrie que dans la prose. . . . [Les rimes] y sont amenées pour flatter l'oreille et pour favoriser le chant.

(But if you agree that [the Psalms] were made to be put into music and sung, you would also have to agree that they must be provided with more grace in the different modulations of song, with a mixture of long and short syllables arranged with more art and symmetry than in prose. . . . [Rhyme] is introduced to appeal to the ear and to favor singing.)[15]

He adds that a "symmetrical mixture of stanzas of unequal length forms a harmonious contrast" (mélange symmétrique de strophes inégales formerait un contraste harmonieux) and that poetry must "imitate music, whose charm consists in a melodious variety of tones and accords" (imiter la musique, dont le charme consiste dans une mélodieuse variété de tons et d'accords).[16] The critic Robert Finch, as indicated near the beginning of this article, is particularly sensitive to the musical quality of the *Poésies sacrées*, comparing the various poems to musical compositions consisting of movements vivace, adagio, and moderato: "like music, especially music of the time, these lyrical movements can hardly be appreciated in short snippets but must be followed throughout their changing web of orchestration from beginning to end." Indeed, Finch believes the first four books of the *Poésies sacrées*, including the *Hymnes*, are "admirably suited for the purpose, there is little doubt [Le Franc] hoped they might be set to music."[17]

As we have seen, throughout the *Hymnes,* Le Franc uses lines of five and seven syllables, anticipating by more than a century what the great poet Paul Verlaine will say explicitly in *L'Art poétique.*

He also introduces an extraordinary variety of meters and strophic forms, as Finch observes:

---

15. Pompignan, *Discours préliminaire*, xli.
16. Ibid., liv–lv.
17. Finch, *The Sixth Sense*, 195.

No two poems in the [first] four books are identical in form. Their length ranges from three to thirty stanzas, each of which may have anywhere from three to fifteen lines. Eight, twelve, six, seven and (in the *Hymnes*) five and four syllable lines are used uniformly, or in combination, throughout a stanza. A poem may consist of a single type of stanza or of several intermingled types. A total of one hundred thirty-five stanza-forms, all but twenty-nine being irregular, are used, and each form heightens or reflects the sense or feeling it embodies.[18]

We have also seen that harmony is not just an element in the musicality of poetry; it is also the union of a thought or an image and its expression, what I am calling Proportionality. In certain cases, and in particular in the *Odes* and the *Prophéties*, the subject matter and the Hebrew text (but not necessarily the Latin text of the Vulgate) call for powerful images, which I have characterized as Muscularity (see note 4). The nature of the hymns does not lend itself very well to this aspect of Le Franc's poetic register. But it does pay attention to proportionality and to the appropriateness of the words for many of the feast days it sings.

I have tried to demonstrate, following Finch, the extraordinary variety of meters which characterizes Le Franc in the hymn for Christmas and others. In the Christmas hymn he mixes lines of six, eight, and twelve syllables, and he includes five-syllable lines to add a bit of lilt to the rhythm of the poem. I have also pointed out how the words reply to the meaning he wants to associate with this feast day. Another hymn showing this kind of harmony between the meaning of the day being celebrated and the emotions associated with it can be seen in Hymn XIII, "For All Souls Day." For this day he wants the music to be lugubrious but consoling.

> Ecoute, Dieu puissant, le cri de ma douleur;
> Autour de moi la mort a déployé son ombre.
> De nos iniquités si tu comptais le nombre,
> Qui pourrait soutenir le poids de ta fureur?

---

18. Ibid., 197.

Ah! suspends tes coups redoutables;
Contre des humains misérables
Quelle haine peut t'inspirer?
Voudrais-tu foudroyer l'argile
Dont tu formas l'être fragile
Que ton souffle fit respirer?

Que l'homme est malheureux, que sa vie est cruelle!
Il naît comme la fleur, il est foulé comme elle;
Ses maux sont mille fois plus nombreux que ses jours.
Il disparaît, semblable à la vapeur légère,
　　Ou tel que l'ombre passagère,
Qui fuit au même instant qu'elle marque son cours.

(Listen, God almighty, to my painful cry;
All around me Death has cast its shadow.
If you counted the number of our iniquities,
Who could sustain the weight of your fury?

Ah ! hold back your fearful blows;
Against miserable human beings
What hatred can inspire you?
Would you strike with thunder the very clay
With which you created the fragile being
That your breath gave life to?

How unfortunate is man, how cruel is his life!
He is born like the flower, he is trampled on as it is;
His misfortunes are a thousand times more numerous than
his days.
He disappears, akin to the fleeting vapor,
　　Or like the fleeing shadow,
That disappears at the very instant it can be seen.)

To illustrate the terrifying aspect of the day of the dead, Le Franc chose to compose a passage in odd-numbered syllables, which seems to rush toward the most frightening conclusion of all: eternal life in the torments of Hell:

O jour de colère,
Terribles moments!
O jour de misère,
De pleurs, de tourments!

La foudre dévore
La terre et le Ciel.
Nous voyons éclore
L'effroyable aurore
Du jour éternel.

O jour de colère,
Terribles moments!
O jour de misère,
De pleurs, de tourments!

Vengeur de nos crimes,
Où fuir? où cacher
Les tristes victimes
Qu'au fond des abîmes
Ta main va chercher?

O jour de colère,
Terribles moments!
O jour de misère,
De pleurs, de tourments!

(O Day of wrath,
Terrifying moments!
O Day of suffering,
Of tears, of torments!

Lightning and thunder devour
Heaven and Earth.
We see the start
Of the frightening dawn
Of the eternal day.

O Day of wrath,
Terrifying moments!

O Day of suffering,
Of tears, of torments!

Avenger of our crimes,
Where can we flee, where can we hide
The bitter victims
Whom in the depths of abysses
Your hand will go to seek?

O Day of wrath,
Terrifying moments!
O Day of suffering,
Of tears, of torments!

He ends his hymn in harmony with the meaning he sees in the feast day, consolation. The short final stanza consists of lines of five and seven syllables:

Âmes des fidèles,
Reposez en paix.
Que les portes éternelles
Pour vous s'ouvrent à jamais.
Âmes des fidèles,
Reposez en paix.

(Souls of the faithful,
May you rest in peace.
May the gates of eternity
Be forever open for you.
Souls of the faithful,
May you rest in peace.)

The end of the world is pictured in hymn XIV, "For the first Sunday of Advent." This hymn, which the poet calls "Ode on the Last Judgment," shares most of the characteristics of the Hymn for All Souls Day, including the use of five-syllable lines, normally lyrical, but used here to paint a terrifying event, the end of time. The rapidity of the events suggests that of the Last Judgment. Even the angels tremble with fear at the sight of the end of creation:

Les monts se renversent
Sur le sein des flots;
Les vents se dispersent
Sur les vastes eaux;
Les ondes se percent
Des chemins nouveaux.
Les tonnerres grondent,
Quels embrasements!
Les Cieux dissous fondent;
Leurs écoulements
Allument, confondent
Tous les elements.

(The mountains crumble
In the bosom of the sea;
The winds are dispersed
Over the vast oceans;
The waters are pierced
With new pathways.
The thunder rumbles,
What fiery lightning!
The heavens, dissolved, melt away;
Their debris
Burns and mixes together
All the elements.)[19]

Here, having arrived at the end of time, I must take leave of my gentle reader, even though we have not been engaged together in an analysis of all the poems. I thought it would be more interesting, and more useful, to present certain aspects of the work of this poet who is too little known even in France in the twenty-first century, and who is much better than his reputation. Jean-Jacques Le Franc de Pompignan produced, for the

---

19. Le Franc de Pompignan, *Oeuvres*, I, 305–8.

first time in 1751, a text, which he called *Poésies sacrées*, which was doubled in size in 1763 and which he published for the last time the very year of his death, 1784. This text consisted of two parts, an Introduction or *Discours préliminaire*, which contains many pages of Le Franc's theory of poetry and especially of religious poetry, and five books of poems, the fourth of which, the *Hymnes*, the subject matter of this article, is derived from New Testament sources and the lives of the saints (the other books—Odes, Canticles, Prophesies, Philosophical Discourses—are translations or paraphrases of Old Testament sources). I have tried to show how he applied his theories to his poems, and I hope I have shown that his poetry, even the hymns (which I had always considered to be the weakest of the five books, but which I now find, after several years of close reading, to be a worthy companion to the other books) illustrate his theories. Like most Catholic hymns of the period, these were not intended as songs sung by the congregation, but rather as performances given by trained singers, accompanied by several instruments. But unlike most of the hymns written in the period, they were written in the vernacular, in French, so that the parishioners could understand the words they were hearing. Unfortunately, we have not yet discovered the musical settings for these hymns, which remain, to us at least, songs without music.

The Elect Methodists: Calvinistic Methodism in England and Wales, 1735–1811

A Review by Isabel Rivers
Queen Mary University of London

The Calvinistic Methodists have received far less attention from historians than the Wesleyan or Arminian Methodists, and this book sets out to remedy that neglect. The imbalance is not surprising—Methodism of the Wesleyan kind became and remains a multimillion, worldwide movement, with many variants that retain the Wesleyan emphasis on holiness and salvation open to all, whereas eighteenth-century English Calvinistic Methodism is now represented only by the Countess of Huntingdon's Connexion, active on a small scale in England and Sierra Leone, while its Welsh co-movement became the Welsh Calvinistic Methodist Church, now known as the Presbyterian Church of Wales. The aim of the authors is for the first time "to tell the story of English and Welsh Calvinistic Methodism woven into a single analytic narrative," organized chronologically, exploring how the movements overlapped and interpenetrated and yet never fully merged, and asking why the Welsh movement went from strength to strength while the English movement ran out of steam. They "hope to reflect the remarkable complexity of the eighteenth-century evangelical revival"(xiv–xv). This is a readable, clearly written, and scrupulously referenced account, which is in many ways an invaluable guide to its tricky terrain but which oddly misses some important opportunities when dealing with the English movement.

The three authors are extremely well qualified for the task. David Ceri Jones has previously published a detailed account of the early stages of the Welsh revival, *'A Glorious Work in the World': Welsh Methodism and the International Evangelical Revival, 1735–1750* (2004); Boyd Stanley Schlenther has published a biography of the Countess of Huntingdon, *Queen of the Methodists: The Countess of Huntingdon and the Eighteenth-Century Crisis of Faith and Society* (1997), and edited *Calendar of the Trevecka Letters* (2003) with Eryn Mant White; and White has published *The Welsh Bible* (2007). All three have published relevant articles, with several of White's in Welsh; indeed, it is one of the strengths of the book that the findings of so much scholarship in Welsh is now made available to English readers, presumably through White's mediation.

The book's opening date refers to the conversions of George Whitefield (1714–70), Howel Harris (1714–73), and Daniel Rowland (1711?–90) in 1735, and its closing date to the ordination of Welsh Methodist preachers as ministers in 1811, marking the Methodists' break with the Church of England and the establishment of a new denomination in Wales. The English figures discussed in most detail are Whitefield and the Countess of Huntingdon (1707–91), with attention given where appropriate to their relations with John Wesley (1703–91) and to other figures such as John Cennick (1718–55), Rowland Hill (1744–1833), and Thomas Haweis (1734?–1820); the main Welsh figures in addition to Harris and Rowland are William Williams (1717–91), Howell Davies (1717?–70), Thomas Charles (1755–1814), and Peter Williams (1723–96). The topics covered include the rise of the revival in England and Wales in the 1730s; the split into Moravian, Wesleyan, and Calvinist factions in 1740–41; the varieties of predestinarianism among the Calvinists, and the theological disputes with the Wesleyans in the 1740s and 1770s; Harris's role in the 1740s as Whitefield's deputy, his attempt to unite the English and Welsh Calvinistic Methodists, and his expulsion; Whitefield's influence and dependence on Lady Huntingdon; the disparate nature of English Calvinistic Methodist groups (a very useful attempt has been made to track down Whitefieldian societies in 1747); the development of Methodism in different parts of Wales and the shift of the center of gravity from the southwest to the north; the importance of publishing in Welsh for the support of Welsh-speaking Methodist societies.

A recurring and essential question is that of the relationship of the Calvinistic Methodists to the Church of England. Whitefield, despite his irregularities as an itinerant in Britain and North America, never made any move to leave the Church and join the dissenters, and hence, it is argued here, he had an ambivalent attitude to the movement he had created (47); Lady Huntingdon found herself on the wrong end of ecclesiastical law in her claim that her huge public chapel at Spa Fields was private and, in 1782, made the decision to leave the church, register her chapels as dissenting, and create a new denomination, despite the fact that she opposed a settled ministry, unlike the dissenters, and always favoured itinerancy, one of the hallmarks of Methodism. Harris and Rowland argued from the outset that the Welsh Methodists should not take actions that would lead to secession, and this view was still held by Rowland and William Williams in the 1780s. After 1800 the mood changed, partly because there were not enough ordained Welsh clergy of Methodist sympathies to administer the sacraments, and the lay preachers pressed for ordination. No suggestion is made here that the split of the Wesleyan Methodists from the Church of England for similar reasons in the 1790s after Wesley's death might have been a precedent, although such a comparison could have been illuminating.

The least convincing part of the book is that dealing with the supposed disintegration of English Calvinistic Methodism. There is some inconsistency on the question of Whitefield's capacity or otherwise for organization (at which Wesley was a past master): at one point it is said that Whitefield did put in place an effective structure for his societies, contrary to the usual assumption of historians, but could not oversee it when in America (62), but elsewhere he is said to have had no taste for administration (149). More is needed on the afterlife of Whitefield and of the Countess of Huntingdon's Connexion. It is stated that after Whitefield's death most chapels in his connexion joined the Independents, but no attempt is made to assess his great impact on English evangelical dissenters or to consider the work of those who took over his Tabernacle, such as Matthew Wilks. The heroic portrait of Whitefield as George Fervidus in *Christian Memoirs: or, A Review of the Present State of Religion in England* (1776) by William Shrubsole, minister in Sheerness, Kent, is not mentioned. No account is given of the long publishing history and usage of Whitefield's *Collection of Hymns for Social Worship*, well into the nineteenth century.

Lady Huntingdon comes out of the story very badly. There is a good account of her Connexion in chapter 8, but her educational legacy is not properly assessed. No one can deny that her college at Trevecca in Wales was badly run and that her students were inadequately educated, nor that her support for slavery in Georgia (like Whitefield's earlier, but in strong contrast to Wesley) was reprehensible. However, the brief picture given of Cheshunt College in Hertfordshire, the successor to Trevecca after her death, is too negative (216): it became in the course of the nineteenth century an important interdenominational college serving both her Connexion and Congregationalism. John Eyre, one of her students, a Church of England clergyman who took part in the opening of Cheshunt in 1792 and founded the enormously influential *Evangelical Magazine* in 1793, is not mentioned (indeed the *Evangelical Magazine* is only referred to as the model for the Welsh equivalent, *Trysorfa Ysprydol*). The movement of Calvinistic Methodism in England into dissent is judged as a failure, in contrast to the establishment of the Welsh Calvinistic Methodist Church as a new dissenting denomination.

Jones, David Ceri, Boyd Stanley Schlenther, and Eryn Mant White. *The Elect Methodists: Calvinistic Methodism in England and Wales, 1735–1811*. Cardiff: University of Wales Press, 2012. Pp. xvii + 307.

David Hume: The Philosopher as Historian

A Review by Richard Kleer
University of Regina

Judging a book by its cover would give especially misleading results in this case. From its title, readers might expect a general introduction to Hume's scholarly work. Instead, they will get an account mainly of Hume the historian. The volume was originally commissioned as part of "a series of short books by historians writing about their favourite historians" (5). First published by Avon (in Britain) and St. Martin's (in the United States), it is now reprinted by Penguin and Yale. The rerelease may have a lot to do with the apparent popularity (judging by the many reviews, at least) of Phillipson's volume on Adam Smith, released by the same two publishers in 2010. The new edition is very much like the old. The most noticeable change is the addition of a few pages in the final chapter about why Hume eventually decided not to add to his *History of England* a volume on the reigns of William III and Anne.

Phillipson positions Hume's *History* as the practical fruition of a lifelong campaign to preserve civilization in Britain by teaching its citizens to rise above faction, xenophobia, and religion in order to think calmly and rationally about their constitution. He sees Hume as heir to Defoe, Addison, and Steele, who strove, he alleges, to develop a language of politeness that would improve the manners of their numerous readers. But Hume did not think good manners sufficient to preserve civilization. He wanted to go further and encourage rational discussion of politics and history as well: "Only then would it be possible to unscramble the ideological confusions and enthusiasms which had fuelled the factionalism of Walpolean politics and that continued later in the eighteenth century to threaten Britain with the prospect of revolutionary unrest" (27).

The book's subtitle—"The Philosopher as Historian"—is no accident. Phillipson maintains that Hume's historical writing was built from an analytical foundation set out in *A Treatise of Human Nature*. Loathing the false certainties of Christianity, Hume sought in the *Treatise* to show that beliefs, theological and otherwise, originated in imagination and everyday experience. Constitutions too rested on contingent beliefs—mere opinions formed over time about the appropriateness and necessity of obeying political authority. So if people wanted to understand themselves and their societies, they needed to study history.

Hume began the move from theory to practice with his *Essays, Moral and Political,* seeking to translate his metaphysical position into party-political language. The most natural form of government was monarchical, not a mixed constitution. Government was supported not by abstract constitutional principles but by considerations of interest and habit. All governments were originally established by force and sustained by a deference that had become habitual. It was religious enthusiasm that had dislodged the monarchy, not a failure of the royals to honor an original contract with the people. Modern politicians needed corruption to forge a degree of the natural deference that had been destroyed by factionalism.

Having failed to win popular acclaim for his *Essays,* Hume sought to teach the same practical lessons in a more popular and accessible manner by writing a new history of England in which James I attempted to rule on the basis of an abstract theory of divine right, failing to understand that the absolute obedience Elizabeth had won was owing to her mastery of the politics of consent. The Petition of Right to which Charles I was forced to agree in 1628 likewise rested on the pure fiction of original consent, which was the recent invention of Puritan enthusiasm. Civil war was inevitable. Elizabeth, by contrast, succeeded by deliberately and carefully protecting her people as much as possible from the strains that theological controversy threatened to thrust on them. It was her prudent governance, not providence, that had preserved England from the religious wars roiling the continent. The feudal constitution was not the font of political liberty Hume's contemporaries had made of it. Originally built to preserve the personal authority of kings who led a highly militaristic society, it could not support any movements toward a more impersonal system of justice. Instead, with each king's death, the country collapsed into schism and disorder. In such a world, liberty was best preserved not by undermining kings but by supporting their claims to absolute power.

I do not find persuasive Phillipson's attempt to position Hume's historical writing as an exercise in refining the tastes of the middling ranks or in working out the practical consequences of his theory of politics and history. The scarlet thread running throughout Hume's work is more likely his iconoclasm; always he wrote against the prepossessions of his day. The *Treatise* established that reason was not the queen of human nature, the *Essays* (among many other things) that corruption had a legitimate role to play in politics, the *Enquiry* that morals were not divinely ordained, and the *History* that the broad sweep of English history could not be told as a story about the ebb and flow of an ancient constitution. Of any broader and more systematic aims than this we should follow Hume's lead and remain skeptical.

Phillipson is at his best when writing of Hume's *History*. He helps us understand what would have stood out for Hume's contemporaries when reading that book. "The history of civilization in England could no longer be told in terms of the fortunes of an ancient constitution. It was now the story of a nation whose people's political behaviour had been shaped by laws and customs, by property, religion and culture, and by the securities and insecurities of the ages in which they lived" (133). Phillipson's book also serves well in whetting our appetite to read the *History of England* ourselves.

Phillipson, Nicholas. *David Hume: The Philosopher as Historian*. New Haven, CT: Yale University Press, 2012. Pp viii + 157.

Imagining Methodism in Eighteenth-Century Britain: Enthusiasm, Belief, and the Borders of the Self

A Review by Robin Runia
Xavier University of Louisiana

In her sensitive and thoughtful afterword, Misty Anderson rehearses the investment of literary criticism in "restaging the opposition between a religious past and a secular modernity" (236). She makes clear how the discipline of literary studies has largely refused to acknowledge its own ideology of secularization. Quoting Michael Kauffman, Anderson offers her audience the following call to action: "Anyone constructing a narrative of secularization (even if finally to refute it) needs to evaluate certain ideas, truth claims, or values that may seem more or less spiritual, more or less 'religious'" (236). Following her own thorough consideration of the relationship between Methodism and the modern self, her plea resonates well.

Within this context, Anderson's efforts to define and justify the terms of her study are significant. Referencing Locke, she insists on the centrality of experience to modern conscious self-making and rejects the term *subjectivity*. Accordingly, the wide array of cultural artifacts Anderson considers, including popular prints and engravings, novels and pamphlets, hymns and ballads, personal correspondence and periodical literature, reveal the Methodist self as one "which does not satisfy the demand for autonomy and agency that liberalism articulates as a requirement of modern consciousness" (199). That this refutation of the narrative of secularization does not consistently interrogate the value of autonomy and agency to a liberal modern selfhood reflects the difficulty of challenging such a long and dearly held history. Nevertheless, Anderson's text offers an abundance of analysis and insightful interpretation that successfully reveals the pride of place Methodism claimed in the eighteenth-century British imagination.

Starting with the caveat that her "argument is not that secular and religious capture the complete horizon of possibility in the project of modernity, but that their opposition achieves a cultural dominance that defines the era," Anderson fleshes out her vision of modernity as both project and era by examining texts produced by and about Methodists (11). First, she provides a history of Methodism's origins as a difficult to define group within the Anglican Church. Anderson enumerates Methodism's satirical associations with religious enthusiasm, Catholic mysticism, sacred eroticism, anarchic revolution, and antinomianism. Additionally, she identifies how its emphasis on "spiritual senses" complicates traditional empirical epistemological accounts. Anderson argues that their celebration of justification by faith remained troubling in its potential to undermine traditional notions of social accountability and thereby proved incompatible with modern selfhood.

By detailing historical links to the anti-Methodist satire of Henry Fielding's *The Female Husband*, John Cleland's *Memoirs of a Woman of Pleasure*, Samuel Foote's *The Minor*, and William Hogarth's *Enthusiasm Delineated*, among others, Anderson next establishes the ubiquity of anxieties surrounding Methodists' perceived feminine somatic receptivity to performance technology. She demonstrates how the unruly body threatened to blur the boundaries between spirituality and sexuality. Specifically, Anderson argues that Methodism "function[s] like a sexuality," naturalizing specific behaviors and offering "a system of practices that could consolidate the self" and demanding the maintenance of cognitive distance within an "excremental Real" (99, 167).

In contrast to the anxieties Methodists provoked, Anderson also presents two chapters on the value their practices and behaviors added to the shifting aesthetic and economic landscapes of the later eighteenth century. With brilliant presentations of Wesleyan hymnody and its reliance on popular music and distinct rhetorical forms, Anderson argues on behalf of a Methodist self open to a sublime collectivity. She writes, "Fueled by an intimate poetic sensibility that asked singers to inhabit a range of gendered subject and object positions, these group declarations of religious devotion struck at the core of the emerging liberal notion of agency, grounded in individual consciousness and self-possession" (173). Her last chapter reinforces this theme by considering the social cohesion Methodism offered through affective supplement to early capitalism within Tobias Smollett's *Humphry Clinker* and Richard Graves's *The Spiritual Quixote.*

While Anderson's book, with its reifications of a "primitive" somatic spirituality, maintains the secularization of self myth which it strives to complicate, its fascinating, carefully researched, and astutely argued pages undoubtedly prove the significance of Methodism to the heart and mind of eighteenth-century British identity.

Anderson, Misty. *Imagining Methodism in Eighteenth-Century Britain: Enthusiasm, Belief, and the Borders of the Self.* Baltimore: The Johns Hopkins University Press, 2012. Pp. xii + 279.

Philosophy and Religion in Enlightenment Britain: New Case Studies

A Review by Bob Tennant
Durham University

This collection of twelve individually strong pieces was published in tribute to M. A. Stewart, the former Gifford Lecturer and, until lately, professor of philosophy at Lancaster University. The editor, Ruth Savage, succeeded in putting together an outstanding list of contributors from across Britain, Europe, and North America. This in itself is a tribute to Stewart's eminence in research and evident excellence as a teacher.

The first seven chapters are a miscellany of studies, the range reflecting Stewart's own breadth of activity. Giovanni Tarantino writes about Martin Clifford, the seventeenth-century English deist. A. D. G. Steers offers a piece about the nonsubscribing Irish Presbyterian Samuel Haliday, who continued his career in Scotland. James Moore studies Scottish Presbyterian nonsubscription in relation to Francis Hutcheson and Hutcheson's relationship with his father—a most interesting extension of our knowledge of someone who tends to be remembered as a moral philosopher tout court. The sole chapter about Locke is by Victor Nuovo, in which Nuovo extends backward his earlier work on the contemporary reception of *The Reasonableness of Christianity*, suggesting that that work is underpinned by a Socinian apologetics. Laurent

Jaffro writes about Toland's atheistic Christology, and Udo Thiel revisits human resurrection and personal identity.

It is notable that the authors of two of the most outstanding chapters can claim Stewart's direct assistance, Stewart having either read drafts or supplied references. Isabel Rivers's subject—the Scottish Episcopalian Henry Scougal, author of *The Life of God in the Soul of Man*—is perhaps a minor figure, but the chapter is a considerable piece of painstaking bibliographical and textual scholarship. Most valuably, the chapter is prefaced by the shrewd and not sufficiently proclaimed fact that works of practical religion were more typical, influential, and—for the historian—more reliably fruitful as evidence than were the opinionated writings of controversialists, whose glamour must always be somewhat at odds with the practical religion of the congregations and wider society. Rivers shows how Scougal's book was, at different times and places, published, prefaced, edited, and redacted from three directions: the mysticism of a strain of largely Scottish Episcopalianism, practical Methodism, and the SPCK. Knut Haakonssen, in another cogent piece, also draws on Stewart in his chapter, "Natural Jurisprudence and the Identity of the Scottish Enlightenment." He analyzes the persistence in the Scottish universities' curricula of natural law and natural jurisprudence, "doggedly maintained" (265) well into the nineteenth century. Unlike Rivers's self-contained chapter, Haakonssen's serves as a preface to forthcoming works, in which the later stages of the Scottish Enlightenment in creating "the civic education of a moderately progressive [Scottish] society" (277) are presumably discussed.

In contrast to the book's overall miscellaneous nature are the four chapters about Hume. Aaron Garrett offers thoughts about the relationship between Joseph Butler and Hume, who admired him. This is a matter of record, but suggestions that Butler reciprocated are anecdotal, although plausible enough: Butler was broad-minded. Garrett discusses some of the correspondence between Samuel Clarke and his intellectually massive but personally humble disciple and examines the Fifteen Sermons' too-little analyzed influence on the Scottish school. It is deeply ironic that the atheist Hume should be attracted by someone whose sturdy and subtle empiricism was so saturated in dark, Newtonian metaphysics.

Two chapters publish Hume manuscripts, one very early and one very late. John P. Wright presents Hume's early "Essay on Chivalry," the playfulness of which—a sort of anti-Addison—is so characteristic of his mature work. Following Stewart himself in assigning the "Essay" a relatively late date (ca. 1731), Wright attempts to use the essay as a sort of back-bearing to support readings and critiques of Mandeville, Hutcheson, and Shaftesbury in the Treatise. Moritz Baumstark's publishes a very late Hume letter—August 1, 1775—in which Hume supports American independence because he professes to dislike "these factious colonists." (Butler bubbles under again—Josiah Tucker, whom Baumstark cites, was his chaplain.) Hume also wishes to see the churches converted to riding schools and other useful functions. But since he also anticipates Englishmen (that is, Britons) being forbidden to round the Cape of Good Hope, under pain of death, and the government being unable to raise bonds at 20 percent, we must acknowledge the risk of taking things too seriously. The letter is surely a piece of playfulness; it is the product of a grumpy old man, certainly, but it echoes the playfulness of the early "Essay on Chivalry"—as well as prominent tendencies in the mature works of this philosophe, belle lettriste, ironist, and practitioner (in Wright's phrase) of "conjectural history" (203).

The fourth Hume chapter is written by James A. Harris and addresses "The Early Reception of Hume's Theory of Justice." This work gives a solid account of critiques—developed mainly by Kames (who corresponded with Butler), Smith, and Reid—of Hume's ethics, again usually with Butler as groundwork. Harris's point is well made: "That Butler was English will disturb those who wish to regard the Scottish Enlightenment as having owed little or nothing to the country that lies to the south of the Tweed . . . [we should have] no regard for the sensibilities of cultural chauvinists on either side of the border" (214).

Taking the volume as a whole, the absence of a critique of Stewart's own body of such remarkable work might be regretted, although it would have been beyond Savage's declared remit. The American practice of critical tribute, with its dedicatee's "reply to my critics," is much to be admired.

The individual chapters are stimulating, vivacious, and of a generally high standard of scholarship. Some are really outstanding. The reader does, however, need to bear in mind that, as "case studies," the chapters are unconnected with each other, although there is a certain fellow-feeling in those on Hume (with which Haakonssen's sits comfortably). The book's whole is no greater than the sum of its parts, but, to adapt Butler, it is what it is, and not another thing. It is well worth reading.

Savage, Ruth, ed. *Philosophy and Religion in Enlightenment Britain: New Case Studies.* Oxford: Oxford University Press, 2012. Pp. x + 289.

The Truth of the Christian Religion, with Jean Le Clerc's Notes and Additions

A Review by Robert G. Walker
Washington and Jefferson College

Paul L. Maier, in his introduction to a recent translation of *The Church History* of Eusebius, has some refreshing advice: regarding Eusebius's long lists of bishops' names and dates, "the reader is urged to scan or to skip this material, since it can all be found in Appendix 2" (20). I can enthusiastically recommend the book under review, a new edition of what is generally known as the first work of Protestant apologetics, with no expectation that many people on the planet will read every word. To become familiar with this book, however, is to go far toward an understanding of the various arguments about religious beliefs both on the continent and in Britain from the beginning to the end of what historians are now calling the long eighteenth century. I have expanded Grotius, the author of the book, chronologically and geographically—Hugo de Groot was born in Delft, Holland, in 1583 and died in a shipwreck in 1645—but Professor Antognazza's stellar introduction suggests this is not a stretch too far.

Antognazza is as good at navigating the treacherous waters of religious arguments as she is at detailing the complicated publication history of *De Veritate Religionis Christianae*—this is the title of the second edition of the Latin prose work published in 1629. The first edition (1627) had a longer Latin title, and the first version was a poem in

Dutch, written while Grotius was imprisoned for life and published in 1622, after his escape. Although fourteen editions in four languages appeared during Grotius's life, "this was . . . only the tip of the iceberg. By the middle of the nineteenth century there had appeared sixty-four editions in Latin, seven in German, forty-five in English, eight in French, seven in Dutch, four in Scandinavian languages, three in Welsh, one in Hungarian, one in Polish, and one in Italian, plus six in Oriental languages, clearly meant as missionary tools" (xv). The present text is of a 1743 English edition, translated by John Clarke (1682–1757), an Anglican clergyman and the younger brother of the better-known Reverend Samuel Clarke. But intervening between Grotius and most subsequent editions, including Clarke's, is Jean Le Clerc (1657–1736), born and reared in Geneva, transplanted to France, brief resident of London, and "befriended by John Locke" (xix). By the time of Le Clerc's third and final edition (1724), he had expanded Grotius's six books to eight, added several epistles designed to highlight Grotius's affection for the Anglican Church, and supplemented Grotius's annotations. This final version of Le Clerc's editing Grotius, then, was published in English translation by Clarke in 1743.

All this detail regarding the publication history is important, I think, for one of the implicit arguments of the introduction, namely, that Grotius's work was so enormously popular throughout the West that it must have represented the dominant religious view of its time. When scholars look back on a period, the natural tendency is to find an early appearance of what eventually becomes the dominant view—well and good, so long as the earlier dominant view is not lost in the search for a unique, early vision. Said another way, a scholar focusing on the middle of the eighteenth century, for example, would probably do better to become familiar with Grotius than with Hume, assuming the scholar's goal is to understand what was being read by everyone, including Hume, prior to Hume's innovative notions.

Grotius was nothing if not clear about his basic point, expressed as follows by Antognazza: "Division among Christians could and should be overcome on the basis of the distinction between fundamental and nonfundamental articles of faith coupled with the crucial claim that all fundamental articles are explicitly contained in Scripture" (xvii). But such clarity soon fell victim to the realpolitik of the age, as the work was attacked by rightwing Calvinists for what it did not contain, namely, a specific defense of the Trinity. Antognazza notes the irony: "Those who vociferously denounced the absence of dogmas were the representatives, not of the Roman church so often stigmatized for its zeal for rigid doctrinal definitions, but of a branch of Reformed Protestantism which regarded itself as an unyielding defender of Calvinist orthodoxy" (xvii). So much for the simplicity of *sola Scriptura*, so often cited as the defining characteristic of the Protestantism of the period. When the hard-line Dutch Calvinists called for a general synod on international Calvinism to rid their church of the Remonstrants (Grotius's party), "the principle of church authority—thrown out through the door by the Protestant Reformation in favor of sola Scriptura—was coming back through the window in order to settle this intra-Calvinist dispute arising from the vexed question of what in fact Scripture taught" (xi).

Religious treatises with "truth" in their titles are usually far from ecumenical, so Grotius's tactics are worth a word. He saw attempts to establish *the whole truth and nothing but the truth* of religion as misguided and counterproductive. This italicized phrase about truth is telling: it is modern, too modern for the celebrated jurist that Grotius was to understand it, even in a strictly legal context. In a religious context, Grotius found Christianity both true and certain, but he acknowledged "that different things must have different kinds of Proof; one sort in Mathematicks, another in the Properties of Bodies, another in doubtful Matters, and another in Matters of Fact" (135-36). Those truths of Christianity essential for man to work out his salvation had been revealed in scripture, allowing Grotius to finesse the disputes among Christians by regarding them as nonessential matters. Grotius seems to have attributed disputes among Christians to political rather than religious motives: "There began to be as many Schemes of Religion as there were Parties of Men who had different Judgment, and got the Power into their Hands" (15). To his strategy of declaring religious differences among Christians' indifferent issues, he coupled a "common enemy" approach to unite all Christians as he devoted a book each to arguing the error of the beliefs of "Paganism, Judaism, or Mahometanism" (167). Perhaps the most interesting of the three books treats Judaism; just as Eusebius had done thirteen centuries earlier, Grotius regards the nation's troubles as punishment for "their despising the Messiah" (215). Grotius balances this, at least from his Christian viewpoint, with an introductory address—"I desire the *Jews* . . . would not look upon us as Adversaries"—and a concluding prayer that God "would enlighten the minds of the *Jews* with his own Light" (189, 229). The treatment of Judaism, a ticklish topic for any Christian apologist, seems to have interested Le Clerc quite a bit, as his annotations of this section frequently sparkle.

And Le Clerc is not inconsequential in this work. Certainly what we have here is mostly Grotius, but Antognazza's intelligent formatting allows us easily to separate Le Clerc's important role. Her annotations to the text are few, thankfully, as we already have Grotius's notes and Le Clerc's, with a very occasional note by the translator Clarke. Antognazza identifies the particular author of any note where it is not obvious, but instead of additional notes, she has provided a thirty-two-page appendix (although not so titled) of "Authors and Works Cited by Grotius and Le Clerc," as well as a detailed index. The book is handsomely designed, as is typical for the Liberty Fund.

Le Clerc's admiration for Grotius is apparent, yet his notes are not always complimentary, and the reader who skips them will miss some interesting knuckle-rapping. For example, when Grotius mentions a prophecy of the Messiah by "a *Hebrew* Teacher *Nehemiah*," Le Clerc's note does not disguise its displeasure at the vagueness of the reference: "*Grotius* ought to have told us whence he had this" (210). Another time, Grotius gets in the weeds as he attempts to explain the resurrection of the body after it has physically deteriorated and, in fact, become parts of other bodies, but Le Clerc's note rescues him: "For he will be as much the same Man, though his Soul were joined to Matter which it was never before joined to, provided it be the same Soul; as a Decrepit Old Man is the same as he was when a Child crying in the Cradle" (111).

Le Clerc's other major importance is his role in linking Grotius with the Anglican church through calling attention to other writings where "the ancient Church-Government [Episcopacy] was highly esteemed by *Grotius*, without condemning others [i.e., Presbyterian]" (273). Le Clerc explains that Grotius "highly approved of [the Episcopacy] in the Manner it is maintained in *England*" (273–74). The letters Le Clerc prints at the end of his edition make the same point: "It appears plainly from them, that this very great Man had the highest Opinion of the Church of *England*, and would most willingly have lived in it, if he could" (289). The link Le Clerc forged, or highlighted, among Grotius, avoidance of religious controversy among Christians, and the Church of England would show up in various places over the next hundred years, including in an early biography of Sir Thomas Browne by his contemporary, John Whitefoot, and in the thought of Samuel Johnson. In 1830, the linkage was still vibrant enough to nettle the other side, as William Orme, a Scottish Congregational minister, wrote waspishly in his biography of Richard Baxter, "The religion of Grotius must have been of a very equivocal kind, for as many sects seem to have contended for him as cities about the birth of Homer" (*The Practical Works of The Rev. Richard Baxter*, 1:644).

Grotius, Hugo. *The Truth of the Christian Religion, with Jean Le Clerc's Notes and Additions*, translated by John Clarke (1743) and edited by Maria Rosa Antognazza. Indianapolis, IN: Liberty Fund, 2012. Pp. xx + 361.

Religious Dissent and the Aikin-Barbauld Circle 1740–1860

A Review by Nigel Aston
University of Leicester

There has been a remarkable rise of interest during the last decade in Anna Letitia Barbauld's (née Aikin) significance in the formation of Romantic literature, and *Religious Dissent and the Aikin-Barbauld Circle 1740–1860* places her appropriately within the thriving nexus of her intellectually creative Dissenting family. This volume of nine essays has its origins in a conference at Dr. Williams's library, currently the engine room of many initiatives into British dissenting history. The Aikins were a talented, hardworking, group of men and women down several generations, sparking off each other, inspired by their non-trinitarian Christian faith, and making complex contributions to British culture for more than a century. In the first chapter, Felicity James introduces the "Circle": men and women of sensibility and aimiable conversation at one level, but not in the least escapist; they were ready to stand up for the ideals of the French Revolution as well as for scientific advance. David L. Wykes then treats the, as it were, founding father of the Circle, John Aikin senior (1713–80). John was a product of Philip Doddridge's Academy in Northampton and King's College in Aberdeen. In time, he set up his own school at Kibworth Harcourt in Leicestershire. Before he moved on to teach at that celebrated flagship of Rational Dissent,

RAE, vol. 5, 2015
Copyright © 2015 AMS Press, Inc

Warrington Academy, John had built up a formidable pedagogical reputation for Kibworth and connected it fully into the nationwide Dissenting network. Wykes argues forcefully for seeing John's school years rather than his Warrington years as making "the greater contribution to Dissent and education" (43).

In chapter 3, William McCarthy, her biographer, discusses "How Dissent made Anna Letitia Barbauld, and what she made of Dissent." McCarthy insists, plausibly enough, on the importance of her father's liberal and didactic parenting, as well as pointing to the lifelong impact on Anna of friendship with Joseph and Mary Priestley at Warrington in the 1760s. McCarthy, unsurprisingly, finds feeling rather than doctrine supremely present in Anna's life and works, as he trawls through her much reprinted *Hymns in Prose for Children* (1781); she reads at times as more pantheist than Christian.

Kathryrn Ready chooses to present John Aikin junior as a literary physician. Ready looks through the prism of his various writings and his own educational formation as a surgical apprentice and a student at both Edinburgh and Leiden. The result of John's development was "a medico-moral discourse" (85) that was as unsettling for establishment politicians as it was for establishment physicians. The many-sided John Aikin junior is also the principal subject for Stephen Daniels and Paul Elliott in chapter 5. They consider John's geographical imagination by focusing on *England Delineated* (1788) and *Geographical Delineations* (1806) as cultural texts. Daniels and Elliot view John's perspective as a progressive landscape, quietly patriotic, proud of commercial circulation, and rising above narrowly Dissenting geographies.

The last four chapters deal with the less familiar later Aikins. In chapter 6, Ian Inkster considers Arthur Aikin (1773–1854) and the character of English industrialization. This Aikin was Secretary of the Royal Society of Arts between 1817 and 1839, keen to publicize inventions and technical discoveries and disseminate useful information on industrial technology. Inkster shows how Arthur's achievement can be understood only within the integrated contexts of progressive Unitarianism and science in the 1790s and 1800s. In chapter 7, Michelle Levy recovers and reassesses Lucy Aikin's history writings, three two-volume court histories on Elizabeth I, James I, and Charles I, published between 1818 and 1833. These histories were much valued in their day for Lucy's lively writing and her willingness to identify what was wrong about past regimes. Lucy spared neither Mary I nor Elizabeth I from criticism for their attacks on religious freedom, and she cast archbishop Laud as the archvillain. In chapter 8, Felicity James looks at Lucy Aikin's *Memoirs* in a narrative that "to some extent resists Barbauld's achievements as woman writer" (185). Lastly, Anne F. Janowitz offers an extended retrospective on the Aikin family in the light of the previous contributions.

The whole volume is nicely balanced in its coverage and shows a critical awareness of the Aikin family's self-presentation that was less evident in earlier treatments, notably Betsy Rodgers's *Georgian Chronicle: Mrs Barbauld and her Family* (1958). Without exception, the contributors are alert to the nuances of Rational Dissent and its capacity for strenuous but enlightened outreach to those in wider society who were broadly in sympathy with its progressive agendas. The Aikin-Barbauld Circle was an important site of religious sociability, but that religious dimension kindled those other varied forms of creativity over several generations that this volume illuminates. One would hope that the model of study deployed here could be adapted for wider use, for instance for Anglican familial networks.

James, Felicity, and Ian Inkster, eds. *Religious Dissent and the Aikin-Barbauld Circle 1740–1860*. Cambridge: Cambridge University Press, 2012. Pp. xiii + 257.

Re-Envisioning Blake

A Review by Joshua Davis
Ohio University

Born out of a conference commemorating its subject's 250th birthday, *Re-Envisioning Blake* surveys the state of contemporary Blake scholarship and invites new and challenging readings of one of British literary history's most renowned iconoclasts. The book's introduction reviews three principal strains in Blake studies—the bibliographic, the hermeneutical, and the historicist—and seeks to locate points of convergence, sites of overlap, in order to imagine not just the future of Blake studies but the future of literary studies as well.

Although the editors take a suitably Blakean synthetic approach, some of the essays collected here do appear to advocate the importance, if not the superiority, of their own methodologies. For instance, Keri Davies and David Worrall argue that much work done on William Blake suffers from an ill-founded reliance on the poet's status as a Dissenter. Arguing for the inaccuracy of this assumption, these critics provide an alternate religious history for Blake rooted in his mother's temporary but noteworthy membership in the Moravian Church—a thread explored more deeply by Craig Atwood, who, like Davies and Worrall, suggests that Blake's rejection of Christianity may have been, in fact, an embrace of the female principal typical of Moravian worship. This conclusion, based in part on their own archival efforts, the archival efforts of M. K. Schuchard, and their own retranslation and reappraisal of an article on Blake written by Henry Crabbe Robinson, produces a convincing and perhaps much-needed corrective to what critics take for granted as Blake's renunciation of Christian orthodoxy. Meanwhile, these efforts contribute to the body of the work, striving toward the enrichment of cultural history rather than textual interpretation. In this way, much of *Re-Envisioning Blake* is actually a re-envisioning of Blake's contexts.

Alongside Davies and Worrall, Mark Crosby and Angus Whitehead work in a decidedly historicist mode. As a result, their earnest recuperation of Catherine Blake devotes less attention to close reading of one of her surviving paintings than it does to close readings of secondhand accounts of how well Catherine Blake assisted her husband, although apparently she was "hardly a passive creature" (90). Even now, Blake's mother and his wife, one concludes, remain accessible to us exclusively through church records and the hearsay of those who knew them rather than by what they may have said or may have written about themselves. Whether this misfortune results simply from a lack of available evidence or from a lack of looking for such evidence remains unclear, but in the generative spirit of its project, the book welcomes and even demands further inquiry into the lives of these women whose impact on Blake bears so much significance.

Separate from the strain that galvanizes the discussion of Blake's historical moment is the strain that positions Blake against our own historical moment. Shirley Dent explores the appropriation of Blake's "Jerusalem" by extreme political groups, progressive and conservative alike. She begins with lines of thinking descended from Edmund Burke and Thomas Paine, but also includes a counterintuitive attachment to the poem on the part of fascists. In so doing, Dent takes stock of Blake's position in the popular imagination and dramatizes the implications of misreading. Dent's most impressive contribution, however, concerns her recommendation that Blake scholars attempt to account for the potentially troubling malleability and susceptibility of Blake's verses and to "look again at the neutrality of Blake's myth-making in the stories told, retold, and reinvented about England" (62). Like all the best essays in this volume, Dent's essay concludes with a clear sense of concerns yet to be satisfied and, more to the point, a clear sense of critics' responsibility to address these contentions.

John Grant and Mary Lynn Johnson supply careful treatments of Blake's paintings and thereby deepen and widen the book's scope. After the historicist-heavy chapters, the formalist approaches these critics take provide opportunities for the reader to participate in intimate interaction with the art itself. Better still, without doing so explicitly, Johnson's investigation into Blake's depictions of the death and ascent of the Virgin Mary actually lends greater credibility and complexity to the chapters that trace potential Moravian influence on Blake's life and work.

Whereas the book's introduction strikes a hopeful tone, the afterword strikes an apologetic one. Focusing on the humanity—and, therefore, on the fallibility—animating editorial decisions, Morris Eaves's closing remarks appear to beg for a margin of error, a margin necessary in part because of "how much Blake has already been deleted from the record" (226). But laying aside the inevitable loss or downright inscrutability of primary sources, it is difficult to understand what the afterword offers other than a rather gloomy nod toward the impermanence of the very material editors labor to preserve and disseminate.

Ultimately, *Re-Envisioning Blake* emerges as a readable collection of essays that attains its aspirations—to invigorate the immediate present as a locus of fruitful reading and thinking dedicated to Blake and to propose that the future of Blake studies resides in a fusion of the methods that have brought Blake studies this far.

Crosby, Mark, Troy Patenaude, and Angus Whitehead. *Re-Envisioning Blake*. New York: Palgrave Macmillan, 2012. Pp. 262.

Anglican Church Policy, Eighteenth Century Conflict, and the American Episcopate

A Review by Christopher J. Fauske
Salem State University

Perhaps the most charming aspect of Kenneth Elliott's *Anglican Church Policy, Eighteenth Century Conflict, and the American Episcopate* is its author's propensity to take at face value the statements made in the voluminous correspondence, the many pamphlets, and the occasional published sermons on the subject of whether a resident bishop would help secure the Church of England in the North American colonies and whether such an outcome was in any case desirable.

Oversight of the church in North America fell—largely by a series of administrative compromises and stopgap decisions—to the bishop of London, but, as Elliott's study makes clear, most of those bishops were not themselves convinced they had the authority to exercise control over the church in the colonies. Nor were they necessarily interested in promoting a resolution to the confused status quo. In that latter regard, they had allies in the various governments of the day in most, if not all, of the colonies and in Westminster. In short, the Church of England's relationship with the colonies, and with the governors of the colonies, was based on something other than a strategic plan.

Whenever an appeal was issued for an episcopal presence in the colonies—and the majority of such appeals came from colonial

RAE, vol. 5, 2015
Copyright © 2015 AMS Press, Inc

churchmen—responses were shaped by secular relationships, relationships often defined in England by domestic considerations and in the colonies by issues of trade, demography, and self-determination. It would have been impossible to design a structure acceptable to a majority of those affected, and many of those involved knew this. That knowledge, however, did not mean church officials could afford to disabuse advocates for a resident bishop, hence the constant refrain from apparently sympathetic clerics in England of support couched with advice about the need to proceed with patience and caution. Regardless of the language of the debate around each proposal—language Elliott takes as his guide—religious considerations themselves were never the deciding factor.

The greatest of the prevaricators among the bishops of London was Edmund Gibson (Bishop of London, 1723–48), who upon his translation sent out "Queries to be Answered by Persons who were Commissaries to my Predecessor," John Robinson. What Gibson wished to know was upon what grounds, and to what extent, he exercised authority over the colonies. The definitive answer seemed to come from Bermuda, which reported that "there was no document linking the bishop's authority back to [William] Laud," as had been suggested. Furthermore, "it was at the discretion of the particular governors whether to allow a commissary to operate within their province" (38–39).

Gibson ultimately appealed to George II for clarification. This appeal, however, came only after consultation with colleagues on the bishops' bench in the House of Lords and after sounding out Robert Walpole as to what might be acceptable. Gibson, who was decidedly conservative on many church matters, was hesitant about the establishment of a colonial suffragan bishopric. More significantly, Gibson recognized the importance of preserving good relations with Walpole as the church sought to limit the spread of toleration. Ultimately, George granted a warrant for the "exercise of only a 'Spiritual and Ecclesiastical Jurisdiction'" (39). The benefit to the church was that the warrant now vested that authority in the bishopric of London, rather than in a particular person, but it also severely restricted the scope of the church to act in the colonies.

In concentrating on the religious aspects of the public debate, Elliott downplays the importance of the secular and political components of the decision-making process. In the case of Gibson, for example, both Norman Sykes and various studies of Walpole offer context and analysis that Elliott eschews to prejudice the religious. It is not that the churchmen involved were not men of faith; it is that their faith was not blind to political reality. Sykes's book is cited in the bibliography, but, as with so many titles therein listed, it is not clear where Elliott draws on the works in his text or what aspects of the works he found influential. The index, perhaps a related editorial tic, is so perfunctory as to be of little, if any, use.

Elliott's account of Gibson's activities is indicative of the challenges faced by any author looking to examine the three components promised in the title: *Anglican Church Policy, Eighteenth Century Conflict, and the American Episcopate*. This is too vast a project to be undertaken in one slim volume.

The study, for example, does not once mention the Church of Ireland, which is important in this context because it was a constant reminder to all parties in England of what could happen if a church hierarchy had its own geographic and cultural identity. Perceived as meddling in both secular Irish and Anglo-Irish affairs, native-born Church of Ireland bishops caused considerable attention to have to be paid to the management of the Irish Houses of Parliament and to episcopal appointments there. Irish claims aside, there is evidence of a diversion to Ireland of promising clerics in England. Church of England managers and civil authorities were loath to consider the possibility of having similarly to divert talent to a new colonial bishopric.

In Scotland, the bishops of the Episcopalian church had chosen disestablishment and exclusion rather than affirm William III and Mary II as monarchs. Perhaps inaccurately, Scottish Episcopalians were identified with Jacobitism and were seen, more accurately, as a succor and a moral justification to the Non-jurors in England. The risk inherent in creating a church in the colonies capable of sustaining an episcopal line of succession after rejecting British civil authority was, likewise, not something the English wished to entertain.

Elliott mentions the Scottish church only in the final pages, when he recounts the route by which Samuel Seabury secured his postrevolution elevation to the bishopric; however, experience with both the Irish and Scottish churches, almost as troublesome to the Church of England as to the government in Westminster, limited enthusiasm even among putative supporters for a colonial bishop. Additionally, as Elliott notes, after the demise of Queen Anne, there was no regal support for Church of England expansion, but the secular domestic political consequences of a loss of royal support for an extraterritorial bishop is not an area Elliott explores. Such absences help reinforce Elliott's reading of the correspondence and pamphlets as essentially complete records when they are, rather, guides to a far more substantive debate.

The book offers significant insight into the day-to-day experiences of church commissaries, clergy, and lay people in the colonies, whose isolation from England, in addition to the requirement for would-be clerics to travel to England for ordination—a principal argument for the appointment of at least one colonial bishop—almost ensured the failure of the Church of England to secure its presence in the colonies.

Elliott's extensive examination of local reactions to attempts to bring a bishop to the colonies is the most significant component of this book. Demands for respect of local practices led to an increasingly energetic response from advocates. By 1760 Samuel Johnson (1696–1772), first president of King's College (now Columbia University), a convert from Congregationalism, and the first Church of England minister in Connecticut, was asking "whether it is for the best public good, that the Charter Governments should continue . . . as the people are nearly rampant in their high notions of liberty, and hence perpetually running into intrigue and faction" (138). Not surprisingly, people such as Jonathan Mayhew (1720–1766), the near Unitarian minister of Boston's West Church, responded with observations about the "monstrous hierarchy" of the Church of England and offered the opinion that Charles I was a "martyr . . . not because he bravely suffered death in the cause of truth and righteousness but because he died an enemy to liberty and the rights of conscience" (158).

As the American public sphere expanded the consequence of a polemic that had initially been designed to exploit British uncertainty about colonial public opinion, the rhetoric of Johnson and of Mayhew became absorbed in the broader discourse that led to 1776, and the debate about bishops and the Church of England in the American colonies was, ultimately, decided by events that owed little to the pre-varications, hesitations, and uncertainties that had kept the Church of England from endorsing the concept in more than vague principles. It would turn out, of course, that that refusal to take a stance was what likely saved the Church of England and permitted Seabury to travel to Scotland after the Revolution and return a bishop, accepted not only by his coreligionists but tolerated by those who not so many years earlier had opposed the very idea of an American bishop.

Elliott, Kenneth R. *Anglican Church Policy, Eighteenth Century Conflict, and the American Episcopate*. New York: Peter Lang, 2011. Pp. viii + 227.

Index

A

Adams, John, 157
Addison, Joseph, 36–37, 44, 50, 53, 299
Aglionby, William, 5
Aikin, Arthur, 318
Aikin, John, Jr., 102, 318
Aikin, John, Sr., 317–18
Aikin, Lucy
  history writings of, 318–19
  sexless soul, 85–86
Anderson, Misty, 303–5
Anne (queen), 23, 299–328
Antognazza, 311–14
Aquinas, 63–64
Aretino, 238
Ariès, Philippe, 103
Aristotle, 176–77
  pity and self-reflection, 172
  rhetoric of, 166
  sexless soul, 61–62
Atwood, Craig, 321
Augustine, Saint, 150
  allegorical hermeneutics, 166–69
  and Campbell, 161, 170–71, 177–79
  De doctrina Christiana, 160, 162, 176, 178–79
  caritas, 161–64, 169–70, 180
  uti (use) and *frui* (enjoy), 164–66
  enthymeme, 176
  sexless soul, 63–64
Aulard, François-Alphonse, 259–60, 267

B

Bach, Sebastian, 281, 285
Bacon, Francis, 39–41, 48
Barbauld, Anna Laetitia, 100, 107, 108
  Dissent, 106, 317–19
  Evenings at Home, 102
  providential empiricism, 109–10, 118
  children's books, 110–11
  godly pedagogy, 120–22
  Lockean self, 107–8, 111–13
Barre, François Poulain de la. *See* Poulain, François
Barry, James, 23
Baumstark, Moritz, 309
Baxter, Richard, 315
Bayle, Pierre, 35, 44, 224, 237
Bell, Andrew, 103
Berkeley, George, 33
  and King, 44–45, 47–48
  convergence of Truth, 34
  materialism, rejection of, 45, 51

Bernard of Clairvaux, 64
Bingen, Hildegard von, 65
Blair, Hugh, 174
Blake, Catherine, 322
Blake, William, 90, 321–23
Boethius, 29
Boreman, Thomas, 101
Boyle, Robert, 30, 34, 37–39
Brassens, Georges, 281
Browne, Thomas, 315
Buckminster, Joseph Stevens, Jr.,
    192–94
Bunyan, John, 118
Burke, Edmund, 322
Butler, Joseph, 308–9

C

Calas, Jean, 211, 215–16
Calas, Madame, 216, 226
Calas, Marc-Antoine, 216
Calas, Pierre, 216
Campbell, George
    and Augustine, 167, 170
    and Locke, 171
    enthymeme, usefulness of,
        176–78
    faculty psychology, 158–59
    influence on, 159–61, 163
    miracles and testimony, 173–74
    modernizing rhetoric, 158
    Philosophy of Rhetoric, The,
        157–58, 171, 178–79
    sympathy, 171–72, 176, 178
    translation of the Gospels,
        175–76

Carracci, Annibale, 6, 10–11, 17,
    20
Carroll, Lewis, 103
Cary, Samuel, 182, 187
    death of, 207
    heir apparent of Freeman, 193
    English's letter to, 198–201
    rebuttal of English, 196–98
    rebuttal of English, criticism of,
        203
Cennick, John, 296
Channing, William Ellery, 182,
    187
    English's letter to, 198–99
    later involvement of, 207
    popularity of, 193
    Two Sermons on Infidelity,
        194–96
Charles I, 319, 328
Charles, Thomas, 296
Cheselden, William, 3
Cicero, 29, 160, 162, 172, 177
Clarke, John, 312, 314
Clarke, Samuel, 308, 312
Cleland, John, 304
Clifford, Martin, 307
Clotilde, Saint, 278
Coleridge, Samuel Taylor, 86, 90
Collins, Anthony, 190
Colman, Henry, 196
Cooper, Ashley. *See* Shaftesbury,
    3rd Earl of
Cooper, Mary, 101
Cordes, Henrik, 26
Countess of Huntingdon, 295–98

Crébillon, 231, 242
Cromwell, Oliver, 22
Crosby, Mark, 322
Cruz, Juana Inés de la, 68

D

Daniels, Stephen, 318
Dante, 29
Darwin, Erasmus, 118
David, Jacques-Louis, 263
David (municipal magistrate of
　Toulouse), 215
Davies, Howell, 296
Davies, Keri, 321
Day, Thomas, 102, 118
Defoe, Daniel, 105, 299
Denon, Vivant, 231, 253, 255
Dent, Shirley, 322
Derham, William, 29, 34, 50, 53
　Astro-theology, 25, 28
　biography of, 26–27
Desan, Susan, 275–76
Descartes, René, 150, 224
　and King, 40
　Meditations, 66
　mind-body dualism (sexless
　　soul), 69
　passion, moderation of, 226
　soul and mind, 76
Desorgues, Théodore, 263
Dickens, Charles, 102
Dickinson, Emily, 103
Diderot, 232, 237
d'Orléans, Philippe, 238
Drake, Judith, 70

E

Eaves, Morris, 323
Edgeworth, Maria, 100, 102
Edwards, Jonathan, 158, 170
Effendi, Mohamed. *See* English,
　George Bethune
Elizabeth I, 300, 319
Elliott, Kenneth, 325–28
Elliott, Paul, 318
Emerson, Ralph Waldo, 184
Enfield, William, 84
English, George Bethune,
　181–209
Euripides, 256
Evelyn, John, 5
Everett, Edward, 182–85, 193,
　207–9
　Defence of Christianity, 202–6
Eyre, John, 298

F

Fenn, Ellenor, 102
Fichte, Johann Gottlieb, 149, 154
　and Kant, 126–27, 136–39, 151,
　　153
　conditional necessity of revela-
　　tion, 127–35
　rational-religious conciliation,
　　124–25
　theology and religion, 137–38
Fielding, Henry, 102, 304
Fielding, Sarah, 118–19
Finch, Robert, 277–87
Fleetwood, William, 3

Fontenelle, 237
Fontenelle, Bernard le Bovier de,
29, 37, 53, 224
Foucault, Michel, 249, 250
Franklin, Benjamin, 103
Freeman, James, 193
Freud, Sigmund, 234
Fuller, Margaret, 91, 94

G

Garrett, Aaron, 308
Garrick, David, 118
Gay, John, 3
Genette, Gérard, 263, 273–74
Genevieve, Saint, 278
George II, 326
Gibson, Edmund, 326–27
Godwin, William, 84
Gorgias, 166
Gossec, François-Joseph, 263
Gournay, Marie de, 66–67
Grant, John, 323
Graves, Richard, 305
Grew, Nehemiah, 49
Gribelin, Simon, 8, 19
Grimké, Sarah, 91–92
Grindon, Leopold Hartley, 94–95
Grotius, Hugo, 43, 311–15

H

Haakonssen, Knut, 308
Haan, Benedict, 26
Handel, George, 281
Harris, Howel, 296–97
Harris, James A., 309

Harvey, William, 27
Haweis, Thomas, 296
Hawkins, Laetitia, 87
Hearn, Thomas, 87
Hegel, 127
Henry III, 217
Henry IV, 211, 217
Hercules, 19–20
Hildegard. *See* Bingen, Hildegard
von
Hill, Rowland, 296
Hobbes, 172
Hooke, Robert, 25
Hume, David, 124, 177, 312
as historian, 299–301
Campbell, influence on,
159–60,
Joseph Butler, relationship
with, 308
manuscripts of, 309
miracles, scientific validation
of, 172–75
Hutcheson, Francis, 44–46, 159,
171, 307, 309
Huygens, Christiaan, 28–29

I

Inkster, Ian, 318
Isocrates, 166

J

Jacobi, 150
Jaffro, Laurent, 307
James, Felicity, 317, 319
James I, 300, 319

Janeway, James, 101
Janowitz, Anne F., 319
Johnson, Joseph, 73
Johnson, Mary Lynn, 323
Johnson, Samuel, 102, 118, 315, 328–29
John the Baptist, Saint, 278
Jones, David Ceri, 296
Julian of Norwich, 65

K

Kant, Immanuel, 134, 149
  and Fichte, 126–27
  inward miracle, 150–51
  moral disposition, 139–43
  moral rectitude and religion, 124
  mutual corruption, 143–48
  radicalization of Fichtean evil, 135–38
  reflective judgment, 152–54
Keats, John, 90
Kemp, F. A. Van de, 206
Kilner, Dorothy, 102
King, William, 47, 53–54
  De origine mali (*An Essay on the Origin of Evil*), 35–36, 46
  Divine Predestination and Foreknowledg, Consistent with the Freedom of Man's Will (sermon), 48–49
  God and man, relationship between, 36–37
  nature of evil, 27–28, 34
    moral evil, 42–43
    natural evil, 38–41

predestination and free will, 35, 48, 50–52
representative theory of perception, 44–46, 51–52

L

Laclos, Choderlos de, 231
Lancaster, Joseph, 103
Laud, William, 319, 326
Law, Edward, 36
Le Clerc, Jean, 312, 314–15
Le Franc de Pompignan, Jean-Jacques, 277, 293
  biblical poetry, 278
  harmony, 279–80, 288
    hymns, music with, 280
    pleasing and tender qualities, 283–86
    syllables (meter), 282
    variety of tone and form, 286–88
  Hymn XIII, 288–92
  Pour le Jour de la Nativité du Seigneur, 281, 283–86
Leibniz, Gottfried Wilhelm von, 35, 44, 125
Lely, Peter, 22
Lessing, Gotthold Ephraim, 125
Levy, Michelle, 318
Lewis, C. S., 29
Locke, John, 307
  and Anderson, 303
  and Barbauld, 107–8, 111, 114
  and Campbell, 159, 161, 170–71

and Drake, 70
and King, 42–43
and More, 99
and Richardson, 1, 9
and Sherwood, 107–8, 114
and Wollstonecraft, 107–8, 114, 116
educational philosophy of, 101, 104–5
moral relativism, 110
tabula rasa, 69, 98, 108, 111, 114
theory of the self, 106–8, 112
Louis, Saint, 278
Louis XIV, 211, 218, 237
Luke (the apostle), 268–70

M

Machaut, Guillaume, 281
Madame de Beaumont, 100
Madison, James, 157–58
Mahomet, 190–91, 199
Maier, Paul L., 311
Mandeville, 309
Mansfield, Edward D., 92
Mary I, 319
Mary II, 327
Mathiez, Albert, 259–60
Matteis, Paolo, 19
Mayhew, Jonathan, 328–29
McCarthy, William, 318
Mead, Richard, 3
Méhul, Étienne-Nicolas, 263
Michelet, Jules, 267
Milton, John, 3, 29, 42

Molyneux, Samuel, 42–44, 52
Montesquieu, 237
Moore, James, 307
More, Hannah, 103, 115
and Locke, 99–100
sexless soul, 88
Morse, Jedidiah, 206
Mott, Lucretia, 92
Murray, Judith Sargent, 84–85

N

Nerciat, Andréa de, 237
Newbery, John, 101
Newman, John (cardinal), 174
Newton, 37–39, 41
Nicholls, William, 3
Nodier, Charles, 266
Nuovo, Victor, 307

O

Orme, William, 315
Ozouf, Mona, 261–72

P

Paine, Thomas, 74, 322
Parker, Theodore, 184
Pascal, 224
Paul, Saint (the apostle), 7–8, 22
Pernot, Laurent, 179
Peter (the apostle), 268–72
Petrie, Alexander, 26
Petty, William, 38
Phillipson, 299–301
Piles, Roger de, 9

Plato, 61–63, 66, 150
  and Marie de Gournay, 66–67
  sexless soul, 61–63
Polwhele, Richard, 89
Pope, Alexander, 3, 35–36, 102
Poulain, François, 69–70
Poussin, Nicolas, 10
Price, Richard, 74
Priestley, Joseph, 318
Priestley, Mary, 318
Priestly, Joseph, 73
Prior, Matthew, 3
Pufendorf, Samuel von, 43
Pythagoras, 61

Q

Quinet, Edgar, 259
Quintilian, 162, 177

R

Raphael, 7–8, 10
Ready, Kathryrn, 318
Reid, 173
Reynolds, Joshua, 23
Richardson, Jonathan, 1, 4
  and Shaftesbury, 14–16, 18–21
  art and religion, 5–12, 21–22
  British Protestant view of
      paintings, 12, 17, 21–23
  connoisseurship, 5, 12–17
  life of, 3
  paintings, proper approach to,
      9–10, 18
  virtue, conception of, 20–21
Rivers, Isabel, 308

Robespierre
  Feast of Pentecost, 267–68,
      269–72
  festival of the Supreme Being,
      260, 261, 263–67
Robinson, Henry Crabbe, 322
Robinson, John, 326
Rodgers, Betsy, 319
Rousseau, 76, 80, 86, 244, 257
Rowland, Daniel, 296–97
Rowson, Susan, 88
Rush, Benjamin, 87

S

Sade, Marquis de, 231–32, 239,
      242, 245, 253
Saint-Évremond, 237
Salmon, William, 5
Savage, Ruth, 307
Schlenther, Boyd Stanley, 296
Schuchard, M. K., 321
Schurman, Anna Maria van, 68
Scott, John, 13
Scougal, Henry, 308
Seabury, Samuel, 328
Seward, Anna, 118
Shaftesbury, 3rd Earl of, 5, 14, 16,
      18–21, 309
Shelley, Mary, 89
Shelley, Percy Bysshe, 90
Sherwood, Mary Martha, 106–8,
      113, 117–19
Shrubsole, William, 298
Silliman, Benjamin, 55
Sloane, Hans, 3

Smith, Adam, 299
Smith, Charlotte, 102
Smollett, Tobias, 305
Somers, John, 14–15
Sor Juana. *See* Cruz, Juana Inés
de la
Spalding, Johann Joachim, 125
Sparks, Jared, 208–9
Spinoza, 127
Stanton, Elizabeth Cady, 91–94
Steele, Richard, 3–4, 299
Steers, A. D. G., 307
Sterne, Laurence, 46, 48
Stewart, M. A., 307–9
Stockton, Annis Boudinot, 85
Stott, Anne, 99
Stuart, Moses, 202–3
Swift, Jonathan, 31–34, 41, 44,
179
Sykes, Norman, 327

T

Talleyrand-Périgord, Charles
Maurice de, 75
Tarantino, Giovanni, 307
Tennyson, Alfred, 90, 102
Thornhill, James, 10
Toland, John, 30, 32–33, 40, 308
Trimmer, Sarah, 100, 102
Tucker, Josiah, 309

V

Valmont (fictional character),
242, 244, 256

Van Dyck, 10
Van Leeuwenhoek, Anton,
25–27, 29, 49–50
Verlaine, Paul, 282, 287
Voetius, Gisbertus, 68–69
Voltaire, 123, 211, 232, 237
affaire Calas, 215–16
defence of justice, 211
fanaticism, 212–13
dogmatic beliefs, 214–15
superstitious beliefs, 213
religion, 212, 225, 229
civilized manners, 219–20
freedom, 217–218
love and charity or gentleness
and forgiveness, 225–27
social solidarity between
religion and state, 221–22
tolerance, 220–21, 230
true versus false, 223–24

W

Walpole, Robert, 3, 326
Ware, Henry, Sr., 181–82, 194,
201
Watts, Isaac, 3, 39, 97–98, 102–3,
111
Wesley, John, 46, 296–97
West, Benjamin, 23
White, Eryn Mant, 296
Whitefield, George, 296–98
Whitefoot, John, 315
Whitehead, Angus, 322
Wilkins, John, 49–50

Wilks, Matthew, 298
William III, 28, 30, 299, 327
William of Orange. *See* William
    III
Williams, Peter, 296
Williams, William, 296–97
Wollstonecraft, Mary, 96, 106,
    115
  and Elizabeth Cady Stanton,
      91, 93–94
  and Leopold Hartley Grindon,
      94–95
  and Margaret Fuller, 91, 94
  and Sarah Grimké, 91–93
  Lockean self, 107–8, 113
  providential empiricism, 114,
      116–18
  sex and gender, 59–60
  sexless soul, 55–58, 79, 80–83
  sexless soul, origin of, 61
  sexless soul, responses to,
      83–89
  social circle of, 73–74
  soul and body, relationship of,
      77–79
  soul, meaning of, 75–77
  tabula rasa, 114
  writing for children, 107, 114,
      117, 120
Wordsworth, William, 90
Worrall, David, 321
Wright, John P., 309
Wright, Susanna, 83
Wykes, David L., 317–18

Y

Yorick, 46–47

Z

Zayas, María de, 67–68